The Philosophy of Viśiṣṭādvaita Vedānta

The Philosophy of Viśiṣṭādvaita Vedānta

A Study Based on Vedānta Deśika's Adhikaraṇa-Sārāvalī

S.M. SRINIVASA CHARI

MOTILAL BANARSIDASS PUBLISHERS
PRIVATE LIMITED • DELHI

Reprint: Delhi, ***2016***
First Edition: Delhi, 2008

ISBN: 978-81-208-3180-3

MOTILAL BANARSIDASS
41 U.A., Bungalow Road, Jawahar Nagar, Delhi 110 007
8 Mahalaxmi Chamber, 22 Bhulabhai Desai Road, Mumbai 400 026
203 Royapettah High Road, Mylapore, Chennai 600 004
236, 9th Main III Block, Jayanagar, Bangalore 560 011
8 Camac Street, Kolkata 700 017
Ashok Rajpath, Patna 800 004
Chowk, Varanasi 221 001

Printed in India

by RP Jain at NAB Printing Unit,
A-44, Naraina Industrial Area, Phase I, New Delhi–110028
and published by JP Jain for Motilal Banarsidass Publishers (P) Ltd,
41 U.A. Bungalow Road, Jawahar Nagar, Delhi-110007

To

The revered memory of

my ācārya

Srī. Goṣṭīpuraṃ Sowmyanārāyanācārya Swāmī

with profound respect and gratitude

CONTENTS

CHAPTER THREE
THE DISTINGUISHING CHARACTERISTICS OF BRAHMAN 53

CHAPTER FOUR
BRAHMAN AS THE CAUSE OF THE UNIVERSE 101

CHAPTER TEN

FOREWORD

प्रकृतस्य 'विशिष्टाद्वैतम्' इत्येद्ग्रन्थस्य महतः प्रणेतारः एते श्री. उ.वे. S.M. श्रीनिवासाचार्याः, बहोः कालात्पूर्वमेव श्रीमन्निगमान्तमहादेशिकविरचितामतिप्रौढां शतदूषणीमधिकृत्य महान्तं शोधनप्रबन्धं विधाय Ph. D. उपाधिं प्राप्तवन्त इति जानीयुः विद्वांसः।।

एते हि सुप्रसिद्धमहानुभावानां महात्मनां श्रीमदुभयवेदान्तेत्याद्यन्वर्थविशेषणानां श्रीगोष्ठीपुरं स्वामिचरणानां सन्निधौ संप्रदायक्रमेण वेदान्तशास्त्रमधीत्य, ततः स्वीयज्येष्ठभातृभ्यः प्रसिद्धमहाविद्वद्भ्यः श्री उ.वे. सरगूर् श्रीनिवासवरदाचार्येभ्यः मननादिक्रममपि जानन्तः उभयभाषाप्रवीणा विराजन्त इति सर्वविदितम्।।

भारतीयसर्वकारस्य परदेशीयदूतावासेष्वनेकेषु संस्कृतिविभागे बहुकालमनेकविधं स्थानं निर्वहन्तः, विश्रान्ताश्चैते। परदेशावासकाले एते तदा तदा पाश्चत्यपण्डितैस्साकं दर्शनविचारादिकमकुर्वन् यदा, तदैतेषां मनसि, "पाश्राश्चात्यदेशेषु अद्वैतसिद्धान्तवत्, विशिष्टा (सविशेषा) द्वैतस्य स्थानं कुतो न दृश्यते?" इति विचारमग्नास्तत्कारणादिकमपि सम्यङ्निश्चित्य ज्ञातवन्त एते।।

उद्योगाद्विश्रान्त्यनन्तरं तदर्थमेव कृतभूरिपरिश्रमा एते भगवद्रामानुजस्य विशिष्टा (सविशेषा) द्वैतदर्शनं बहुधाऽधीत्य, सर्वसंमानानार्हान् बहून् ग्रन्थान् विरच्य, प्रकाश्य चैतत्सिद्धान्तस्यानितरसाधारणीं सेवां कुर्वन्तः, जन्मैव सार्थकीकुर्वन्तो विराजन्तः, प्रशंसनीयचरिता विलसन्तीति सर्वविदितमेव।।

अद्य प्रकटीक्रियमाणोऽयम् 'विशिष्टाद्वैतम्' इति ग्रन्थः पूर्वमेभिरेव प्रकटीकृतात् उपनिषत् ब्रह्मसूत्रविचारग्रन्थापेक्षयाऽत्यन्तं विलक्षणः। अत्र हि भगवद्भाष्यकारैः स्थापितस्यास्य सिद्धान्तस्य श्रीमद्वेदान्तदेशिकैः कवितार्किकसिंहैः दर्शनत्वेन प्रापितप्रचारस्य प्रक्रियां विमर्शपूर्वकं अतिसरलक्रमैः अधिकरणसारावल्यां

प्रतिपादितक्रममनुसृत्य, एते श्री श्रीनिवासाचार्याः अधिकरणसारावलीं प्रधानाधरत्वेन स्वीकृत्य स्वीयं विमर्शप्रबन्धं रचयामासुः। अत एवायं सिद्धान्तः न केवलं मतरूपः, किन्तु दर्शनरूप एवेति सम्यगवगन्तुं शक्यत इत्ययमंशो विशेषेणावधानमर्हति विदुषाम्।

एतेषामसाधारणविमर्शसरणिः, भाषाद्वयपान्डित्यमित्यादिकम् एतादृशमहत्तमकार्यसाधनक्षममभूदिति न संशयलेशोऽपि। एवमेवैते आरोग्यादिसंपन्नाः एतत्सिद्धान्तस्य प्रकाशने इतोऽपि बहुधा सेवां कृत्वा विराजन्तुतरामिति भगवन्तं प्रार्थये।

नव्यमङ्गलाभिजनो वरदाचार्यः

K.S. Varadacharya

Mahāmahopādhyāya, Śāstraratnākara, Paṅditaratnam, Mysore

PREFACE

The *Brahma-sūtra Bhāṣya* of Śrī Rāmānuja, traditionally revered as *Śrī-Bhāṣya,* is a monumental commentary on the *Vedānta-sūtras* of sage Bādarāyaṇa. In this work, Rāmānuja has expounded in detail the doctrines of Viśiṣṭādvaita Vedānta with adequate support of the Upaniṣads. Vedānta Deśika, an illustrious successor to Rāmānuja wrote two independent philosophical treatises, *Tattva-muktā-kalāpa* and *Adhikaraṇa-sārāvalī* with the main objective of establishing Viśiṣṭādvaita as a sound and most acceptable system of Vedānta. Both these works are written in the form of verses containing 500 and 562 verses respectively, composed in the rhythmic *sragdharā* metre. The *Tattva-muktā-kalāpa* discusses comprehensively all the theories of Viśiṣṭādvaita – epistemological, ontological, cosmological and eschatological – and establishes their soundness by examining critically the corresponding theories of rival schools of thought including Advaita Vedānta. The *Adhikaraṇa-sārāvalī,* on the other hand, is confined to the study of the *Brahma-sūtra Bhāṣya* of Rāmānuja and it presents the essential teachings of each *adhikaraṇa,* or section dealing with specific topics of *Brahma-sūtra,* as interpreted by Rāmānuja. In the *Tattva-muktā-kalāpa,* Vedānta Deśika does not enter into the discussion of the Scriptural texts for the obvious reason that he wanted to prove the soundness of the Viśiṣṭādvaita theory more on a logical basis than on the Scriptural authority. But in the *Adhikaraṇa-sārāvalī*, which directly deals with the *Śrī-Bhāṣya*, he attempts to establish that the doctrines of Viśiṣṭādvaita are in full accord with the Upaniṣadic teachings and the *Vedānta-sūtras*. These two classics are complementary and are comparable, in the words of Vedānta Deśika, to the two hands supporting each other (*anyonyahastapradam*). A study of both these works is considered essential for a fuller understanding of Viśiṣṭādvaita Vedānta in all its aspects.

My book "*Fundamentals of Viśiṣṭādvaita*", published earlier covers the study of the *Tattva-muktā-kalāpa* and attempts to show that Viśiṣṭādvaita is a sound philosophical system. In order to justify that Viśiṣṭādvaita Vedānta also conforms fully to the Upaniṣads and *Vedānta-sūtras*, unlike Advaita Vedānta, I have now undertaken the present work on the basis of an in-depth study of *Adhikaraṇa-sārāvalī*.

This book does not attempt to render into English the 562 verses with explanatory notes nor does it deal with the 156 *adhikaraṇas* in the same order as it is found in the original text. Its scope is confined to enunciate the doctrines of Viśiṣṭādvaita Vedānta as outlined in the *adhikaraṇas* of the *Brahma-sūtras*. For this purpose the selected *adhikaraṇas* which have direct bearing on the philosophical doctrines of Viśiṣṭādvaita are discussed in a logical sequence and presented as a coherent system of philosophy.

In the preparation of this book, I have drawn material mostly from the original texts '*Adhikaraṇa-sārāvalī*' and the two learned commentaries on it titled *Adhikaraṇa-cintāmaṇi* contributed by Śrī Kumāra Varadācārya, the son of Vedānta Deśika and *Padayojanā*, written by Śrī Śaṭakopa Rāmānuja-yati, the 34th pontiff of Ahobila Maṭham. Among the contemporary traditional scholars, Sri Uttamur Veeraraghavacharya has also written a detailed commentary named *Sārārtha Ratnaprabhā*. Another book under the title *Śārīraka Adhikaraṇa Ratnamālā* by Mm. Kapisthalam Desikacharya presents in lucid Sanskrit the essential teachings of the *adhikaraṇas* with a statement of *pūrvapakṣa* and *siddhānta*. I have made use of these works. For purposes of elucidation, wherever necessary, I have also taken material from the *Śrī-Bhāṣya* of Rāmānuja and the learned commentary on it titled *Śrutaprakāśikā*, by Sudarśana Sūri and also Vedānta Deśika's *Tattva-muktā-kalāpa* and *Śatadūṣaṇī*.

It is for the first time, such an attempt is made to publish in English an authentic treatise on Viśiṣṭādvaita Vedānta based on original source books. It is hoped that this volume will be found useful for an in-depth study of Viśiṣṭādvaita Vedānta as expounded in the *Śrī-Bhāṣya* and the *Adhikaraṇa-sārāvalī*.

I must pay my respects to my revered Acharya, the late Sri Gostipuram Sowmyanarayanacharya Swami to whom I owe my knowledge of Vedānta. I must also pay my respects to the late Sri Madhurantakam Veeraraghava-charya Swami and the late Mm. Saragur Madabhushi Varadacharya Swami, under whom I studied *Śrī-Bhāṣya, Tattva-muktā-kalāpa* and *Adhikaraṇa-sārāvalī* in the traditional manner. I am deeply indebted to them. I have derived help and guidance for understanding the crucial *adhikaraṇas* of the Vedānta-sūtras from traditional scholars Mm. N.S. Ramanuja Tatacharya, Mm. V. Srivatsankacharya and Mm. K.S. Varadacharya. I express my grateful thanks to them. I should also thank my esteemed friends Sri Ananthanarasimhachar, Dr. N.S. Anantharangachar and Sri S. Srinivasachar who have gone through the major part of the typescript and offered useful suggestions for improvement. I also express my grateful thanks to the eminent scholar Mm. K.S. Varadacharya for writing a foreword to the book.

Bangalore
Date: 9th August, 2006 S.M. Srinivasa Chari.

ABBREVIATIONS

Acc.	According to
Ait. Up.	Aitareya Upaniṣad
As.	Adhikaraṇa-sārāvalī
A&V.	Advaita and Viśiṣṭādvaita–A Study based on the Śatadūsaṇī
BG.	Bhagavad-gītā
Br. Up.	Bṛhadāraṇyaka Upaniṣad
Ch. Up.	Chāndogya Upaniṣad
FVV.	Fundamentals of Viśiṣṭādvaita–A Study based on Tattvamuktākalāpa
Isa Up.	Īśāvāsya Upaniṣad
Ka. Up., also Kaṭha Up.	Kaṭha Upaniṣad
Kau. Up.	Kauṣitakī Upaniṣad
MB.	Madhva Bhāṣya on VS.
Mu. Also Muṇḍ. Up.	Muṇḍaka Upaniṣad
NS.	Nyāyasiddhāñjana
RB.	Rāmānuja Bhāṣya on VS.
SB.	Śaṅkara Bhāṣya on VS.
SS.	Sarvārthasiddhi
Sub. Up.	Subāla Upaniṣad
Svet. Up.	Śvetāśvatara Upanisad
Tait. Br.	Taittirīya Brāhmaṇa
Tait Up.	Taittirīya Upaniṣad
Up.	Upaniṣad
VP.	Viṣṇupurāṇa
VS.	Vedānta-Sūtra of Bādarāyaṇa

INTRODUCTION

Meaning of the term Viśiṣṭādvaita

The system of Vedānta as expounded by Śrī Rāmānuja is designated as Viśiṣṭādvaita. The term Viśiṣṭādvaita signifies that the Ultimate Reality, named Brahman in the Upaniṣads is one as organically related to the sentient *jīvas* (*cit*) and the non-sentient cosmic matter (*acit*). On the basis of the Upaniṣadic teachings, this school of thought acknowledges three real ontological entities namely, Brahman or *Īśvara*, the *jīvātman* or the individual self and the *prakṛti* or the primordial cosmic matter. Though all the three are different from each other, Brahman being inseparably related to the sentient souls as well as non-sentient matter is ultimately one as a qualified Reality. As Vedānta Deśika states, though there is absolute difference between *Īśvara* and the two other ontological entities and also among the individual selves and cosmic matter, the ultimate Reality is considered as one from the standpoint of its being a *Viśiṣṭa tattva: (viśiṣṭasya advaitam)*[1].

Historical Development of Viśiṣṭādvaita

Though all the schools of Vedānta owe their origin to the Upaniṣads, *Brahma-sūtras* and the *Bhagavadgītā*, the three basic source books, Viśiṣṭādvaita as a well formulated philosophical system or *darśana*, with properly developed epistemology and ontology on logical ground as well as on the basis of correct interpretation of the Scriptural statements and allied texts, was expounded by Rāmānuja in his monumental commentary on the *Vedānta-sūtras* known as *Śrī-Bhāṣya.* In view of this, Rāmānuja may be regarded as the founder of the Viśiṣṭādvaita system. But Rāmānuja himself does not claim this distinction. In the opening para of the *Śrī-Bhāṣya,* he says that he is writing a commentary on the *sūtras* in accordance with the views contained in an elaborate and extensive *vṛtti* or glossary written by Bodhāyana which was abridged by earlier teachers[2]. Though *Bodhāyanavṛtti* as well as the works of these ancient teachers are not extant, there is ample internal evidence to show from the quotations cited by Rāmānuja that there were already eminent exponents of Viśiṣṭādvaita Vedānta such as Bodhāyana, Ṭanka, Dramiḍa, Guhadeva, Kapardi and Bhāruci[3]. In his *Vedārtha Saṅgraha,* Rāmānuja mentions the names of all these ancient exponents. He also quotes a few statements of Bodhāyana who is also known as *vṛttikāra* and also by the name of Upāvarṣa, according to Śaṁkara. This establishes beyond any doubt that the system of Vedānta developed by Rāmānuja follows faithfully an ancient tradition (*śiṣṭa-parigṛhīta-purātana-veda-vedānta-vyākhyāna*). Such evidence is not forthcoming either in the Śaṁkara's *Sūtra-bhāṣya* or Madhva's *Brahmasūtra-bhāṣya.*

According to Vedānta Deśika, Nāthamuni, who lived in the tenth century was the first exponent of Viśiṣṭādvaita as a system of Philosophy (*nathopajñam pravṛttam*)[4]. He wrote two important works: *Nyāya tattva* and *Yoga-rahasya,* but both these are not extant[5]. However it is evident from the numerous quotations cited by Vedānta Deśika in his *Nyāya-siddhāñjana,* that *Nyāya-tattva* is regarded as an important philosophical treatise which had considerable influence on both Rāmānuja and Vedānta Deśika[6]. According to *Vaiṣṇava* tradition, Nāthamuni inherited his knowledge of Viśiṣṭādvaita Vedānta from a long line of preceptors commencing from Nammāḷvār, the renowned Tamil saint, who is claimed to have lived in the beginning of *Kaliyuga* 2803 B.C.

After Nāthamuni, Ālavandar, also known as Yāmuna, who lived sometime between AD 916-1036 developed the system by contributing a few independent philosophic works (*bahubhiḥ yāmuneya prabhandhaiḥ upcitam*)[7]. He wrote six works and of these the most important is *Siddhitraya* consisting of three parts – *Ātmasiddhi, Īśvarasiddhi* and *Saṃvitsiddhi*, each one being devoted to one of three fundamental doctrines of Viśiṣṭādvaita. The teachings of Yāmuna have greatly influenced both Rāmānuja and Vedanta Deśika as they have extensively used the logical arguments advanced by him in the refutation of Advaita doctrines.

Rāmānuja, who came after Yāmuna, was born in AD 1017[8]. Though he could not become a direct disciple of Yāmuna, he was orally instructed by four of his disciples – Mahāpūrṇa, Tirukkottiyur Nambi, Tirumalai Nambi and Tirumalai Āṇḍān. The works of Yāmuna and the teachings received from his disciples enabled Rāmānuja to further develop and re-establish the Viśiṣṭādvaita as a full fledged system of Vedānta on strong foundation (*tratuṁ samyag yatīndraiḥ*)[9].

From the foregoing brief account, it may be observed that Viśiṣṭādvaita Vedānta was not a new system founded by Rāmānuja. On the contrary, it was already in existence from the time of Bādarāyaṇa who compiled the *Vedānta sūtras* on the basis of the Upaniṣadic teachings and also sage Bodhāyana, who wrote the first authoritative glossary on it. At the time Rāmānuja was born, there was a long felt need for consolidation and systematization of the apparently conflicting interpretations of the Upaniṣads. Earlier than Rāmānuja, Śaṁkara, Bhāskara and Yādavaprakāśa, among the extant schools of Vedānta, had attempted to interpret the Upaniṣads and the *Vedānta-sūtras* through scholarly *Bhāṣyas*. But the doctrines presented by them were not found acceptable. Śaṁkara's doctrine of *Māya* on the basis of which the *Nirviśeṣa Brahmādvaita* with the denial of reality to the individual souls and the universe is developed was not found philosophically sustainable. The *Bhedābheda vāda* of Bhāskara and Yādava was also not tenable since this concept conceived by them involved self-contradiction. It therefore became necessary for Rāmānuja to develop a more rational system of Vedānta by properly interpreting the *Vedānta-sūtras* and the connected Upaniṣadic texts and by refuting the doctrines which were opposed to the main tenets of Viśiṣṭādvaita. He successfully accomplished this task assigned to him[10] by writing the monumental *Bhāṣya* on the *Brahma-sūtras*. He also wrote several other works. These are *Vedānta-dīpa, Vedānta-sāra,* which are brief commentaries on *Vedānta Sūtras, Vedārtha-saṁgraha,* containing the quintessence of the Upaniṣads, the *Gītā Bhāṣya,* a commentary on the *Bhagavad-gīta,* three lyrics named as *Śaraṇāgati-gadya, Śrīraṅga-gadya* and *Vaikuṇṭha-gadya* and lastly *Nitya-grantha* mainly dealing with the mode of worship of the image of God. Of these works, the commentary on *Brahma-sūtra,* named *Śri-Bhāṣya* is the magnum opus of Rāmānuja in which the Viṣiṣṭādvaita doctrines are thoroughly discussed. This will mainly engage our attention in the present book.

For nearly two centuries after Rāmānuja, there was no significant contribution to the Viśiṣṭādvaita system by way of major philosophical works. The *ācāryas* who succeeded Rāmānuja, though some of them were eminent *vedāntins* such as Parāśara Bhatta, Viṣṇucitta, Vātsya Varada, Sudarśana Sūri and Ātreya Rāmānuja, confined their attention primarily to the dissemination of the philosophy of Rāmānuja by teaching *Śrī-Bhāṣya* or writing further glossaries on it. The *Śrutaprakāśikā,* written by Sudarśana Sūri is an outstanding commentary on *Śrī-Bhāṣya.* Some of the Ācāryas, such as Pillān, Nanjīyar, Periavāccān Pillai, Vaḍakkutiruvīdi Pillai, who were attracted by the devotional hymns of the Āḷvars in Tamil engaged themselves in writing elaborate commentaries on them. During this period the theological aspect of Viśiśṭādvaita received much greater emphasis and importance than its philosophy.

Besides, the Viśiṣṭādvaita system itself seems to have been exposed to the criticism by rival schools of thought and in particular from the Advaitins. Though Rāmānuja had vigorously attacked *Māyāvāda* of Śaṁkara in his *Śrī-Bhāṣya*, the Advaita scholars of post-Rāmānuja period had attempted to defend their doctrines against the criticisms of Rāmānuja. Thus there was a clearly felt need for another great philosopher to consolidate the teachings of Rāmānuja and establish the Viśiṣṭādvaita system of philosophy on a stable foundation.

This need was fulfilled by Venkatanātha, popularly known as Vedānta Deśika and also *Vedānta Ācārya*, who was born in the year 1268[11]. It is said that Vedānta Deśika's future role as the re-establisher of Rāmānuja's philosophy was prophesied even when he was a child of five by Vātsya Varadācārya, a spiritual descendent of Rāmānuja. The story goes that when the child accompanied by his maternal uncle met the *ācārya* for the first time, the latter was so attracted by the extraordinary intelligence of the boy, that he blessed him in the following words: "May you establish the Vedānta on a firm basis, vanquishing the theories of rival schools of thought; may you become the respected of the orthodox *Vedāntins* and the abode of abundant auspiciousness"[12]. Vedānta Deśika himself acknowledges with gratitude the blessings received from his spiritual guru in the opening verses of *Tattva-muktā-kalāpa* and *Adhikaraṇa-sārāvalī*, the two major philosophical treatises devoted to the exposition of Viśiṣṭādvaita Vedānta on a solid foundation[13].

Vedānta Deśika was a prolific writer and he wrote more than hundred works not only in the realm of philosophy and religion but also in the field of poetry and drama. His chief philosophical works are: *Nyāya-pariśuddhi, Nyāya-siddhāñjana, Tattva-muktā-kalāpa* along with *Sarvārthasiddhi* (his own commentary), *Adhikaraṇa-sārāvalī, Seśvara-mīmāṁsā, Mīmāṁsā-pādukā, Śatadūṣaṇī*. His other philosophical works which are in the form of commentaries are *Tattva-ṭīka* (an incomplete commentary on *Śrī-Bhāṣya*),

Tātparya-candrikā (a gloss on Rāmānuja's *Gītā-bhāṣya), Īśāvāsyopaniṣad-bhāṣya* (a commentary on Īśāvāsyopaniṣad), *Gītārtha-saṁgraha-rakṣā* (a commentary on Yāmuna's *Gītārtha-saṁgraha), Rahasyarakṣā,* a commentary on Yāmuna's *Stotra-ratna, Catuḥślokī* and Rāmānuja's *Gadyatraya.*

Among the philosophical works, *Nyāya-pariśuddhi, Nyāya-siddhāñjana, Śatadūṣaṇī, Tattva-muktā-kalāpa* and *Adhikaraṇa-sārāvalī* are important since in these works the doctrines of Viśiṣṭādvaita are expounded. *Nyāya-parīśuddhi* is an epistemological work devoted primarily to the discussion of the nature of the *pramāṇas* and other epistemological theories of Viśiṣṭādvaita. In the *Nyāya-siddhāñjana,* the ontological theories of Viśiṣṭādvaita are presented in detail. The *Śatadūṣaṇī,* which is a polemical work (*vāda-grantha*) is devoted to the refutation of the doctrines of Śaṁkara's Advaita Vedānta by adopting dialectical arguments with a view to establishing the soundness of the theories of Viśiṣṭādvaita. The *Tattvamuktākalāpa,* which is written in verse containing 500 verses composed in *sragdharā* metre is intended primarily to present the Viśiṣṭādvaita doctrines by critically evaluating the corresponding theories of rival schools of thought. Unlike *Nyāya-siddhāñjana,* it is a comprehensive philosophical classic of Viśiṣṭādvaita Vedānta covering all topics in the realms of Metaphysics, Ontology, Theology, Epistemology, Cosmology and Eschatology. As Vedānta Deśika claims, there is no topic in Philosophy which is not covered in this work and what is not considered here cannot be found elsewhere (*yannāsmin kvāpi naitat*)[14]. It is indeed the magnum opus of Vedānta Deśika[15].

The *Adhikaraṇa-sārāvalī,* is an equally important philosophical treatise written in the same style as *Tattva-muktā-kalāpa* in *sragdharā* metre. It is primarily devoted to the discussion of the different *adhikaraṇas* or sectional topics of *Brahma-sūtras* as interpreted by Rāmānuja in his classical *Śrī-Bhāṣya.* In this work Vedānta Deśika, while summarizing the contents of each *adhikaraṇa,* attempts to establish that the doctrines of Viśiṣṭādvaita as developed by Rāmānuja are philosophically sound and well rooted in the Upaniṣads. While the main objective of *Tattva-muktā-kalāpa* is to establish the soundness of the Viśiṣṭādvaita theories on a logical basis by way of proving the untenability of the corresponding theories of rival schools of thought, the main focus of the *Adhikaraṇa-sārāvalī* is to establish that Viśiṣṭādvaita fully conforms to the Upaniṣadic teachings and the Vedānta-sūtras, unlike the Advaita of Śaṁkara. In view of this, Vedānta Deśika states that the two philosophical treatises are complementary, comparable to the two hands supporting each other (*anyonyahasta-pradam*). Thus, among the philosophical works of Vedānta Deśika, the *Tattva-muktā-kalāpa* and *Adhikaraṇa-sārāvalī* constitute the outstanding Vedānta classics which provide a comprehensive knowledge of Viśiṣṭādvaita system.

Adhikaraṇa-sārāvalī – its Scope and Contents

The *Adhikaraṇa-sārāvalī,* as its title suggests deals with the essential teachings contained in each *adhikaraṇa* of *Brahma-sūtra*. Bādarāyaṇa has codified the philosophical teachings of the Upanisads in the form of *sūtras* or concise aphoristic sentences expressed in a few cryptic words. The total number of *sūtras,* according to Rāmānuja, is 545. These are divided into four *adhyāyas* or chapters. Each *adhyāya* is subdivided into four *pādas* or pārts. Each *pada* is further subdivided into *adhikaraṇas* or sections dealing with specific subject covered in a single or group of *sūtras*. *Adhikaraṇa* is a technical name for a section devoted to discuss a specific subject or topic by following the five-fold methodology adopted in the traditional philosophical disputation[16]. The five stages of discussion are:

1. *Viṣaya* or the subject matter of discussion is to be stated.
2. *Saṃśaya* or all possible alternative views relating to it are to be mentioned.

3. *Pūrvapakṣa* or the prima facie view about it is to be presented.
4. *Uttara* or a suitable reply to it is to be given after a methodical discussion and refutation of *pūrvapakṣa*.
5. *Prayojana* or the usefulness of the discussion by way of the establishment of the conclusive view (*siddhānta*).

This methodology of discussion of a subject was introduced by the Pūrva-mīmāṁsakas in respect of *Mīmāṁsā-sūtras* which deal with the interpretation of the ritualistic portion of the Vedas. Though Bādarāyaṇa, who has framed the *sūtras* to codify the teachings of the Upaniṣads has not grouped them into *adhikaraṇas,* the commentators on *Vedānta-sutra* accepted this methodology and named the *adhikaraṇas* by grouping the *sūtras* dealing with the specific subject. There is great advantage in following such a methodology. First it becomes easier to comprehend a variety of subjects covered by Bādarāyaṇa in a large number of *sūtras*. More importantly, it provides a logical justification for arriving at a conclusive view on the basis of a critical evaluation of the possible alternative theories.

The number of *adhikaraṇas* is 156 according to Rāmānuja, whereas it is 196 for Śaṁkara and 222 for Madhva. This wide variation arises as a result of the manner in which the *sūtras* are grouped with reference to the subject matter acknowledged by the commentators.

The names of *adhikaraṇas* and the subject covered in them are given in the Appendix I. The *adhikaraṇas* are generally titled after the key word of the *sūtra,* which indicates its subject matter. Thus, for instance, the *Jijñāsādhikaraṇa* which covers the first *sūtra* is named after the term *jijñāsā* mentioned in the *sūtra 'athāto brahma jijñāsā'*. Wherever an *adhikaraṇa* covers several *sūtras,* as in the case of the *Ānandamayādhikaraṇa* dealing with the subject of Brahman as blissful, it bears the title of the keyword of the principal *sūtra* viz. *'ānandamayo abhyāsāt'*. With the exception of a few, most of the *adhikaraṇas* cover more than one *sūtra* and in some cases 10-15 *sūtras*, depending upon the nature of the subject to be discussed. It is therefore considered necessary for a commentator to discuss the subjects dealt with in the *sūtras* in the order of *adhikaraṇas* rather than individually.

The sequence of the *adhikaraṇas* is also the same as followed in the *sūtras* by Bādarāyaṇa. As will be seen presently, there is perfect coherence (*saṅgati*) not only between the four *adhyāyas* and the four *pādas* under each *adhyāya*, but also betw een the different *adhikaraṇas* under each *pāda*. According to the traditional commentators, even the *sūtras* are also inter-connected.

The central theme of the *adhikaraṇas* and the subject matter covered in them are the same as found in the *Brahma-sūtras*. The main subject of *Brahma-sūtras* as its title suggests, is Brahman. Though each *adhyāya* and each *pāda* of it covers different topics, these are directly or indirectly related to Brahman.

According to Rāmānuja, the first *adhyāya* which is named as *Samanvayādhyāya*, is primarily devoted to establish the correlation of various texts of the Upaniṣads with Brahman as the primary cause of the universe. It directly deals with Brahman after providing the needed justification for the enquiry into the nature of Brahman (*Brahma-jijñāsā*), a clear definition of Brahman, the proof for its existence and usefulness of the Upaniṣadic texts for knowing the Supreme Goal to be attained. It also discusses the essential nature of Brahman as a sentient being, as blissful (*ānandamaya*), as distinct from *jīvātman* and all other celestial beings, and also from the non-sentient cosmic entities such as ethereal space (*ākāśa*), vital breath (*prāṇa*), the cosmic light (*jyotis*). All these points are covered in eleven *adhikaraṇas*(1-11) included in the first *pāda* of *Brahma-sūtra*.

The second *pāda* deals with the distinguishing characteristics of Brahman. According to Vedānta Deśika, it establishes on the authority of the Upaniṣadic teachings the following points:

I) Brahman as the Self of all (*Sarvātmā*),
II) Brahman as the devourer of the entire universe (*Attā*),
III) Brahman as the *Puruṣa* abiding for ever in the eye (*Akṣinityasthitiḥ*)
IV) Brahman as the Inner Controller of all (*Antaryāmin*),
V) Brahman as the Imperishable Reality (*Akṣara*)
VI) Brahman as *Vaiśvānara.*

These subjects are covered in the *adhikaraṇas* 12 to17.

The third *pāda* brings out a few more important characteristics of Brahman after critically examining the Upaniṣadic passages which prima facie appear to lend support to the theory that *jīva* is Brahman. These are:

I) Brahman as the Support of heaven and earth (*Āyatana*).
II) Brahman as Infinitely great (*Bhūmā*).
III) Brahman as the *Ādhāra* of the universe (*viśvādhāra*).
IV) Brahman as the Object of Enjoyment of *muktas* (*mukta bhogyaḥ*).
V) Brahman as the subtle space within the heart (*daharākāśa).*
VI) Brahman as the Controller of all (*Sarvaniyantā*)
VII) Brahman as the Object of meditation for celestial deities (*Devādīnāṁ upāsyaḥ*)
VIII) Brahman as the *Nāma-rūpa Nirvahitā.*

All these points are covered in the *adhikaraṇas* 18-27 of the third *pāda*.

The fourth pāda of the first *adhyāya* is devoted to establish that Brahman as the primary cause of the universe is the Ultimate Reality by way of refuting the claims of the ancient Sāṁkhya school of thought, according to which *prakṛti,* also named as *pradhāna* and also described as *avyākṛta,* is the cause of the universe. It also takes up for critical examination the views of the later Sāṁkhya school which claims that the *jīvātman*, which is the twenty fifth principle and is other than *prakṛti*, is the cause of the universe. In the same strain, it also refutes the theory that the liberated self (*muktātmā*), is Brahman. In this connection, it also examines critically the view of the Yoga school which upholds that *Īśvara* is only instrumental cause (*nimitta kāraṇa*) and establishes that Brahman is the material cause of the universe (*upādana-kāraṇa*) and also the instrumental cause (*nimitta kāraṇa*). These topics are dealt in *adhikaraṇas* 28 to 35 of the fourth *pāda*.

The second *adhyāya* of *Brahma-sūtra* is named as *Avirodhādhyāya* or the chapter which proves the absence of contradictions. It is primarily devoted to uphold the main thesis of the first *adhyāya* viz that Brahman is the primary cause of the universe. For this purpose Bādarāyaṇa refutes the theories advanced by the rival schools of thought which were prevalent during his time and which stood opposed to the Vedānta theory of Reality. The schools which come up for critical examination in the order in which it is stated in the *Brahma-sūtra* are: Sāṁkhya, Yoga, Nyāya-vaiśeṣika, Buddhism, Jainism, Pāśupata (the ancient Śaiva school) and Pāñcarātra.

In the first *pāda* of this *adhyāya*, the arguments advanced by the schools of Sāṁkhya and Yoga against the possibility of accepting Brahman as the cause of the universe are discussed and set aside. In this conn41ection the theory of causality as conceived by the Vaiśeṣikas viz. that cause and effect are distinct is discussed with a view to establish the causal relationship between Brahman and universe. A few objections raised against the Vedanta theory of Brahman as the material cause of the universe are also answered. All these topics are dealt in *adhikaraṇas* 36 to 46.

The second *pāda* of second *adhyāya* examines critically the other schools of thought including Sāṁkhya, Nyāya-vaiśeṣika, Bauddha, Jaina, Pāśupata and Pāñcarātra. In the case of Sāṁkhya it highlights the self- contradictions involved in their teachings. Regarding Nyāya-vaiśeṣika, Buddhists and Jainas, the impossibility of *paramāṇus* or subtle atomic elements becoming cause of the universe is demonstrated.

It also refutes the *śūnyavāda* of the Mādhyamika Buddhists. In the case of Pāśupata, the theory of *Īśvara* as the only *nimitta kāraṇa* is refuted. In the case of Pāñcarātra, it is proved to be acceptable as its teachings are in conformity with the Vedas. All these issues are covered in *adhikaraṇas* 47 to 53.

The third *pāda* of second *adhyāya* is far more important as it deals among other topics with the nature of *jīvātman*. Out of seven *adhikaraṇas* included in this part, five are devoted to establish that *jīvātman* is eternal (*nitya*), it is the subject of knowledge (*jñātā*) and also the agent of action (*kartā*). It also discusses in detail the relation of *jīva* to Brahman in terms of difference and non-difference and affirms that *jīva* is an *aṁśa* or integral part of Brahman. This *pāda* also examines the evolutes such as *viyat* (ether), *tejas* (fire) and *vāyu* (air) and establishes that they have an origin unlike *jīvātman*. All these are covered in the *adhikaraṇas* 54 to 60.

The fourth *pāda* of this *adhyāya* takes up for consideration the nature of the sense organs (*indriyas*), their number, their atomic character, the nature and role of *prāṇa vāyu* (vital breath). An important subject which comes up for discussion is the manner in which the physical universe consisting of variety of living beings and non-sentient entities is created through the process of quintuplication of five elements (*pañcīkaraṇa*). It is shown that the creation of the physical universe is brought about through the media of *caturmukha Brahmā* by *Paramātman*, as stated in the Upaniṣads. These issues are dealt with in the *adhikaraṇas* 61 to 68.

The third *adhyāya* of *Brahma-sūtra* is named as *Sādhanādhyāya*, since it primarily deals with the *sādhana* or the ways and means of attainment of Brahman. According to Bādarāyaṇa, *upāsanā* or unceasing mediation on Brahman, which is termed as *vidyā,* is the direct means to the attainment of Brahman. Prior to embarking on meditation, the spiritual aspirant is required to develop *vairāgya* or a sense of non-attachment to worldy and heavenly objects and also a deep craving for attainment of Brahman. For this purpose, the first *pāda* of this *adhyāya* and early part of second *pāda,* describes the transmigration of the soul, the manner of its rebirth and also its condition in different states such as dream, deep sleep (*suṣupti*) and swoon (*murcchā*). In the later part of the second *pāda,* the nature of Brahman as totally free from all defects and also endowed with auspicious attributes (*ubhayaliṅga*) is presented in detail as it is considered necessary to know that Brahman is the worthy object of meditation. In this connection it is also pointed out that Brahman is the highest Reality (*para*) and the bestower of the Supreme Goal for the attainment of which *upāsanā* is laid down. All these subjects are covered in the *adhikaraṇas* 69 to 82.

The third *pāda* of this *adhyāya,* which is the longest in the *Brahma-sutra* comprising 26 *adhikaraṇas,* deals with the different types of *vidyās* or modes of meditation for realization of Brahman. The Upaniṣadic passages prescribe 32 types of meditation. These are not different paths for *mokṣa* but are regarded as alternative means since the goal to be attained is the same. They are, however, named differently since certain attributes (*guṇas*) with which Brahman is to be meditated upon are different for each *vidyā*. The discussion of this subject in the different *adhikaraṇas* is generally centered round the issues relating to what *guṇas* are to be included and what are to be excluded. This *pāda* is therefore titled *guṇopasaṁhāra pāda* or the part dealing with the inclusion or exclusion of *Brahma-guṇas*. All these topics are covered in the *adhikaraṇas* 83 to 108.

The fourth *pāda* of the third *adhyāya* is of some importance as it straight-away discusses the nature of the means for attaining the Supreme Goal (*puruṣārtha*) and the place of *karma* vis-a-vis *upāsanā*. It sets aside the view of Mīmāṁsakas who lay greater emphasis on *karma* or observance of ritutals and regards that *jñāna* or *upāsanā* is subordinate to it. Bādarāyaṇa emphasizes the need of the observance of the prescribed rituals by all the aspirants for *mokṣa* and also the cultivation of ethical virtues such as *śama, dama* etc. as necessary pre-requisites for *upāsanā*. These points are all covered in the *adhikaraṇas* 109 to 123.

The fourth *adhyāya*, which is named *Phalādhyāya* or the chapter dealing with the spiritual Goal, considers the manner in which the prescribed *sādhana* is to be practised, *utkrānti* or the exit of the individual soul from the physical body at the time of liberation from bondage, the description of the path (*arcirādi gati*) through which the liberated soul passes to reach the ultimate Goal and the nature of the Goal attained by the *jīva* after final liberation from bondage. These points are covered in the four *pādas* of this *adhyāya* comprising a total of 33 *adhikaraṇas* (124 to156).

In the *Adhikaraṇa-sārāvalī*, Vedānta Deśika deals with all the 156 topics and discusses them in the same order as found in Rāmānuja's *Brahma-sūtra Bhāṣya*. As stated earlier, it is written in the form of verses composed in the dignified *sragdharā* metre. It is difficult to present a philosophical discussion in poetic style with the statement of prima facie view (*pūrvapakṣa*), criticism of the same and establish a conclusive theory (*siddhānta*). But Vedānta Deśika, being a gifted poet (*kavi*) and logician (*tārkika*) has successfully accomplished this task, as he has done in the *Tattva-muktā-kalāpa*.

This treatise is not a mere summary of the contents of the *adhikaraṇas* as found in the *Śrī-Bhāṣya*, as the term '*Sārāvalī*' denotes. Its scope is much wider. So also the method of presentation of the subject is different. It does not attempt to present in a stereotyped manner, as in the *Śutra-bhāṣya*, the details of the *pūrvapakṣa* along with the *viṣayavākya* or the Upaniṣadic statements which form the basis for the *sūtra*, and the dialectical arguments and counter-arguments advanced to establish a conclusive theory with the supporting scriptural authority. If it were a mere repetition of what is already stated in the *Śrī-Bhāṣya,* then *Adhikaraṇa-sārāvalī* would be a mere duplication of the effort made by Rāmānuja and it would not be of any special value. Vedānta Deśika himself seems to be aware of this possible objection, which is evident from the fact that at the commencement of the work, he attempts to justify this arduous undertaking. In the opening verse he states that he would defend the title of *Vedāntācārya* conferred on him by Lord Raṅganātha, the presiding deity of Śrīrangam (*tena devena dattāṁ vedāntācārya saṁjñāṁ ...sārtham anvarthayāmi*). If we closely study the work, we find that this claim made out of modesty is well founded by establishing the doctrines of Viśiṣṭādvaita enshrined in the *sūtras* and expounded in the *Śrī-Bhāṣya* by Rāmānuja on a more solid ground not only with the support of Scriptural texts but also on the basis of logic through the discussion of the issues arising as a result of the interpretation of the *sūtras* and the connected Upaniṣadic texts. Unlike Rāmānuja, he does not go into the details of the *pūrva-pakṣa* and answer them step by step in a dialectical manner. On the other hand, he concentrates on the main issue or issues related to the doctrine enshrined in the *sūtras* and after examining them with the relevant arguments, he sets down the *siddhānta* in a precise and clear way. In the *Śrī-Bhāṣya,* a reader often gets lost in the elaborate discussion on the views of the *pūrvapakṣa* with arguments and counter arguments and miss the essential theory that needs to be established. Vedānta Deśika, in his *Adhikaraṇa-sārāvalī* avoids such an elaborate discussion and confines his attention to the disputed issue which is directly related to the topic and answers it with a clear statement of the final view on the subject. This method of discussion enables us to grasp the essential points relevant to a doctrine. A comparative study of the manner of treatment of the *adhikaraṇas* such as *Jijñāsādhikaraṇa, Samanvayādhikaraṇa,*

Ānandamayādhikaraṇa and *Ārambhaṇādhikaraṇa* in *Śrī-Bhāṣya* and *Adhikaraṇa-sārāvali* will bear out the observation made above. If we take note of these facts, it becomes evident that *Adhikaraṇa-sārāvalī* is not a mere summary of the contents of the *adhikaraṇas* of *Brahma-sūtra* but is a distinctive philosophical treatise aimed to present the essential teachings contained in the *adhikaraṇas*.

There are a few other characteristic features of *Adhikaraṇa-sārāvalī*. The first and foremost is the attempt made by Vedānta Deśika to establish the *saṅgati* or connection not only between one *sūtra* and the other but also between the four *adhyāyas*, the four *pādas* of each *adhyāya* and more importantly between the *adhikaraṇas*. On the face of it, it appears that the *sūtras* and *adhikaraṇas* under which they are grouped are somewhat disconnected. But it is not so according to the author of the *sūtras*, who has conceived a perfect sequence. The entire work of *Brahma-sūtra* is a well-knit treatise. Though all the commentators are generally agreed on this point, Vedānta Deśika makes a special effort to establish a close and meaningful connection (*saṅgati*) between the *sūtras*. Though for modern scholars, this may not be of any special importance, the traditional scholars accord great significance to it since it provides a rational justification for formulating a *sūtra* in certain order and sequence from the beginning to the end.

Another important feature of this treatise, as Vedānta Deśika himself points out, is that it clarifies the doubts or minor criticisms raised by some critics on the *Śrī-Bhāṣya* such as repetition of what is already stated elsewhere (*paunarukti*), negation of what is stated (*uktabādha*), irrelevance of the teachings (*mandatva*), absence of proper saṅgati or connection between *adhyāyas*, *pādas* and *adhikaraṇas*, opposition to the accepted *pramāṅas* (*mānabādha*) etc.. According to Vedānta Deśika the *Adhikaraṇa-sārāvalī* reveals that the *adhikaraṇas* of *Brahma-sūtra Bhāṣya* of Rāmānuja is free from these defects. He says that those who read these verses carefully with an open mind will be delighted to find that it is free from defects[17].

It may be observed from this brief contents of the *adhikaraṇas* in the preceding pages that the text in original is very extensive comprising 562 terse verses in Sanskrit and covering 156 *adhikaraṇas* related to a variety of philosophical and allied topics. For persons not well acquainted with Sanskrit, an English translation of the verses with explanatory notes may provide some idea of the contents of the book. But an English translation having its own limitation cannot bring out the spirit of the original text. It does not also provide to the reader a comprehensive and consolidated account of the doctrines of Viśiṣṭādvaita Vedānta in a sequential order. Therefore, neither any attempt is made to present a translation of this original work nor a summary of the *adhikaraṇas* is given in the same order as found in the original text. Some of the *adhikaraṇass,* particularly those which are included in the third *pāda* of third *adhyāya* dealing with different types of *vidyās* and the issues relating to what *guṇas* or attributes of Brahman are either to be included or excluded in respect of the *upāsanā*, would not be of any special philosophical significance. The main objective of the book is to present the important doctrines of Viśiṣṭādvaita Vedānta as expounded in the classic *Sūtra-bhāṣya* of Rāmānuja on the basis of the Upaniṣad and the *sūtras* in a logical order. For this purpose we have confined our attention to the discussion of the selected *adhikaraṇas* that have a direct bearing on the fundamental doctrines of Viśiṣṭādvaita.

Though the central theme of the *Brahma-sūtra* is Brahman, it deals with three major subjects. These are *Tattva* or Brahman, the *Sādhana* or the means of its attainment and *Puruṣārtha* or the Supreme Goal. Under these three major subjects, the following doctrines are discussed in the various *adhikaraṇas*.

The Doctrine of Brahman

1. The essential nature of Brahman
2. The distinguishing characteristics of Brahman
3. Brahman as the cause of the universe

The Doctrine of Universe and Brahman

1. Brahman as the material cause of the universe
2. The relation of the universe to Brahman
3. The theory of cosmic creation

The Doctrine of *Jīva* and Brahman

1. The essential nature of *jīva*
2. The relation of jīva to Brahman
3. The theory of the transmigration of *jīva*
4. The different states of *jīva*

The Doctrine of *Sādhana* or the Means of attainment of Brahman.

1. Brahman as the worthy object of Meditation.
2. *Vidyā* (*upāsanā*) as the direct means of attainment of Brahman.
3. *Karma* as subsidiary means to *Vidyā*.
4. The nature and components of *Upāsanā*.

The Doctrine of *Parama-puruṣārtha*.

1. The nature of the liberation of *jīva* from bondage.
2. The theory of *utkrānti*.
3. The theory of the pathway to *mokṣa* (*Arcirādi-mārga*).
4. The status of *jīva* in the state of *mukti*.

In the present book we shall deal with the *adhikaraṇas* which are related to the above doctrines in a sequential order with the main objective of expounding Viśiṣṭādvaita philosophy as developed by Rāmānuja in the *Brahma-sūtra* Bhāṣya and as further elucidated by Vedānta Deśika in the *Adhikaraṇa-sārāvalī*. We shall not attempt a comparative and critical study of these theories with reference to the commentaries of Śaṁkara and Madhva on the *adhikaraṇas,* since this task has already been accomplished in the book *'The Philosophy of the Vedāntasutra – A study based on the comments of Śaṁkara, Rāmānuja and Madhva'*. We shall not also take up a comparative study of the corresponding theories of other schools of thought to establish the soundness of the Viśiṣṭādvaita doctrines, since this task is undertaken in the book *'Fundamentals of Viśiṣṭādvaita- A study based on Vedānta Deśika's Tattva-muktā-kalāpa.* This book is primarily aimed to give an exposition of Viśiṣṭādvaita Vedānta established in conformity with the Upaniṣads and *Brahma-sūtras* as evidenced by the *Adhikaraṇa-sārāvalī* of Vedānta Deśika.

---

1. *See* NS p1. *Prakāra-prakāriṇoh prakārāṇām ca mitho atyanta bhede api viśistaikyādi vivakṣaya ekatva vyapadesaḥ*
2. RB 1.1.1. *Bhagavat bodhayāna kṛtam brahmasūtra vṛttim pūrvācāryāḥ sanchikṣupuḥ tanmatānuśareṇa sūtrākṣaraṇi vyākhyāsyante*
3. Vedārtha Saṅgraha – p.100
4. TMK V-136 *nāthopajñam pravṛttam*
5. In recent years a book under the title *'Yoga-rahasya'* is published by Sri T.V.K. Desikachar who claims that it is the same *'Yoga-rahasya'* of Nāthamuni, which was revealed to his father, Sri T. Krishnamacharya, during the state of trance at Alwar Tirunagari, the birth place of saint Nāmmālwar. This claim is questionable since the *Yoga-rahasya* of Nā thamuni which was not available to such eminent *Ācāryas,* Rāmānuja and Vedānta Deśika could have been discovered by a person of the present century.
6. TMK IV-10 and V-59
7. TMK – V-136
8. For an authentic account of the biography and the works of Rāmānuja, see the author's article in the *'History of Science, Philosophy and Culture in Indian Civilization'* – Vol II – part 3. pp. 70-105.
9. *See* TMK V-136
10. According to the tradition, one of the commands of Yāmuna was that Rāmānuja should write a proper commentary on the *Vedānta-sutras.*
11. For a biographical sketch of Vedānta Deśika and his works, *see* author's *'Advaita and Viśiṣṭādvaita'* pp. 1-4 and also the volume

mentioned under fn. 8.

12. *pratiṣṭhāpitavedāntaḥ pratikṣipta bahirmataḥ; bhūyaḥ traividyāmanyastvam bhūri-kalyanabhajanam.*
13. TMK I-2. *Varadagurukṛpālaṃbitoddamabhumā...* See also AS. verse 2. *Varadācārya Rāmānujābhyam samyagdṛṣṭeṇa sarvam.*
14. TMK V-134
15. For further details regarding *Tattvamuktākalāpa* see Fvv. Introduction.
16. It is defined as follows: *viṣayo saṁśayaścaiva pūrvapakṣaḥ tathottaram; prayojanam ca pañcāṅgam pañco adhikaraṇam viduḥ.* Vedānta Deśika offers another definition of *adhikarana* which is an expansion of the five stages of discussion into ten: *sangatiḥ viṣayaścaiva saṃśayotthāna kāraṇam; saṃśayaśca prakārāśca tadarthā ca vicāraṇa; tasyam phalaphalitvam ca nyāyau dvau pakṣayordvayoḥ, nirṇayas-tat phalam ce'ti bodhyany-adhikratau daśa.*
17. *See* AS verse 3. *hṛdyā padyavaliyam hṛdayam-adhigatā sāvadhānāt dhinotu (santuṣṭān karotu)*

Chapter One

THE STUDY OF VEDĀNTA

Brahma-sūtra is primarily concerned with the study of Brahman, which is the ultimate metaphysical Reality. Bādarāyaṇa therefore rightly commences his classic treatise on Vedānta with four aphorisms to justify the need and importance of the philosophic study for obtaining the knowledge of Brahman. These *sūtras* deal with four important subjects viz., a) enquiry into the nature of Brahman, b) definition of Brahman as the primary cause of the cosmic functions, c) *śāstra* as the only source of knowing Brahman, and d) the main purport of the Upaniṣads is Brahman. The first four *adhikaraṇas* named as *Jijñāsādhikaraṇa, Janmādyadhikaraṇa, Śāstrayonitvādhi-karaṇa* and *Samanvayādhikaraṇa* cover these subjects respectively. These *adhikaraṇas* which constitute one unit (*peṭikā*) are regarded by the commentators as a preface (*upodghāta*) to *Brahma-sūtra* since they affirm the value and importance of the Vedānta study by way of refuting the general objection that the study of Vedānta is futile. As explained by the commentators, Bādarāyaṇa has in mind four possible objections prevalent during his time against the study of Vedānta. These are: (a) The Upaniṣadic texts which teach about Brahman which is an existent (*siddhapara*) are not purportful; (b) the definition about Brahman offered by the Upaniṣad is not satisfactory and hence Brahman cannot be known; (c) since the existence of Brahman can be proved by inference, Sacred texts cannot teach anything new; and

(d) the knowledge of Brahman derived from the Upaniṣads does not serve any useful purpose.[1] The details of these criticisms will be explained when we discuss the relevant *adhikaraṇas*. For the present it may be noted that these are implied in the relevant *sūtras* and that Bādarāyana, as explained by the commentators, attempts at the very outset to refute them in order to establish the value of Vedānta study. We shall discuss these four topics in the present chapter.

I. Brahma-jijñāsā

Regarding *Brahma-jijñāsā*, the *sūtra* reads: *Athāto brahma-jijñāsā*[2]. It means: 'Then, therefore, the enquiry into Brahman'. Each word in the *sūtra* has far reaching implications. *Jijñāsā* means desire to know (*jñātum icchā*). It refers to the object of desire viz., knowledge of Brahman which is more important than desire itself. The term Brahman denotes, according to Rāmānuja, the Supreme Person (*Puruṣottama*) who by nature is endowed with infinite auspicious attributes and is also free from all imperfections.[3] The word *atha* means soon after (*anantara*) and implies, as interpreted by Rāmānuja, that *Brahma-jijñāsā* is to be undertaken after completing the study of *Pūrva-mīmāṁsā* dealing with the ritualistic portion of the Vedas. The word *ataḥ* means 'therefore' and it implies the reason for pursuing the study of Vedānta after one has realized the futility of the fruits of the rituals and come to know the eternal value of the spiritual goal to be attained by the study of Vedānta. The fuller meaning of the *sūtra*, as explained by Rāmānuja, is that the enquiry into the nature of Brahman is to be undertaken by a spiritual aspirant after he has completed the study of *Pūrva-mīmāṁsa*, which deals with the ritualistic portion of the Vedas and realized the impermanent value of the fruits achieved by the Vedic rituals and the eternal value of the Supreme Goal to be attained by the study of *Uttara-*

mīmāṁsa, which deals with the later portion of the Vedas (Upaniṣads)

This view has for its support the teaching of the Muṇḍaka Upaniṣad on the basis of which the *sūtra* itself is formulated. Thus it states:

Parīkṣya lokān karmacitān brāhmaṇo nirvedamāyāt. Nastyakṛtaḥ kṛtena. tadvijñārthaṁ sa gurumeva abhigacchet samitpāṇiḥ śrotriyam brahmaniṣṭham. Tasmai sa vidvān upasannāya saṁyak praśāntacittāya samanvitāya. Yenākṣaram puruṣam veda satyam provāca taṁ tattvato brahmavidyām[4]

"After having examined the fruits obtained by the performance of the prescribed rituals, a *Brāhmaṇa* (one who has studied the *Vedas*) should become dejected by realizing that what is eternal (*Paramātman*) cannot be attained from the non-permanent fruits of the rituals. In order to know that (Reality), he should approach with a token gift a preceptor who is learned in the *Vedas* and is also well established in the knowledge of Brahman. To such a pupil, who has approached the preceptor with his senses restrained and equipped with mental tranquility, the *guru* (preceptor) should impart the knowledge of Brahman by means of which the eternal and imperishable Reality is realized".

The above passage clearly indicates that the study of *Vedānta* for gaining the knowledge of Brahman is to be taken up after the study of *karma-kāṇḍa*. This view is also supported by the authoritative statement of Bodhāyana, an ancient commentator on *Brahma-sūtra*. Thus, it is stated: *vṛttāt karmādhigamāt anantaram brahma vividiṣā.*[5] "Soon after the comprehension of the knowledge of the rituals has taken place, there follows the enquiry into Brahman.

II. Pūrva-mīmāṁsā and Uttara-mīmāṁsā

The first question that is raised in this connection is whether there is any connection between *Pūrva-mīmāṁsā* and *Uttata-mīmāṁsā*. It is contended that these two are distinctive parts of the *Vedas* dealing with separate subjects, the former with the rituals and the latter with Brahman. There is difference in respect of their authors, contents, aim and the persons eligible for their study. There is also opposition between *karma* or observance of rituals which is the main theme of *Pūrva-mīmāṁsā* and *jñāna* or knowledge of Brahman, which is the central theme of the *Vedānta*. Besides, the study of *Pūrva-mīmāṁsā* is not of any use for the study of *Vedānta* and hence the study of *Pūrva-mīmāṁsā* is not a necessary precedent to the study of *Vedānta*.

These issues are discussed in great detail by Rāmānuja in the *Śrī-Bhāṣya* while commenting on the first *sūtra* and also by Vedānta Deśika in the *Adhikaraṇa-sārāvalī* and the *Śatadūṣaṇī*. These are refuted on the basis of three strong arguments. First, the enquiry into the meaning of the Vedic texts which comprises the ritualistic as well as Brahman portion should cover the study of both *Pūrva-mīmāṁsā* and *Uttara-mīmāṁsa*. Secondly, the knowledge of *Pūrva-mīmāṁsā* is very essential for the study of *Vedānta*. Thirdly, the two *Mīmāṁsas* - *Pūrva* and *Uttara*- form one integral whole.

Regarding the first argument, it is pointed out that the Scriptural injunction demands the study of the entire Vedas including the Upaniṣads along with the anciliary texts (*Vedāṅgas*). Its meaning also should be grasped with the aid of the rules of interpretation and other logical arguments since with the understanding of the meaning only, it is possible to determine the subsequent action. The enquiry into their meaning (*arthavicāra*) may be initiated either through a specific injunction, as the *Mīmāṁsakas* maintain, or it may take place out of one's own desire (*rāgataḥ*). In either case, Vedānta Deśika argues, that it covers the entire portion of the Vedas, as it cannot be restricted to any one part. Though it may be possible to restrict the enquiry that is undertaken due to a specific injunction, it is not possible to do so in the case of an enquiry initiated out of one's own desire. It cannot be restricted to Brahman since one may desire to know all the four human goals (*puruṣārthas*) and a desire to know all the four *puruṣārthas* naturally leads to the enquiry into the meaning of the entire Scriptural texts including the Upaniṣads. Consequently, one realizes in a general way from the Scriptural statements that *svarga* etc., achieved through prescribed sacrifice are of impermanent nature and that the knowledge of Brahman obtained through the study of the Upaniṣads lead to eternal Spiritual Goal (*akṣayaphala*).

Regarding the second argument, Vedānta Deśika points out that the *Pūrva-mīmāṁsā* actually aids the *Uttara-mīmāṁsā*. The aid is in the form that Vedānta requires the arguments and the principles of *Pūrva-mīmāṁsā* (*nyāyopajīvanam*). The first *adhyāya* of *Pūrva-mīmāṁsā* establishes that Vedas are authoritative. This in general is very essential for *Vedānta*. The second *adhyāya* named *Bhedādhyāya* discusses the nature of difference etc. This is useful to the study of the third section of the third *adhyāya* of the Vedānta titled *Guṇopasaṁhāra pāda*. Again the third *adhyāya* of the *Pūrva-mīmāṁsā* which deals with the principles of interpretation is useful throughout the study of *Vedānta*. *Prayukti* or that which discusses the purpose of each ritual which comes under the fourth *adhyāya* of *Pūrva-mīmāṁsā*, is helpful in ascertaining whether the religious duty connected with the caste etc., is meant for the purpose of Brahman-knowledge or confined to the *āśrama* itself. Again in the fifth *adhyāya* of *Pūrva-mīmāṁsā*, the topic dealing with the succession of rituals (*kramaḥ*) is helpful in studying the third section of the last chapter of *Brahma-sūtra*. The discussion relating to the nature of the agent etc., which is taken up in the sixth *adhyāya* of *Pūrva-mīmāṁsā* is useful for the discussion about the eligibility of persons to the study of *Vedānta*. Likewise the other *adhyāyas* of *Pūrva-mīmāṁsā* are also useful either directly or indirectly to the study of Vedānta. Thus, the meaning of *Vedānta* texts is ascertained with the help of the principles and arguments set forth in the *Pūrva-mīmāṁsā* and hence the knowledge of *Pūrva-mīmāṁsā* is indispensible for *Uttara-mīmāṁsā*.

Vedānta Deśika further contends that there is absolutely no contradiction between *Pūrva-mīmāṁsā* and *Uttara-mīmāṁsā* either in respect of content or end or aspirant. The aspirant is one and the same. He who has studied the *Pūrva-mīmāṁsā* and understood the finite and impermanent character of the fruits of *karma* enters on the study of Vedānta which refers to the Supreme Goal. As regards the subject matter, though there are minor differences there is an inherent unity between the two subjects. Ritualism is preliminary and philosophic quest is subsequent development. One is apprenticeship and the other is adeptship. One clarifies and illuminates the other. Thus, there is organic unity between the two treatises (*śāstras*). As will be shown, presently the two constitute one single treatise.

Nor is there any opposition between *karma* or the performance the prescribed *rituals* and *jñāna* taken in the sense of the knowledge of Brahman or *upāsanā* (meditation) on Brahman. As will be seen in the later chapters, the performance of rituals is helpful in acquiring the desire to know Brahman (*vividiṣā*), as the Advaitin admits and it is a subsidiary means to *upāsanā*, as the Viśiṣṭādvaitin maintains. The ritualistic observances cannot be dispensed with as it serves as the purificatory programme and aids Brahman-enquiry.

But how could the two treatises be considered to be one, while they have been composed by different authors? This is an important objection raised by the critic. Vedānta Deśika exposes the hollowness of this objection. One and the same person can plan a project and successfully execute many endeavours, many schemes; or again countless persons by combined effort may accomplish a single project as in the case of the construction of a tower of a temple. Even in respect of a literary work, one scholar can compose a number of independent treatises. Or as in the case of the commentary on Pāṇini *sūtras*, even though different authors are involved, the treatise continues to be the same.

It may be argued that in many of the *Vedānta-sūtras* the position taken by Jaimini is indicated as *pūrva pakṣa*, that is, a position to be repudiated. Does not this indicate that the two are incompatible? How then can they coalesce into a single unity?

This objection is baseless, argues Vedānta Deśika. The differences referred to between Bādarayāṇa and Jaimini relate to minor matters, almost to trivial formalities (*atyalpatara apradhānārtha*). If in a portion of a building some part is removed and reconstructed the main unity of the building is not destroyed. On the other hand, the removal of the part and its reconstruction add to the beauty of it. Likewise it should be understood that the *Pūrva-mīmāṁsā* has been corrected by the *Uttara-mīmāṁsā*. Or again the differences between Jaimini and Bādarāyaṇa may be understood in a different way. It may be taken that Jaimini has given expression to such views not with the intention of opposing the views of Bādarāyaṇa but to demonstrate his capacity to establish the truth on grounds conceding the opponents' assumptions (*vaibhavokti*). Bādarāyaṇa reexamines them with the idea that laymen may not mistake them for truths. The position of Jaimini is, therefore, quoted with approval for removing likely doubts, for clarification of the issues and also for a reasoned reinforcement of the main doctrines. All this is amply evidenced by references like 'So said Jaimini'. More than that, in many contexts Bādarāyaṇa refers to Jaimini by name for supporting his own views.[6] Similarly Jaimini to support his own conclusion refers to Bādarāyaṇa and his authority.[7] These reciprocal references must prove convincingly that the two brances of the literature dealing with *karma-kāṇḍa* and *Brahma-kāṇḍa* constitute a totality.

Now we come to the third important argument in support of the theory upheld by Rāmānuja that the study of the *Pūrva-mīmāṁsā* should precede the study of *Vedānta*. According to the tradition, *Mīmāṁsā-śāstra*, which is concerned with the interpretation of the *Vedas*, is one single *śāstra* comprising three parts. The first part is named as *karma-kāṇḍa* consisting of 12 *adhyāyas* which deal with the nature and manner of performing the various rituals. The *Pūrva-mīmāṁsā sutras* of Jaimini constitute this part and it is generally acknwoledged as the basic *Mīmāṁsā* treatise. The second part is known as *Devatā-kāṇḍa* consisting of four *adhyāyas* which deal with the nature and status of celestial deities referred to in the Vedas. It is also called *Saṁkarṣaṇa-kāṇḍa,* named after its author, Saṁkarṣaṇa. This work is not extant. However, there are references made to it in other works. The concluding *sūtra* of this *kāṇḍa* which refers to Viṣṇu, the Supreme Deity and who is equated with Brahman is quoted by Vedānta Deśika and also by Madhva. The relevant *sūtra* reads: *sa viṣṇurāha hi..taṁ brahmetyācakṣate taṁ brahmetyācakṣate.* "He is known as Viṣṇu and that he is called Brahman". The mention of Brahman in the concluding *sūtra* of *Saṁkarṣaṇa kāṇḍa* also establishes its connection to the opening *sūtra* of the *Brahma-sūtra.* The third part of *Mīmāṁsā śāstra* is the *Brahma-sūtra* of Bādarāyaṇa consisting of four *adhyāyas.* The three constitute one single *śāstra,* though they are divided into three parts, each one being authored by three different sages. Keeping this fact in mind, the author of the *Bodhāyana Vṛtti* states: *saṁhitam-etat śārīrakam jaiminīyena ṣoḍaśa lakṣaṇena iti śāstraikatva siddhiḥ.* (Quoted by Rāmānuja in the *Śrī-Bhāṣya*). "The *śārīraka* (*Vedānta-sūtra*) of four chapters forms a textual totality with the sixten-chaptered *Pūrva-mīmāṁsā* of Jaimini."

To give prominence to Jaimini, Saṁkarṣaṇa is not mentioned by name by Bodhāyana, as Vedānta Deśika explains. But it is implied by the word *ṣoḍaśalakṣaṇa* or 16 chapters, since Jaimini's *Mīmāṁsā-sūtras* cover only 12 *adhyāyas,* as accepted by all the Mīmāṁsakas. On the authority of Bodhāyana who is the reputed ancient commentator on *Brahma-sūtra, Rāmānuja* affirms that Mīmāṁsā is a single *śāstra* beginning with *'Athāto dharma-jijñāsā' and ending with 'Anāvṛtti śabdāt'*, divided into three parts: *Karma-kāṇḍa* of twelve chapters, *Devatā-kāṇḍa* of four chapters, and *Para-devatā-kāṇḍa* of four chapters. This twenty-chaptered literature is throughout dominated by a central plan and execution. In view of these facts it is considered necessary that the study of *Pūrva-mīmāṁsā* should necessarily precede the study of *Vedānta*.

According to the Advaita Vedānta, *Pūrva-mīmāṁsā* is not a pre-requisite for the study of *Vedānta*. There are four factors which are considered necessary for the study of *Vedānta*. These are: discrimination of eternal and non-eternal *(nityā-nityavastu vivekaḥ)* possession in abundance of calmness, equanimity and other such means *(śama damādi sādhana sampat)*, non-attachment to the enjoyment of fruits here and hereafter *(ihāmutraphalabhoga virāgaḥ)* and desire for release *(mumukṣatvam)*.

Vedānta Deśika rejects the above theory on the ground that the four factors in question do not invariably precede the enquiry into Brahman. The main point of his criticism is that the discrimination of things eternal and non-eternal becomes possible only after one has made a study of *Vedānta* and hence it cannot be a pre-requisite to the study of *Vedānta*.[8] It cannot be said that this knowledge of discrimination arises from the study of other systems, which one would have completed before commencement of the study of Vedānta. In that case, the study of Vedānta would become superfluous since the knowledge that is to be obtained from it would have already been derived from the study of other systems. Similarly if the possession of *śama, dama* etc., is taken to imply perfect control of sense organs, this would be possible only after one has studied Vedānta and embarked on the *sādhana* for the realization of the Self (*darśana*). This is evident from the following Upaniṣadic text: "Hence having become possessed of calmness, equanimity, turning away from the objects of pleasure and the desire to abandon them, one seeing the Self in the self (mind) alone, sees everything".[9] As regards the non-attachment to the fruits here or hereafter and the desire for release, though these may be needed for the study of *Vedānta*, it is more appropriate, contends Vedānta Deśika, that the study of *Pūrva-mīmāṁsā* is accepted as the pre-requisite to the enquiry into Brahman for more than one reason. First, it suggests the order in which a person proceeds to study Vedānta. Secondly, it makes evident that an individual who enters into the study of Vedānta has clearly understood the arguments that are required for the purpose of knowing the nature of Brahman as well as contemplation thereon. Thirdly, it also facilitates an unhindered enquiry into Brahman through the removal of the prima facie superficial knowledge that the ritualistic deeds lead to the infinite and permanent result. The Scriptural text to which we have already referred also states: "Let a Brahmin after he has examined all these worlds (fruits of *karma*), obtain freedom from all desires and approach a qualified *guru* to obtain knowledge of Brahman".[10]

Another serious objection is raised by the *Mīmāṁsakas* questioning the usefulness of the study of Vedānta. In fact this constitutes the prima facie view (*pūrvapakṣa)* for the *sūtra* enjoining *Brahma-jijñāsā,* as interpreted by the commentators. According to *Prābhākara Mīmāṁsā,* words convey their meanings only as related to specific action. The process by which the meanings of words are derived is explained by an illustration. An elderly person asks a younger person to bring a cow and take it back. A child nearby observes the younger person carrying out the command and comes to understand that the word cow mentioned in the statement refers to the animal 'cow'. From this it is concluded that in the first stage words convey their meanings through such injunctive statements of elderly persons involving action *(ādyā vyutpattiḥ kārya eva).* On the basis of this, the Prābhākaras uphold that words convey their meanings only as related to specific action. The implication of this theory is that only Vedic statements of injunctive character are purportful, whereas the Upaniṣadic statements which refer to the existent or what is already established (*siddhapara)* cannot be taken as valid except as complemental to the injunctive statements. In view of this, the study of *Vedānta* is not of any use.

Following the criticisms offered by Rāmānuja in *the Śrī-Bhāṣya*, Vedānta Deśika refutes this theory. He explains how at the initial stage words derive the meaning without any reference to activity in respect of existents. Thus, a person pointing his finger at a cow tells his child that it is called cow and the child learns to associate that word with the object 'cow'. The child then understands the meaning of words without those words having any reference to activity. To give another example, an individual, who is aware of the fact that the news about the birth of a child causes pleasure, conveys such news to the father of the newly-born child, and the latter feels happy after hearing the statement of the former. It is obvious that the statement of the first individual conveys the meaning to the second individual and as such he reacts with joy. It is not therefore necessary that, in order to be meaningful, statements should have a direct bearing on activity.

Vedānta Deśika further explains how in the subsequent periods too, words convey their meaning in respect of existents. A person who is already acquainted with the meaning of certain words, understands on the basis of previous experience that such and such words have specific meanings and vice versa. With the knowledge of limited number of words, he also understands the meaning of more connected words in our ordinary experience. Whatever meanings are attached to the words in our ordinary experience, the same also hold good in respect of Vedic vocabulary. When however, there are Vedic words which do not bear the meaning current in our ordinary experience, their meaning is to be understood with the help of *Nirukta*, the treatise containing etymological interpretation of Vedic words.

Vedānta Deśika therefore concludes that words and the Upaniṣadic statements about Brahman are purportful even in respect of the existent.[11] Hence the study of Vedānta is to be undertaken after the study of *Pūrva-mīmāṁsā*, as enjoined in the *Brahma-sūtra*.

III. Definition of Brahman

This is the subject of the *adhikaraṇa* named as *Janmādya-dhikaraṇa* covering the second *sūtra* in which Brahman, the object of *jijñāsā* is defined by Bādarāyaṇa. The *sūtra* reads: *janmādy-asya yataḥ*[12]. The word *janma* means creation *(sṛṣṭi)* and the affix *ādi* implies *sthiti or* sustenance and *laya* or dissolution. The word *asya* refers to the variegated universe including the souls. The total meaning of the *sūtra* is that from which proceed the creation, sustenance and dissolution of the universe is Brahman. Thus, Brahman is defined by Bādarāyaṇa as that which is the cause of the creation, sustenance and dissolution of the universe.

This *sūtra* is formulated with reference to the passage of the Taittirīya Upaniṣad which offers the definition of Brahman. Bhṛgu requests his father Varuṇa to teach him about Brahman. In reply, Varuṇa states:

Yato vā imāni bhūtāni jāyante, yena jātāni jīvanti, yat prayanti abhi-saṁviśanti, tad vijijñāsasva, tat brahmeti[13].

"That from which these beings are born, that from which when born they live, and that unto which when departing, they enter, seek to know that; that is Brahman."

In the context of the Upaniṣadic teaching there is no vagueness regarding the definition of Brahman offered by Bādarāyaṇa. The *sūtra* clearly lays down the three-fold cosmic function *(jagatkāraṇatva)* as the criteria for determining an ontological entity as Brahman.

In this connection an important issue is raised by the critic. There are two ways by which an object is defined. It can be defined in terms of its essential attributes (*viśeṣaṇas*) or qualifications per proprium. It can also be described with reference to certain identity marks (*upalakṣaṇas) or* qualifications per accidens. The moon in the distant sky, for instance, can be identified with reference to its abundant luminosity. It can also be identified through the moon visible as if close to the branch of a tree. The first kind of definition is known as *svarūpa lakṣaṇa* or definition in terms of its essential qualities belonging to the object. The second type is named as *taṭastha lakṣaṇa* or description offered by using certain identity marks (*upalakṣaṇas*) which do not actually belong to the object. The question to be considered is whether the present Upanisadic text defines Brahman through the *viśeṣaṇas* or the *upalakṣaṇas*. The prima facie view is that in either case, Brahman cannot be defined. If the three cosmic functions are taken as *viśeṣaṇas*, these are different in nature and as such they denote three different entities as each one being qualified by a particular function. This view is based on the assumption that different *viśeṣaṇas* are applicable to different *viśeṣyas* or substances. On the contrary, if these functions are taken as *upalakṣaṇas*, even then Brahman is not defined. The *upalakṣaṇa* can convey the knowledge of the *upalakṣya* or the object denoted by it when the latter (Brahman) is already known in some way. Since Brahman is not already known, the *upalakṣana* in the form of cosmic functions cannot convey the knowledge of Brahman. Hence the definition given in the Upaniṣad does not help us to know Brahman. It is therefore futile to undertake *Brahma-jijñāsā*.

In reply to this general criticism, Vedānta Deśika points out that Brahman as the Supreme Being and as the primary cause of the universe is already known through other Scriptural texts, particularly in the *Puruṣasukta* passage of the Vedas. It is only such a Brahman that is being taught by Varuṇa to Bhṛgu in the Taittirīya Upaniṣad. This is evident from the two pronouns *yataḥ* and *tat* used in the passage. The word *yat* implies what is well established as the creator of the universe and *tat* refers to such a Brahman.[14]

The Advaitin advances a different criticism. If all the three cosmic functions are regarded as *viśeṣaṇas*, then Brahman denoted by them cannot be one undifferentiated Being. This view is based on the logical principle adopted by the Advaitin that different *viśeṣaṇas* mentioned in a statement about the *viśeṣya* or substance break up the unitary character of the *viśeṣya (viśeṣaṇānam viśeṣyabhedakam)*. The example given in support of this view is the statement describing the cow as one without horn, with broken horn and with full horn *(khaṇḍo muṇḍah pūrṇaśrañgo gauḥ)*. This statement does not convey the idea of one cow but three different ones. In the same way the definition of Brahman as that which is the cause of the creation of the universe, as the cause of its sustenance and as the cause of its dissolution does not denote one Brahman. This criticism also applies to the definition of Brahman as *satyam, jñānam* and *anantam* which is regarded as *lakṣaṇa vākya* or statement offering a definition. In this statement, if the three terms are taken as attributes, Brahman cannot be one undifferentiated Being.

To avoid this difficulty, if one of the cosmic functions alone is taken as *viśeṣaṇa* denoting Brahman, then the other two functions mentioned in the Upaniṣad become irrelevant. If all the three together denote Brahman, then Brahman cannot be distinguished from entities other than Brahman. According to the Advaitin, each term in the statement should serve the purpose of distinguishing Brahman from what it is not, as in the case of *satya* from what is *anṛta* or unreal, *jñāna* from what is *jaḍa* and *ananta* from what is finite. Hence the definition of Brahman in terms of three cosmic functions taken as *viśeṣaṇas* is unsatisfactory similar to the statement on cow as *khaṇḍo muṇḍaḥ pūrṇasrañgaḥ*.

The above criticism is untenable, contends Vedānta Deśika. The three cosmic functions Viz. *janma, sthiti and pralaya* are not mutually opposed as in the case of the cow with broken horn, without horn and with horn. Wherever the characteristics are not mutually opposed, the object to which these are applicable does not become disintegrated. That is, the object denoted by different attributes which are not mutually opposed (*aviruddha)* is one and the same as qualified by them, as in the statement that Devadatta is *śyāma* or of dark complexion, *yuvā* or youth and *lohitākṣaḥ* or having brown eyes. In the statement 'The cow with broken horn, without horn and with full horn', the qualifications attributed to the cow are mutually opposed. Besides this fact is also evident to our experience. The important point to be noted is that in a judgment where the terms stated in apposition connote different qualities which are not opposed to each other and which can also inhere in the same substance, the object denoted by them is not disintegrated. Where the terms connoting different qualities that are opposed to each other and which do not inhere in the same substance, the object denoted by them is not one and the same *(viruddhameva viśeṣaṇam viśeṣyabhedakam, na punaḥ aviruddham viśeṣaṇam)*[15]. The three cosmic functions mentioned in the Upaniṣadic text are therefore applicable to Brahman.

It may be still questioned how the three cosmic functions, which are different in nature, are applicable to one Brahman? The same Brahman which is the creator of the universe cannot also be its destroyer. In reply to this objection, Vedānta Deśika points out that the same one Brahman can perform different functions at different times *(kālabhedena)*. It is possible to define Brahman in terms of one function only. That is, Brahman is that which causes the creation of the universe. Yet all the three functions together are adopted as the criteria of the definition in order to eliminate the possibility of mistaking other lower deities such as Brahmā, Rudra etc., as Brahman.[16]

An objection is also raised against the definition of Brahman through the *upalakṣaṇa,* that is, in terms of the cosmic functions taken as identity marks. When an object is defined through *upalakṣaṇa,* some aspect of the *upalakṣya* or the object to be defined is required to be known. The illustration cited to explain this point is the paddy field of Devadatta which is being identified through the tree on which a *sārasa* bird is sitting. In this illustration the tree associated with the *sārasa* bird sitting on it serves as the *upalakṣaṇa* for the identification of the field of Devadatta. In this case the field is known but what is not evident is that it belongs to Devadatta. The tree associated with the bird is made use of to identify Devadatta's field. In the case of Brahman, which is to be made known through *upalakṣaṇa,* it is not possible to specify what aspect of it is known and what aspect is unknown (*jñātājñātāṁśa bhedastu durabhilapaḥ).* If Brahman is known, it is then possible to say that the term Brahman denotes it. If it is not known, the query about Brahman does not arise.

The above dialectical argument is set aside by Vedānta Deśika. That Brahman as the Ultimate Reality is infinitely great is well established in several *Śruti* and *Smṛti* texts such as *'Brahma parivrīḍam sarvataḥ', 'bṛhati brahmayati tasmāducyate paraṁ brahma' etc.,* What is not known is that among the various other deities referred to in the *Śruti* and *Smṛiti* texts such as Brahmā, Viṣṇu, Rudra etc.,it is not known which particular Deity is the Supreme Being. In order to remove this doubt, the Upaniṣad teaches in a specific way that which is the cause of the creation, sustenance and dissolution of the universe is Brahman[17]. All the three cosmic functions are not attributable to any other Vedic Deity than Brahman. Similarly in the *Puruṣa-sūkta* passage, the term *Puruṣa* is used in a general way in the earlier part. In order to specify who this *Puruṣa* is, the later part of the passage (*uttarānuvāka*) states that Goddess *Śrī* and *Bhū* are His consorts. The mention of *Śrī* and *Bhū* as His consorts eliminates the possibility of *Puruṣa* being any other Deity than the Supreme Being designated as *Nārāyaṇa* who is equated with *Para Brahma* in the Taittirīya Nārāyaṇa Upaniṣad.

As we have stated earlier, there are two ways of defining an object, either by means of *viśeṣaṇas or upalaksaṇas.* The definition of an object in terms of its characteristics which refer to the nature of the object (*svarūpa*) is called *svarūpa lakṣaṇa.* The definition of an object by means of certain identity marks, as for example, the description of the moon seen in the distant sky through the moon seen as if close to the branch of a tree, is known as *taṭastha lakṣaṇa*. According to the Advaitin, the definition of Brahman in terms of the three cosmic functions is regarded as *taṭastha lakṣaṇa*. The definition of Brahman as *satyaṁ, jñānaṁ and anantaṁ is svarūpa lakṣaṇa*. This distinction is maintained by the Advaitin since Brahman being *niriviśeṣa* or devoid of all determinations cannot be defined in terms of characteristics. *Jagatkāraṇatva* as a *viśeṣaṇa* cannot be attributed to higher Brahman which is undifferentiated. The terms *satya, jñāna and ananta* in the other definition refer directly to the *svarūpa* of Brahman.

This view is rejected by Vedānta Deśika as unsound. As Rāmānuja has pointed out, *jagatkāraṇatva* taken either as *upalakṣaṇa or viśeṣaṇa*, can serve the purpose of knowing Brahman directly. According to Madhva, both the definitions are *svarūpa lakṣaṇas* since they reveal the nature of Brahman.

Logically an object is defined in terms of its essential characteristics. We distinguish one object from another only with reference to its essential characteristic. Brahman is defined as the origin of three comic functions to distinguish it from other sentient and non-sentient entities. Similarly in the case of the definition of Brahman as *satya, jñāna and ananta*, the three terms which refer to three distinguishing characteristics of Brahman denote Brahman as qualified by them.

The above explanation is in conformity with the grammatical rule laid down by Pāṇini Mahābhāṣya and also the principle of interpretation adopted by the Seśvara Mīmāṁsakas. According to the Grammarian, in a sentence or judgment where the terms are stated in apposition (*samānādhikaraṇa)*, though each term connotes different qualities, they denote one entity as qualified by them[18] This principle applies to the definition of Brahman as *satya, jñāna and ananta.*

According to the principle governing the interpretation of Vedic statements adopted by the Mīmāṁsakas, the words in a sentence bearing different imports are applicable to the same one entity or act. There is a Scriptural statement which reads: *aruṇayā ekahāyinyā piṅgākṣyā somam krīṇāti.* It enjoins that soma plant (for *yāga*) is to be bought in exchange for a cow of red colour, one year old and tawny eyed. The question raised in interpreting this statement is whether both the terms *aruṇa* denoting the quality of redness (*guṇa*) and *ekahāyin* referring to one year old cow (*dravya*) are applicable to the cow. The prima facie view is that they are not applicable to the cow and the sentence is therefore to be broken up into two since redness being a general quality is not necessarily applicable to one year old cow. This view is rejected by the Seśvara Mīmāṁsaka and it is established that the act of buying the cow being one, both the quality (*guṇa*) and the *dravya* or object referred to are applicable to the same one cow.[19]

The Upaniṣadic text offers the definition of Brahman in terms of the three cosmic functions viz., *sṛṣṭi, sthiti and laya.* As Rāmānuja has stated, the mention of the three cosmic functions may be taken either as *upalakṣana or viśeṣaṇa.* Either way, the definition provided by the Upaniṣad conveys the knowledge of Brahman. The implication of this stand taken by Rāmānuja, as Vedānta Deśika explains, is that *jagatkāraṇatva* taken either as *upalaksana* or *viśeṣaṇa,* does not make any difference in respect of knowing the *svarūpa* of Brahman. The *viśeṣaṇas* necessarily inhere in the object defined, whereas the *upalakṣaṇas,* though not belonging to the object, serve the purpose of identifying it as in the case of the moon seen through the branch of the tree. Vedānta Deśika, therefore, concludes that the Upanisadic text offering the definition of Brahman is sound and it conveys the knowledge of Brahman. Hence the study of Vedānta is justified.

IV. Proof for the Existence of Brahman

This is the subject-matter of a separate *adhikaraṇa* named *Śāstrayonitvādhikaraṇa* covering the third *sūtra* which reads: *śāstra-yonitvāt*[20]. It means that *śāstra* is the source for knowledge of Brahman. The word *śāstra* is taken in the broad sense to mean the Vedas including the Upaniṣads and all the allied sacred texts such as *Vedaṅgas, Itihāsas* and *Purāṇas*. The term yoni means *kāraṇa* or source (*pramāṇa*) for the knowledge of Brahman. The fuller implication of the *sūtra,* as interpreted by Rāmānuja, is that Brahman cannot be known either by means of perception (*pratyakṣa*) or inference (*anumāna*) and that *śāstra* is the only *pramāna* for knowing it (*śāstraika pramāṇam).*

The Naiyāyikas attempt to prove the existence of God by means of inference. They have advanced several logical arguments for this purpose. Of these the most important one is the cosmological argument based on the idea of causation (*kāryatā)*. The universe is an effect and must have been produced by an agent or creator called *Īśvara*. The argument is expressed in the following syllogistic form: 'This physical universe must have been caused by an agent, because it is an effect, just as a pot.' (*Pṛthivyādikam sakartṛkam, kāryatvāt, ghaṭavat)*. By further qualifying the *kartā* or agent as one endowed with omniscience, it is attempted to prove the existence of God. Thus, if the existence of God can be proved by means of inference, there would be no need to undertake the study of Vedānta for knowing Brahman which is already established by other *pramāṇas*. Anticipating such an objection, Bādarāyaṇa has formulated the *sūtra* to affirm that Brahman can be known only through *śāstra* and not by any other means.

This syllogistic argument is subjected to detailed critical examination by Rāmānuja in the *Śrī-Bhāṣya* and also by Vedānta Deśika in the *Tattva-muktā-kalāpa* and it is proved to be fallacious. In the *Adhikaraṇa Sārāvalī,* Deśika points out that the syllogism in whatever manner it is modified to overcome the logical fallacies, cannot prove on the basis of the present probans viz., *kāryatvāt,* the existence of an omniscient God as the creator of the universe. All that it can establish is that a super individual (*jīva*) possessing unlimited capacity and knowledge acquired through penance could be the creator of the universe and not an omniscient and omnipotent Supreme God, as taught in the Upaniṣads. Hence Bādarāyaṇa states that *śāstra* is the only source for knowing the existence of Brahman.

The important point to be noted is that *anumāna* by itself cannot conclusively prove the existence of God or Brahman as conceived in the Upaniṣads. Apart from the fact that it suffers from various logical fallacies, it is possible for one to advance syllogistic arguments to disprove what is asserted by means of inference. As Vedānta Deśika points out, it is neither possible to prove the existence of God nor disprove His existence solely by means of inference.[21]

This does not imply that logic has no place in *Vedānta.* Logic is accepted to supplement what is stated in the *Śruti.* Sage Parāśara in Viṣṇupurāṇa uses logical arguments to prove the existence of Viṣṇu as the Supreme Deity. These arguments are intended to support what is stated in the Upaniṣads. The Taittirīya Upaniṣadic text teaching about Brahman as the cause of the universe is not to be construed as supplementing the *anumāna* adopted to prove the existence of God. On the contrary, it is a restatement about Brahman already well known in other Scriptural texts, as is evident from the preposition *yataḥ (yata iti ca sadādi uktisiddha anuvādāt).*[22]

V. The Upaniṣads and Brahman

This is the subject-matter of the *adhikaraṇa* named *Samanvayādhikaraṇa* covering the fourth *sūtra* in which Bādarāyaṇa affirms that the Upaniṣads which teach about Brahman are valid and meaningful. The *sūtra* reads: *Tat-tu samanvayāt*[23]. Its general meaning is that Brahman is known through the *śāstra* because all the Upaniṣadic texts proclaim it as their purport (*tātparya*). Every word in the *sūtra* is of special significance. The word *tat* means Brahman. To be more specific, it refers to the thesis maintained in the previous *sūtra* viz., that *śāstra* is the only source (*pramāṇa*) for knowing Brahman. The word *tu* which is a conjunction means 'but' and it implies that the view upheld by Bādarāyaṇa differs from that of the *Pūrva-mīmāṁsakas* who do not consider the Upaniṣadic texts as purportful. According to them only Scriptural texts which are in the form of injunctions and which involve human endeavour such as the performance of a *yāga* leading to the attainment of a desired goal are meaningful. The Upaniṣads, on the contrary, teach about Brahman, which is an existent and accomplished fact (*siddhavastu*) and not something to be achieved by human effort, and these are not therefore purportful. Bādarāyaṇa rejects this view on the ground that all the Upaniṣadic texts are purportful since they teach about Brahman as the Supreme Goal of attainment. This is the implication of the word *samanvayāt (samyak paramapuruṣārthabhūtasya brahmaṇaḥ abhideyatayā anvayāt),* as interpreted by Rāmānuja.[24]

The commentary of Rāmānuja on this *sūtra* is very elaborate. He presents the arguments advanced by the ancient *Mīmāṁsakas* and the counter replies to them by the *Bhedābhedavādins* as well as the school of Advaita Vedānta in great detail. All these are refuted as untenable. The theory of the Advaitin that knowledge generated by the study of Scriptural texts *(vākyārtha-jñāna),* secures *mokṣa* through the removal of *avidyā,* comes up for special consideration. In the *Adhikaraṇa-sārāvalī,* Vedānta Deśika does not go into all these details. He highlights only the essential points of criticism to establish that the Upaniṣads are valid and meaningful. We may take note of these points.

According to the Mīmāṁsakas, words convey their meanings only as related to specific action. On the basis of this principle, they contend that Vedic statements of injunctive character are purportful, whereas those which refer to an existent (*siddhapara)* cannot be taken as purportful since they do not serve the purpose of achieving any fruitful result. Thus for instance, the Vedic injunction *'svargakāmo yajeta'* or one who desires to attain *svarga* should perform a *yāga* is purportful, whereas the statement that a crow possesses eight teeth, referring to a matter of fact, does not serve any useful purpose. It may be argued that even a statement not involving some action is fruitful in so far as it generates some joy to the listener. For instance, a person makes a statement that there is hidden treasure in the house and the person who hears it derives some joy. This statement is therefore purportful. This will not do, since one can also make a false statement to this effect. Though it may cause some joy to the person, it is not of any use since the object referred to does not actually exist. It cannot be said that the Upaniṣadic texts become meaningful by making them as part of the injunctive statement, as in the statement 'One who desires to attain the highest goal should observe meditation on Brahman' *(paro prāptikāmaḥ brahma vidyāt)*. Even then what is sought for may not be true, as in the case of the meditation on mind as the symbol of Brahman. Hence the mere study of Brahman for gaining its knowledge is of no practical value.[25]

Against these criticisms, Vedānta Deśika contends that even if the Scriptural text referring to Brahman as *satya, jñāna* etc., is taken as part of the injunctive statement enjoining the *upāsanā* on Brahman for attaining the Supreme Goal, it would not become purportless similar to the statement 'The crow has eight teeth.' Even if a false statement is made by a person, it can still cause some joy to the person as long he believes it to be true. If the listener knows that it is false, he cannot possibly derive any joy. When a child, for instance, hears a false statement made by a person that its father is safe, it becomes delighted since the child is not aware that it is false. Taking the Scriptural statement that Brahman is *ānanda,* the disciple who hears it, surely becomes delighted. If he thinks that it is a false statement, he would not react to it with joy. But this would not render the Scriptural text meaningless. Vedānta Deśika therefore states that even if a statement is false and it is made only for the purpose of causing joy, it does not necessarily imply that the object referred to by it is false. As long as the listener believes that such a statement is true, he derives joy from hearing it and to this extent it is meaningful, even though it is not injunctive in character. The sweet words uttered to a child to pacify it causes delight even though they may not be true. It is not therefore correct to say that the Upaniṣadic texts teaching about Brahman as *satya, jñāna, ananta, ānanda etc.,* are false because these statements generate interest in seeking Brahman. Besides, these statements are not contradicted either by perceptual knowledge or other Scriptural texts. Vedānta Deśika therefore concludes that the Upaniṣads are valid and meaningful in teaching about Brahman.[26]

There are other theories which attempt to justify the validity of the Upaniṣdic texts. These are: *i) Niṣprapañca niyoga vāda, ii) Dhyāna-niyoga vāda* and *iii) Advaita vāda.* According to the first theory, held by the ancient Advaitins (*jaranmāyāvādī*) who follow the *Mīmāṁsakas,* Brahman which appears to be associated with the illusory universe, is to be realized as dissociated with the universe (*niṣprapañca*),by means of continuous meditation on Brahman. The Upaniṣadic texts become meaningful by subordinating them to the main injunction '*brahma niṣprapañcaṁ kuryāt*' or 'Brahman is to be dissociated with the universe.'

According to the second theory, which is also advanced by the ancient Advaitins, Brahman is to be realized through a '*niyoga*' or special potency in the form of *adṛṣṭa* generated by the observance of continuous meditation on Brahman. The Upaniṣadic texts teaching about Brahman are regarded valid since they are subordinate to the main injunction enjoining meditation.

According to the third theory advanced by the Advaita

Vedānta of Śaṁkara, the realization of the identity of the individual self and Brahman is the sole means to *mokṣa*. All the Upaniṣadic texts are purportful since they generate the direct intuitive knowledge *(aparokṣa jñāna)* of this identity which removes the cosmic ignorance (*avidyā*) leading to *mokṣa*.

As mentioned earlier, these theories are subjected to detailed criticism by Rāmānuja in the *Śrī-Bhāṣya*. Vedānta Deśika briefly refers to them and summarily rejects the same as unacceptable since these views are opposed to the teaching of the Upaniṣads, besides being self-contradictory (*svapakṣa-svavacana vihatiḥ*).[27]

An objection may be raised against the stand taken by the Viśiṣṭādvaitin in respect of the *pūrva-kāṇḍa* and *uttara-kāṇḍa* of the Vedas. In the *pūrva-kāṇḍa* dealing with rituals, the glorificatory statements (*arthavādas)* are accorded validity (*prāmāṇya)* by treating them as subordinate to the injunctive statements, whereas in the *uttara-kāṇḍa*, he establishes *prāmāṇya* for them (*arthavādas*) on the basis that they serve the useful purpose of directly teaching about Brahman *(svātantryeṇa)*. How then the two parts of the *Mīmāṁsā* be regarded as one treatise?

Vedānta Deśika replies that there would be no opposition between the two, if the principle of general and exceptional (*utsarga apavāda nyāya)*is adopted. In the *pūrva-kāṇḍa*, the glorificatory statements are accorded validity following the general rule laid down by the *Mīmāṁsaka* that they are subordinate to the injunctive statements. In the case of the *uttarakāṇḍa*, particularly in the *Samanvayādhyāya* of *Brahma-mīmāṁsā*, the Upanisdic texts of glorificatory nature are accorded validity since they serve the purpose of knowing more about the nature of Brahman (*bodhamātrāt pumarthe)*. The stand adopted in respect of *pūrva-kāṇḍa* is of a general nature (*utsarga)*, whereas the stand taken in respect of *Uttarakāṇḍa* is exceptional.[28]

Vedānta Deśika proves the validity of the Upaniṣadic

texts on a different ground. There are injunctive statements in the *pūrva-kāṇḍa* enjoining the performance of certain types of *yāga* such as *kārīya* for rain fall which is a seen result of mundane character (*aihika phala)*. There are also injunctive statements such as the performance of the prescribed sacrifice for securing *svarga* or heaven, which is an unseen result (*adṛṣṭa phala)* to be attained in a higher realm. There are references to the good and bad effects of good and bad omens, and also astrological forecasts of future events. Pious individuals well versed in the Vedic knowledge observe religious acts with the belief of obtaining higher spiritual benefits. If all these are accepted as valid and meaningful, there is no reason why the Upaniṣadic texts teaching about Brahman and the Supreme Spiritual Goal should not be accorded the same validity. In fact the entire Vedic texts including the Upaniṣads are valid and purportful since they are free from defects and are also not ascribed to any human author. Otherwise it would amount to denouncement of the Vedic way of life (*naigamādhvāpalāpaḥ*[29]).

By way of summing up the discussion of the four *adhikaraṇas* dealing with the subject-matter of the first four *sūtras*, which constitute one unit *(peṭika)*, Vedānta Deśika points out that these are intended to justify the study of Vedānta to secure the knowledge of Brahman for the purpose of attaining the Supreme Goal. The first *adhikaraṇa* establishes that *Brahma-jijñāsā* is to be undertaken after completing the study of *Pūrva-mīmāṁsā* and realization of the futility of the fruits of the ritualistic deeds and the permanent value of the Spiritual Goal to be attained by the study of Vedānta. The second *adhikaraṇa* establishes that the definition offered by the Upaniṣad provides the knowledge of Brahman directly. The third *adhikaraṇa* proves that *śāstra* is the only source for knowing Brahman. The fourth *adhikaraṇa* establishes that all the Upaniṣadic texts are valid and purportful since they teach that

Brahman which is endowed with infinite bliss is the Supreme Goal to be attained.

---

1. *See*. AS. verse 22. *See* also Cintāmaṇi on AS. *Uktam ca pūrvācāryaiḥ: vyutpattyabhāvāt pratipatti-dausthyād-anyenasiddheḥ aphalatvataśca; amātvam āśaṅkya nirācakāra nyāyaiḥ caturbhiḥ pratipādya tattat.*
2. VS I-1-1
3. *See* RB I-1-1. *Brahma-śabdena ca svabhāvataḥ nirasta-nikhila-doṣaḥ, anavadhikātiśaya asaṁkhyeya-kalyāṇa-guṇagaṇah, puruṣottamo abhidhīyate*
4. Mu. Up. I-2-12 and 13.
5. Quoted in RB I-1-1.
6. *See*, V.S. I-2-29; I-2-32; I-4-18; III-4-40.
7. *See*, *Śatadūṣaṇī*, *vāda* 3.
8. *See* Śatadūṣaṇī, vāda 8. for further details. Also A&V, chapter 8.
9. Br. Up. VI-4-23. *tasmāt evam vit śānto dānta uparataḥ titikṣuḥ samāhito bhūtva ātmanyeva ātmānaṁ paśyet.(The references to Br. Up. is in accordance with Rangarāmānuja Bhāṣya)*
10. *See* fn.4
11. *See* AS verses 28 and 33.
12. VS I-1-2
13. Tait. Up. III-1
14. *See Padayojanā* on Verse 35. *Yato jagatsṛṣṭyādikam prasiddham tad brahmetyāha*
15. *See* AS verse 36.
16. AS verse 37.
17. AS verse 38. *Nānā āgamodyad-viṣaya śamanataḥ śrīmati brahmatokteḥ.* See also *Padayojanā* on verse 38.
18. *See*. *Mahābhāṣya* on *Pāṇini-sūtra*. *Binna pravṛttinimittānāṁ śabdānām ekasmin arthe vṛttiḥ sāmānādhikaraṇyam.*
19. *See Pūrva Mīmāṁsā Sūtra* III-1-12. *Arthaikatve dravyaguṇayoḥ ekakarman-niyamaḥ syād.* See also RB.I-I-13 and AS verse 40.
20. VS I-1-3.
21. *See*. TMK. III-24. See also VS II-1-11, *tarkāpratiṣṭhānādapi.*
22. *See* AS. verse 45.
23. VS I-1-4.
24. RB. I-1-4.
25. AS verse 46.
26. AS verse 48. *Trayyantāḥ Satya-nitya-adbhuta paramasukha brahma-niṣṭhāḥ pramāṇam*
27. AS verse 49.
28. AS verse 50.
29. Ibid 52. *Śabde tasmāt ca bodhe sati paraviṣaye doṣabhāva-vyapete mānam tatra svato asau.*

Chapter Two

THE DOCTRINE OF BRAHMAN

In the preceding chapter we have seen how Bādarāyaṇa has justified the need to undertake the study of Vedānta for gaining knowledge of Brahman. In the subsequent *sūtras* of the first *pāda* of the first *adhyāya*, he proceeds to outline the essential nature *(svarūpa)* of Brahman. The next seven *adhikaraṇas* are devoted to bring out the following points relating to the *svarūpa* of Brahman:

1. It is distinct from *pradhāna* or the non-sentient primordial cosmic matter.
2. It is different from the *jīvātman* or the individual self.
3. It is distinct from the celestial deities such as *Āditya-puruṣa, Akṣi-puruṣa* etc, taken as exalted *jīvas*.
4. It is also distinct from non-sentient cosmic entities such as *ākāśa, prāṇa and jyotiṣ*.

We shall discuss these topics in the present chapter.

I. Brahman as Sentient Being

The *Īkṣatyadhikaraṇa* deals with this subject. It is based on the *sūtra* which reads: *Īkṣateḥ na aśabdam*[1]. The word *aśabdam* means, according to Rāmānuja, that which is not proved by Scripture but established by inference *(ānumānika)*. It implies the *pradhāna* or the primordial cosmic matter accepted by the Sāṁkhyas as the cause of the universe.

The word *na* negates it. That is, the *pradhāna* as conceived by the Sāṁkhyas is not the cause of the universe. The reason for the denial of this theory is contained in the word *'ikṣateḥ'*. This term derived from the root verb *īkṣaṇa* means the function of seeing or resolving. The fuller meaning of the *sūtra* is that *pradhāna* admitted by the Sāṁkhyas on the basis of the inference cannot be the cause of the universe since the function of resolving to create the universe, as stated in the Upaniṣad, cannot be ascribed to it. It is Brahman that is the cause of the universe. Thus, Bādarāyaṇa seeks to establish that Brahman is a sentient Being and as such it is different from non-sentient cosmic matter.

The justification for bringing up the theory of Sāṁkhya for criticism and thereby assert that Brahman is the cause of the universe is found in the context of the passage of the Chāndogya Upaniṣad which teaches that *sat* is the cause of the universe. Thus it states: *Sadeva saumya idam agra āsīd ekameva advitīyam...tad aikṣata bahusyāṁ prajāyeyeti. Tat tejo asṛjata*[2] - "In the beginning (prior to creation), my dear, this universe existed as *sat* only, one only, without a second. That *sat* resolved, 'May I become many'. Then it created *tejas* etc."

It is possible to construe this passage in favor of the Samkhya theory of *pradhāna* as the cause of the universe , the word *sat* being interpreted as the unmanifested causal state of the manifold universe. According to the Sāṁkhyas, this variegated universe consisting of three *guṇas, sattva, rajas and tamas,* existed prior to the state of creation as unmanifest, when the three *guṇas* were in equilibrium. With the disturbance of the equilibrium, the unmanifest *pradhāna* evolved itself into the manifest universe through the process of evolution. The main logical argument advanced in support of this view is that whatever is the nature of the effect (*kārya*), the same should be the nature of the causal substance (*kāraṇa*). It is only on the basis of the non-difference between cause and effect, that it is possible to explain that by the knowledge of the causal substance, the products made out of it can be understood, as in the illustration of the clay and its products cited in the Upaniṣad.

The above view is rejected by Bādarāyaṇa, the main reason being that the expression *'aikṣata'* or resolved mentioned in the Upaniṣadic text, does not hold good in respect of the non-sentient *pradhāna*. That is, *īkṣaṇa* or the the function of resolving to become many cannot be ascribed to the non-sentient entity such as *pradhāna*.

Against this view, it may be argued that the function of thinking (*īkṣaṇa*) is not to be taken in its primary sense. It is to be understood in a figurative sense (*gauṇa*) to mean that prakṛti is in the state of readiness to evolve itself into its manifest form. In the same passage it is said that the *sat* created *tejas* (*tat tejo asṛjata*). There are statements such as 'The trees look forward to rainfall'[3] in which even non-sentient entities are described to have the function of thinking. It is therefore appropriate to ascribe *īkṣaṇatva* to *sat* taken as *pradhāna*. Further, as pointed out earlier, the causal substance should be of the same nature as its effects. Otherwise it would not be possible to substantiate the general principle stated by the Upaniṣad viz., by the knowledge of the one, the many become known. The illustration of the clay and its products cited by the Upaniṣad to substantiate it fully supports the inferential argument adopted by the Sāṁkhyas to prove that *sat* referred to in the passage is *pradhāna* as the cause of the universe.

These arguments are untenable, contends Vedānta Deśika. As explained by Rāmānuja in the *Śrī-Bhāṣya*, the illustration cited in the Upaniṣad does not serve the purpose of the probans (*hetu*) for the syllogistic argument advanced by the Sāṁkhyas. As will be pointed out later in the chapter on the universe, it is not necessary that the cause and effect should be of the same nature. In fact Brahman which is the material cause of the universe is not of the same nature as the non-sentient universe.[4] Further, in the concluding passage of the Chāndogya dealing with *Sadvidyā*, *sat* is identified with Ātman (*aitadātmyam idam sarvaṁ tat satyaṁ, sa ātmā*)[5]. Hence the non-intelligent *pradhāna* cannot possess the power of thinking even in a figurative sense.

There are other arguments which are advanced by Bādarāyaṇa to prove that *sat* is not the *pradhāna* of the Sāṁkhya. In this Upaniṣadic passage it is taught that the person who meditates on *sat* (Brahman) attains *mokṣa* soon after he is liberated from bondage. If *sat* were *pradhāna*, then it would amount to the attainment of non-self, which is not what is sought after (*tanniṣṭasya mokṣopadeśāt*[6]). Besides, as already stated, it would run counter to the statement made in the beginning of the passage viz., 'All that is not known becomes known by the knowledge of the ātman.'(*yena aśrutaṁ śrutaṁ bhavati*) The implication of this statement is that by the knowledge of the causal substance, all its effects become known, as in the instance of clay and its products. If *pradhāna* were the causal substance, the *jīvas* which are not its products cannot be known.

In the same passage, we come across a statement, which says that the individual soul during the state of deep sleep merges itself in *sat* which is its source.[7] If *sat* were *pradhāna*, such a merging would not be possible because the Sāṁkhyas do not admit *pradhāna* as the causal substance for the sentient souls.[8]

The most important point which goes against the claim of the Sāṁkhyas, is the crucial Upanişdic text *"Tattvamasi'* "Thou art that', which is the final teaching of Uddālaka to Śvetaketu. If *'tat'* which refers to *sat* were *pradhāna*, then *'tvam'* referring to *jīva* should be one with pradhāna, a non-sentient entity. This would amount to the wrong philosophical teaching (*heyatva vacanācca*[9]).

It is also stated in the Upaniṣad that *sat* which is Brahman enters itself along with *jīva* into all that is created and gives names and forms to all the entities created by it (*anena jīvenātmanā anupraviśya nāmarūpe vyākaravāṇi*[10]). If *sat* were *pradhāna,* its *anupraveśa* along with *jīva* is inconceivable.

More importantly, all the Upaniṣadic texts speak of only a sentient Being as the cause of the universe. Thus states the Aitareya Upaniṣad: *ātmā vā idam eka eva agra asīt, sa īkṣata lokānnu sṛjā iti*[11]. The Taitirīya *says: so' kāmayata bahusyāṁ prajāyeya iti.*[12]

Taking all these points into consideration, Vedānta Deśika affirms that the *īkṣatyadhikaraṇa* brings out an important nature of Brahman viz., it is the cause of the entire universe through the operation of its free will (*sveccātaḥ sarvahetuḥ).*[13]

II. Brahman as Ānandamaya

This is the subject-matter of a separate *adhikaraṇa* named *Ānandamayādhikaraṇa.* In the previous *adhikaraṇa,* it was shown that Brahman as a sentient Being is different from the non-sentient cosmic matter. In the present *adhikaraṇa,* Bādarāyaṇa establishes that Brahman is blissful in nature and as such it is distinct from the sentient individual self (*jīvātman*). The reason for taking up this particular topic is two-fold. First, if *pradhāna* of the Sāṁkhyas cannot be the cause of the universe, since *īkṣaṇatva* in its primary sense cannot be ascribed to it, the question is raised whether *jīvātman* which is sentient can be admitted as the cause of the universe. Secondly, in the same Chāndogya passage teaching *Sadvidyā,* we come across the famous statement *'tat-tvamasi'* which prima facie, implies that *jīva* is identical with Brahman. Anticipating such an objection, Bādarāyaṇa points out that Brahman is essentially of the nature of bliss and that it is different from *jīvātman,* which being subject to affliction in the state of bondage, cannot be the cause of the universe.[14]

The main *sūtra* reads: *Ānandamayo abhyāsāt.*[15] It means that Brahman is constituted of bliss because of the repetition of the term *ānanda* in respect of Brahman in the Upaniṣad. The fuller implication of the *sūtra* can be understood with reference to the passage of the Taittirīya Upaniṣad on the basis of which it is formulated. This passage teaches about the nature of Brahman for the purpose of easy comprehension in five concrete forms as *annamaya* or consisting of essence of food, as *prāṇamaya* or consisting of vital breath, as *manomaya* or consisting of mind, as *vijñānamaya* or of the nature of knowledge and *ānandamaya* or constituted of bliss. Brahman is first conceived as *annamaya* because food sustains the body in which the self resides. But this is transcended by the concept of Brahman as *prāṇamaya* because life breath is of greater importance for the sustenance of life. This is further transcended by Brahman as *manomaya* because mind is important for the function of the body. This is superseded by *vijñānamaya* since *vijñāna,* understood as the individual self, is more important than the *manas.* Brahman as *vijñānamaya* is further transcended by the concept of *ātman* (Brahman) as *ānandamaya.*

Each one is described as *puruṣa* in a human form having head (*śiraḥ*), right and left side (*pakṣaḥ*), middle part (*ātmā*) and foundation (*puccha*). It also states that *prāṇamaya ātmā* is other than *annamaya puruṣa.* The *manomaya ātmā* is other than *prāṇamaya.* Distinct from *manomaya* is *vijñānamaya ātma.* After the description of *vijñānamaya,* the Upaniṣad mentions the *ānandamaya ātmā,* which is considered other than *vijñānamaya.* Thus says the Upaniṣad: *tasyaiṣa eva śārīra ātmā, yaḥ pūrvasya tasmād vā etasmāt vijñānamayāt anyontara ātmā ānandamayaḥ.*[16] It means: "He who is the Self of the preceding one is the Self related to the *vijñānamaya* also. As compared with this *vijñānamaya,* there is another self which is constituted of bliss."

While each one of these forms other than *annamaya* is stated to be higher and different from the preceding one, the Upaniṣad does not mention any other principle higher than *ānandamaya.* Hence *ānandamaya ātmā* is admitted as Brahman. Further, the concluding passage of the Upaniṣad refers to the different gradations of bliss. It commences with the statement: *saiṣā ānandasya mīmāṁsā bhavati.*[17] It means, "Now commences the enquiry concerning bliss." It first mentions what the measure of one human bliss is (*eko mānuṣa ānandaḥ)* in terms of youthful energy, sound body and mind and full of wealth. One hundred times of this human bliss is one unit of bliss of human *gandharvas* (*manuṣya gandharva*); one hundred times of *manuṣya gandharva* is one unit of bliss of divine *gandharva* (*deva gandharva*). What is one hundred times of the bliss of divine *gandharva* is one measure of the bliss of manes who dwell in the enduring world (*pitṛloka*). In this manner the Upaniṣad goes on mentioning by upward gradations the *ānandas* of gods born in the *ajāna* heaven, of *karma devas* (sacrifical gods), of the *devas* (celestial deities), of Indra, of *Bṛhaspati*, and of *Prajāpati*. Finally it states that one hundred times of the bliss of *Prajāpati* is the one unit of bliss of Brahma, the word *brahma* being understood as Brahman, as interpreted by Rāmānuja.

This description of *ānanda* of Brahman by comparing it progressively with all other beings, commencing from human being to the highest celestial deity, provides the justification for affirming that Brahman is *ānandamaya* or infinitely blissful. This is what is implied by the words *'ānandamayo abhyāsāt'* in the *sūtra*.

A few objections are raised against this conclusion of Bādarāyaṇa. The major objection is that what is described as *ānandamaya* is the *jīvātma-svarūpa*. This is based on the assumption that *jīva* and Brahman are not essentially different. This view constitutes the *pūrva-pakṣa* or prima facie view, according to Rāmānuja. He therefore devotes special attention to the examination of this theory and refutes it. In this connection he discusses in great detail the true import of the famous Upaniṣadic statement *'tat-tvamasi'*, which prima facie supports the Advaitin's doctrine of the non-difference between *jīva* and Brahman and establishes that *jīva* is distinct from Brahman and that *ānadamaya ātmā* is Brahman. Vedānta Deśika does not go into all these details in the *Adhikaraṇa-sārāvalī*. He confines his attention to the following general criticisms made against the conclusion of Bādarāyaṇa:

1) The affix *mayaṭ* to the term *ānanda* implies the sense of *vikāra* or modification, as in the case of the term *annamaya*, whereas Brahman is *nirvikāra*.
2) The Upaniṣad describes the *ānadamaya ātmā* as *śārīra-ātmā* which means that it is a soul encased in the physical body (*śarīra sambandha jīvātmā*) as in the case of *annamaya ātmā* which refers to the physical body of an individual soul.
3) The *ānandamaya ātmā* is conceived in a human form with a head (*śiraḥ*), sides (*pakṣaḥ*) and tail (*puccha*).[18]

Regarding the first objection, Vedānta Deśika points out that the affix *mayaṭ* does not necessarily imply the sense of modification as in the case of the concept of *annamaya*. Thus, in respect of the concept of *prāṇamaya*, we do not take it in the sense of *vikāra*. Here it is understood as essentially of the nature of *prāṇa*. In the same way, the term *ānadamaya* in respect of Brahman should be understood in the sense of abundance (*prācurya*), that is. Brahman is essentially of the nature of *ānanda*. *Ānandamaya* taken in the sense of modification is not applicable even in respect *jīvātman* or the higher Brahman as conceived by the Advaitin since the higher Brahman is *nirvikāra* or not subject to modification. It is also not correct to understand the word *prācurya* in the sense of predominance, since in that case it would imply that there exists a small amount of suffering (*duḥkālpatva*). Brahman which is described by the Upaniṣad as the one who dispels the fear or suffering of the devotees cannot have an iota of *duḥka*. Hence it is essentially and wholly constituted of bliss.[19]

Regarding the second objection viz. the description of it as *śārīrātmā*, Vedānta Deśika contends that this description is very appropriate in respect of Brahman. The statement *'tasyaiṣa eva śārīrātmā yaḥ pūrvasya'* is intended to point out that as in the case of the earlier concept of Brahman conceived as *annamaya* etc, the *ānadamaya ātmā* does not have for it another *antarātmā* or the Indwelling Spirit but on the contrary, Brahman itself is the *antarātmā* for it. Brahman being the Self of the entire universe which is its *śarīra*, as well established in the *Antaryāmi Brāhmaṇa*, it can be regarded as *śārīrātmā*. In fact, as Vedānta Deśika points out, the description of *ānandamaya ātmā* as *śārīrātmā* is most appropriate in its fullest sense since *Paramātman* is the only one who is the Self (*śarīrī*) of the entire universe. (*śarīroktiḥ tasmin akhilatanutayā syād asaṅkocaḥ vṛttiḥ).*[20]

The third objection, viz the description of *ātmā* in human form with head, sides (arms), tail, etc is of some significance. In fact, Śaṁkara also in his interpretation of the relevant *sūtra* of this *adhikaraṇa* takes the stand that the *ānandamaya brahma* cannot be the higher Brahman since it is *nirvikāra* and *niravaya*. The statement *Brahmapucchaṁ pratiṣṭhā* implies, according to him, that Brahman is transcendental support of all empirical souls. (*pucchavat pucchaṁ pratiṣṭhā parāyaṇam ekaniḍam*).[21] This is the true Brahman which is the higher Reality (*para brahma*) and not the *ānadamaya ātman*, which according to him, is the lower Brahman (*apara brahma*). He advances sufficient arguments in support of this theory.

Rāmānuja refutes all these arguments. He rejects the view that *puccha* Brahman is different from *ānandamaya* Brahman. The same *ānandamaya* Brahman is symbolically described in terms of head, arms, *puccha*, etc. for the purpose of meditation.[22] As an additional point of criticism, Vedānta Deśika points out that if the description of higher Brahman in terms of *puccha* is acceptable to Advaitin, why should he have any objection to the view of the Viśiṣṭādvaitin who admits that the *ānandamaya* Brahman is symbolically presented by the Upaniṣad in terms of human form with head, arms and *puccha*? The expression *'Brahma pucchaṁ pratiṣṭhā'* means that Brahman itself is the foundation for itself. That is, it does not have to depend on any other ground than itself. It is self-existent (*anitarādhāra*)[23]. Elsewhere in the Upaniṣad in reply to the query *'sa bhagavaḥ kasmin pratiṣṭhitā'*, it is stated *'sve-mahimni'*[24] that is, it exists by its own power. It is therefore not inappropriate to describe Brahman in terms of *Brahma puccham pratiṣṭhā*. Thus, it is concluded that Brahman is essentially constituted of infinite bliss (*ānadamaya*) and it is distinct from *jīvātman*.

III. Brahman as endowed with Spiritual Body

This is the subject-matter of the *Antarādhikaraṇa* which establishes that Brahman as *ānadamaya* also possesses a spiritual body. The relevant *sūtra* concerned with this subject reads: *Antaḥ taddharmopadéśāt.*[25] The word *antaḥ* means within or what abides inside and it implies with reference to the two passages of the Chāndogya Upaniṣad that the *puruṣa* who resides within the orbit of the sun and also in the eye (*akṣi*) is Brahman. The expression *tad-dharmopadeśāt* means because the passages speak about the characteristics that are only applicable to Brahman. The fuller meaning of the *sūtra* can be understood with reference to the concerned passages of the Upaniṣad on the basis of which this *sūtra* is formulated. The main objective of the *sūtra,* as explained by Rāmānuja, is to prove that Brahman as a spiritual Being is not only distinct from *jīvātman* but it is also different from exalted *jīvas*.

The following passages dealing with the meditation on *Udgītha,* a hymn of Sāmaveda covering the syllable *'Aum'* refer to the *puruṣa* who is seen within the orbit of the sun and also within the eye with vivid description: *atha ya eṣo antarāditye hirarṇmayaḥ puruṣaḥ dṛśyate hiraṇyasmaśruḥ hiraṇyakeśa ā-praṇakhāt sarva eva suvarṇaḥ; tasya yathā kapyāsaṁ puṇḍarīkam evamakṣiṇī; tasyoditi nāma, sa eṣa sarvebhya pāpmebhya uditaḥ, udeti ha vai sarvebhyaḥ pāpmabhyaḥ. Ya evam veda.*[26]

"Now this Golden Person (*puruṣa*) who is seen within the sun, has a golden beard and golden hair, who is golden to the very tip of his nails. His eyes are like a red lotus flower. His name is *ut*, for he has risen above all evil. He who knows this, raises above all evil."

The other passage states: *atha ya eṣo antarakṣiṇi puruṣo dṛśyate, saiva ṛk, tat sāma, tad uktham tad yajuḥ, tad brahma tasyaitasya tadeva rūpam. yadamuṣya rūpam, yāvamuṣya geṣṇau tau geṣṇau yannāma tannāma.*[27] "Now this person (*puruṣa*) who is seen within the eye is the hymn (*ṛk*). He alone is the chant (*sāman*), the recitation (*uktha*), the sacrificial formula (*yajus*), is Brahman. The form of this one is the same as the form of that (person seen in the sun). The songs of the former are the songs of this. The name of this one is the same as the other".

The description of the *puruṣa* in terms of physical body with golden colour, with eyes similar to the lotus, etc gives room for the doubt whether such a Being could be Brahman. It is therefore possible to advance a theory on the basis of these passages that the *puruṣa* in question is an exalted *jīvātman*, who has risen to such a position by virtue of the accumulation of excessive *puṇya* and who can function as *Īśvara* or Ruler of the universe in cyclic succession at each epoch like the celestial Deity, Indra and create the universe with the aid of the body and intellect. This is the prima facie view that is advanced against the *sūtra*.

Bādarāyaṇa rejects this view and affirms that the *puruṣa* seen in the sun and also in the eye is Brahman who possesses a spiritual lustrous body. The main reason for refuting this view is that certain characteristics mentioned in the passage in respect of the *puruṣa* are applicable only to Brahman and not to *jīvātman* even if it is exalted. Secondly, what abides within the orbit of the sun is *Paramātman,* as is evident from the *Antaryāmī Brāhmaṇa* of the Bṛhadāraṇyaka Upaniṣad.[28]

By way of elucidating the reason advanced by Bādarāyaṇa against the prima facie view, Vedānta Deśika points out, that the body of golden colour (*hiraṇmayaḥ*) with eyes similar to the lotus does not refer to the physical body caused by *karma* (*akarma utthita divyākṛtiḥ)* but it is a spiritual divine body constituted of *śuddha-sattva.*[29] It is a body assumed by the Supreme Deity out of His own will for the benefit of the devotees who desire to meditate on Him. It is such a Supreme Person who is endowed with glory and associated inseparably with Goddess Lakṣmī (*nityaśrīḥ*) and who is also the Ruler of the entire universe that is referred to in the Upaniṣadic passage as residing in the orbit of the sun. This *puruṣa* in the orbit of the sun is not different from the *puruṣa* abiding in the inner recess of the heart *(ya eṣo antarhṛdaya ākāśaḥ; tasminnayaṁ puruṣo manomayaḥ, amṛto hiraṇmayaḥ).* The Taittirīya Upaniṣad also states the same. *(sa yaścāsau āditye, sa ekaḥ)*

It may be argued that the statement in the passage viz., the *puruṣa* abiding in the sun is free from all *pāpas,* does not rule out the possession of some *puṇya.* Such a Being associated with *puṇya* cannot be considered to be one free from *karma,* since *karma* in Vedānta consists of both *puṇya* and *pāpa*.

This objection is untenable, contends Vedānta Deśika. Several other Scriptural texts declare that Brahman is free from both *puṇya* and *pāpa.* In fact, the term *pāpma* in the Upaniṣadic parlance includes *puṇya* too. Further, Brahman who has unchecked freedom confers the fruits of the deeds to all individuals in accordance with their *puṇya* and *pāpa*[30].

An objection may be raised against the view that *Īśvara* possesses a body. Even if this body is regarded as non-material and divine in character it may be subject to modification. In reply to this objection, Vedānta Deśika points out that it is made of spiritual substance which is of the nature of pure *sattva* (*śuddha sattva*) unmixed with the element of *rajas* and *tamas.* The existence of transcendental realm constituted of spiritual substance as different from the material world is warranted by several Scriptural texts[31]. It is *nitya* or everlasting in the sense that it is not subject to decay or destruction (*nāśarahitam*). The Scriptural text says that Viṣṇu, the Supreme Deity with such a divine form is eternally seen by the *nitya-sūris* or divine sages (*tadviṣṇoḥ parmaṁ padaṁ sadā paśyanti sūrayaḥ*) Such a Supreme Being manifests Himself out of His own free will in different incarnated forms (*avatāras*) such as *vyūhas, vibhāvas, arcā* and *antaryāmin* without abrogating His transcendental spiritual character purely for the purpose of the protection of the pious devotees (*sa devaḥ puṁsāṁ saṁsāra śāntyai vipariṇamati vyūhapūrvaiḥ vibhāgaiḥ*[32]). Vedānta Deśika therefore contends that as against a strong Scriptural authority supporting the possession of a Divine body, the inferential arguments denouncing the body for *Īśvara* on the basis of the probans such as *dehatvāt* or because it is a body and *aṁśatvāt* or because it is divisible into parts, stand sublated. If the Divine Being in His incarnated human form behaves like a human being as if affected by grief, it is all a mere enactment, similar to the acting of a person on the theatrical stage in different roles (*svecchā avatāreṣu abhinayati*).

The description of the *puruṣa* with eyes similar to a lotus (*puṇḍarīkākṣa)* is regarded by Rāmānuja as Supreme Deity in the name of Nārāyaṇa or Viṣṇu since the *Itihāsas* and *Purāṇas* speak of such eyes exclusively in respect of Viṣṇu.

IV. Brahman as Distinct from Non-Sentient Cosmic Entities

In the preceding sections, it is observed that Brahman is distinct from the individual souls as well as the exalted *Puruṣas* in the sun and in the eye. In the same way, Bādarāyaṇa regards that Brahman is also different from ontological entities such as *ākāśa* or ether, *prāṇa or* breath and *jyotis* or cosmic light. These three are specifically mentioned in the Upaniṣadic passages which prima facie give the impression that they are the very cause of the universe (in the case of *ākāśa* and *prāṇa)* and the highest Spiritual Being (in the case of *jyotis*). This matter is therefore examined in three separate *adhikaraṇas* named

Ākāśādhikaraṇa, Prāṇādhikaraṇa and *Jyotiradhikaraṇa* with a view to determining the nature of Brahman as distinct from all physical entities.

a. Ākāśa as Brahman

This is the subject of the *Ākāśādhikaraṇa* which deals with the question whether the term *ākāśa* mentioned in the following passage of the Chāndogya refers to the etherial space which is generally the accepted meaning of it, or does it refer to Brahman. The *sūtra* framed on the basis of the passage reads: *ākāśah tallingāt.*[33] It means that *ākāśa* is Brahman since the characteristic marks mentioned in the passage about *ākāśa* are applicable to it.

In reply to the query 'what is the goal of this universe' the Upaniṣad states: *ākāśa iti hovāca, sarvāṇi imāni bhutāny ākāśādeva samutpadyante, ākāśam pratyastam yānti, ākāśohy evebhyo jyāyān, ākāśaḥ parāyaṇam.*[34]

"It is *ākāśa*, for all these beings originate from *ākāśa* and return to *ākāśa*. *Ākāśa* is greater than these. Therefore, *ākāśa* is the goal."

The term *ākāśa* generally means the etherial space. Besides, in the Taittirīya Upaniṣad it is stated that from *ātman* (Brahman) *ākāśa* is brought into existence (*ātmanaḥ ākāśaḥ sambhūtaḥ*). As a product of *Ātman*, it cannot be Brahman itself. Hence, its description in this passage as the origin of the universe and as the goal, gives room for the doubt whether it could be Brahman.

But there should be no room for such a doubt, contends Vedānta Deśika' because in the statement '*sarvāṇi ha vā bhūtāni ākāśādeva samutpadyante*' the expression *ha vā* implies the acceptance of special meaning of the term on the basis of the established principle viz. that the general term should bear the meaning of the special term. Thus, in the passages dealing with causation of the universe, the general terms such as *sat, ātmā*, Brahman which are employed in them, are taken to denote the meaning of the special term

'Nārāyaṇa' mentioned in the Mahopaniṣad in the same context.[35]

Besides, the passage describes *ākāśa* as the highest of all beings and also their goal (*ākāśo jyāyān ākāṣaḥ parāyaṇam)*. This description is not applicable to the etherial space (*bhūtākāśa*). Further in the Taittirīya text it is stated that *ākāśa* is brought into existence from the *ātman* (*ātmanaḥ ākāśaḥ sambhūtaḥ*). The *ātmā* referred to here stands contextually to Brahman mentioned at the commencement of the passage which is described as *vipaścit* or all-knowing (*vividham paśyaccitva*) or omniscient Brahman. This *bhutākāśa* which is the product of Brahman is different from *Ākāśa* mentioned in the Chāndogya Upaniṣad. *Ākāśa* is Brahman in the sense that it illumines everything else (*ākāśayati*) and it also shines everywhere (*ākāśate*).

b. Prāṇa as Brahman

This is the subject of the *Prāṇādhikaraṇa* which discusses the issue whether the term *prāṇa* employed in the Chāndogya passage stands for the vital breath or Brahman. The passage states: in reply to the query made to *prastotā* priest regarding the deity connected with *prastāva,* it is said: *prāṇa iti hovāca, sarvāṇi ha vā imāni bhūtāni prāṇameva abhisaṁviśanti prāṇam abhyujjihate, saiṣā devatā prastāvam anvyāyattā.*[36]

"The *prāṇa* is that deity, for all these beings merge in the *prāṇa* alone and from *prāṇa* alone do they depart. This is the deity which is connected with *prastāva*."

The *sūtra* which is framed with reference to this passage says: *Ata eva prāṇaḥ.*[37] It means for the same reason, that is, the reason offered in respect of *ākāśa* in the earlier *sūtra,* namely that the characteristics of Brahman mentioned in the Upaniṣad holds good in respect of Brahman.

The doubt arises in respect of *prāṇa* because *prāṇa* is taken in the commonly understood sense of fivefold vital breath. In the case of *ākāśa* the commonly accepted meaning (*ruḍhyartha)* of the term *ākāśa* is rejected since it is not known to be the origin of all living beings. Hence it is not appropriate to reject the commonly accepted meaning for *prāṇa* and attach a special meaning to it in favour of Brahman.

Bādarāyaṇa rejects this argument. The main reason for its rejection, as elucidated by Vedānta Deśika, is that as in the case of the passage on *ākāśa* as Brahman the expression *ha vā* used in the statement, *"sarvāṇi ha vā imāni bhūtāni prāṇameva abhisaṁviśanti..."* implies that *prāṇa* here is the source (cause) of all beings in the universe. That which is the source of all beings cannot be the ordinary vital breath but Brahman which sustains life of all entities both sentient and non-sentient, such as wood, rocks, (*kāṣṭha śilādiṣu*). Such a power or capacity to sustain life of all entities is not found in vital breath. Further, as in the case of *ākāśa*, the *Śruti* texts speak of Brahman as *prāṇasya prāṇaḥ, amṛtasya prāṇa*. More importantly, the Taittirīya states that no one else other than Brahman can sustain life of all. Brahman is therefore admitted as *prāṇa* in the sense that it sustains all life (*nikhila prāṇana* or *prāṇayati sarvāṇi bhūtāni*). Hence *prāṇa* denotes Brahman.[38]

c. Jyotis as Brahman

This is the subject of *Jyotiradhikaraṇa* which establishes that the *jyotis* or self-luminous light referred to in the Upaniṣad denotes Brahman and not the cosmic light. The *sūtra* covered by this *adhikaraṇa* reads: *Jyotiś-caraṇābhidhānāt.*[39] It means: 'The cosmic light is Brahman because of the mention of the feet or part (in the Upaniṣadic passage connected with cosmic light.)

In the Chāndogya Upaniṣad, a passage refers to the cosmic entity named as *jyotis*, in connection with the meditation on *gāyatrī*. It states:

Atha yad ataḥ paro divo jyotir dīpyate viśvataḥ pṛṣṭheṣu sarvataḥ pṛṣṭheṣu anuttameṣu uttameṣu lokeṣu, idam vāva tad yaḥ idam asminnantaḥ puruṣe jyotiḥ tasyaiṣa dṛṣṭiḥ.[40] - "Now the light which shines above the heaven, above all, above everything, in the highest worlds beyond which there are no higher worlds; verily that is the same as the light which is here within the person."

The question raised in this connection is whether the *jyotis* mentioned in the passage refers to the physical light radiated by the sun and other luminaries or Brahman which is the Supreme Spiritual Light. The prima facie view is that it is the extraordinary light of the sun and the like, which is the well established meaning of the term. As Vedānta Deśika explains, there are certain favourable factors in support of this view. First, unlike in the passage referring to the *ākāśa* and *prāṇa*, there is no mention in this passage that *jyotis* is the cause of the universe, so that the meaning commonly accepted for the term can be overlooked, as *Śruti* is stronger than *liṅga or* descriptive identity mark. Secondly, the *jyotis* of the higher realms is equated with the digestive fire within one's body (*jaṭharāgni*). Though *agni* as the cause of the universe is stated elsewhere in the Upaniṣad dealing with *Vaiśvānaravidyā*, it is not mentioned in the present passage. Hence it is appropriate to accept the well-established meaning of *jyotis* as physical light and not Brahman.

The above arguments are not tenable, contends Vedānta Deśika. As Bādarāyaṇa states, the *jyotis* denotes Brahman because of the mention of the feet. The *sūtra* reads: *caraṇābhidhānāt*[41]. The fuller implication of it is that the earlier part of the passage, which deals with the manner of mediation on the *gāyatrī mantra*, the following statement of the *Puruṣasūkta* is reiterated:

etāvānasya mahimā, ato jiyāyāṁśca puruṣaḥ, pādosya viśvābhūtāni, tripādasya amṛtam divi.[42]

"Such is the greatness of it; greater than it is the Supreme Person (*puruṣa*). One part of it represents all the beings in the universe, while the other three parts (*tripād*) cover the immortal higher domain (*amṛtam divi*)".

The same Supreme Person who is connected with the three quarters of the higher abode is referred to in the present Upaniṣad as the Light (*jyotis*) connected with the higher domain (*atha paro divo jyotiḥ).* This fact cannot be overlooked. *Jyotis,* therefore, denotes Brahman.[43]

An objection may be raised against this conclusion. At the commencement of the passage, it is said that all this is *gāyatrī (gāyatrī vā idam sarvam)*. In the later part of the passage, the *jyotis* in the higher domain is described as having four parts. Since *gāyatrī mantra* also has four metrical quarters, it is possible to say that *jyotis* referred to in the passage is *gāyatrī* and not Brahman.

This objection, which is anticipated by Bādarāyaṇa also[44], is set aside. The teaching about *gāyatrī* is intended for the purpose of meditating on Brahman as having four parts similar to the four (metrical) quarters of *gāyatrī*. The four parts of Brahman represent the totality of the *jīvas* denoted by the term *bhūta* or the living beings, *pṛthivī* or earth, which is the field of experience, the physical body which is the accessory for experience and the *hṛdaya* or the inner recess of the heart in which *ātman* resides. The *bhūtas* taken to mean all beings together cannot actually be the *pāda* or part of *gāyatrī*. Hence the reference to *paraṁjyotis* is to be understood as referring to Brahman. Brahman also stands for the Supreme Light since it gives light to all other luminaries. Thus states the Muṇḍaka Upaniṣad : *Tameva bhāntaṁ anubhāti sarvaṁ tasya bhāsā sarvaṁ idam vibhāti*[45] - "Him the shining one, everything shines after; by this light all this is lighted". The Bṛhadaranyaka also says: "Him the Gods worship as the light of the lights, as the immortal (*Taddevā jyotiṣāṁ jyotir-āyur hopāsate aṛtam*[46])).

V. Brahman as Antarātmā of Indra-prāṇa.

This is the subject-matter of *Indra-prāṇādhikaraṇa* which discusses the issue whether the terms *Indra*, the chief of the celestial deities and the *prāṇa* referred to by him, which are employed in an important passage of the Kauṣītakī Upaniṣad, denote Indra himself as the Ruler of the universe or Brahman which is the *antarātmā* of all entities. We have seen in the preceding *adhikaraṇas* (*Antaradhikaraṇa* and *Prāṇādhikaraṇa*) that Brahman is distinct from the celestial deities such as *āditya-puruṣa* or the *puruṣa* seen in the sun taken as exalted *jīvātman* and also *prāṇa* taken as vital breath. The Indra and *prāṇa* concepts are allied to the issues related to the *āditya-puruṣa* and *prāna* respectively and hence Bādarāyaṇa takes it up for consideration as a separate topic.

The relevant *sūtra* states: *prāṇaḥ tathānugamāt*[47]. It means, according to Rāmānuja , that the word *prāṇa* (referred to by Indra) denotes Brahman because it is correlated with the terms such as *ānanda, ajara* and *amṛta* referred to in the passage. This *sūtra* has direct reference to the passage of Kauṣītakī Brāhmaṇa dealing with *Pratardana vidyā*. In a dialogue between Indra and Pratardana, the former being pleased with the performance of extraordinary deeds by the latter, asks Pratardana to choose a boon as a reward for his good act. But Pratardana does not name the boon and prays to Indra to confer what he himself deemed most beneficial to mankind. (*yaṁ tvaṁ manuṣyāya hitatamaṁ manyase.*) Indra tells him: *māmeva vijānīhi, etadeva ahaṁ manuṣyāya hitatamaṁ manye* - "Understand me only; that is what I deem most beneficial for mankind[48]". He first narrates his exploits and glories and thereafter says: *prāṇo'smi prajñātmā taṁ māṁ āyur amṛtam iti upāsva, āyuḥ prāṇaḥ, prāṇo vā āyuḥ.*[49]

"I am *prāṇa,* meditate on me as the intelligent self, as life, as immortality; life is *prāṇa* and *prāṇa* is life". In the concluding passage it is stated that *prāṇa* is *prajñātmā, ānanda, amaraḥ, amṛtaḥ.*[50]

The question which is raised in this connection is whether the meditation suggested by Indra is on the individual soul denoted by the term *prāṇa* or on Brahman which is distinct from it. The prima facie view is that *prāṇa* here refers to the individual soul, since Indra instructs Pratardana to meditate on him as *prāṇa* and as the intelligent self. Such a meditation is considered most beneficial for mankind (*hitātamā*). Besides, the passage also commences with this matter. Hence Indra who is credited with heroic achievements is to be accepted as the Ruler of the universe (*viśvakartā*). According to the principle of interpretation, what is stated at the commencement (*upakrama*) is stronger than the conclusive statement describing *prāṇa* as *amṛta, ajara, ānanda* etc.

Following the explanation offered by Rāmānuja, Vedānta Deśika refutes the above prima facie view. There are three kinds of *upāsanā* on Brahman for the attainment of the highest goal: a) Brahman as related to *jīvātman*, b) Brahman as related to *acit* or cosmic matter c) Brahman in its essential nature (*tredhā hi upāsyaṁ bahuvidhā cid-acid-kañcukaṁ svātmanā ca).*[51] The *upāsanā* enjoined in the present passage on *Indra-prāṇa* is to be treated as *upāsanā* on Brahman as related to the *jīva* of Indra. The description of Indra with the glory of his achievements is intended to bring out the great qualities of Indra, who represents the *viśeṣaṇa* or body of Brahman in a technical sense, as the object of meditation for attaining the most beneficial goal of human endeavor.

Regarding the point mentioned in support of the prima facie view, it is true that the opening statement of the passage is stronger than the conclusive statement. But in the present passage there is no conflict between the two statements, since the opening statement referring to Indra *prāṇa* also stands for Brahman as qualified by Indra *prāṇa* (*Indraviśiṣṭa Paramātmā*).

An objection, which is raised by the *Śutrakāra* himself is how Indra, who is the main spokesman (*vaktā*) and who is fully aware of himself being an individual soul, can mean by his *prāṇa* Brahman. The reply is that Indra is justified in advising Pratardana to meditate on him on the basis of the *śāstradṛṣṭi*, that is, the knowledge leading to the comprehension that *jīvātman* is the *śarīra* (body) of *Paramātman*, as taught in the *Antaryāmi Brāhmaṇa* and other Scriptural texts. Indra as an enlightened person was gifted with this spiritual knowledge and he can therefore advise Pratardana to meditate on his soul which denotes the *Paramātman* as the *Antaryāmi* of the soul. Bādarāyaṇa cites the example of the Vedic sage Vāmadeva who was gifted with such a knowledge as stated in the Bṛhadāraṇyaka Upaniṣad[52].

In this connection, Vedānta Deśika explains why the criteria adopted in interpreting the general terms such as *ākāśa, prāṇa, jyotis, Indra-prāṇa* etc., in favour of Brahman is not uniformly the same and it differs in accordance with the subject-matter and the context in which the Upaniṣadic statements are made (*viṣayabhedena*). If the object or entity denoted by a term such as *ākāśa* is found to be a product or what is brought into existence (*kārya),* the commonly accepted meaning (*rūḍhyartha*) is to be rejected and the etymological meaning (*yaugikārtha)* conveyed by it is to be adopted. Wherever a sentient Being denoted by a term is known to be subject to *karma* (*karmavāsya*), as for instance *Prajāpati,* a higher celestial deity, the same principle of interpretation holds good. This is the reason for interpreting *ākāśa* and *āditya puruṣa* mentioned in the Upaniṣad as Brahman. In the case of *jyotis* and Indra, the commonly accepted meaning is not admitted since the descriptions provided in the later part of the passages do not conform to them. Thus for instance, the identification of *jyotis* with the *agni* as physical fire and its meditation for attainment of higher goal cannot be reconciled. As regards Indra the description about his exploits, cannot be explained by accepting Indra as Supreme Being. Hence in both these cases, *jyotis* is taken to mean Brahman as qualified with self-luminous light (*jyotiviśiṣṭa brahma)* and *Indra* is Brahman as the *antaryāmin* of *Indra.* The same principle is followed in respect of the two famous statements: *ahaṁ brahmāsmi* and *tattvamasi. Ahaṁ* which denotes the *jīva* is understood as *svātmā viśiṣṭam paramātmā* or one's self as *śarīra* of *Paramātmā*. Similarly *tvaṁ* refers to the *jīva* of Śvetaketu and *tvamasi* means *abhimukha cetana viśiṣṭa Paramātmā,* that is, *Paramātman* as qualified by Śvetaketu. Such an interpretation, Vedānta Deśika contends, is fully justified according to the principle of interpretation laid down by the Mīmāṁsakas. There is a Vedic statement: "*aindryā gārhapatyam*". *Gārhapatya* is the name of sacrificial fire and Indra means in the accepted sense, a celestial deity. In this instance, Indra cannot be regarded as *agni* in the primary sense and hence Indra is understood in a secondary sense as *agni* since Indra is associated with sacrifice. But etymologically Indra can also be understood as *Īśvara* since the root word *Ind* denotes the quality of *Īśvara*.[53] The principle of interpretation followed by the Viśiṣṭādvaitin is summed up as follows: *Vyutpattyā paramātmānaṁ tattaduktiḥ prakāśayet; tallinga ananaythāsiddhau tadvīsiṣṭāvalambanī*. It means: "The terms employed in such passages denote *Paramātman* with reference to their etymological meaning. If the descriptive statements in the passage about them do not corroborate that meaning, we have to interpret them in favour of *Paramātman* qualified by them.

By way of summing up the preceding *adhikaraṇas* dealing with the nature of Brahman, Vedānta Deśika points out how each *adhikaraṇa* brings out an important aspect of Brahman. The first four *adhikaraṇas* – *Jijñāsādhikaraṇa*, *Janmādy-adhikaraṇa*, *Śāstrayonitvādhikaraṇa*, and *Samanvayādhikaraṇa* – are intended to justify the study of Vedānta (*śāstra ārambha samarthana)* and hence these are treated as Introductory. The actual teaching of *Vedāntaśāstra* commences from the fifth *adhikaraṇa* named *Ikṣatyadhikaraṇa*.[54] The important point brought out in this *adhikaraṇa* is that *Paramātman* is the creator of the universe out of His own free will (*svecchātaḥ sarvahetuḥ)*, as indicated by the term *Īkṣaṇa* and supported by the Upaniṣadic statement '*tadaikṣata bahusyāṁ prajāyeyeti, tat tejo asṛjata*'. The sixth *adhikaraṇa* named *Ānandamayādhikaraṇa* highlights that Brahman who is endowed with auspicious attributes is constituted of *ānanda* par excellence (*śubha guṇavibhava ananta nissīma harṣaḥ*.) The *Antaradhikaraṇa* reveals that Brahman possesses a divine form (body) which is constituted of *śuddha-sattva* or spiritual substance which is assumed out of His free will and which is not subject to karma (*śuddha akarmottha-divyākṛtiḥ*). This point is supported by the Chāndogya text: *atha eṣo antarāditye hiraṇmayaḥ puruṣaḥ*. The *Ākāśādhikaraṇa* establishes that Brahman is of the nature of self- illumination (*prakāśa*) par excellence and illumintates every thing in the universe (*anupadhika-ākāśanādi svabhāvaḥ*) and that it is also the highest Goal, as evidenced by the Scriptural text '*ākāśo jyāyān ākāśo parāyaṇam*'. The *Prāṇādhikaraṇa* emphasizes that Brahman is the giver of life or sustenance (*sattā*) to everything in the universe, both living beings and non-sentient objects such as wood, rocks, etc., (*saprāṇa aprāṇa bheda vyatikarabhidura jagataḥ prāṇanaḥ*). This is evident from the Upaniṣadic statement: *sarvāṇi ha vā imāni bhūtāni prāṇameva abhisaṁviśanti prāṇam abhyujjihate*). The *Jyotiścaraṇādhikaraṇa* reveals that Brahman is of the nature of transcendental spiritual Light (*divya dīptiḥ*). The Chāndogya statements '*atha paro divo jyotiḥ dīpyate*', *uttameṣu lokeṣu* etc supports this. The last *adhikaraṇa* known as *Indraprāṇādhikaraṇa* brings out the fact that Brahman is the *antarātmā* or Indwelling Self of celestial deities such Indra and non-sentient entities such as *prāṇa* (*prāṇendriyādy antarātmā*). The main objective of these *adhikaraṇas* and also those which are covered in the *pādas* 2 and 3 of first *adhyāya*, which deal with Brahman, according to Vedānta Deśika, is to highlight the *guṇas* or attributes of *Paramātman* (*sarveṣām api adhikaraṇānāṁ tattat bhagavadguṇa prādhānakṛtyam*). The other details contained in these *adhikaraṇas* are meant for critical evaluation of prima facie views for the purpose of supporting the main thesis.[55]

1. VS I-1-5
2. Ch. Up. VI-6-1 and 3
3. Cp. *Vṛṣṭi-pratīkṣāḥ śālayaḥ*
4. AS verse 56.
5. Ch. Up. VI-8-7
6. VS I-1-7
7. *See* Ch. Up VI-8-1. *satā somya tadā sampanno bhavati*
8. *See* VS I-I-10. *Svāpyayāt*

9. VS I-1-8.
10. Ch. Up. VI-3-2
11. Ait. Up. I-1
12. Tait. Up. II-6
13. *See* AS. Verses 57 and 78
14. *See* AS. Verse 58.
15. VS. I-1-13
16. Tait. Up. II-5
17. *Ibid* II-8.
18. *See* Tait. Up. II-5. *sa vā eṣa puruṣa vidhaḥ...tasya priyameva śiraḥ, modo dakṣiṇaḥ pakṣaḥ, pramoda uttaraḥ pakṣaḥ, ānanda ātmā, brahma puccham pratiṣṭhā...*
19. *See* AS verse 59.
20. AS. Verse 60
21. SB I-1-19.
22. *See* RB I-1-13. *Brahmaiva svabhāva viśeṣaṇa puruṣavidhatvarūpitam śiraḥ-pakṣa-puccha-rūpeṇa vyapadiśyate.*
23. AS verse 61. *Brahmaṇi ātmapratiṣṭhāvacanam anitarādhāratā khyāpanāya.*
24. *See* Ch. Up. VII-24-1
25. VS I-1-21
26. *See* Ch. Up. I-6-6 and 7
27. *Ibid* I-7-5
28. *See* Br. Up.V-7-9. *ya āditye tiṣṭhan, yasya ādityādantaraḥ, yasya ādityaḥ śarīram*
29. AS verse 62.
30. *See* VS, III-2-37 *phalam ataḥ upapatteḥ*. See Also BG IX-24. *ahaṁ hi sarvayajñānāṁ bhoktā ca prabhureva ca*
31. *See puruṣa sūkta*: *padosya viśvā bhūtani, tripādasya amṛtaṁ divi.. tamasaḥ paramo dhātā*
32. *See* AS verse 64
33. VS I-1-23.
34. Ch. Up I-9-1
35. *See* FVV pp.224-25.
36. Ch up I-11-5
37. VS I-1-24
38. AS verse 70
39. VS I-1-25
40. Ch. Up. III-13-7
41. VS I-1-25
42. Tait. Āraṇyaka III-12
43. *See* A.S. verse 72. *puṁsūkta-vākyodita parapuruṣa pratyabhijñapty-abādhāt.*
44. *See* VS I-1-26
45. Muṇḍ. Up II-2-10

46. Br. Up. IV-4-16
47. VS I-1-29
48. Kau. Up III-1
49. *Ibid* III-2
50. Kau. Up III-9. *sa eṣa prajñātmā ānando ajaro amṛtaḥ*
51. AS verse 74
52. Br. Up III-4-10 *Taddhaitat pāsyan ṛsir-vāmadevaḥ aham manurabhavam, aham kakṣīvān, sūryaśca ...aham ṛṣirasmi...pratipedire*
53. *Indratvam agnau gauṇam syād yajñasambandha kāritam; indathyarthānusārādvā svakārya so'pi hi Iśvaraḥ*
54. According to Madhva even this adhikaraṇa is treated as part of the *upodghāta* or introduction.
55. *See* AS verse 78. *See* also *Padayojanā*.

Chapter Three

THE DISTINGUISHING CHARACTERISTICS OF BRAHMAN

In the preceding chapter we have outlined the essential nature (*svarūpa*) of Brahman as enunciated by Bādarāyaṇa in the first *pāda* of *adhyāya* I of *Brahma-sūtra*. In the present chapter we shall present the distinguishing characteristics (*dharmas*) of Brahman as brought out by Bādarāyaṇa on the basis of the Upaniṣadic teachings dealing with Brahman.

The important passages of the principal Upaniṣads contain statements which are not clear as to whether they refer to Brahman or some other ontological entities such as *jīvātman* and *prakṛti*. According to Rāmānuja, such Upaniṣadic texts are of three kinds: 1) *aspaṣṭa jīvādiliṅgaka vākyas*, or the statements which are not clear as to whether they teach about *jīvātman*. 2) *spaṣṭa jīvādiliṅgaka vākyas* or the statements which appear to speak clearly about *jīvātman*. 3) *spaṣṭatara jīvādilingaka vākyas* or the statements which appear to teach more clearly about either *jāvātman* or *prakṛti*. If the main purport of the Upaniṣads is Brahman, as established in the *samanvayādhikaraṇa*, it would be necessary to examine these statements to clear the doubts and establish that the Upaniṣadic texts teach about Brahman and its *dharmas*. The remaining three *pādas* of first *adhyāya* are devoted to the consideration of this important matter. Accordingly, the second *pāda* deals with the statements which are vague (*aspaṣṭa*), the third *pāda* deals with statements which are unambiguous (*spaṣṭa*) and the fourth *pāda* deals with texts which appear to point out more clearly that either *prakṛti or jīvātman* is the cause of the universe (*spaṣṭara*). By way of critically examining the prima facie views advanced by the critics of Vedānta either on the basis of their own accepted theories or on certain assumptions, Bādarāyaṇa brings out the following important *dharmas* of Brahman:

1) Brahman as the Self of all (*Sarvātmā)*
2) Brahman as the Devourer of the entire universe (*Attā)*
3) Brahman as the *Puruṣa* abiding in the eye (*Akṣisthiti puruṣa)*
4) Brahman as the Inner Controller of all (*Antaryāmin)*
5) Brahman as the Imperishable Reality (*Akṣara)*
6) Brahman as the Ruler of all souls (*Vaiśvānara)*
7) Brahman as the Support of heaven and earth (*Āyatana*)
8) Brahman as Infinitely great (*Bhūmā)*
9) Brahman as the *Ādhāra* of the universe (*Viśvādhāra)*
10) Brahman as the object of enjoyment for *muktas* (*Muktabhogya*)
11) Brahman as the subtle space within the heart (*Daharākāśa*)
12) Brahman as the *anguṣṭamātra Puruṣa* is the Ruler of All (*Sarvaniyantā*)
13) Brahman as the object of meditation for celestial deities (*Devādīnām upāsyaḥ).*
14) Brahman as the *Nāmarūpakartā* of the universe
15) Brahman as the Cause of the universe
16) Brahman as *Ubhayaliṅga*

The *adhikaraṇas* of the second and third *pādas* deal with the topics 1 to 14. We shall discuss each of these in the present chapter. Regarding the topic 15, this subject is covered in the *adhikaraṇas* of the fourth *pāda*. As these are mainly concerned with the establishment of the Vedānta theory that Brahman is the cause of the universe by way of refuting the views of the Sāṁkhya and Yoga, as reflected in some of the Upaniṣads, it will be considered separately in the next chapter. Regarding the topic 16, it is covered in the *adhikaraṇa* named *Ubhayaliṅgādhikaraṇa*, which is included in the third *adhyāya* and which establishes the two-fold characteristic of Brahman as endowed with attributes and also free from defilements. As this is an important subject having a bearing on whether Brahman is the worthy object of meditation, it will be discussed in the chapter on *Sādhana*.

I. Brahman as the Self of All

This is the subject-matter of the *Sarvatra-prasiddhyadhikaraṇa*. The main *sūtra* related to it reads: *Sarvatra prasiddhopadeśāt*[1]. The word *sarvatra* means everywhere, that is, in all the Upaniṣads. Rāmānuja offers another meaning viz. everything in the universe (*sarvasmin jagati*). *Prasiddha upadeśa* means a teaching or theory which is well established in the Upaniṣads. The fuller implication of the *sūtra* will become clear from the famous passage of the Chāndogya Upaniṣad dealing with *Śāṇḍilya Vidyā* or the meditation prescribed by Śāṇḍilya on Brahman as the primary cause of the universe. The passage commences with the following statement: *Sarvaṁ khalu idaṁ brahma tajjalān iti śānta upāsīta.*[2]

"Verily, all this is Brahman, because all this originates from, ends in, and is sustained by Brahman. Thus knowing one should mediate with calm mind." The subsequent statement says: *Atha khalu kratumayaḥ puruṣo yathā kraturasminn-loke puruṣo bhavati tathetaḥ pretya bhavati, sa kratuṁ kurvīta, manomayaḥ prāṇa śarīraḥ bhārūpaḥ.*[3]

"Man is indeed of the nature of thought (mediation); he becomes in his supra mundane state after departing from this life, what he meditates upon in his life. Let him therefore practise meditation. Let him meditate on that which consists of mind (*manomaya*), which has *prāṇa* or vital breath as its body (*prāṇaśarīra*) and whose form is light (*bhārūpaḥ*)"

The opening sentence of the passage refers to the meditation on Brahman since the compound word *'tajjalān'* employed in it implies that from which the universe originates (*tajjatvāt*), that in which the universe is dissolved (*tallatvāt*) and that in which everything is sustained (*tadanatvāt*). These are the three cosmic functions that are attributed to Brahman only and not to any other ontological entity. This fact that Brahman is the primary cause of the universe is well established in all the Upanisads (*sarvatra prasiddha*), as is stated in the *sūtra*.

In the subsequent statement, it is said that meditation is to be observed on that which is *manomaya, prāṇaśarīra,* and *bhārūpa*. This description of meditation in terms such as *manomaya, prāṇaśarīra,* and *bhārūpa* gives room for doubt as to whether the object of meditation is the individual self (*jīvātman*) or the Supreme Self (Brahmaṇ). The prima facie view is that it refers to the individual self because *manas* or mind and *prāṇa* or breath are associated with *jīva*. The word *'manomaya'* is taken to mean as that which consists of mind and *prāṇaśarīra* as that which has breath (*prāṇa*) as its body. Accordingly, what is referred to in the Upaniṣad is *jīva* since *manas* and *prāṇa* belong to it. It cannot be Brahman since according to the Upaniṣad Brahman is devoid of both *manas* and *prāṇa*. Thus says the Upaniṣad: *aprāṇohy amanāḥ śubraḥ*[4] -" Brahman is devoid of mind and *prāṇa*'

This view is rejected by the author of the *sūtra*. The reason for rejection, as explained by Rāmānuja, is that the same Brahman which is referred to in the opening sentence is to be meditated upon as qualified with *dharmas* such as *manomayatva, prāṇamayatva,* etc which are well established in all the Upaniṣads. Thus says the Muṇḍaka Upaniṣad: *manomayaḥ prāṇa śarīra netā* - "He who is made of mind, the guide of the body of breath." The Kena Upanisad says: "He is the Ruler of *prāṇa*."[5] The term *manomaya* is applicable to Brahman because Brahman is to be apprehended only by purified mind (*viśudhena manasā grāhyatvam*). *Prāṇaśarīra* means that Brahman is the Supporter and Ruler of *prāṇa* (*prāṇasyāpi ādhāratvam niyantṛtvam ca).*

The above explanation is offered by Rāmānuja to answer the objection that the second statement in the passage refers to the meditation on *jīvātman* since it is described as *manomaya, prāṇaśarīra,* etc. As pointed out by Vedānta Deśika, there is another prima facie view, according to which the entire passage covering both the opening sentence and the subsequent one refer to the meditation on *jīvātman* and not Brahman. In the opening statement, *"sarvaṁ khalu idaṁ brahma" brahma* can also mean *jīvātman* since *jīva* takes birth due to *karma* in variety of forms in the universe. Hence it is equated with the universe by the expression *'idaṁ sarvaṁ'*. It is such a *jīva* on which one has to meditate as *manomaya, prāṇamaya,* etc.

This view is untenable, contends Vedānta Deśika. As pointed out by Rāmānuja, the entire passage speaks about the meditation on Brahman. Though *jīva* exists in a variety of forms in the universe, it cannot be the cause of the creation, sustenance, and dissolution of the entire universe, as expressed in the phrase *'tajjalān'* Secondly, the word *sarvatra* taken in the sense of everything in the universe (*sarvasmin jagati* or *vastuni*), according to the second interpretation of Rāmānuja, implies that Brahman is the entire universe in the sense that it is the *Ātman* or the Self of everything in the universe which constitutes the *śarīra* or body of Brahman in a technical sense viz that it is sustained and controlled by Brahman. *Jīva* which is finite in character and part of the universe cannot be the Self of the universe in this sense.

The terms *manomaya, prāṇaśarīra,* etc. constitute the *dharmas* or attributes of Brahman. The meditation on Brahman as the cause of the universe which is enjoined in the opening statement in a general way is made more specific in the subsequent statement by indicating that

Brahman as qualified by attributes of *manomayatva, prāṇaśarīratva,* etc is to be meditated upon. It is not a separate injunction (*vidhi*) but it is a restatement of what is already enjoined in a more specific way. *Prasiddha upadeśa* in the *sūtra* means, according to this interpretation, that it is so well established in the Taittirīya and other Upaniṣads and *sarvatra* means that Brahman is the Self (*ātmā*) of all entities in the universe. The expression '*sarvaṁ idaṁ brahma* 'therefore implies that Brahman is the universe in the sense that it is the Self of all (*sarvātmā*). This qualification does not apply to *jīvātman*.

A few other arguments are advanced to prove that the object of meditation is Brahman. The various attributes which are mentioned in the passage such as *sarvakarma, sarvagandhaḥ, sarvarasaḥ, ākāśātmā,* etc.[6], for purpose of mediation are only applicable to Brahman. In a later part of the passage[7] it is stated that this (Brahman) is my Self[8]. This statement conveys the difference between *jīva* and Brahman and hence it cannot be *jīva*. Its description as smaller than the smallest (*aṇīyān*) is intended to convey that Brahman abides in one's heart for the purpose of *upāsanā* (*nicāyatvāt*).[9]

The important point to be noted in this *adhikaraṇa* is that Brahman is *Sarvātmā* or the Self of everything in the universe. That is, Brahman abides in all entities in the universe as Ātman (Indwelling Self) by controlling them from within (*svādhīna-aśeṣa-sattā-sthiti yatanatayā sarvabhāvena tiṣṭhan*[10]).

II. Brahman as the Devourer of the Universe

This is the subject-matter of the *adhikaraṇa* named *Attrādhikaraṇa.* A passage in the Kaṭha Upaniṣad describes *ātman* symbolically as the one for whom *Brāhmaṇas* and *Kṣatriyas* are food and death is itself the condiment. Thus it states: *yasya brahma ca kṣatram ca ubhe bhavata odanaḥ; mṛtyuḥ yasya upasecanam*[11] - "For Him *brahma* (*Brāhmaṇa*) and *kṣatra* (*kṣatriyas*) are food and death (*mṛtyu*) is the condiment. No body really knows how and where He is." In this verse *brahma* and *kṣatriya* which mean *Brāhmaṇas* and *Kṣatriyas* represent the entire universe of movables and immovables. *Mṛtyu* represents the God of death. The words food and condiment suggest that the *Ātman* referred to here is the *attā* or devourer. Based on this passage Bādarāyaṇa has framed the *sūtra* which reads: *attā carācara grahaṇāt*[12]. It means that the eater is Brahman because of the mention of what is movable and what is immovable.

The question arises whether such a physical activity of eating is applicable to Brahman. The prima facie view is therefore advanced that the individual self (*jīva*) is the *attā* or eater, since normally a *jīva* who is subject to *karma* is the eater of the food. The *sūtra*, as interpreted by Rāmānuja, rejects it and upholds that it is the Supreme Self or Brahman which is *attā*, because the terms *'brahma* and *'kṣatra'* together with *mṛtyu* used in the Upaniṣad symbolically represent the entire universe comprising the movable (*cara*) and immovable (*acara*) entities. *Jīva* cannot consume the entire universe. Brahman is therefore the *attā* or devourer. That is, it is the *Saṁhartā* or the cause of the dissolution of the universe.

The act of eating here symbolically represents the dissolution (*saṁhāra*) of the entire universe by Brahman. As the primary cause of the creation and sustenance of the universe, Brahman also withdraws it from the state of manifestation into itself. In this sense the characteristic of *attratva* is attributed to Brahman.

Vedānta Deśika also points out that in the same context, the Upaniṣad brings out that the *jīva* is distinct from *Paramātman* (Brahman) (*jīvavyāvartam ca prakaraṇa viditam*[13]). The question of regarding *jīva* as *samhartā* of the universe does not therefore arise.

However, an objection is raised against the theory of Brahman as *attā* on the basis of a later passage of Kaṭha Upanisad in which it is said that two *ātmans* (*jīva* and Brahman) who have entered the cave (heart) drink the fruit of *karma* (*ṛta*). The relevant passage says: *Ṛtam pibantau sukṛtasya loke guhāṁ praviṣṭau parame parārdhe; chāyā'tapau brahmavido vadanti*[14] -"The two of the nature of sunshine and shadow having entered the cave drink the fruit of *karma* (ṛta) in the world of good deeds." If the two who have entered the cave are Brahman and *jīva*, the question arises whether Brahman can be the enjoyer of the fruits of *karma* (*sukṛta*). If Brahman is not the *bhoktā* unlike *jīva* how can it enjoy the fruits of *karma*? This issue may be resolved by treating the two who have entered the cave as *buddhi* and *kṣetrajña (Paramātman)* respectively. Such a view is also supported by a statement in *Paiṅgī Rahasya Brāhmaṇa* dealing with the same matter. Thus it is stated: *Tayoranyaḥ pippalam svādvatti iti sattvam. Sattva* here is interpreted as *buddhi* which experiences *karma*.

Bādarāyaṇa has anticipated this objection and replied to it. The relevant *sūtra* reads: *guhāṁ praviṣṭau ātāmnau hi tad-darśanāt*[15]. It means that the two who have entered into the cave are two souls, the individual self and the Supreme Self, because it is stated so in the Upaniṣad. The two, according to the Upaniṣadic statement, as interpreted by Rāmānuja, are the individual self and Brahman since both of them enter into and dwell in the heart which is symbolically expressed as *guhā* or cave. The individual soul being subjected to *karma* actually drinks the *ṛta* in the sense of reaping the benefits of good deeds. *Paramātman* is regarded as the one who drinks the *ṛta* in a figurative sense by virtue of his companionship with the drinking *jīva*. This is explained on the analogy of the statement '*chattriṇo gacchanti*' which literally means those holding the umbrella move (walk). Actually only one person holds the umbrella but the others who have been walking under its shade are regarded as going with umbrella. The Upaniṣadic statement can also be understood in the sense that *Paramātman* as *preraka* or the impeller causes the *jīva* to drink the fruits of *karma*, while *jīva* actually enjoys it as impelled by Him (*prerya*). That is, *jīva* who actually enjoys the fruits of *karma* is the one who is impelled to do so by *Paramātman* in accordance with his *karma*. As the controller or impeller of jīva, *Paramatman* is figuratively regarded as *bhoktā* while the actual *bhoktā* is *jīva*.

Regarding the *Paingī Śruti* quoted in support of the two selves as *buddhi* and *Paramātman* respectively, Vedānta Deśika points out that even this particular text which elucidates the *Kaṭha* text referring to two birds sitting on a tree, one eating the fruit and the other sitting as passive observer, uses the word *sattva* as qualifying the word anyaḥ (*tayor-anyaḥ pippalaṁ svādvatti sattvam*). The term *sattva* stands for *jīvatman* and not *buddhi*, as wrongly interpreted. *Sattva* means *jantu* or a living being, according to *kośa*.[16] A *jantu* is one which experiences the fruits of *karma* and accordingly it cannot be regarded as *buddhi* (*jantau ca sattva śrutiḥ iyam ucitā karma-bhuk*[17]).

Thus the *Attrādhikaraṇa* brings out the important characteristic of Brahman as the *saṁhartā* or the one who dissolves the universe. Though in an earlier *adhikaraṇa* (*Janmādyadhikaraṇa*) dealing with the definition of Brahman, it is established that Brahman is the cause of the dissolution of the universe, this subject is separately considered in order to prove that Brahman is not the *bhoktā* or experiencer of the fruits of *karma*, unlike *jīva*, though it abides in the heart.

III. Brahman as the Puruṣa Abiding in the Eye

This is the subject matter of a separate *adhikaraṇa* named *Antarādhikaraṇa* which discusses the issue whether the *puruṣa* abiding in the eye seen by the Yogins, as stated in the Upaniṣad, is Brahman or some other being. This *adhikaraṇa* is different from the *Antarādhikaraṇa* discussed earlier which deals with the *puruṣa* seen in the orbit of the sun (*ādityapuruṣa*) and also in the eye (*akṣipuruṣa*). The former is part of the *Upakosala-vidyā* narrated in the Chāndogya and the latter is part of the *Antarādityavidyā* mentioned in the same Upaniṣad in a different context. The present *adhikaraṇa* is aimed to prove that Brahman abides in the eye in the same way as it abides in the inner recess of the heart to enable a *upāsaka* to meditate on it. The previous *adhikaraṇa* (*Antarādhikaraṇa*) on the other hand, is intended to prove that the *ādityapuruṣa* and *akṣipuruṣa* are not the higher celestial deities but Brahman.

The Chāndogya Upaniṣad teaching *Upakosala-vidyā* states: *ya eṣo akṣiṇi puruṣo dṛśyate, eṣa ātmā iti hovāca, etad amṛtam abhayaṁ etad brahmeti, tad yady apyasmin sarpir vodakaṁ vā siñcati, vartmani hy eva gacchati*[18].

"This person (*puruṣa*) who is seen in the eye, He is the Self (*ātmā*). This is the immortal, the fearless (*abhayaṁ*), this is *brahma*, that is why if one drops melted butter into the eye, it flows out."

The question raised with reference to this statement is: who is that *puruṣa* referred to as seen directly (by the yogins) in the eye. Four alternatives are possible. Either it is the reflection of the *jīva*, since it is so explicitly stated to have been perceived directly by the *yogins*; or it is the *jīvātman*, since on the basis of the function of the eye, the presence or absence of (life) is determined; or it can be the presence of a deity (*sūrya devatā*) who is stated to be present in the eye through the rays; or it is the very *Ātman* (Brahman).

Bādarāyaṇa rejects the first three views and affirms that the *puruṣa* seen in the eye is Brahman. The relevant *sūtra* reads: *Antara upapatteh.*[19] It means: The person seen inside the eye is Brahman because of the relevance of the attributes mentioned in the Upaniṣad. That is, the *puruṣa* seen in the eye is Brahman because the Upaniṣad describes it as *ātman* and it is *amṛta* or immortal, *abhaya* or fearless and *brahma* or infitintely great. These attributes are not applicable to either *jīvātman* or its reflection or to the celestial deity. That the *puruṣa* in the eye is Brahman is further confirmed by the subsequent statement which refers to the following other attributes of Brahman:

etam samyadvāma ity ācakṣate, etaṁ hi sarvāṇi vāmāni abhisaṁyanti, sarvāṇi enaṁ vāmāny abhisaṁyanti, ya evaṁ veda...eṣa u eva vāmāniḥ eṣa u eva bhāmānīḥ, esa hi sarveṣu lokeṣu bhāti.[20]

"This they call *saṁyad vāma* since all desirable things go towards Him. All desirable things go to him who knows this." "He is *vāmāniḥ* since he bestows all blessings to living beings. "He is *bhāmāni* for He shines in all worlds." Both these terms *vāmāni* and *bhāmāni* (describing Brahman) signify that Brahman who is the object of meditation bestows all blessings to living beings and that it shines in all the worlds. These attributes are applicable to Brahman who abides in the eye for the purpose of meditation by the *upāsaka*.

In the earlier part of this passage referring to the instruction imparted by the sacrificial fires (fire Gods) to Upakosala who was made to stay in the hermitage of the sage Satyakāma Jābāli while he was away, the following teaching was imparted to Upakosala : *prāṇo brahma kaṁ brahma khaṁ brahma* - "The *prāṇa* is Brahman, joy (*kaṁ*) is Brahman, ether (*khaṁ*) is Brahman." By way of clarification of what is *kaṁ* and *khaṁ*, it is further stated: *yadvāva kaṁ tadeva khaṁ, yadvāva khaṁ tadeva kaṁ iti; prāṇam ca hāsmai tadākāśaṁ ca ūcuḥ*[21] - "What is joy(*kaṁ*) that itself is *ākāśa* (*khaṁ*). What is *ākāśa* (*khaṁ*) that itself is the joy (*kaṁ*). They (*agni* Gods) taught him about *prāṇa* and *ākāśa*.

The term *prāṇa* 'as interpreted by Rāmānuja' refers to Brahman since it is the giver of life to the entire universe. The term *kaṁ* means joy and the word *khaṁ* means infinite and the two terms taken together as qualifying each other imply that Brahman denoted by *prāṇa* is infinitely blissful (*jagat prāṇayitṛtvena prāṇa viśiṣṭam yad Brahma tadeva aparicchinna sukharūpeṇa ca...*[22])

The point to be noted is that the mention of the essential characteristic of Brahman as *kaṁ* and *khaṁ* supports the view that the *akṣi-puruṣa* mentioned in the Chāndogya passage denotes Brahman and not *jīva* or any other entity. Bādarāyaṇa also mentions this fact in the *sūtra* reading '*Ata eva ca sa brahma.*'[23] It means that because of the mention of *ka* and *kha* as qualifying characteristic of *prāṇa,* the Upaniṣadic statement refers to Brahman.

Two other arguments are advanced by Bādarāyaṇa in support of this view. In the Antaryāmī Brāhmaṇa of Bṛhadāraṇyaka Upaniṣad it is stated that *Paramātman* dwells in the eye as the inner controller (*ya cakṣusi tiṣṭhan*). In view of this, the *puruṣa* seen inside the eye by the *yogins* is Brahman. Besides, the Chāndogya Upaniṣad dealing with *Upakosala-vidyā* mentions the *arcirādi mārga.* This pathway is prescribed only for those *upāsakas* who meditate on Brahman (*sthitiniyatibalāt arcirādi yuktitaśca*[24]). The *akṣipuruṣa* referred to here is therefore Brahman.

A minor objection is raised against the theory of *akṣipurusa* being regarded as the object of meditation in *Upakośala-vidyā.* The *puruṣa* who is seen in the eye could be a reflection of the person and such a reflected Being (*pratikṛti-puruṣa*) is not capable of giving any fruitful result. Can it be considered as a worthy object of meditation?

Vedānta Deśika refutes this argument. In matters enjoined by the Scriptural texts which enjoy supreme authority, we have to accept them in good faith irrespective of the fact whether or not the object of meditation leads to good result. (*svātantrya uttaṁsitastu śrutiṣu na phaladaśaiva vedyatva vādaḥ*[25]). Thus for instance, we accept on the authority of the Scriptural text that the performance of *jyotiṣṭoma* sacrifice is *dharma* and the killing of a Brahmin is *adharma.* There are statements which say that seeing auspicious objects after waking in the morning such as gold, diamond, sandal paste, white cow, the flower etc, is the portender of good event. We accept them on the authority of the sacred texts without questioning whether the object seen is real or unreal. The seeing of such objects irrespective of its reality or otherwise yields the good result. In the same way the meditation on the *akṣipuruṣa,* even if it is taken as a reflected image, can confer good result since it is enjoined by the Scriptural text.

From the foregoing details, Vedānta Deśika concludes that the *Antarādhikaraṇa* establishes that Brahman always abides in the eye (*akṣinityasthitiḥ*), as stated in the *Antaryāmi Brāhmaṇa*.

IV. Brahman as the Inner Controller of All

This is the subject matter of the *Antaryāmyadhikaraṇa* which brings out explicitly that Brahman is the *Antaryāmin* of all entities in the universe, both sentient and non-sentient. The relevant *sūtra* reads: *Antaryāmyadhidaiva adhiloka ādiṣu tad-dharma vyapadeśāt.*[26] The term *antaryāmī* means one who controls from within or the Inner Controller. *Adhidaivādiṣu* means the deities and other entities referred to in the Upaniṣadic statements. The word *adhiloka* added by Rāmānuja on the basis of the *Mādhyandina* recension of the Bṛhadāraṇyaka Upaniṣad means the worlds and others. The word *taddharmopadeśāt* means because of the mention of the attributes applicable to Brahman. The total meaning of the *sūtra*, as interpreted by Rāmānuja, is that *Antaryāmin* or the Inner Controller of the deities and other entities mentioned in the Upaniṣadic passage is Brahman because the attributes stated in the passage are only applicable to Brahman.

This *sūtra* is based on the significant passage known as the *Antaryāmi Brāhmaṇa* of the Bṛhadāraṇyaka Upaniṣad. In a discourse between the Sage Yājñavalkya and Uddālaka, Uddalaka asks Yājñavalkya to tell him about Antaryāmin who controls from within this world as well as the next world and all things: *Vetta nu tvam antaryāminam. Ya imāṁca lokaṁ paraṁ ca lokaṁ sarvāṇi bhūtāni yo antaro yamayati.* In reply Yājñavalkya states: *yaḥ pṛthivyām tiṣṭhan pṛthivyā antaraḥ, yaṁ pṛthivī na veda, yasya pṛthivī śarīraṁ, yaḥ pṛthivīm antaro yamayati, yeṣa ta ātmā antaryāmy amṛtaḥ.*[27]

"He who dwells in the earth, who is within the earth, of whom the earth does not know, whose body the earth is, who controls the earth from within, He is your self (*ātmā*), the Inner Controller (*antaryāmī*), the immortal (*amṛtaḥ*)."

In the same strain Yājñvalkya repeats the statement twenty times covering in each statement the following other entities viz. *ap* (water), *agni* (fire), *antarikṣa* (sky), *vāyu* (air), *divi* (heaven), *āditya* (sun), *dik* (quarters), *candra-tāraka* (moon and stars), *ākāśa* (ether), *tamas* (darkness), *tejas* (light), *sarvabhūta* (all beings), *prāṇa* (life breath), *vāk* (organ of speech), *cakṣus* (ther eyes), *śrotra* (the ear), *manas* (the mind), *tvak* (the skin), *vijñāna* (the individual self) and *retas* (semen). The above enumeration of the entities is according to the recension of the *Kāṇva*. The Mādhyandina recension of the Upaniṣad lists a few more additional entities viz. *sarvaloka, sarva veda* and *sarva yajña*. Besides, in place of *vijñāna*, it uses the term *ātman*, or the individual self. Thus it is stated: *ya ātmani tiṣṭhan, ātmano antaro, yam ātmā na veda, yasyātmā śarīram, ya ātmānam antaro yamayati, sa ta ātmā antaryāmī amṛtaḥ.*[28]

This significant passage covers in an exhaustive way both the sentient and non-sentient entities including the individual self denoted by the term *vijñāna* and *ātman*. In each it is described that *Paramātman* (Brahman) dwells in them (*tiṣṭhan*) and also abides within them (*antaraḥ*), none of the entities know Him (*na veda*), But they constitute His body (*sarīram*). Paramātman controls them from within (*antaro yamayati*). It is also stated that this *Paramātman* is your Self (*yeṣa ta ātmā*), who is *Antaryāmin* and immortal (*amṛta*).

After narrating in a grand way the immanence of *Paramātman* in all the entities of the universe, Yājñavalkya makes the following statement:

Adṛṣṭo draṣṭā, aśrutaḥ śrotā, amanto mantā, avijñāto vijñātā, nānyato'sti draṣṭā, nānyato'sti śrotā, nānyato'sti mantā, nānyato'sti vijñātā, eṣa ta ātmā antaryamī amṛtah ato anyad ārtam.[29]

It means according to Rāmānuja: "He (*Antaryāmin*) is not seen but He sees all. He is not heard but hears everything. He is not comprehended but He comprehends everything. He is not perceived but He perceives everything. There is no other seer but He. There is no other hearer but He. There is no other cognizer but He. There is no other knower but He. He is your *Ātmā* (self) the inner controller, and the immortal. Everything else is a source of misery (*ārtam*).

An important question raised with regard to this passage is whether this *Antaryāmin* referred to here is *Paramātman* or is it *jīvātman*? According to the prima facie view, it is *jīvātman*. The main argument in support of it is that towards the end of the passage it is described as *draṣṭā*, one who sees, *śrotā* or one who hears etc. Besides it is also mentioned that there is no one else who is the seer, no one else who is the hearer etc. These descriptions do not fit with *Paramātman* but only with *jīva*. The act of hearing or seeing is possible through the media of respective sense organs and only a *jīva* associated with the mind and sense organs can have such functions.

Bādarāyaṇa rejects this view and affirms that the *Antaryāmin* referred in this Upaniṣad is Brahman. The reason advanced in favour of this conclusion is that the *dharmas* or the attributes mentioned in the passage are directly applicable to *Paramātman* (*taddharma vyapadeśāt*). The first important characteristic, which is well brought out in the Upaniṣadic statements, is that He controls all the deities, all the worlds and all the entities by virtue of His being their *Antarātmā* or indweller. Such a *dharma* cannot belong to anyone other than *Paramātman*. What is said in these statements viz. that all entities in the universe are controlled by *Paramātman* by virtue of His being inherent in them and that the respective entities do not know this fact, is repeated in the following statements by way of conclusion at the end of the passage : *Adṛṣṭo draṣṭā na anyato'sti draṣṭā , aśruto srotā etc.*, The implication of it is that *Paramātman* cannot be seen through the eyes, and he cannot be heard through our ears etc. But such a *Paramātman* is the true seer (*draṣṭā*) and the true hearer (*srotā*) in the sense that He directly intuits all things in the universe without the aid of the sense organs, unlike a *jīvātman (tattatkaraṇa sāpekṣatvābhāve'pi svābhāvika tattat viṣaya sākṣātkaraṇa*[30] *)*

Further, both the Kānva and Mādhyandina recension of *Antaryāmi Brāhmaṇa*, emphatically state that *Paramātman* indwells in *jīvātman*[31] denoted by the synonymous terms *vijñāna* and *ātman*, and that *jīvātman* is the *śarīra* of *Paramātman* in the technical sense, as explained by Rāmānuja, viz., that it is sustained (*ādheya*) and controlled (*niyāmya*) by Him. The final statement *'sa te ātmā antaryamī amṛtaḥ'* also draws a clear distinction between the *jīvātman* and *Paramātman*. Hence the *jīvātman* cannot be the *Antaryāmin*.

It may be still argued that the terms *vijñāna* and *ātman*, though they may have the same meaning, may be taken in the sense of *buddhi* or intellect in which *Paramātman* dwells. It is therefore not possible to advance the theory of body-soul relation (*śarīrātmabhāva*) between *jīva* and *Paramātmā* on the basis of *Antaryāmi Brāhmaṇa*. In reply, Vedānta Deśika points out that this is a wrong interpretation (*apārtha*). It is well established in all the Scriptural texts and also in the ordinary empirical usage, that the terms *vijñāna* and *ātman* are applicable to a sentient being and not to an insentient object. For instance, in the Upaniṣadic statement *'vijñanaṁ yajñaṁ tanute'*, the term *vijñāna* does not mean mind but the individual self. In the text of the Kaṭha Upaniṣad, *'ātmānaṁ rathinaṁ viddhi'*, the term *ātmā* means *jīva*. There is no compelling reason to adopt a secondary meaning to *ātmā* as *buddhi*. The final statement *'sa ta ātmā'*, or He is your Self, stands well explained by taking *Paramātman* as the *Antaryāmin* of the individual self. *(sa ta ityādibhiḥ sāmarasyam)*[32].

Vedānta Deśika therefore comes to the conclusion that this *adhikaraṇa* establishes that all entities in the universe constitute the body (*śarīra*) of Brahman by virtue of its being the Inner Controller (*akhila tanuḥ*[33]).

V. Brahman as the Imperishable Reality (Akṣara)

This is the subject-matter of the *adhikaraṇa* named *Adṛśya-tvādi-guṇakādhikaraṇa*, which discusses the issue whether the metaphysical principle termed as *akṣara* which is described by the Muṇḍaka Upaniṣad as *adṛśya* or that which is not perceived, as *agrāhya* or that which is not grasped etc. refers to Brahman or some other entity either *prakṛti* or *jīvātman*. This doubt arises since the relevant passage of the Muṇḍaka Upaniṣad on which the *sūtra* is framed contains statements about *akṣara*, which do not clearly reveal whether this *akṣara* denotes Brahman. Hence Bādarāyaṇa takes up this subject for consideration. The relevant *sūtra* reads : *Adṛśyatvādi gunako dharmokteḥ*[34]. It means: The entity denoted by *akṣara* in the Upaniṣad which is qualified by the attributes such as imperceptibility (*adṛśyatva*) is Brahman, since the characteristics (*dharmas*) mentioned in the Upaniṣadic texts belong to Brahman. The fuller implications of the *sūtra* will be evident from the examination of the concerned passage of the Muṇḍaka Upaniṣad.

The Upaniṣad commences with a significant passage in which sage Aṅgiras teaches Śaunaka about the nature of the ultimate principle, by knowing which everything else becomes known. After explaining the two types of *vidyās* which are to be known for this purpose, Angiras makes the following statement:

Atha parā yayā tadakṣaram adhigamyate, yat tad adṛeśyam agrāhyam agotram avarṇam acakṣuḥ śrotraṁ tad apāṇipādaṁ nityaṁ vibhuṁ sarvagataṁ susūkṣmaṁ tad avyayaṁ yad bhūtayoniṁ paripāsyanti dhīrāḥ.[35]

'Now this *parāvidyā* by means of which the *akṣara* is to be comprehended; that which is imperceivable, ungraspable, without family, without caste, without eyes or ears, without hands or feet, which is eternal, all pervading, omnipresent, exceedingly subtle, that is the imperishable (*avyayaṁ*) which, the wise perceive as the source of beings (*bhūtayoni*)."

Later in the second section of the Upaniṣad, it states: *"divyo hi amūrtaḥ puruṣaḥ sa bāhyābhyantaro hy ajaḥ, aprāṇo hy amanāḥ śubhro akṣarāt parataḥ paraḥ."*

'The *Puruṣa* is divine. He is formless (*amūrtaḥ*), He is pervading within and without, unborn. He is without *prāṇa* and mind (*amanāḥ*) He is higher than *akṣara (akṣarat parataḥ paraḥ)."*[36]

Taking into consideration both the statements, a doubt arises as to whether the term *akṣara* mentioned in the opening statement and also in the later statement refers to the *prakṛti* and *jīva* respectively or to *Paramātman*. According to the prima facie view, the qualities described in the Upaniṣadic texts appropriately apply to the *prakṛti* of the Sāṁkhya. The text of the second section of the Muṇḍaka speaks of something higher than *akṣara* and this *akṣara* cannot possibly be Brahman. It may refer to *jīva*, since *jīva* is higher than *prakṛti (akṣarāt parataḥ paraḥ).*

Bādarāyaṇa rejects this view and affirms that *akṣara* referred to in the beginning of the passage, which is also regarded as *bhūta-yoni* or the source of the universe is Brahman and not either *pradhāna* or *jīva*. The main reason in support of it is that the *akṣara* mentioned at the commencement of the passage is described later on as *sarvajña* and *sarvavit*, the two important attributes which are applicable only to *Paramātman*. *(sarvajñatvādi dṛṣṭeḥ prathama samuditam akṣaram brahma śuddham*[37]*).*

In the second statement, *'akṣarāt parataḥ paraḥ'*, *akṣara* refers to the *prakṛti* for the reason that there cannot be anything greater than *akṣara* taken as Brahman. In this statement, *akṣarāt parataḥ paraḥ*, three principles are referred to: *prakṛti*, *jīva* and *Paramātman*. *Akṣarāt paraḥ* means greater than *prakṛti* is *jīva*; the words *parataḥ paraḥ* imply, greater than *jīva* is Brahman (*para*[38]). Hence, *akṣara* in the later statement denotes *prakṛti*.

As Rāmānuja has explained, the entire passage teaches about Brahman. A few important points are mentioned in the passage, which support this view. First, *akṣara* is described as *bhūtayoni* or source of the universe, that is, the material cause of the universe, as explained by the analogies of spider and the web created by it, the herbs growing on earth, and the growth of hairs on the body of a living person. Secondly, it is also stated that from *akṣara* originates *prāṇa, manas* and the sense organs and all elements.[39] It is also mentioned that the *puruṣa* is divine, formless and pervading within and without. The passage also states that the heaven, moon, sun, the *dik, vāyu, pṛthivī* and the entire universe represent parts of His *śarīra* and that *Paramātman* is *antarātmā* of all entities.[40] All these points unmistakably reveal that *akṣara* referred to in this passage of the Muṇḍaka is no other principle than Brahman. Thus, this *adhikaraṇa* brings out the fact that *akṣara* as qualified with negative qualities such, as *adreśyatva* is Brahman.

VI. Brahman conceived in its Cosmic form is the Ruler of all Souls (Vaiśvānara)

This is the subject-matter of *Vaiśvānaradhikaraṇa* which discusses whether *vaiśvānara ātmā* referred to in the Chāndogya Upaniṣad denotes Brahman or some other principle.

The relevant passage commences with the narration of five sages who are desirous of knowing "what is our Self (Inner Controller), what is Brahman" (*ko na ātmā kiṁ brahma*). They first approach Uddālaka who in turn takes them to Aśvapati Kaikeya who is reputed to know it better. On meeting Kaikeya, they request him with these words: *'Ātmānameva vaiśvānaram sampraty-adhyeṣi tameva no brūhi.'*[41]

'You know at present that *Vaiśvanara* Self. Tell us that'. With a view to finding out how much the sages already knew, Kaikeya asks each one of them to tell what they have been presently meditating. In reply each one mentions that he meditates on *Vaiśvānara* conceived as one of the following entities respectively: *divi* (heaven), *sūrya* (sun), *vāyu* (air) *ākāśa* (ether), *ap* (water) and *pṛthivī* (earth). Realizing that this amounts to the meditation of *Vaiśvānara* as limited by a part only and not its complete form, Kaikeya makes the following statement:

Tan hovāca ete vai khalu yūyam pṛthagivemam ātmānaṁ vaiśvānaraṁ vidvāṁso annam attha, yastu etaṁ evaṁ prādeśamātram abhivimānam ātmānaṁ vaiśvānaraṁ upāsāte, sa sarveṣu lokeṣu sarveṣu bhūteṣu sarveṣu ātmasu annam atti[42]

"Then he (Aśvapati) said to them: you meditate this *vaiśvānara ātmā* in part only as if it were many and you eat your food (that is, obtain limited material benefits). But he who meditates on the *vaiśvānara ātman* measured by a span or part (*prādeśa mātra*) as *abhivimāna* (as unlimited, pervading the entire universe) eats the food in all worlds, in all beings, in all selves. That is, he enjoys Brahman which abides in all places and in all beings."

Based on this passage, which does not convey the import of the term *Vaiśvānara*, Bādarāyaṇa introduces the following *sūtra*: *Vaiśvānaraḥ sādhāraṇa śabda viśeṣāt*[43]. The word *Vaiśvānara* means Brahman. The reason for regarding it as Brahman is contained in the next words of the *sūtra* '*sādhāraṇa śabda viśeṣāt*'. Its meaning is that the common word is qualified by distinctions. By way of elucidation, it is pointed out that this is regarded as the common word because it applies to more than one thing. It can mean either the digestive fire (*jaṭharāgni*), or elemental fire (*bhūtāgni*), or its presiding deity (*tadabhimāni-devatā*) or even *Paramātman*. We come across Scriptural texts using them in these different senses. The doubt therefore arises as to which one of these is applicable to the term *vaísvānara* employed in the Upaniṣad. As stated by Bādārāyaṇa, this term denotes only Brahman because it is qualified by distinguished attributes (*viśeṣāt*).

How does the common word (*sāmānya śabda*) become distinguishable (*viśeṣa*)? According to the explanation offered by Rāmānuja, the common word *Vaiśvānara* is further qualified by distinguishing marks, which are applicable to Brahman. Taking this entire passage into consideration, it may be noted that it commences with an enquiry by the five sages about Brahman and the person who teaches it is also reputed to have that knowledge. Both the subject of enquiry and the contents of the teaching imparted by Kaikeya is also related to Brahman. The terms *ātmā* and Brahma used in the opening statement '*kona ātmā kiṁ brahma*' are replaced later on in the passage by *ātmā* and *vaiśvānara* respectively. The term *Vaiśvānara* which replaces Brahman denotes that it is the same as Brahman. Besides the fruits of the meditation as described in the later part of the Upaniṣad and also the fact that the knower of *vaiśvānara* becomes free from all sins[44] clearly confirms that the term *vaiśvanara* denotes Brahman.

Further, in this passage, *Vaiśvānara* is personified and described for purposes of meditation as possessing different parts of the universe viz., *divi* as its head, *āditya* as its eye, *vāyu* as its *prāṇa*, *ākāśa* as its body, water as its bladder (*vasti*) and *pṛthivī* as its feet.[45] Such a description is appropriate only in respect of *Vaiśvānara* as Brahman and not *jīvātman*, since the entire universe consisting of sentient and non-sentient entities is the *śarīra* or body of Brahman, as declared in the *Antaryāmi Brāhmaṇa* (*paramātmanaḥ prapañca śarīrakatayā anyatra prasiddheḥ*[46]).

An objection is raised against this conclusion. In one of the Scriptural texts of the *Vājasaneya śākhā*, dealing with *Vaiśvānara-vidyā*, it is stated that *agni* is *Vaiśvānara* (*sa eṣo agnir vaísvānaraḥ*), thus equating *Vaiśvānara* with *agni* or fire. In the present passage of Chāndogya too, the *upāsaka* on *Vaiśvānara* is required to regard one's own heart as the altar or basis for *gārhapatya* sacrificial fire and offer oblations to it (mentally) in the name of *prāṇa* and its other forms. This *agni* is conceived in a human form as abiding inside one's body. From these descriptions it follows that the term *Vaiśvānara* mentioned in the passage is *jāṭharāgni* or digestive fire inherent in one's body which carries out the functions of digestion. Hence it is not possible to state conclusively that *Vaiśvānara* is *Paramātman.*

Bādarāyaṇa himself has anticipated this objection and given a suitable reply to it.[47] As explained by Rāmānuja, the same *Vaiśvānara* who is Brahman in its universal form, that is, as having the entire universe as its body, is to be regarded as *jāṭharāgni* or digestive fire, as inherently related to *Paramātman* (*jāṭharāgni -śarīraka paramātmā*). The contemplation on *jāṭharāgni* or digestive fire inside the body is not the mere physical aspect of *agni* but that which constitutes the body of *Paramātman.* This explanation is justified because the mere *jāṭharāgni* cannot be the *puruṣa* or the Supreme Person in his cosmic form comprising all entities in the universe as His body. For the same reason, it cannot be either mere elemental fire or its presiding deity.[48] One other explanation is that the term *agni,* according to etymological meaning, denotes directly Brahman, (*agraṁ nayatīti agniḥ).* This interpretation is also supported by Jaimini. According to him, there is no objection in taking the term *Vaiśvānara* to denote Brahman directly (*Sākṣād api avirodham jaiminiḥ*[49]). According to the grammatical rule, the term *vaiśvānara* is formed out of the word *Vaiśvānara,* which means one who is the Ruler of all human beings or souls (*viśveṣām narāṇām netāra*). Thus this *adhikaraṇa* brings out the fact that Brahman conceived as *Viśva-śarīraka* is the Ruler of all souls (*Vaiśvānara*).

VII. Brahman as the Support of Heaven and Earth (Āyatana)

This is the subjectmatter of the *adhikaraṇa* named as *Dyubhvādy-adhikaraṇa* which establishes another important characteristic of Brahman viz. it is the *Āyatana* or Support of the heaven (*dyu*), earth (*bhū*), sky (*antarikṣa*) and other entities such as mind (*manas*) and breath (*prāṇa*), as stated in the Muṇḍaka Upaniṣad. In a significant statement made about the *Ātman,* the Upaniṣad says: *Yasmin dyauḥ pṛthivī ca antarikṣam otam manaḥ saha prāṇaśca sarvaiḥ; tamekaṁ jānatha ātmānam anyā vāco vimuñcatha, amṛtasya eṣa setuḥ*[50].

'He in whom the heaven, earth and the sky along with the mind and the vital breath (*prāṇa*) are woven; know Him alone as the *Ātman* and abandon all other talk; He is the bridge (*setu*) to the immortality."

In the subsequent statement, the Upanisad says: *arā iva ratha nābhau saṁhatā yatra nāḍyaḥ sa eṣa antaḥ carate bahudhā jāyamānaḥ*[51] -"In the heart, the nāḍis are fixed like the spokes of the wheel on the hub of the chariot."

With reference to this passage, the question is raised whether that which is described as the support of heaven, earth and so on is Brahman or *jīvātman*. According to the prima facie view, it is *jīvātman*. The main argument in support of it is that *manas* and other sense organs are woven in it and whereas *Paramātman* is devoid of sense organs (*aprāṇo hi amanāḥ*). Besides in the later statement it is said that it is the main support (*ādhāra*) for the *nāḍis*, similar to the central hub on which the spokes of the wheel rest and that it also moves inside the bodies (*antaḥ carati*) and takes birth in different forms (*bahudhā jāyante*). Taking all these descriptions, it follows that what is referred to in the passage is *jīvātman*.

This view is rejected by Bādarāyaṇa. Thus says the *sūtra*: *dyubhvādyātanaṁ sva śabdāt*[52]. The compound word *dyubhvau* (*dvyauśca bhūśca dyubhvau*) means heaven and earth. The suffix *ādi* implies other entities such as sky (*antarikṣa*), mind (*manas*) and vital breath (*prāṇa*) mentioned in the Upanisadic text. *Āyatana* means that which provides the support. The total meaning of the fourth part of the *sūtra* is that Brahman is the support of the heaven, earth and so on. The reason for maintaining this view is expressed in the word *sva śabda* which means that the very term *Ātman* is specifically mentioned in the Upaniṣadic passage.

By way of elucidation it is pointed out that the term *Ātman* in its primary sense denotes Brahman (*āpnoti iti ātmā*). The words *dyu* and *pṛthivī* referred in the text are illustrative of the entire universe. As clearly stated in the Upaniṣadic text, only Brahman can be *āyatana* of the universe. More importantly, it is described as the *setu* for attaining immortality. The term *setu* is to be understood in the sense of *prāpaka* or the one who enables the person to attain immortality (*setuḥ amṛtasya prāpakaḥ*) It can also be understood, as explained by Rāmānuja, to mean that which leads towards immortality that lies beyond the ocean of *saṁsāra* or bondage in the same way as a bridge leads to the other side of the river bank. The characteristic of *āyatanatva* therefore belongs to Brahman only.

The above conclusion is further affirmed by Bādarāyaṇa himself with additional arguments on the basis of the statements of the Muṇḍaka Upaniṣad. Firstly, the Upaniṣad itself states that the released soul attains the state of *mokṣa*[53]. The relevant text says: *yadā paśyaḥ paśyate rukmavarnaṁ kartāram īśaṁ puruṣam brahma yonim; tadā vidvān puṇya pāpe vidhūya nirañjanaḥ paramaṁ sāmyam upaiti.*[54]

"When the knower of Brahman (*jīvātman*) sees the *Puruṣa* (*Paramātman*) who is of the golden colour, who is the Ruler of the universe, the cause of the *prakṛti*, then the knower of Brahman shaking off good and evil and becoming free from defilements, attains the Supreme equality with the Lord."

In a later passage it is specifically said that the liberated soul attains the Divine *Puruṣa* who is higher than both *prakṛti* and *puruṣa* (*tathā vidvān nāmarūpād vimuktaḥ parātparam puruṣam upaiti divyam*[55]). Further, this Upaniṣad also speaks of the difference between Brahman and *jīva* by citing the analogy of two birds sitting on the same tree, one abiding as the passive observer (*anaśnan*) and the other enjoying the fruits of *karma*.[56] More importantly, the subject-matter of the entire passage is related to Brahman only (*prakaraṇataḥ*). There is no mention of either *jīva* or *prakṛti* as the *āyatana* or support of the heaven, earth etc. Hence it is concluded that Brahman is *āyatana* or the Support of the entire universe.[57]

Vedānta Deśika further points out that the description of the mind and senses being woven in the all-pervasive Brahman should not be regarded as inconceivable. Though *Paramātman* is not subject to birth caused by *karma,* He can assume many forms out of His will. As *Antaryāmin* or one who indwells in the body of an individual, He can be the *ādhāra* or the support for the numerous *nāḍis,* similar to the hub of the chariot in which the spokes rest (*arā iva ratha nābhau saṁhatā yatra naḍyaḥ*). The presence of Brahman in the body as *Antarātmā* is warranted by the Bṛhadāraṇyaka and other Upaniṣads. The *antaścaraṇa* or the movement of Brahman in the body is to be understood in the sense of Brahman being the supporter of everything in the universe (*adhiṣṭhāna mātram*) by virtue of His *svarūpa* pervading everywhere.[58] It is in this sense that the Subāla Upaniṣad also uses the word *antaścaraṇa* (*yaḥ pṛthivīm antare sancaran*).

VIII. Brahman as Infinitely Great (Bhūmā)

This is the subject-matter of the *Bhūmādhikaraṇa* which brings out the characteristic of Brahman as *bhūmā* or infinitely great on the basis of the passage of Chāndogya Upaniṣad .The term *bhūmā* is derived from the root word *bahu* (immense) but with the addition of the suffix *imnic,* it becomes *bhūmā.* It therefore, means *bahutva* or immensity in terms of quality and not quantity, as contrasted to *alpatva* or smallness. As a quality it should inhere in a substance or entity. What is that entity which is described as *bhūmā* in the Upaniṣad?

According to Bādarāyaṇa, the term *bhūmā* refers to Brahman. Based on the passage of the Chāndogya Upaniṣad, the *sūtra* says: *Bhūmā saṁprasādāt adhyupadeśāt.*[59] *Bhūmā* refers to Brahman. The reason for regarding it as Brahman is given in the next compound word of the *sūtra,* viz. *Samprāsadāt adhyupadeśāt. Samprasāda* means, according to the interpretation of Rāmānuja, *jīvātman,* since the Chāndogya Upaniṣad elsewhere uses this word as synonymous with *jīva (eṣa samprasādaḥ asmāt śarīrāt samutthāya*[60]). The word *adhyupadeśāt* means that *bhūman* which is identified with *satya* or Brahman is taught in addition to the *jīvātman* which is termed as *prāṇa* in the passage.

The fuller implication of the *sūtra* can be understood with reference to the passage of the Chāndogya Upaniṣad. This passage covers an interesting dialogue between Sanatkumāra and his pupil, Nārada. It commences with the request made by Nārada to teach him *ātma-vidyā* or knowledge of Brahman, which is the means to overcome bondage (*tarati śokam ātmavit*), To facilitate the realization of *Ātman*, Sanatkumāra first suggests the meditation on a series of the entities conceived as symbols of Brahman in an ascending order beginning with *nāma*, or name, followed by *vāk* or speech, *manas* or mind, *saṁkalpa* or will, *citta* or mental state, *dhyāna* or contemplation, *vijñāna* or comprehension, *bala* or strength, *anna* or food, *apa* or water, *tejas* or fire, *ākāśa* or ether, *smara* or memory, *āśā* or hope and lastly *prāṇa* or individual self (according to Rāmānuja). In enumerating these fifteen entities for the purpose of meditation as the symbols of Brahman, Sanatkumāra extols each one of them as worthy object of meditation leading to the acquisition of certain higher material benefits. In reply to Nārada's query, he also states that each one, commencing with *vāk*, is higher than the preceding one. But with regard to the meditation on *prāṇa*, no further query is made by Nārada as to whether there is anything higher than *prāṇa*. Nor does Sanatkumāra suggest any other principle as superior to it. On the other hand, he glorifies the meditation on *prāṇa* to a greater extent than the others. He also says that *prāṇa* is everything (*prāṇo hy eva etāni sarvāṇi bhavanti*). He who knows *prāṇa* is considered as *ativadi* or one who can speak of its greatness (*ativādī bhavati*[61]).

After extolling the meditation on *prāṇa*, Sanatkumāra mentions the greatness of *satya* or Reality. *Satya* is extolled with the words: "He who speaks about *satya* surpasses everything else. Thus he says: *eṣa tu vā ativadati yaḥ satyena ativadati.*[62] It means: "But in reality he is an *ativādī* who has become an *ativādī* by the knowledge of *satya.*"

In the above dialogue culminating with *prāṇa,* after which no further query from Nārada is made regarding anything higher than *prāṇa* and Sanatkumāra also does not make any categorical statement to the effect that *satya* is higher than *Prāṇa,* a doubt arises whether *prāṇa* can be *bhūman.* According to the prima facie view, *prāṇa* itself is *bhūmā.* The main argument in support of this view is that Sanatkumāra who was approached by Nārada seeking the *Ātma jñāna* ends up with the teaching about *prāṇa.* The glorifying description provided in the Upaniṣad about *prāna* as everything, that it is father, mother, *ācārya* etc. and that if one ill treats them, he is considered to be harming them, lends support to the theory that *prāṇa* is *jīvātman* and that itself is *bhūman.*

This view is rejected by Bādarāyaṇa. The term *bhūmā* does not refer to *jīvātman* denoted by the word *prāṇa* but to Brahman. The reason given is that after culminating the teaching with *prāṇa,* the Upaniṣadic passage proceeds to extol *satya* with the words:

Eṣa ṭu vā ativadati yaḥ satyena ativadati. "But in reality he is an *ativādī* who has become an *ativādī* by the knowledge of the *satya.*"

The implication of this statement soon after extolling *prāṇa* is that *satya* is greater than *prāṇa* and one who speaks of the glory of this is a true *ativādī.* As Rāmānuja explains, in the text *"eṣa tu vā ativadati"* the word *'tu'* implies that some higher principle than *prāṇa* is going to be emphasized. Though there was no query on the part of Nārada as to whether there is anything higher than *prāṇa,* Sanatkumāra on his own mentions *satya* as the highest object with the intention of teaching Nārada that the meditation on *satya* leads to liberation from bondage. The term *satya* stands for Brahman. Nārada also readily responds by saying that he would become an *ativādī* by the knowledge of *satya.* In response to the desire expressed by Nārada to know *satya,* sanatkumāra instructs him to meditate on *satya* (*satyam tveva vijijñāsitavyaḥ*[63]). He also instructs him the various steps to be taken for realization of *satya* (Brahman). Further, *satya* is identified with *Bhūmā*. *Satya* therefore denotes Brahman and on that basis it is concluded that *Bhūman* is Brahman and not *jīvātman* or *prāṇa*. Besides, *Bhūman* is also described as *sukha* or bliss (*yo vai bhūmā tat sukham*[64]). This implies that Brahman is essentially of the nature of infinite bliss (*niratísaya-sūkha-rupa*).

Another reason for regarding *Bhūman* as Brahman is that this Upaniṣadic passage ascribes several attributes to *Bhūman*. These are besides *sukha* (bliss), *satyatva*, *amṛtatva* or immortality, *ananyādhāratva* or not being dependent on anything else for its existence than its own greatness (*sve mahimni pratiṣṭitatva*[65]) and *sarvātmakatva* or that it is the Self of all (*sa eva idaṁ sarvam*[66]). All these *dharmas*, as stated by Bādarāyaṇa, are applicable only to Brahman and not to *jīvātman*. It is therefore concluded that the passage dealing with the theory of *Bhūman* brings out the characteristic of Brahman as infinitely great (*anantabhūmā*). As the Inner Controller of all it is higher than all the fifteen entities including *prāṇa* as stated in the Upaniṣad in an ascending order. (*prāṇaḥ satyaḥ parātmā sakala niyamitā gamyate bhūma vākye*[67]).

IX Brahman conceived as Akṣara is the Ādhāra of the Universe (Vísvādhāra)

This is the subject-matter of the *adhikaraṇa* named as *Akṣarādhikaraṇa* which establishes that *akṣara* referred to in the Bṛhadāraṇyaka Upaniṣad is Brahman by its being the *ādḥāra* or main support of the entire universe by virtue of its supreme commanding power (*praśāsana*). In an earlier *adhikaraṇa* titled *Adṛśyatvādhikaraṇa*, the same ontological principle termed as *akṣara*, which is described by the Muṇḍaka Upaniṣad as qualified with negative attributes such as *adṛśyatva* etc. was proved to be Brahman on the basis of the fact that it is described as *sarvajña* and *sarvavit*.

In the present *adhikaraṇa*, the same concept of *akṣara* which is described in the Bṛhadāraṇyaka with negative qualities such as *asthūla, anaṇu* etc. is proved to be Brahman on a different ground viz. It is *ādhāra* or supporter of the universe by virtue of its supreme power to command everything in the universe (*praśāsana*). The purpose of taking up this issue separately is to establish that *akṣara* referred to in the teaching of Yājñavalkya to Gārgi is neither *prakṛti* nor *jīvātman*.

The relevant *sūtras* relating to this subject read : *Akṣaram ambarānta-dhṛteḥ* and *sā ca praśāsanāt.*[68]

The first *sutra* means, according to Rāmānuja, that *akṣara* is Brahman because it is stated in the Upaniṣad that it is the supporter *(dhṛti)* of the entire universe beginning from the gross element of earth and culminating in the subtlest unmanifest *ākāśa (sūkṣma-bhūta ākāśa)*. The second *sūtra* means that *akṣara* is the supporter of all that exists because of its supreme command (*praśāsanāt)*. The fuller implication of the *sutras* can be understood with reference to the passage of the Bṛhadāraṇyaka Upaniṣad dealing with the teaching of Yājñavalkya to Gārgi on the nature of *akṣara*. Gārgi poses two searching questions to Yājñavalkya. The first question is:

Yad ūrdhvam, yājñavalkya, divaḥ, yadarvāk pṛthivyāḥ yad antarā dyāvā pṛthivī ime, yad bhūtam ca bhavacca bhaviṣyaccety ācakṣate; kasmin tad otam ca protaṁ ca iti.[69]

"O Yājñavalkya, what is it in which woven like warp and woof that which is above the heaven, which is beneath the earth, that which is between the two, the heaven and earth, that which was in the past, that which is in the present and that which will be in the future."

Yājñavalkya replies that it is the unmanifest ether *(ākāśa)* in which all these are woven like warp and woof *(ākāśa tadotam ca protam ca*)

Gārgi then poses (as her second question) " In what is *ākāśa* woven like warp and woof?" In reply Yājñavalkya makes the following statement describing *akṣara* in negative terms:

Sa hovāca, etad vai tad akṣaraṁ, Gārgi, brāhmaṇā abhivadanti, asthūlam, anaṇu, ahṛasvam, adīrghaṁ, alohitaṁ, asnehaṁ, accāyaṁ, atamaḥ, avāyu, anākāśam, asaṅgaṁ, avaśaṁ, agandhaṁ, acakṣuṣam, aśrotraṁ, avāk, amanaḥ, atejaskaṁ, aprāṇam, amukhaṁ, amātram, anantaraṁ, abāhyaṁ, na tad aśnāti kiṁcana, na tad aśnāti kaścana[70]

"He said: O Gārgi, the knowers of Brahman call that *akṣara* the imperishable, it is neither gross not subtle, neither short nor long, neither red nor adhesive, it is neither shadow nor darkness, neither air nor space, it is unattached, without taste, without smell, without eyes, without ears, without organ of speech, without mind, without radiance, without breath, without mouth, without measure, having no interior or exterior, it does not eat anything, nor is it eaten by any one."

In the subsequent passage, the same *akṣara* is described by Yājñavalkya in positive terms. Thus he says:

"etasyā vā akṣarasya praśāsane Gārgi sūryā candramasau vidhṛtau tiṣṭhataḥ; etasya vā akṣarasya praśāsane gārgi dyāvāpṛtihvyau vidhṛte tiṣṭhataḥ; etasy va akṣarasya praśāsane gārgi, nimeṣā muhūrtā ahorātrāṇi, ardhamāsā māsā ṛtavaḥ saṁvatsarā iti vidhṛtaḥ tiṣṭhanti[71] *"*

'Verily, at the command of this *akṣara*, Gārgi, the sun and the moon are held in their respective positions; at the command of this *akṣara*, Gārgi, heaven and earth are held in their respective positions; at the command of this *akṣara*, the moments, hours, days and nights, fortnights, months, seasons stand in their respective positions'

While concluding this teaching about *akṣara*, Yājñavalkya states:

"Tadvā etadakṣaraṁ, Gārgi, adṛṣṭaṁ draṣṭṛ, aśrutaṁ srotṛ, amataṁ mantṛ, avijñātaṁ vijñātṛ, nānyad ato' sti draṣṭṛ, nānyad ato'sti śrotṛ, nānyad ato'sti mantṛ, nānyad ato'sti vijñātṛ; etasmin khalu akṣare Gārgi ākāśa otaśca protaśca"[72]

'Verily, that *akṣara*, O Gārgi, is unseen but is the seer, is unheard but is the hearer, unthought but is the thinker, unknown but is the knower. There is no other seer but this, there is no other hearer but this, there is no other thinker but this, there is no other knower but this. But this *akṣara*, Gargi, is the ether (*ākāśa*) woven like a warp and woof.'

In the above passage, it is not quite clear what the term *akṣara* denotes. It may be *pradhāna* or the primordial cosmic matter from which the manifest universe evolves. Or it may be the *jīvātman* which is the basis for *prakṛti* or it may be *Paramātman* (Brahman). According to the prima facie view, it is the *pradhāna*, since at the commencement of the passage it is stated to be the basis for *ākāśa* and its other modifications. The description in terms of physical qualities such as *asthūla, anaṇu* etc. is applicable to it. Besides the word *akṣara* is also used in the sense of *pradhāna*.

Alternatively, *akṣara* can stand for *jīvātman*, since it is the basis of everything which is non-sentient such as *pṛthivī*. The term *akṣara* is also employed in the Upaniṣad in the sense of *jīvātman* (*avyaktam akṣare līyate*).[73]

Bādarāyaṇa rejects both these views and affirms that *akṣara* is Brahman because of the two characteristics mentioned in the *sūtras* viz. *Ambāranta-dhṛtatva* or the capacity to sustain the entire universe and *praśāsanatva* or its power to command everything in the universe. These characteristics do not apply either to the non-sentient *prakṛti*, or to the *jīvātman* (*anitaraniyata*). The passage brings out vividly how Brahman holds everything in the universe in their respective places through its supreme commanding power. Another important reason in support of this view is that *akṣara* is stated in the passage as *dṛṣṭā* or seer, as *śrotā* or hearer and as *vijñātṛ* or the knower and that there is no other seer, hearer or knower than this *Akṣara*. This point is also mentioned in the subsequent *sūtra* which reads: *Ananyabhāva vyāvṛtteśca*[74], meaning that the very Upaniṣad makes out the difference between *akṣara* as Brahman and the other two entities viz. *prakṛti* and *jīvāṭman* (*drastṛantarasya vyudāsanam iha tattulya tad draṣṭrapohaḥ*)[75].

The important point brought out in this *adhikaraṇa*, as summed up by Vedānta Deśika, is that Brahman who is designated as *akṣara* is *niyamana dhṛtikṛt*, which means that it is *ādhāra* or supporter of all entities in the universe by virtue of its command (*niyamanena śasanena sarva kāryādhāraḥ*).[76]

X. Brahman as the Object of Enjoyment for Muktas

This is the subject of a separate *adhikaraṇa* named as *Īkṣatikarmādhikaraṇa* which establishes that Brahman is the object of realization through meditation on the syllable *'Aum'* mentioned in the Praśnopaniṣad. This is different from the *Īkṣatyādhikaraṇa* discussed earlier in which *pradhāna* of Sāṁkhya is ruled out as the cause of the universe on the ground that the function of *īkṣaṇa* or will to create the universe is not attributable to it. In the present *adhikaraṇa*, the subject of discussion relates to the question whether the object realized through the *upāsanā* on *praṇava* or the syllable *'Aum'* is Brahman or the celestial deity named as *Hiraṇyagarbha*, also known as *Caturmukha Brahmā*. The relevance of bringing up this issue, as explained by Vedānta Deśika, is that in the preceding *adhikaraṇa*, *akṣara* was proved as Brahman on the basis of the description as *adṛṣṭo draṣṭā* or that which though not seen visually is a seer, But in the statement of the Praśnopaniṣad, it is stated that the *Paramapuruṣa* or the Supreme Being is visualized by the *upāsaka* on *praṇava* (*puruṣam īkṣate*), How can then such a *Puruṣa*, who becomes the object of vision is regarded as Brahman. To meet this objection Bādarāyaṇa introduces the following *sūtra* based on the passage of Praśnopaniṣad: ***Īkṣati karma vyapadeśāt saḥ***[77].

It means: "The object of *īkṣaṇa* or vision is Brahman only", because the Upaniṣadic statements directly convey this fact." The fuller implication of the *sūtra* can be understood with reference to the relevant passage of the Praśnopaniṣad. The fifth section of the Praśnopaniṣad dealing with the meditation on the syllable *'Aum'* with all the three letters (*tisromātra*) becomes free from sins and beholds *Parama puruṣa* as dwelling in one's heart. The relevant passage reads *'ya punaḥ etaṁ trimātreṇa aum iti etaineva akṣareṇa parama puruṣam abhidhyāyīta, sa tejasi surye saṁpannaḥ yathā padodaras tvacā vinirmuktaḥ sa sāmabhir unnīyate brahma lokam; sa etasmāt jivaghanāt parātparam puriśayam puruṣam īkṣate'.*[78]

"He who meditates on the Highest person (*Parama puruṣam*) with this very syllable with three letters (*a,u,ma*) becomes united with the effulgent sun. As the snake becomes free from its old skin, in the same way he is freed from the sins. He will be lead by *Sāma* (chants) to the *Brahmaloka*. He beholds the Supreme Self (*Puruṣa*) who is higher than the *Jīvaghana* and who dwells in the body (*puriśayam*).

With regard to this passage, doubt arises whether the *Parama Puruṣa* mentioned at the commencement as the object of meditation and also the *puruṣa* referred to at the end of the passage described as the object of *īkṣaṇa* or realization is Brahman or some other celestial deity such as *Hiraṇyagarbha*. According to the prima facie view, it is the *Hiraṇyagarbha* because he is stated to be higher than *prakṛti* and *jīva* (*jīvaghanāt parāt paraṁ puruṣa*). Besides the *Brahmaloka* to which the person meditating on *Parama Puruṣa* is first taken is the abode of *caturmukha brahmā*. According to the passage those who meditate on two syllables of *Aum* attain higher heavenly felicity. But one who meditates on the *puruṣa* with all the three letters reaches *Brahma-loka*. *Brahma-loka*, which is above *antarikṣa-loka*, represents the region of *caturmukha Brahmā* or *Hiraṇyagarbha*.

The above theory is rejected by Bādarāyana on the ground that the object of *īkṣaṇa* or what is visualized by the *upāsaka*, is Brahman. By way of explaining the reason advanced in the *sūtra* in favour of this view, Rāmānuja points out that according to *tatkratu nyāya*, whatever is the object of meditation, the same is attained. If the *upāsaka* meditates on the Supreme Brahman with the support of the syllable *Aum* with all the three letters, he should attain the same Brahman and not *Hiraṇyagarbha* or the lower Brahman, as Śaṁkara contends. Besides, the Upaniṣad states that the *upāsaka* becomes free from all sins, that is, he is liberated from bondage and it is but appropriate that the liberated soul attains the Brahman proper. Further, at the conclusion of the passage, the Upaniṣad points out that the *upāsaka* attains through the path of *Auṁkāra*, Brahman which is described as tranquil (*śāntam*), unaging (*ajaram*), immortal (*amṛtam*) and fearless (*abhayam*). The relevant statement reads : *Taṁ auṁkāreṇaiva-āyatanena anveti vidvān yat tat śāntam ajaram amṛtam abhayaṁ paraṁ ca*[79]. These characteristics do not apply to *Hiraṇyagarbha*. All these *dharmas* in their primary sense are applicable only to Brahman. The statement *'jivaghanāt parāt param puriśayam puruṣam īkṣate'*, which bears the same meaning as the Muṇḍaka Upaniṣad text *'nāmarūpād vimuktaḥ parāt paraṁ puruṣam upaiti divyam'*, conveys clearly that what is attained by the liberated soul is *Paramātman* (Brahman) and not *Hiraṇyagarbha*. Vedānta Deśika therefore concludes that the *Īkṣatikarmādhikaraṇa* establishes that Brahman is the object of attainment by the *muktas* (*Muktabhogyasvabhāvaḥ*[80]).

XI. Brahman as the Subtle Space within the Heart (Daharākāśa)

This is the subject-matter of the *Daharādhikaraṇa* which discusses the question whether the concept of *Daharākāśa* or the subtle space within one's heart mentioned in the famous Chāndogya passage as the object of meditation along with certain attributes refers to Brahman or some other entity such as *bhūtākāśa* (ethereal space) or *jīvātman*.

The Upaniṣad states:

'Atha yad-idam asmin brahmapure daharaṁ puṇḍarīkaṁ veśma, daharośmin antarākāśaḥ tasmin yadantaḥ, tad-anveṣṭavyam tad vāva vijijñāsitavyam'[81]

"Now, herein this city of Brahman is an abode, a small lotus (of the heart), within it is the small *ākāśa*; what is within that small *ākāśa*, that should be sought; that is what one should desire to know."

In this statement couched in a symbolic language, the word *brahmapura*, as explained by the commentators, refers to the human body since it is chosen by Brahman as its residence to enable the *upāsaka* to mediate on it. *Brahmaveśma* or the abode of Brahman is the human heart which is figuratively described as lotus-like abode (*puṇḍarīkaveśma*); Within this heart of the body, there is a small or subtle space known as *dahara ākāśa* (*dahara* meaning *alpa* or small). The *daharākāśa* along with what it contains within it (*tasmin yadantaḥ*) is to be meditated upon.

What is this *daharākāśa*? The Upaniṣad itself comes up with the following description:

"Yavān vā ayam ākāśaḥ tāvān eṣo antarhṛdaya ākāśaḥ, ubhe asmin dyāvāpṛthvī antareva samāhite; ubhau agniśca vāyuśca sūryā candramasau ubhau, vidyun nakṣatrāṇi, yacca asti yacca nāsti sarvaṁ tad asmin samāhitam." [82]

As far as this (ethereal) space extends, so far extends the space within the heart. Within it are contained both heaven and earth, both fire and air, both sun and moon, lightning and the stars; and whatever there is in this world and whatever is not, all that is contained within it (the *ākāśa* in the heart).

The question is raised: if everything that exists is contained in this city of Brahman, then what is left of it when old age overcomes it or when it perishes?

In reply the Upaniṣad says:

"Nāsyā jarayā jīryati, na vadhenāsya hanyate etat satyam brahmapuraṁ, asmin kāmāḥ samāhitāḥ, eṣa ātmā apahatapāpmā vijaro vimṛtyuḥ vísoka vijighatso apipāsaḥ satyakāmaḥ satyasaṁkalpaḥ."[83]

"With old age of the body this (*daharākāśa*) does not age; with the death of the body, it does not die. It is eternal (*satyam*). In it all desires (auspicious qualities) are contained.

It is the *ātmā* which is free from evil, free from old age, death, grief, hunger, thirst, whose needs are fulfilled and whose desires are not obstructed."

What does this *daharākāśa* which is to be meditated denote? There are three possible views. It can be the physical space (*bhūtākāśa*), since the word *ākāśa* is commonly understood in that sense. It can also denote *jīvātman* since the eight attributes mentioned in the passage can also be ascribed to it. Besides in the later part of the passage a reference is made to jīvātman by the word *'eṣa ātmā'*. The description of the *daharākāśa* as subtle entity also supports the theory of *jiva*. The third alternative is that *daharākāśa* refers to *Paramātman*.

Bādarāyaṇa rejects the first two alternatives and upholds that *daharākāśa* enjoined for meditation is *Paramātman* (Brahman). The relevant *sūtra* reads : *dahara uttarebhyaḥ*[84]. The word *dahara* means the subtle space and it is regarded as Brahman. The word *uttarebhyaḥ* means on account of the reasons provided in the later statements of the Upaniṣad (*uttarebhyo vākyagatebhyo hetubhyaḥ*). The first important reason in support of it is that the Upaniṣad states clearly that this *ātmā* (*eṣa ātmā*) is free from evil (*apahata pāpmā*), free from old age, death, grief, hunger, whose needs are always fulfilled (*satyakāma*) and whose desires are not obstructed(*satyasaṁkalpaḥ*). *Ātmā* in its primary sense refers to Brahman. The attributes, particularly, the *apahata pāpmatva, satyakāmatva, satyasaṁkalpatva* are applicable only to *Paramātman* and not to *bhutākāśa*. The second reason in support of it is that the subtle *ākāśa* within the heart is stated to be of the same magnitude and excellence as the *ākāśa* outside and within it are contained the heaven and earth, the *agni* and the *vāyu*, the sun and the moon, the stars and the lightning. Such a description does not fit with the *bhūtākāśa*. Further as Vedānta Deśika points out, the term *ākāśa*, in Upaniṣadic parlance is well known to imply *Paramātman (śrautī ca syāt prasiddhiḥ bhagavati)*. Thus in the statement of the Taittirīya Upaniṣad *'yadeṣa ākāśa ānando na syāt'*[85] the word *ākāśa* clearly refers to Brahman.

Besides, the *Brahmapura* is regarded as *satya (etat satyaṁ brahmapuram)* and that it is also *ātmā (eṣa ātmā)*. These expressions are not applicable to *bhūtākāśa. (satyātmabrahma śabda nabhasi kathamapi anvayam na prāpnuvanti).*[86] In the same passage it is also stated in reply to the question, what is there to be sought within *daharākāśa (kim tadantaḥ vidyate yad anveṣṭavyaḥ)*, the Upaniṣad says that all desires are contained in *it (kāmāḥ samāhitāḥ). kāmās* here refer to the auspicious attributes of *Paramātman (kāmyante iti kāmāḥ).* What is thus enjoined in the passage is the meditation on *daharākāśa* as Brahman along with the eight attributes mentioned in the Upaniṣadic statement (*tadguṇaḥ cintyamānaḥ*). The *daharākāśa* cannot therefore be *bhūtākāśa.*

If the *daharākāśa* cannot be the *bhūtākāśa*, it may be possible to regard it as *jīvātman*. Two arguments are advanced in support of this view. First, eight attributes mentioned in the passage can be ascribed to it. Secondly, in the later passage dealing with the teaching of Prajāpati to Indra, a reference is made to *jīvātman* and its status after it is liberated from bondage. Besides, the description of the *ākāśa* in terms of *alpatva* or smallness in magnitude also favours the theory of *jīva*.

These arguments are untenable, contends Vedānta Deśika. It is true that *jīva* is also stated to be free from evil (*apahatapāpmā*), free from old age, death etc. and also it is *satyakāma* and *satyasaṁkalpa*. But these eight *guṇas* are ascribed to *jīva* only after it is totally liberated from bondage. The author of the *sūtra* states: *Uttarāt cet āvirbhūta svarūpastu.*[87] It means: If it is said that from the subsequent passage *jīva* is referred to, it is intended to convey the fact that the *jiva* manifests itself with all these attributes after it is liberated from bondage and attains Brahman. These *guṇas* are natural (*svābhāvika*) in respect of *Paramātman,* but not so in the case of jīvatman. In the state of bondage, these *guṇas* are eclipsed due to *karma* and they become manifest after it is liberated from bondage out of the grace of the Supreme Being (*Paramātma prasādena jīvasya satyasaṇkalpatvādikam*). The Chāndogya also states: *Evam evaiṣa samprasādo asmāt śarīrāt samuṭhāya paraṁ jyotir upasaṁpadya svena rūpeṇa abhiniṣpadyate.*[88]

It means: "The serene being *(jīva)* after having risen from the body and having attained the Supreme Light manifests itself in its true form."

Only in the state of *mokṣa, jīva* manifests itself with these eight qualities. The Muṇḍaka also states that the *jīva,* when it is free from bondage, attains an equal status with that of Brahman[89]. Further, the *daharākāśa* is stated to be the support for the entire universe (*viśvaikadhāraka)* and this special feature is not applicable to *jīvātman.* The smallness or the subtle nature (*alpatva*) of *Paramātman* is due to the limitation of the inner recess of the heart (*aupādhikī*) and it is assumed by *Paramātman* by His will for the sake of meditation by the *upāsakas.* It is not therefore His natural form *(svābhāvika).* Hence the possibility of *daharākāśa* being *jīvātman* does not arise[90].

The question is raised as to why in this Chāndogya passage dealing with the meditation on *daharākāśa* as Brahman, the theory of *jīvātman* comes up in the later part of the passage in which Prajāpati instructs Indra about *jīvātman.* Are these two teachings about the meditation on *jīvātma* different? Or are they the same thing? The commentators also differ in their views regarding this matter. Vedānta Deśika, on the basis of Rāmānuja Bhāṣya, explains that the two teachings are interconnected. The later passage containing Prajāpati's teachings is subordinate to the earlier teaching on *daharākāśa.* The purpose of bringing up the teaching about *jīvātman* in this context is to show that meditation on *daharākāśa* as Brahman confers *mokṣa* to the *upāsaka*[91] and also to explain the nature of the goal to be attained by the *jīva (prāpya niṣkarṣaṇārtham*[92]*).* There is no conflict or contradiction between the *dahara vidyā* dealing with meditation on *Paramātma* and *Pratyagātma-vidyā* as contained in the teachings of Prajāpati. The latter is not a separate teaching unconnected with the former. According to Rāmānuja, the knowledge of *jīvātman* is useful and also serves as a subordinate means *(aṅga)* for the attainment of *Paramātman,* which is the Supreme Goal. The Chāndogya text also says *'yastam ātmānam anuvidya vijānāti*[93]*'* – "He who has known this *ātman* (*jīvatman*) and meditates on it (*vijānāti*) attains all desires."On the basis of the foregoing discussion. Vedānta Deśika comes to the conclusion that the *Daharādhikaraṇa* reveals that Brahman which abides in the inner recess of the heart as subtle space *(daharākāśa)* is the support of the entire universe (*Dahara svādhāra sarva lokaḥ*[94]).

XII. Brahman as Anguṣṭhamātra Puruṣa is Sarvaniyantā

This is the subject-matter of a separate *adhikaraṇa* named *Pramitādhikaraṇa* which discusses whether the *puruṣa* abiding in one's heart limited to the size of a thumb of a human being *(anguṣṭha-mātra puruṣa),* as described in the Kaṭha Upaniṣad refers to Brahman or *jīvātman*. There is a particular reason for taking up this subject for consideration. In the preceding section it was shown that *dahara-ākāsa,* though it is of the smallest magnitude, is Brahman because Brahman abides in that form in the inner recess of the heart for the purpose of meditation by the spiritual aspirants. The question arises whether the description of *puruṣa* in the Kaṭha Upaniṣad as of the magnitude of a human thumb and as abiding within one's heart could be Brahman. In order to clarify this point, Bādarāyaṇa introduces the following *sūtra* based on the concerned statement of the Kaṭha Upaniṣad: *Śabdādeva pramitaḥ*[95]. It means: "The *Puruṣa* of the size of the human thumb is *Paramātman* (Brahman) because the very Scriptural text speaks about it in terms applicable to Brahman. The following Upaniṣadic passage of Kaṭha Upaniṣad makes this point clear:

'anguṣṭhamātraḥ puruṣo madhya ātmai tiṣṭhati; īśāno bhūtabhavyasya na tato vijugupsate, etad, vai tat'[96]

"The *puruṣa* who is only of the size of the thumb abides in the centre of the body; He is the Ruler of the past and future and He is not affected by it in any way. This is that."

A doubt arises with regard to this statement as to whether this *puruṣa* who is said to be of the size of the thumb could be *Paramātman*. In the Śvetāśvatara Upaniṣad we come across the following statement:

'Prāṇādhipaḥ samcarati svakarmabhiḥ anguṣṭhamātrah[97]'- "The ruler of the *indriyas* (sense organs) of the size of only the thumb functions in accordance with his *karmas.*" If this statement is taken into consideration, it follows that the *puruṣa* described as of the size of the thumb is *jīvātman,* since it is associated with the sense organs and it functions in accordance with its past *karmas*. This is the prima facie view.

This view is rejected by Bādarāyaṇa. The main reason is that the very Upaniṣadic text describing *puruṣa* as *anguṣṭa-mātraḥ* states that this *puruṣa* is the Ruler of all that exists in the past, present and future. Such a *puruṣa* as *Īśāna* cannot be *jīvātman* but only *Paramātman* (Brahman).

The reason for describing Brahman as of the size of the thumb is that Brahman resides in the heart of a human being to enable him to meditate on it. The human heart is conceived as of the size of the thumb of a human being only for the purpose of meditation. *Paramātman,* who indwells in it is therefore regarded as of the size of the thumb. This limitation imposed on the Brahman does not constitue His natural form. It is assumed by Him out of His free will for the sake of the *upāsakas* to enable them to meditate on Him who is present within own's heart. As Bādarāyaṇa states Brahman is described as of the size of *anguṣṭha* only with reference to the human heart, since only human beings are eligible for *upāsanā* on Brahman. The relevant *sūtra* reads: *Hṛdyapekṣayā tu manuṣyādhikāratvāt.*[98] This rules out the possibility of the presence of Brahman as of the size of *anguṣṭha* in other living beings, such as animals, reptiles, insects etc. since they do not have the capacity for *upāsanā*. Such a Brahman who resides in the heart of the *upāsakas* is regarded by the Upaniṣads as *Īśāna* or Controller of all beings (*sarvaniyantā*).

XIII. Brahman as the Object of Meditation for Devatās

As allied to the concept of Brahman as *anguṣṭhamātra puruṣa*, the question is raised whether the celestial deities (*devatās*), who are regarded as higher category of beings, are eligible for *upāsanā*. Among the *devatās*, there is a special category of celestial deities known as *vasus, rudras, ādityas, maruts* and *sādhyas* who have attained a special status on account of their having already done some good deeds. Among the human beings also, one category of persons who, according to the Hindu caste system, are regarded as *śūdras*, are not eligible for the study of the Vedas and Vedānta. The author of *Brahma-sūtra* considers the question of the eligibility of all these categories of individuals – the *devatās* in general, the special devatās such as *vasus* and the *śūdras* – for the *upāsanā* on Brahman. There are three *adhikaraṇas* dealing with these matters. These are named as:

1) Devatādhikaraṇa
2) Madhvādhikaraṇa
3) Apaśūdrādhikaraṇa

The first topic has reference to the theory advanced by Jaimini, the exponent of *Pūrva-mīmāṁsā*, who does not admit the possibility of *upāsanā* for the *devatās* on the ground that they do not possess physical body and *indriyas* unlike human beings and hence do not have the capacity and required eligibility for meditation on Brahman. But Bādarāyaṇa rejects this view of Jaimini and upholds that *devatās* too have the knowledge of Brahman and eligibility to observe meditation. They also possess body and the sense organs, as is evident from the Scriptural texts.

The second *adhikaraṇa* has reference to the passage in Chāndogya dealing with *Madhuvidyā*.[99] The prima facie view advanced regarding this matter is that the special deities such as *vasus* etc. are themselves the objects of meditation and hence these deities are not required to do the meditation on Brahman. This view is also rejected by Bādarāyaṇa on the ground that they can meditate on Brahman as their *Antaryāmin*. The relevant *sūtra* reads: *Bhāvaṁtu Bādarāyaṇo asti hi.*[100]

Regarding the third topic, this has reference to the Chāndogya passage dealing with *Saṁvarga-vidyā*[101] or meditation on *vāyu* as *saṁvarga*. In this passage containing a dialogue between the sage Raikva and Jānaśruti a *kṣatriya*, who does not possess Brahman knowledge, Raikva addresses Jānaśruti as *śūdra* in the sense of one who is afflicted with grief due to lack of Brahman knowledge (*asya śuk sūcyate iti śūdraḥ*). In this connection the question is raised whether the *śūdras*, the persons belonging to the lowest caste, are eligible for meditation on Brahman, since they are not permitted, according to the Vedic tradition, for recitation of Vedas. Bādarāyaṇa takes the view on the authority of the Scriptural texts that *śūdras* are not eligible for Brahma-vidyā. The relevant sūtra reads: *Śravaṇādhyanārtha pratiṣedhāt*[102] - "Because *śūdras* are prohibited by *Srutis* from hearing Vedas and studying them."

All these topics are not of philosophical significance. Even according to the author of the *Brahma-sūtra*, these are incidental topics (*prāsangika*). We need not therefore go into the details of these *adhikaraṇas*. We shall only take note of the following conclusions drawn by Vedānta Deśika with reference to these *adhikaraṇas*, as far as Brahman is concerned:

1) Brahman is the object of meditation for the *devatās (devādīnam upāsyaḥ)*
2) The *vasus* and other deities meditate on Brahman as their *Antaryāmin* (*vasumukha-vibudhaiḥ svātmabhāvena sevyaḥ*)
3) *Śūdras* are not eligible for meditation on Brahman (*śūdrād yopāsty-anarhaḥ*[103])

XIV. Brahman as the nāma-rūpa Nirvahitā

This is the subject-matter of the last *adhikaraṇa* of the third *pāda* of first *adhyāya* named *Arthāntaratvādi-vyapadeśādhi-karaṇa,* which discusses the issue whether ākāśa described in the Chāndogya as *nāma-rūpa nirvahitā* or that which performs the function of giving names and form to the created objects, is *muktātmā* or *Paramātmā.*

This subject is also incidental to the theory of *daharākāśa* as Brahman discussed earlier with reference to the Chāndogya passage dealing with the meditation on it. Towards the end of the passage dealing with *Daharavidyā,* the Upanisad states: *ākāśo ha vai nāmarūpayoḥ nirvahitā, te yadantarā tad brahmā tad amṛtam sa ātmā'*[104].

"This very *ākāśa* is the one which performs the task of giving names and forms to all that is created. The created universe of names and forms is in Brahman, that is immortal, that itself is *Ātmā.*"

Preceding this text, the following statement is found:

Aśva iva romāṇi vidhūya pāpaṁ candra iva rāhoḥ mukhāt pramucya, dhūtvā śarīram akṛtam kṛtātmā brahma lokam abisambhavāmi[105]

"Shaking off evil as a horse shakes off its hairs, shaking off the body as the moon frees itself from the mouth of *Rāhu,* I as a perfected self obtain the eternal abode of Brahman."

The question that is raised with reference to the later passage is: what does *ākāśa* described as *nāma-rūpa nirvahitā* stand for? Does it refer to the *muktātmā* (liberated self) or *Paramātmā*?

The prima facie view is that the term *ākāśa* here denotes the *muktātmā* since in the preceding statement it is mentioned that the individual self attains *brahma-loka* after totally being liberated from the shackles of bondage. It is but appropriate to admit that the liberated self is *ākāśa* which can be regarded as *nāma-rūpa kartā.* In the state of bondage it was associated with a name and form and the same in the state of liberation exists without a name and form. *Jīvātman* is described as Brahma, that is, it attains *brahma-bhāva* and also *amṛta* or immortality.

This view is rejected by Bādarāyaṇa. The main reason advanced is that the Upaniṣadic text clearly conveys the idea that *ākāśa* referred to here is different from both the bound *jīva* and liberated *jīva*. The relevant *sūtra* reads: *Ākāśo arthāntaratvādi vyapadeśāt.*[106] It means that *ākāśa* is Brahman, because of the indication that it is different from *jīva*. That is, the expression *'nāma-rūpa nirvāhakatva'* or the function of giving names and forms to the different entities in the universe cannot be ascribed either to the bound *jīva* or the liberated *jīva*. The *baddha jīva* in its variety of forms as *devas*, humans, animals etc. derives the names and different forms from *Paramātman* in accordance with the *karma*. Hence it cannot itself perform this function in respect of all the entities in the universe. The *muktātmā* also cannot perform this function because in the state of *mokṣa* it is devoid of the capacity of cosmic functions which exclusively belong to Brahman. It therefore follows that only Brahman is the *nāma-rūpa kartā*. The Upaniṣadic text supports this. Thus says the Chāndogya: *'anena jīvena ātmanā anupraviśya nāma rūpe vyākaravāṇi'*[107] - "Brahman along with the *jīva* enters into the created objects and provides names and forms to them." Hence, the *ākāśa* referred to in the Upaniṣadic statement as *nāma-rūpa kartā* is Brahman.

Further, in the preceding statement, it is stated that the liberated *jīvātman* attains *brahma-loka* (*brahmalokam abhisambhavāmi*). The word *brahma-loka* does not mean the *loka* of Brahman (*brahmaṇah lokaḥ*) but it is interpreted as Brahman itself (*Brahma eva brahmalokaḥ*). It therefore becomes the goal of attainment for *muktātmā*. The term *ākāśa* used in the subsequent statement in the text refers to Brahman which is attained (*Abhisambhāvyaḥ puroktā eva ayaṁ punar-upāttaḥ*[108]). Since *jīva* even in the state of *mokṣa* does not have the capacity to do the cosmic function of giving names and forms to created objects, *ākāśa* in the subsequent passage is to be admitted as *Paramātman* (Brahman).

Further, the *ākāśa* as *nāma-rūpa kartā* is described as Brahma (*etad brahma*). The term *brahma* cannot be understood as *brahmāvasthā* or the state of Brahman, since *jīva* does not attain a new status of *brahmāvasthā* after it is liberated. If what is attained is a new form, then it cannot be eternal. Hence *brahmatva* is not a new *avasthā* (*brahmatvam avasthā na hi*). *Ākāśa* as Brahman eternally exists as Brahman.

Another important reason in support of *ākāśa* as *nāma-rūpa kartā* is that the Upaniṣad itself draws a clear distinction between *jīva* and Brahman (*śrutiṣu yugapad jñāna ajñānatā vibhaktaḥ*[109]). The Muṇḍaka Upaniṣad[110] says that *Īśvara* is *jña* or omniscient, whereas *jīva* is *ajña* or ignorant one. One is Ruler (*īśa*) and the other is the one ruled by *Īśvara*, i.e. *Anīśa*. Hence it is not possible to regard *muktātmā* as *nāma-rūpa kartā*. Vedānta Deśika, therefore, concludes that this *adhikaraṇa* establishes that *ākāśa* as the *nāmarūpa kartā* is Brahman (*nāmarūpaika kartā*).

---

1. VS I-2-1
2. Ch. Up. III-14-1
3. Ch. Up. III-14-1 and 2.
4. Muṇḍ. Up. II-1-2
5. Kena. Up. I-2 *prāṇasya prāṇaḥ*
6. Ch. Up. III-14-2.
7. *Ibid* III-14-3. *eṣa ma ātmā antarhṛdaye aṇīyān vrīhervā yavādvā sarṣapādvā ....eṣa me ātmā antarhṛdaye jyāyān pṛthivyā jyāyān antarikṣāt.*
8. *See* fn. 7 above.
9. *See* VS I-2-7 *See* also As verse 85
10. AS verse 98.
11. Kaṭha Up. I-2-25
12. VS I-2-9
13. AS verse 86
14. Kaṭha. Up. I-3-3
15. VS I-2-11
16. *Dravyāsu vyavasāyeṣu sattvamastrī tu jantuṣu.* The term sattva used in non-feminic gender (astrī), denotes jantu, that is, a living being.
17. *See* AS verse 87
18. Ch. Up. IV-15-1

19. VS I-2-13
20. Ch. Up. IV-15-2 to 4.
21. Ch. Up. IV-10-5
22. RB I-2-16
23. VS II-2-16
24. AS verse 88
25. *Ibid* verse 89
26. VS I-2-19
27. Br Up. V-7-3
28. Br. Up. (Mādhyandina version) V-7-22
29. Br. Up. V-7-23
30. *See* Cintāmaṇi on AS verse 91
31. *See* VS I-2-21 *ubhaye'pi hi bhedenainam adhīyate*
32. *See* AS Verse 92
33. *See* AS verse 98
34. VS I-2-22
35. Muṇḍ. Up. I-1-5
36. Muṇḍ. Up II-1-2
37. AS verse 93
38. *See* Cintāmaṇi – *akṣarāt prakṛteh paratarah jīvāt paraḥ parama puruṣaḥ iti vākya yojanā*
39. *See* Muṇḍ. Up. *Etasmāt jāyate prāṇo manaḥ sarvendriyāṇi ca; khaṁ vāyur-jyotir-āpaḥ pṛthivī viśvasya dhāriṇī.*
40. Mu. Up. II-1-4
41. Ch. Up. V-11-6
42. Ch. Up. V-18-1
43. VS I-2-25
44. *See* Ch. Up. V-24-3. *tad-yathā iṣīkatūlamagnau protam pradūyeta, evam hy-āsya sarve pāpmānaḥ pradūyante*
45. *See* Ch. Up V-12-2 to V-17-2, See also Mund. Up.II-I-4
46. *See* Padayojanā, verse 94
47. *See* VS-1-2-27. *śabdādibhyo antaḥpratiṣthānācca na iti cen na tathā dṛṣṭyupadeśād asambhavāt- puruṣamapi cainam adhīyate*
48. *See* VS I-2-28. *Ata eva na devatābhūtam ca*
49. *See* VS I-2-29
50. Muṇḍ. Up. II-2-5
51. Muṇḍ. Up. II-2-6
52. VS I-3-1
53. VS I-3-2. *muktopasṛpya vyapadeśāt*
54. Muṇḍ. Up. III-1-2
55. *Ibid* III-2-8
56. *See* Muṇḍ. Up. III-1-1 and 2. *See* also VS I-3-4. *bhedavyapadeśāt* and VS I-3-6. *Sthityadanābhyāṁ ca*
57. AS verse 102.
58. *See* Cintāmaṇi on verse 103. *antaryāmitvena adhisthānamātrasyaiva caraṇa-śabda vācyaḥ.*

59. VS I-3-7
60. Ch. Up. VIII-12-2
61. *See* Ch. Up. VII-15-1 to 4.
62. *Ibid* VII-16-1
63. Ch. Up. VII-16-1
64. *Ibid* VII-23-1
65. Ch. Up. VII-24-2. See also As verse 1o6
66. *See* fn. 65 above.
67. AS verse 107
68. VS I-3-9 and I-3-10
69. Br. Up. V-8-7
70. Br. Up. V-8-8
71. *Ibid* V-8-9
72. *Ibid* V-8-11
73. *See* Subala. Up. II-1
74. VS I-3-11
75. AS verse 108
76. *See* AS verse 129
77. VS I-3-12
78. Praśna Up. V-5
79. Praśna. Up. V-7. See also AS verse 109
80. AS verse 129. See also Cintāmaṇi, *muktaiḥ upabhogya* svabhāvaḥ
81. Ch. Up. VIII-1-1
82. Ch. Up. VIII-1-3
83. Ch. Up. VIII-1-5
84. VS I-3-13
85. Tait. II-7
86. AS verse 112
87. VS I-3-18
88. Ch. Up. VIII-3-4
89. Muṇḍ. Up. III-1-2
90. AS verse 114
91. *Ibid* verse 115. *daharākāsa apavarga prada iti gaditum samprasādoktir-atra prājāpatye tu vākye para pari pathanam prāpya niṣkarṣaṇārtham*
92. *See* fn 91.
93. Ch. Up. VIII-7-1
94. AS verse 129
95. VS I-3-23
96. Kaṭha Up. I-4-12
97. Svet. Up. V-7-8
98. VS I-3-24
99. Ch. Up. III-1 to 11
100. VS I-3-32
101. Ch. Up. IV-1 to 3
102. VS I-3-38

103. *See* AS verse 129
104. Ch. Up. VIII-14-1
105. Ch. Up. VIII-14-1
106. VS I-3-42
107. Ch. Up. VI-3-2
108. AS verse 128
109. AS verse 128
110. Muṇḍ. Up. I-9

Chapter Four

BRAHMAN AS THE CAUSE OF THE UNIVERSE

In the preceding two chapters we have presented the nature and distinguishing characteristics of Brahman as enunciated by Bādarāyaṇa in the first three *pādas* of the first *adhyāya* on the basis of the Upaniṣadic teachings. The present chapter is devoted to outline another important characteristic of Brahman viz that it is the sole cause of the universe (*jagatkāraṇa*). Though in the *Janmādhyadhikaraṇa*, while defining the nature of Brahman, it is established that Brahman is the primary cause of the creation, sustenance and dissolution of the universe it is considered necessary to re-establish this theory. This need arises because there are a few important passages in the Upaniṣads, particularly in the Kaṭha, Bṛhadāraṇyaka, Śvetāśvatara and Kauṣītakī, which convey the idea in more unambiguous terms (*spaṣṭatara*) that either the *prakṛti*, also termed as *avyakta* or *puruṣa*, a sentient principle higher than non-sentient prakṛti, is the cause of the universe. These passages, prima facie reflect the theories of Sāṁkhya and Yoga, the two schools of thought which were predominant during the time of Bādarāyaṇa. Bādarāyaṇa therefore devotes special attention to the examination of these passages and shows that even the statements referring to the *prakṛti* and *puruṣa* in these Upaniṣads support the Vedānta theory of Brahman as the sole cause of the universe. The following eight *adhikaraṇas* of the fourth *pāda* of first *adhyāya* deal with this matter.

1. *Ānumānikādhikaraṇa*
2. *Camasādhikaraṇa*
3. *Saṁkhyopasaṅgrahādhikaraṇa*
4. *Kāraṇatvādhikaraṇa*
5. *Jagadvācitvādhikaraṇa*
6. *Vākyānvayādhikaraṇa*
7. *Prakṛtyādhikaraṇa*
8. *Sarvavyākhāynādhikaraṇa*

The first two *adhikaraṇas* attempt to prove that the terms *avyakta* and *ajā*, employed in the Upaniṣad do not support the Sāṁkhya theory of *pradhāna* as the cause of the universe. The third topic explains that the mere enumeration of twenty five principles (*pañca-pañca-janāḥ*) does not imply the Sāṁkhya theory of twenty five categories. The fourth one points out that the concept of *avyākṛta* or unmanifest state of the universe referred to in the Bṛhadāraṇyaka, does not rule out Brahman as the direct cause of the universe. The fifth and sixth *adhikaraṇas* are aimed to prove that neither the *puruṣa* as *baddha jīva* nor the Ātman as *muktātmā* can be the cause of the universe. The seventh *adhikaraṇa* is devoted to refute the Sāṁkhya theory of *Īśvara* as *nimitta kāraṇa* or instrumental cause of the universe and establish that Brahman is the *upādāna kāraṇa* or the material cause and also the *nimitta kāraṇa* or instrumental cause. The eighth *adhikaraṇa* points out briefly that all other Upaniṣadic statements which refer to some of the higher celestial deities imply that Brahman is the sole cause of the universe, in accordance with the principles of interpretation adopted in the earlier *adhikaraṇas*. We shall deal with all these topics except 7, in the present chapter. Regarding topic 7 (*Prakṛtyādhikaraṇa*), it discusses the theory of Brahman as the material cause of the universe. As this is an important subject in Vedānta and is also open to some objections raised by the Sāṁkhyas and Vaiśeṣikas, we shall deal with it separately in the next chapter on 'The Doctrine of universe and Brahman'.

I. Avyakta conceived as prakṛti is not the cause of the universe.

This is the subject of the *adhikaraṇa* named *Ānumānikādhikaraṇa*. The word *ānumānika* means what is proved by inference. In the present context, it refers to *prakṛti,* also termed as *avyakta,* which is established as the cause of the universe by the Sāṁkhyas on the basis of inferential argument (*anumāna*). It is claimed by the Sāṁkhyas that the following passage of the Kaṭha Upaniṣad supports this view:

Indriyebhyaḥ parāhy-arthā arthebhyaśca paraṁ manaḥ; manasastu parā buddhiḥ buddher ātmā mahān paraḥ; mahataḥ param avyaktām, avyaktāt puruṣaḥ paraḥ; puruṣānna paraṁ kiñcit sā kāṣṭhā sā parā gatiḥ[1]

"The (sense) objects are of greater force than the sense organs. The mind is more important than the sense objects. Greater than the mind is the *buddhi* or intellect. More important than *buddhi* is the *mahān-ātmā*. Greater than the *mahān-ātmā* is the *avyakta*. Greater than *avyakta* is the *puruṣa* or the self and there is nothing beyond this."

This passage is construed in favour of the two ultimate principles of Sāṁkhya viz *prakṛti* and *puruṣa*. The *prakṛti* is claimed to be the cause of the universe, since it is stated in the passage that there is nothing higher than *puruṣa*. This is the prima facie view advanced against the Vedānta theory of Brahman as the cause of the universe.

This view is rejected by Bādarāyaṇa on the ground that the term *avyakta* in the passage does not denote the Sāṁkhya concept of *pradhāna,* but on the contrary it refers to the physical body(*śarīra*) in the context of the illustration of the chariot (*ratha*) and the master of the chariot (*rathī*) cited by the Upaniṣad to explain the mode of control of the senses and mind for the purpose of attainment of the highest Spiritual Goal. The earlier part of the Kaṭha Upaniṣad enumerates how the senses, mind and intellect have to be progressively controlled by the spiritual aspirant on the analogy of the master of the chariot (*rathī*) and the chariot (*ratha*). Thus it is stated:

Ātmānaṁ rathinaṁ viddhi śarīraṁ rathameva ca; buddhiṁ tu sārathiṁ viddhi manaḥ pragrahameva ca; indriyāṇi hayānyāhuḥ viṣayāṁsteṣu gocarān[2]

"Know the master of the chariot as the *ātman* (the self in this body), the chariot as the physical body. Know the *buddhi* as the charioteer and the mind as the reins (*pragraha*). The senses are to be regarded as the horses and the objects of the senses as the paths treaded by the horses."

The above analogy of the chariot and the master of the chariot is intended to explain how it is important for the seeker of *mokṣa* to control the mind and the senses in order to attain the Supreme Goal which is described by the Upaniṣad as the Abode of Viṣṇu (*paramapada*). In the context of this analogy of the charioteer and the chariot drawn by the horses, this passage explains the relative importance of the various factors such as the sense objects, the senses, the *buddhi* and the mind which are to be controlled by the spiritual aspirant. (*vividhā vaṣīkārya mukhyakramoktiḥ*[3]). Thus the passage tells that the sense objects are of greater force than the sense organs since the presence of the objects can disturb the senses. The mind is more important than the senses because even in the absence of objects, the mind becomes attracted to them. Greater than the mind is *buddhi* because in the absence of determined will (*adhyavasāya*), mind does not remain controlled. More important than *buddhi* is the *mahān-ātmā* which means acc. to Rāmānuja, the individual self which is the agent of all actions (*kartā*). Greater than *mahān-ātmā* is the *avyakta* which, in the present context denotes the physical body as it is compared to the chariot. Greater than the body is the self which is compared to the master of the chariot (*rathī*). Greater than the self is the *Puruṣa* or the Supreme Self (*Paramātman*) which is the goal to be attained, as stated in the Upaniṣad (*so adhvanaḥ pāram āpnoti tadviṣṇoḥ paramaṁ padam*[4])

In view of these explanations, the *avyakta* referred to in the passage does not denote the *pradhāna* of Sāṁkhya. On the contrary, it denotes the physical body. As stated by Bādarāyaṇa, the body is regarded as *avyakta* since it is the modification or the product of the primordial cosmic matter, which during dissolution assumes the state of *avyakta* or subtle form[5]. Further, the statement 'There is nothing higher than the *puruṣa* and that it is the ultimate Goal' conveys the idea that Viṣṇu (Brahman)as the ultimate Goal is to be attained by the spiritual aspirant. This is evident from the following text.

'So adhvanaḥ param āpnoti tadviṣṇoḥ paramaṁ padaṁ'[6]

Thus there is no room to interpret this passage in favour of the Sāṁkhya theory of *pradhāna*.

Vedānta Deśika points out that the passage taken as it is even without reference to the analogy of *ratha* and *rathi* cannot favour the Sāṁkhya theory. According to Sāṁkhya, there is no causal relationship between sense objects and the senses since the *indriyas* are not the products of objects. Nor is the mind the cause of the objects. *Buddhi* does not cause the mind nor does *buddhi* cause *mahat* because according to the Sāṁkhya theory of evolution *buddhi* itself is *mahat-tattva*. Hence it follows that the term *avyakta* denotes *śarīra* or the physical body and not *prakṛti* (*avyaktoktiḥ śarīre*[7]).

II. Ajā conceived as prakṛti is not the cause of the universe.

This subject is discussed in a separate *adhikaraṇa* named *Camasādhikaraṇa*. In the preceding *adhikaraṇa* it was shown that the term *avyakta* used in the Kaṭha Upaniṣad refers to the physical body (*śarīra*) and not *prakṛti* of Sāṁkhya. The present *adhikaraṇa* discusses whether the term *'Ajā'* employed in the Śvetāśvatara Upaniṣad in connection with the creation of the universe refers to the *prakṛti* of the Sāṁkhya. The prima facie view which is advanced on the basis of the following Upaniṣadic text is that it implies that *prakṛti* which is unborn, that is, not having an origin, is the cause of the universe.

Ajām ekāṁ lohitaśuklakṛṣṇāṁ bahvīḥ prajāḥ sṛjamānāṁ sarūpāḥ; ajo hy eko juṣamāṇonuśete jahāty enāṁ bhukta bhogyām ajonyaḥ[8]

"This one is unborn red, white and black, which gives birth to many creatures similar to itself; and an unborn lies attached to it and enjoys it, while another unborn gives it up having had its enjoyment."

This passage may be construed in favour of the Sāṁkhya theory of *prakṛti* and *puruṣa* since the word *ajā* literally means the 'she-goat' and the second word *'ajā'* as 'he-goat' and the words red, white and black as the three stripes of the she-goat. The first word *'ajā'* can be taken as the *prakṛti* which is constituted of three qualities *sattva, rajas* and *tamas* and the second word *aja* as the individual soul respectively. Both are unborn *(aja)* in the sense that they have no beginning. The soul which is bound (*baddha*) is attached to *prakṛti* whereas the soul which is liberated is free from attachment to it. The word *'sṛjamānām'* or that which gives birth to many creatures, conveys the idea of *prakṛti* as the independent cause of the variegated universe (*svātantryeṇa nikhila-janakatā*), as conceived by the Sāṁkhyas.

Bādarāyaṇa rejects this view. The main reason advanced is that the word *aja* is a general term which only means that it has no beginning. But the Upaniṣadic statement in which it is employed does not specify that *aja*, understood as the *prakṛti* can be the cause of the universe independently, that is, without the guidance or control of Brahman, as Vedāntins maintain (*abrahmātmakā ajāgrahaṇe viśeṣa apratīteḥ*).

The relevant sutra reads *'Camasavat aviśeṣāt'.*[9] *Aviśeṣāt* means unqualified, that is, the term is not used with specific qualifying description. To illustrate this point, the word *camasa* employed in a Vedic statement, is cited. *Camasa* as a general term means a *sādhana* or an article useful for consuming the food used in the yāga. But the later part of the Vedic statement gives a vivid description of it as a vessel having a narrow neck at the top and a small opening at the bottom and with a wide circular base. On that basis, its meaning is determined as a special vessel for drinking the soma juice used in the sacrifice. There is no such description of *aja* indicating that it is an independent cause of the universe.

Besides, as Vedānta Deśika points out, it is well established in the Taittirīya Upaniṣad and also in the Śvetāśvatara that *prakṛti* as controlled by Brahman is the cause of the manifest universe. This is evident from the fact that the same passage found in Śvetāśvatara occurs in the Taittirīya after mentioning the process of creation caused by Brahman. In the Śvetāśvatara also, *prakṛti* which is designated as *māyā* is stated to be the cause of the evolution as controlled by *māyin* or *Paramātman* (*asmāt māyī sṛjate viśvametat*[10])

As regards the statement that *ajā* gives birth to many beings (*bahviḥ prajāḥ sṛjamānāṁ sarūpāṁ*) it does not imply that *prakṛti* creates the universe independently. On the other hand it means that *prakṛti* is the cause of the universe being impelled by *Paramātman*. There are two ways in which *kartṛtva* or being the agent of creation is understood – *prayojya kartā* and *prayojaka kartā*. The former refers to that which is the cause of the creation being impelled by a higher principle. The latter refers to that which actually wills or impels another being to undergo the process of creation. In the case of *prakṛti* it can be the cause of creation of the universe by being impelled by *Paramātman*. In this sense the expression '*sṛjamāṇatva*' by *ajā* is to be understood. This does not contradict *Paramātman* being the sole cause of the creation of the universe (*sṛjati-rapi para-preryatāṁ no'parundhyāt*[11]

III. The term Pañca-pañca-janā does not imply the Sāṁkhya theory of Prakṛti and its Evolutes.

This is the subject of *Saṁkhyopasaṁgrahādhikaraṇa* which discusses whether the term *pañca-pañca-janā* mentioned in a passage of the Bṛhadaranyaka Upaniṣad refers to the Sāṁkhya doctrine of *prakṛti* and its twenty three evolutes along with *Puruṣa*, making a total of twenty five principles which can account for the causation of the universe. The relevant Upaniṣadic statement reads:

yasmin pañca pañca janā ākāśaśca pratiṣṭhitaḥ;
tamevam anya ātmānaṁ vidvān brahma amṛto amṛtam.[12]

"That in which the five into five categories including *ākāśa* is established, the man of wisdom who knows that alone as *ātman* becomes immortal".

The question which is raised in this connection is whether the twenty five principles mentioned here refers to the Sāṁkhya theory of twenty five categories. The prima facie view answers it in the affirmative. *Pañça-pāñca janā*, that is, the five groups of five principles (*pañcānāṁ janānāṁ samūhaḥ pañca-janāḥ*) correspond to the twenty five ontological categories acknowledged by the Sāṁkhyas. Thus says the Sāṁkhya Kārikā:

'mūla prakṛtiḥ avikṛtiḥ mahadādyāḥ prakṛti vikṛtayaḥ sapta; ṣodaśakaśca vikāro na prakṛtiḥ na vikṛtiḥ puruṣa iti'. The *mūla prakṛti* is unmodified. *Mahat* and six other evolutes are causal substances and also the modifications. That is, these are modifications of *prakṛti* but they also serve as causes for other evolutes. There are sixteen other evolutes which are only modifications. The soul is neither causal substance nor a modification.

According to Bādarāyaṇa this view is untenable. The relevant *sūtra* reads: *na saṁkhyopasaṅgrahād-api nānābhāvāt atirekācca.*[13]

It means that even the enumeration of the twenty five principles does not imply the twenty five *tattvas* acknowledged by the Sāṁkhyas because of two reasons. First, what is stated in the Upaniṣad is different from what is admitted by the Sāṁkhyas. That is, in this statement the twenty five principles and also *ākāśa* are stated to be established in Brahman, denoted by the words *'yasmin pratiṣṭhitaḥ'*. Sāṁkhyas do not subscribe to such a theory. Secondly the total number of principles comes to twenty seven if we take due note of *ākāśa* as distinct from twenty five *tattvas* and also Brahman, denoted by the word *yasmin*, which is the ground (*ādhāra*) for all these. Hence the expression *pañca-pañca-janāḥ* or five groups of five in each do not imply the twenty five *tattvas* accepted by the Sāṁkhyas.

What then does the term *'pañca-pañca-janāḥ'* imply? Vedānta Deśika explains that this phrase is to be taken as a technical word implying a group of any five entities similar to the word *'sapta-saptarṣayaḥ'* or seven Ṛṣis. These five entities are the five *jñānendriyas* viz. *prāṇa, cakṣus, śrotrā, anna* and *manas* as is evident from the Bṛhadāraṇyaka Upaniṣadic text *'prāṇasya prāṇam uta cakṣuṣaḥ cakṣuḥ śrotrasya śrotram annasya annam manaso mano ye viduḥ'*[14]. It is not therefore possible to claim that the mere enumeration of twenty five principles support Sāṁkhya theory of *prakṛti* and its evolutes.

IV. Avyākṛta as Prakṛti is not the Cause of the Universe.

This is the subject of a separate *adhikaraṇa* named *Kāraṇatvādhikaraṇa* which examines the passages dealing with the causation of the universe (*viśvopadāna vaktṛ śrutis*) and affirm that Brahman alone is the cause of the universe even though the terms such as *avyakta, ajā, sat, asat* and *avyākṛta* etc. used in these passages may reflect the Sāṁkhya theory of *prakṛti*.

In the previous three *adhikaraṇas* it was shown how the terms *avyakta, ajā* and *pañca-pañca-janā* employed in the Upaniṣads do not favour the Sāṁkhya doctrine. The present *adhikaraṇa* discusses that the concepts of *avyākṛta* and *asat* used in the Bṛhadāraṇyaka and Taittirīya Upaniṣads respectively, also do not support the Sāṁkhya theory.
The Bṛhadāraṇyaka Upaniṣad states:
taddhedaṁ tarhy avyākṛtam āsīt, tan-nāmarūpābhyām eva vyākriyata[15]

"At that time (prior to creation), this universe was undifferentiated and it became differentiated with names and forms"

Similarly, the Taittirīya Upaniṣad states:

'asad vā idamagra āsīt'[16]

"This universe was *asat* prior to the creation."

The term *avyākṛta* means that which is unmanifest. So also the term *asat* denotes what is unmanifest. According to the Sāṁkhyas, the *prakṛti* existed in the unmanifest form prior to its evolution into the manifest universe. If according to these statements *prakṛti* is the source of the universe, the terms such as *sat, ātmā* etc employed in the passages dealing with the causation of the universe are to be interpreted in accordance with Sāṁkhya doctrine. This is the prima facie view.

This is rejected by Bādarāyaṇa. The argument adduced in support of it is that these very passages which employ the terms such as *asat, avyākṛta* etc also point out that a sentient Being endowed with omniscience and omnipotence creates the universe through the operation of its will[17]. Thus for instance, the Taittirīya text where the statement *'asadvā idamagra āsīt'* is mentioned, it is stated in the earlier part of this passage that Brahman described as omniscient (*vipaścitā Brahmaṇā*), wills to become many (*so akāmayata bahusyāṁ prajāyeyeti*). Similarly in the Bṛhadāraṇyaka where the term avyākṛta is employed, it is evident with reference to the earlier context of the same passage that this term implies Brahman as inherently related to the unmanifest universe. (*avyākṛta śabdena avyākṛta śarīraṁ brahmaiva abhidhīyate*).

Vedānta Deśika explains how these terms *'asat', 'avyākṛta'* etc do not denote *prakṛti* but refer to Brahman as the cause of the universe. The statement *'asadvā idamagra āsīt'* signifies only the state of the universe during the stage of dissolution (*vilayāvasthātāmātram uktam*). It does not imply that universe is mere consciousness (*cinmātrarūpa*) as Advaitins contend. Nor does it mean absolute non-existence of the universe (*atyantābhāvarūpatvam*). It does not also convey the idea of non-existent (*atyanta asadrūpatva*). Even the text *'naiveha kiñcana agra āsīt'* does not indicate the absolute destruction of the universe (*vilaya*) since in the

Vedānta system absolute destruction of an entity is not admitted. On the other hand, it refers to the modified state of the universe. The term *avyākṛta* therefore means that the universe in the state of *pralaya* is devoid of names and forms (*nāmarūpa vibhāgābhāva*). In other words it exists in an unmanifest form. Since Brahman is the *antarātmā* or the indwelling Self of all entities even in the state of dissolution (*kāraṇāvasthā*) as in the state of creation (*kāryāvasthā*), it is appropriate to regard the concepts of *avyākṛta, asat* etc in the sense of Brahman as inherently related to them (*avyākṛtādy-avasthā viśiṣṭa tattat pradhānādi dravya-samūha antarātmā parama puruṣa eva*)[18]

V. Puruṣa as Jīva is not the Cause of the Universe

This is the subject matter of the *adhikaraṇa* named '*jagadvācitvādhikaraṇa*' which discusses whether *puruṣa* conceived by the Sāṁkhyas as the twenty fifth ontological principle and also as distinct from *prakṛti*, can cause the evolution of the universe. This question arises because an important passage in the Kauṣitikī Upaniṣad dealing with Bālākīvidyā mentions that the *puruṣa* described as *kartā* and also its *karma* are to be known (*puruṣāṇāṁ kartā yasya vai etat karma sa veditavyaḥ*). If *puruṣa* is taken as *jīvātman* and if that be the ultimate metaphysical principle, the Vedānta doctrine of Brahman as the primary cause of the universe stands refuted. Hence Bādarāyaṇa devotes his attention to this matter and establishes that the *puruṣa* mentioned in this passage refers to Brahman which is the cause of the universe.

The relevant *sūtra* reads: *jagad-vācitvāt*[19]. It means: "It is Brahman because of the mention of the universe created by it". That is, what is referred to in the Upaniṣad is not the finite *jīva* but Brahman because of the mention of the universe which is created by it. The implications of the *sūtra* can be understood with reference to the relevant passages of the Kauṣītikī and Bṛhadāraṇyaka dealing with the teaching about Brahman by Ajātaśatru to Bālāki.

The Kauṣītakī Upaniṣad contains a dialogue between Bālāki, a Brahmin, who has only completed the study of the Vedas and Ajātaśatru, a Kṣatriya having full knowledge of Brahman. Bālāki who proposes to tell about Brahman to Ajātaśatru (*brahma te bravāṇi*) expresses his views about Brahman as the *puruṣa* present in the following entities as their presiding deities on whom he meditates – The *āditya* (sun), *candra* (moon), *vidyut* (lightning), *ākāśa* (ether), *vāyu* (wind), *agni* (fire), *ap*(water), *ādarśa* (person seen in the mirror), *śabda* (sound which follows a person while walking), *chāyā* (shadow of a person), *dik* (the person present in the quarters), *puruṣa* (the soul in the body). But Ajātaśatru considers that the views of Bālāki represent imcomplete knowledge of Brahman since the *puruṣa* presiding over these different entities is not Brahman.

He tells Bālāki: "*yo vai Bālāke, eteṣaṁ puruṣāṇāṁ kartā yasya vai etat-karma sa vai veditavyaḥ*[20]". "You should know the creator (*kartā*) of all these *puruṣas* and also the *karma* (what is created by it).

Bālāki then desired to be instructed about the knowledge of Brahman. As he was not initiated to receive knowledge of Brahman directly, Ajātaśatru took him inside his residence where a person was fast asleep. He addressed the sleeping person by the name of Somarājan which means *prāṇa* but the person did not wake up. He hit the person with a stick and thereafter the person woke up from sleep. At this stage, Ajātaśatru posed the question to Bālāki. "Where was this *puruṣa* sleeping all this time? In what condition did he remain then? From where did he now come back? (*kvaiṣa etat bālāke puruṣo aśayiṣṭa? Kva vā etad abhūt? Kuta edad-āgāt?*). Bālāki could not answer these questions. In this connection, Ajātaśatru explains in detail the state of sleep (*svapnāvasthā*) and also the state of dreamless sleep (*suṣupti*). In the state of sleep, jīva rests in the *purītati nāḍi* which radiates from the centre of the heart (*hṛdayāt purītatam abhipratiṣṭhanti. tāsu tadā supto bhavati*). But in the state of *suṣupti jīva* rests with *Paramātman* in the *purītati nāḍi* when it does not experience any dreams since all sense organs cease to function and the *prāṇa* is united with *jīva* (*prāṇa evaikadhā bhavati*). When he wakes up, all the sense organs including mind and *prāṇa* start functioning. Finally he concludes with the statement that one who knows this *Brahmavidyā* becomes free from all sins and attains the highest Lordship (*svārājyam ādhipatyaṁ*).

After considering all these factors, the question arises whether the *puruṣa* referred to in this passage is *jīvātman* or *Paramātman*. According to the prima facie view, it is jīvātman for the following reasons. First, the statement '*yo vai bālāke, eteṣām puruṣāṇām kartā yasya vai etat karma sa vai veditavyaḥ*' conveys the idea that it is the *jīva* which is subject to karma in the sense of the *puṇya-pāpa karma*. By the influence of the *karma* of the past it can be the creator of other beings (*svakṛta pariṇateḥ puruṣāṇām kartā*). Secondly the acts of awakening the sleeping person, calling him by a name and hitting him with a stick etc corroborate the view in favour of *jīva*. It is also stated that *prāṇa*, the vital breath becomes one with *jīva* in the state of *suṣupti*. *Prāṇa* subsists on *jīva*.

This view is untenable, contends Vedānta Deśika, because it conflicts with the subject matter mentioned at the commencement of the passage (*upakrānti bhagnam*). Ajātaśatru is required to teach Bālāki what he did not already know. Bālāki approaches Ajātaśatru and tells him voluntarily that he will speak to him about Brahman (*Brahma te bravāṇi*). But he tells Ajātaśatru about the *puruṣas* (*jīvas*) presiding over the various entities commencing with *āditya*. Since the *puruṣa* presiding over these entities is not Brahman proper, Ajātaśatru realizes that Bālāki lacks true knowledge of Brahman. He therefore tells him specifically that the *kartā* or the creator of all these entities and the *karma*, in the sense of what is created by Brahman (*kriyata iti karma*) should be known. If Ajātaśatru were to teach about *puruṣa* taken as *jīvātman*, there is no useful purpose in teaching about what is already known by him. What is not known by Bālāki is: what is to be meditated upon is not *jīva* but Brahman, which is the *kartā* in the sense of being the creator of the *puruṣas* presiding over the various entities in the universe. The term *karma* mentioned here (*yasya vai etat karma*) refers in this context to the universe (*jagat*) which is created by Brahman. Etymologically, *karma* can mean what is created (*kriyata iti karma*), that is, the entire *jagat* or universe created by Brahman.

Keeping all these facts in mind, Bādarāyaṇa says in the sūtra: '*jagadvācitvāt*[21]': "What is denoted by *karma* in the Upaniṣadic statement is *jagat* created by Brahman. As Vedānta Deśika points out, the primary import of *karma* with reference to Brahman is *jagat* (*kriyata iti karmeti vyutpattyā jagata īśvarāpekṣaya karmatva vacanam mukhyam*[22])

An objection can be raised to this conclusion. If contextually, the entire passage is considered to be related to the subject of Brahman, why then in the later part of it, the Upaniṣad speaks about *mukhya prāṇa* and that it also becomes one with *jīva*. That is, Ajātaśatru takes Bālāki inside the palace to see the person who is fast asleep and addresses him as 'Somarājan', which is the name for *mukhya-prāṇa*. He also explains that *hitā nāḍi* in which the *puruṣa* rests, is the *svapnasthāna* and the *jīva* resting in *purīti nāḍi* with *Paramātman* is *suṣuptisthāna*. Would not these statements about *mukhya-prāna* conflict with the main subject of the passage viz. Brahman?

Vedānta Deśika points out that there is no conflict involved because the teaching about *mukhya-prāṇa* as related to Brahman is intended for the purpose of meditation on *prāṇa* as the *śarīra* of *Paramātman* (*tadviśiṣṭe upāsā bhavati*[23]). In the Bṛhadāraṇyaka Upaniṣad, *prāṇa* and *jīva* are both regarded as *śarīra* of *Paramātman*, since they depend on *Paramātman* for their existence.

Thus it follows that this *adhikaraṇa* does not support the Sāṁkhya theory of *puruṣa* as the cause of the universe, but on the contrary, it establishes that Brahman is the cause of the universe.

VI. Ātman conceived as Mukta-puruṣa is not the Cause of the Universe.

This is the subject of the *Vākyānvayādhikaraṇa* which discusses whether the term *'Ātman'* employed in the *Maitreyī Brāhmaṇa* of the Bṛhadāraṇyaka Upaniṣad, conceived as the *puruṣa* being totally dissociated with *prakṛti* could be the cause of the universe. In the previous *adhikaraṇa* it was shown that *puruṣa* referred to in the Kauṣītikī Upaniṣad, which is regarded as *jīvātman* in bondage, cannot be the cause of the universe. In the present *adhikaraṇa* Bādarāyaṇa attempts to establish that *'Ātman'* conceived as the liberated *puruṣa* or the *jīvātmā* totally free from the association with *prakṛti* cannot also be the cause of the universe.

The cryptic *sūtra* which is based on an important passage of the Bṛhadāraṇyaka Upaniṣad, enjoining the meditation (*nididhyāsana*) leading to the realization of the self (*ātma darśana*), reads: *'vākyānvayāt*[24]*'*. Its general meaning is that *'Ātman'* (which is to be meditated upon) is Brahman because the statements in the Upaniṣadic passage become well connected. The fuller implications of the *sūtra* can be made out with reference to the passage of *Maitreyī Brāhmaṇa* teaching about *Ātman* by Yājñavalkya to Maitreyī. Yājñavalkya who wishes to renounce the life of a householder and enter that of anchorage proposes to divide his wealth between Maitreyī and his other wife Kātyāyinī. On hearing this, Maitreyī wishes to know if she would be able to attain immortality (*amṛtatva*) with all this wealth. In reply, Yājñavalkya makes it clear that there is no hope of immortality through wealth (*amṛtasya tu na āśā asti vittena*). Thereupon, Maitreyī, realizing the futility of wealth, seeks to know the means to immortality. In this background, Yājñavalkya teaches the following.

na vā are patyuḥ kāmāya patiḥ priyo bhavati
ātmanastu kāmāya patiḥ priyo bhavati
na vā are jāyāyai kāmāya jāyā priyā bhavati
ātmanastu kāmāya jāyā priyā bhavati[25]

"Verily not due to the desire of the husband, the husband

is dear to the wife, but the husband is dear to the wife due to the will of *Paramātman* (acc. to R)."

"Verily not due to the desire of the wife, the wife is dear to the husband, but the wife is dear to the husband due to the will of *Paramātman*."

In the same strain the Upaniṣad mentions several other entities such as son, wealth etc . Finally it says:

Ātmā vā are draṣṭavyaḥ śrotavyo mantavyo nididhyāsitavyaḥ; maitreyī ātmano vā are darśanena, śravaṇena matyā vijñānena idam sarvam viditam bhavati[26]

"O Maitreyī, it is *ātmā* that should be seen, to be heard, to be reflected on and meditated upon. Verily, by seeing of, by the hearing of, by the thinking of, by understanding of the *ātman*, all this is known.

The issue to be considered is whether the *'ātmā'* mentioned at the commencement of the passage and also in the concluding statement as that which is to be realized (*draṣṭavyaḥ*) refers to *jīvātman* or *Paramātman*. According to the prima facie view it denotes *jīvātman* because the passage states at the very commencement that husband wife etc are dear to each other due to the desire of one's self (*ātmanaḥ kāmasiddhaye*). It is the *jīva* that enjoys the fruits of good or bad deeds, according to its past *karma*.

This view is untenable, contends Vedānta Deśika, because it contradicts the statements made both at the commencement of the passage and conclusion (*prakramādi pratīpam*). By way of explanation he points out that the expression *'ātmanastu kāmāya'* does not imply that the husband is dear to the wife due to the desire or will of the husband. On the contrary, the husband is dear to the wife due to the *saṁkalpa* or will of *Paramātman* (*kāmāya* being understood as *saṁkalpāya*). That is, a wife is dear to a husband not because the husband desires but because *Paramātman* wills that the wife should be dear to the husband in accordance with his *karma*. A person or an object becoming dear to one is dependent on the *saṁkalpa* or the will of *Paramātman* (*tattat priyatvam bhagavat-*

saṁkalpāyattam[27]). It is only when *Paramātman* wills that one's wife should be dear to the husband in accordance with his *karma*, the wife becomes dear to the husband. An individual self cannot make a person or object dear to him (*priyatva*). The word *'ātman'* in the statement therefore refers to *Paramātman*. This meaning for *'ātman'* is also appropriate, as Rāmānuja points out, in the context of the teaching about the way of reaching immortality. The mere *darśana* or realization of *jīvātman* cannot confer *mokṣa*. All the Upaniṣads affirm that only the attainment of *Paramātman* is *mokṣa*. Hence the statement *'ātmā vā are draṣṭavyaḥ'* signifies that the realization of *Paramātman* leads to *mokṣa*.

Vedānta Deśika justifies the meaning adopted for *ātman* in favour of *Paramātman*. There are three views in support of this interpretation. The term *'ātman'* etymologically means that which pervades everything (*āpnoti iti ātmā*). Accordingly it primarily means *Paramātman* (*vyutpattyā hi ātmā śabdaḥ prathayati paramaṁ Brahma*). This is the first view. The second view is that it can also mean *Paramātman* according to the well accepted meaning of the term (*yadvā samāsāt svārtho'yam*). The third view is that the term *ātman* which is generally regarded by laymen as *jīva* also denotes *Paramātman* in the sense that *jīvātman* is inherently related to *Paramātman* (*dvāravṛttyā paramaṁ vadati*[28]).

Even during the time of Bādarāyaṇa, differing views about *ātman* were held by ancient *Ācāryas* named Āśmarathya, Auḍulomi and Kāśakṛtsna as is evident by the references made to them by name in the *Vedānta sūtras*[29].

According to Āśmarathya, *jīva* and Brahman are essentially non-different (*vyaktaikya*) and hence *jīva* can also denote *Paramātman*. Auḍulomi maintained the view that *jīva* and Brahman are different in the state of bondage due to *avidyā* which is the limiting adjunct but in the state of *mokṣa* when *avidyā* is eradicated the two are essentially one (*advaita*). Hence it is appropriate to regard *jīva* as Brahman. The third view is ascribed to Kāṣakṛtsna, according to which

Paramātman indwells in *jīvātman* as its *antaryāmin* and hence *jīvātman* can be regarded as *Paramātman* in the sense of its being inherently related to *Paramātman* (*jīva śarīraka paramātmā*).

Vedānta Deśika points out that the views of Auḍulomi that *jīva* becomes Brahman in the state of *mokṣa* is most unsound. This theory is explained on the analogy of ether which is all pervasive, becomes conditioned by several limiting adjuncts such as pots. But with the removal of the limiting adjuncts, space conditioned by the pots becomes one with the ether. In the same way, the *jīvas* are regarded as many when Brahman is conditioned by the limiting adjuncts such as *antaḥkaraṇas* caused by avidyā. When *avidyā* is removed the *jīva* becomes one with Brahman. This theory is untenable because according to the several Scriptural texts, *jīvas* are *nitya* just as Brahman is *nitya* and they are also many. Hence it cannot be said that the two become one in the state of *mukti*.

The Scriptural texts also declare that *jīvas* and Brahman are different by their very nature (*nityam tad bheda dṛṣṭeḥ*). Besides, the Upaniṣadic texts state that in the state of *mokṣa* *jīva* attains equal status with *Paramātman* (*paramaṁ sāmyam upaiti*), which clearly implies the difference between the two even in the state of *mukti*. Hence it is not possible to say that *jīva* and Brahman are essentially the same (*svarūpaikya*). The illustration of clay and its products cited by the Upaniṣad cannot be taken to support the view of non-difference in terms of essential nature (*mṛtsvarūpa*) because according to the Scriptural texts the jīva and Brahman are by their very nature different. Hence the view advanced by Kāśakṛtsna is sounder than the other two theories. According to him, Brahman abides in jīva as its Inner Controller (*jīva īśe taṭsthatvāt*). By virtue of *Paramātman* indwelling in the *jīva*, the term *jīva* denotes *Paramātman*. This is a sound view and stands justified since it upholds that jīva and Brahman are both different and also one in the sense of *jīva* being inherently related to

Paramātman. In the opinion of Vedānta Deśika, this view represents the *vyāsa siddhānta* (*kāśakṛtsno yadiha niravahat vyāsa siddhānta eṣaḥ*)[30]

VII. Īśvara conceived by Yoga school cannot be the Cause of the Universe.

This is the subject-matter of the *adhikaraṇa* named *Prakṛtyadhi-karaṇa*. In the preceding six *adhikaraṇas* the views of the ancient school of Sāṁkhya which maintains the theory of either *prakṛti* or *puṛusa* as the cause of the universe and which are also reflected in a few Upaniṣads, were examined and refuted as untenable. In the present *adhikaraṇa*, the view of the Seśvara Sāṁkhya (yoga school of thought) which admits *Īśvara* or God as the instrumental cause of the universe (*nimitta kāraṇa*) is taken up for consideration. There are two reasons for consideration of this matter separately. First, there are a few Upaniṣadic statements which point out that *prakṛti* as controlled by *Īśvara* is the cause of the universe. Thus says the Śvetāśvatara: *asmāt māyī sṛjate viśvametat* – "The *māyī* (*Īśvara*) creates the universe through the media of *prakṛti* (named as *māyā*)". Secondly Brahman is *nirvikāra* and if it be regarded as the material cause, it would be subject to transformation. Further in the illustration of clay and its products cited by the Upaniṣad, it is seen that clay is the material cause, whereas the potter is the instrumental cause. Thus the material cause is different from the instrumental cause. Accordingly with regard to Brahman and universe which are causally related, it is to be admitted that Brahman is *nimitta kāraṇa* while *prakṛti* is the *upādāna kāraṇa* of the universe.

Bādarāyaṇa refutes this view and affirms that Brahman is both the *nimitta kāraṇa* and the *upādāna kāraṇa* with the support of the Upaniṣadic texts and also logical arguments. He also examines the several objections raised against this conclusion by the Sāṁkhyas and Vaiśeṣikas and shows that they are untenable. The *adhikaraṇas* of the first *pāda* of the second *adhyāya* are mainly devoted to this matter. As this is an important subject in Vedānta, we shall discuss these *adhikaraṇas* separately in the next chapter on the doctrine of Universe and Brahman. For the present, it may be noted that according to Bādarāyaṇa, *Īśvara* is not only the *nimitta kāraṇa* as maintained by the Seśvara Sāṁkhya but it is also the *upādāna kāraṇa*.

VIII. Brahman as the Supreme Deity is the Cause of the Universe.

This is the subject-matter of the last *adhikaraṇa* named *Sarvavyākhyānādhikaraṇa* which covers the single conclusive *sūtra* of the fourth *pāda* of the first *adhyāya*. In the preceding seven *adhikaraṇas*, Bādarāyaṇa has examined the selected Upaniṣadic statements which convey the idea of either the *Pradhāna* or *puruṣa* as the cause of the universe and shown that their true import is Brahman as the sole cause of the universe. Brahman, according to Rāmānuja, is the Supreme Deity in the name of Nārāyaṇa or Viṣṇu, as is evident from the statements of Subāla, Kaṭha, Taittirīya, Nārāyana and Mahopaniṣad. There are a few stray Scriptural statements appearing in the Upaniṣads which prima facie, speak of other deities such as Hiraṇyagarbha, Śiva, Indra, Rudra etc as the higher deity that existed prior to creation. Thus it is stated: *Hiraṇyagarbhaḥ samavartata agre bhūtasya jātaḥ patrireka āsīt*. "Prior to creation, Hiraṇyagarbha existed and that He became the ruler by creating all beings[31]". The Śvetāśvatara says – *yadā tamaḥ tanna divā na rātriḥ na sat na ca asat śiva eva kevalaḥ*[32]. "At the time prior to creation when it was only darkness which was neither day nor night, when there was neither being nor non-being, only *śiva* existed".

These statements give room for the doubts that other than Brahman there are other deities which could be the cause of the universe.

In order to remove such doubts, Bādarāyaṇa states: *etena*

sarve vyākhyātāḥ. It means "All such statements stand explained by adopting the principles of interpretation and logical arguments stated in the preceding *adhikaraṇas* of the earlier *pādas* (*prāgukta nītibhedāt*). That is, if we take into consideration the context in which these statements are made, the main theme or the subject matter of the entire passage and also the sentences at the commencement and conclusion of the passage, it becomes apparent that all the Upaniṣadic statements conclusively establish that Brahman is the only cause of the universe. The details of the interpretation of the texts referring to Hiraṇyagarbha, Śiva etc are given in the *Vedārtha Saṅgraha* of Rāmānuja and other theological treatises of Vedānta Deśika. These are not therefore discussed in the Adhikaraṇa-sāravālī. He mentions only one important point to assert the Supremacy of Viṣṇu as Para Brahman. In the popular concept of *tri-mūrti* or three deities namely Brahmā, Viṣṇu, Rudra – mentioned in the Purāṇas, Viṣṇu referred to here on a par with the other two deities is the incarnated form of Brahman as a *devatā* for the purpose of carrying out the function of *rakṣaṇa* (protection). The Supreme Lord assumes the incarnated form of *Matsya* (fish), *Kūrma* (tortoise), Rāma and Kṛṣṇa (as human forms) for specific purposes on specific occasions without abrogating His original essential nature[33]. Viṣṇu as the incarnated form of a *devatā* is not different from Viṣṇu as the Supreme Deity. Hence it is concluded that all the Upaniṣadic texts teach that Brahman as the Supreme deity is the sole cause of the universe.

---

1. Kaṭha Up. I-3-10 and 11.
2. Kaṭha Up. I-3-3 and 4.
3. AS verse 132
4. Katha. Up. I-3-9
5. *See* VS I-4-2. *sūkṣmam tu tad-arhatvāt* – "The subtle *avyakta* becomes the body, for it is only then that it becomes fit to be useful." See AS verse 133.
6. Katha Up. I-3-9.
7. *See* AS verse 133.

8. Śvet. Up. IV-5
9. VS I-4-8
10. Śvet. Up. IV-9
11. AS verse 134
12. Br. Up –VI-4-17
13. VS-I-4-11.
14. Br. Up. VI-4-8
15. Br. Up. III-4-70
16. Tait. Up. II
17. *See* Ch. Up. VI-2-3. Also AS verse 137. *yatra asatvādi dṛṣṭam, tatra prakaraṇa viditam sarvajñatādyam liṅgaṁ syāt*
18. *See* Padayojanā AS verse 138
19. VS I-4-16.
20. Kau. Up. IV-18.
21. VS I-4-16.
22. Cintāmaṇi verse 139.
23. AS verse 140. *prāṇākhyānaṁ na tena kṣatiriha ca tathā tadvísiṣṭe hy upāsā.*
24. VS I-4-19.
25. Br. Up. IV-4-5
26. *See* Br. Up.IV-4-6
27. AS verse 141. tattad-*bhoga pradātuḥ prathayati hi vibhoḥ kāmataḥ tatpriyatvam.* See also Cintāmaṇi on verse 141 – *tattad putradi nimitta, bhoga pradātuḥ parama puruṣasyaiva saṁkalpāt teṣām putrādīnāṁ pitrādīn prati priyatvam bhagavat saṁkalpāyattam ityarthaḥ.*
28. *See* AS verse 142. See also Padayojanā, *śarīra vācakānāṁ śarīri paryantatva nyāyena dvārabhūta jīva aparityāgena tad-viśiṣṭatayā pratipādayati.*
29. *See* V.S. II-4-20, 21, and 22.
30. AS verse 143.
31. Ṛg Veda. X-121. See also Tattirīya Saṁhitā IV-1-8.
32. Śvet. Up. IV-18.
33. AS verse 150. *etat matsyādibhāveṣviva nija-vibhava anukriyā naṭyam syāt. See* Rāmāyaṇa,VI-104 *tatstvamapi durdarṣaḥ tasmāt bhāvāt sanātanāt; rakṣarthaṁ sarva bhūtānāṁ viṣṇutvam upajagmivān.*

CHAPTER FIVE

THE DOCTRINE OF UNIVERSE AND BRAHMAN

In the previous chapter we have seen how Bādarayaṇa has established by methodical analysis and proper interpretation of the Upaniṣadic texts that Brahman is the sole cause of the universe. In connection with the refutation of the theory of Seśvara Sāṁkhya (Yoga) which admits *Īśvara* as the *nimitta kāraṇa* of the universe, he has upheld the doctrine of Vedānta that Brahman is the *upādāna kāraṇa* of the universe on the basis of the Upaniṣadic teachings. The *Prakṛtyādhikaraṇa* to which we have referred earlier, mainly deals with this subject. Several objections are raised against this theory by the Sāṁkhyas. These are all dealt in the *adhikaraṇas* of the first *pāda* of second *adhyāya*. In this context, the relation of Brahman to the universe comes up for special consideration in the *Ārambhaṇādhikaraṇa* included in the first *pāda* of the second *adhyāya* and also in the *Ahikuṇḍalādhikaraṇa* included in the second *pāda* of the third *adhyāya*. We shall deal with all these matters in the present chapter with a view to presenting a coherent doctrine of universe in relation to Brahman

I. Brahman as the Material Cause of the Universe.

This is an important subject in Vedānta. It is covered in a separate *adhikaraṇa* named *Prakṛtyādhikaraṇa*. The relevant *sūtra* reads: *Prakṛtiśca pratijñā-dṛṣṭāntānuparodhāt*[1]. The word *prakṛti*, as interpreted both by Rāmānuja and Śaṁkara means *upādāna kāraṇa*[2]. The word *'ca'* added to it implies that it is also the *nimitta kāraṇa*. That is, Brahman is both the material and instrumental cause of the universe. The reason for advancing this view is contained in the words of the *sūtra 'Pratijñā dṛṣṭānta anuparodhāt'*. It means that the general statement and the illustrations mentioned in the Upaniṣad in support of it would not be contradicted by the admission of Brahman as both material and instrumental cause. An important passage of the Chāndogya Upaniṣad to which the *sūtra* refers contains statements which point out that by the knowledge of the one Reality everything else becomes known (*eka vijñānena anyat sarvaṁ vijñātam bhavati*). Thus says the Upaniṣad *'uta taṁ ādeśam aprākṣyaḥ yena aśrutaṁ śrutaṁ bhavati, amataṁ mataṁ, avijñātaṁ vijñātam'*[3].

"Have you ever asked that instruction by which that which is not heard becomes heard; that which is not thought becomes thought; that which is not comprehended becomes comprehended."

By way of elucidation of this statement, the Upaniṣad cites three illustrations: *yathā saumya ekena mṛtpiṇḍena sarvaṁ mṛṇmayam vijñātam syātekena loha maṇinā sarvaṁ lohamayaṁ vijñātaṁ syāt; ekena nakha nikṛntanena sarvaṁ kārṣṇāyasaṁ vijñātam syāt*[4]....

"My dear, as by one lump of clay, all that is made of clay is known,....by one nugget of gold, all that is made of gold is known, by a pair of nail scissors, all that is made of iron is known"

The general statement about the knowledge of one (the causal substance) leads to the knowledge of everything else (all the products made of it) is named *pratijñā* or declaration. The illustrations offered by the Upaniṣad to elucidate this are called *dṛṣṭānta*. If we take into consideration the illustrations cited by the Upaniṣad, it is obvious that the knowledge of the material cause leads to the knowledge of the products made out of it. On the same analogy, it is maintained that if Brahman is admitted as the material cause of the universe, everything else caused by it would be known. This is the main justification for affirming that Brahman is the *upādāna kāraṇa*.

In support of the above conclusion, Bādarāyaṇa points out that the very Upaniṣadic texts state that Brahman itself resolved to become the universe in the following words *'tadaikṣata, bahusyāṁ prajāyeya'* – 'It resolved, may I become many'[5]. The Taittirīya Upaniṣad also says *'so'kāmayata, bahusyāṁ prajāyeya*: "It thus resolved, may I become many'. The Taittirīya Upaniṣad also states: *'tad-ātmānaṁ svayam akuruta'*[6] – "It (Brahman) makes itself evolved into the form of the universe". On the basis of these Upaniṣadic texts Bādarāyaṇa states that Brahman itself becomes the universe through modification. The relevant *sūtras* read: *Ātmakṛteḥ, pariṇāmāt*[7]. The word *'pariṇāmāt'* used in the *sūtra* means, as explained by Rāmānuja, *pariṇāma-svābhāvyāt*, that is, Brahman possesses the characteristic of undergoing modification. Its implication is that Brahman is of such a nature as it is capable of undergoing modification without at the same time, its *svarūpa* or intrinsic nature being subject to change. This is possible because, according to Viśiṣṭādvaita Vedānta, Brahman is inseparably related to the souls and the cosmic matter (*cid-acid-viśiṣṭa Brahma*). As explained by Rāmānuja, Brahman is always (*sarvadā*) associated with *cit* and *acit* both in the states prior to creation and also after creation. In the state prior to creation, Brahman is associated with *cit* and *acit* in their subtle state, and the same Brahman, when it wills to become many, manifests itself as associated with *cit* and *acit* in their manifest form. This explanation has the full support of the Scriptural texts. The Bṛhadāraṇyaka Upaniṣad says: *'Taddhedam tarhi avyākṛtam āsīt tan-nāmarūpābhyām eva vyākriyata*[8]*'* – "This universe consisting of souls and matter existed prior to creation in unmanifest form. It then became many with name and form". All the changes apply to *cit* and *acit* and not to Brahman. But Brahman as the substrate of *cit* and *acit* is not affected by the change. This is illustrated by the analogy of a boy growing into youth and the youth attaining manhood etc. In this instance, the different states such as youth, manhood etc involving physical change, actually belong to the body and the soul which is the *ādhāra* or support of the body is in no way affected by it. In the same way, the modification taking place in the *cit* and *acit* do not affect the *svarūpa* of Brahman, which is its *ādhāra*. Brahman is regarded as *upādāna kāraṇa* by virtue of its being the substrate of *acit* which actually undergoes modification. It is only in this sense that *pariṇāma* of Brahman is to be understood in order to maintain its *nirvikāratva*.

By way of defending the above explanation offered by Rāmānuja, Vedānta Deśika points out that the analogy of clay and its products should not be taken literally in respect of the causal relation of Brahman to the universe. It is not necessary that there should be absolute similarity in every respect between *dṛṣṭānta* or illustration and *darṣṭrāntika* or the object to be explained. The analogy is to be made use of to the extent it is plausible (*yathā yogyam sādharmyam*). There are other instances which substantiate how a substance can serve as a material cause without transforming itself into the state of an effect. Thus for instance, the spider causes the web without effecting any change in respect of it. Neither the body of the spider nor its *jiva* undergoes modification but only the spider as associated with the body (*dehaviśiṣṭa ūrṇanābhiḥ*) creates the web[9]. In the same way, it is to be understood that Brahman as associated with *cit* and *acit* undergoes modification without affecting its *svarūpa*.

Vedānta Deśika further points out that there is no inconsistency in respect of Brahman being both the *upādāna* and *nimitta kāraṇa* as this is supported by the Scriptural texts. The general principle (*pratijñā*) viz. the knowledge of the causal substance leads to the knowledge of its effects is sustainable if *kāraṇa* or causal substance is not different from *kārya* or its effects. In order to substantiate that Brahman is *upādānakāraṇa* the Upaniṣad has provided the illustration of clay and its products (*tadanuguṇa udāhari dṛṣṭāntavargaḥ*).

The statement that Brahman itself resolved to become many conveys the idea that it is also *nimitta kāraṇa*. In the context of the creation of the universe, a passage of the Ṛgveda also speaks of Brahman as both *upādāna* and *sahakāri kāraṇa* or accessory cause. Thus it states: *'kiṁsvid vanaṁ ka u sa vṛkṣa asīt, yato dyāvā pṛthivī niṣṭatakṣuḥ, brahma vanaṁ brahma sa vṛkṣa āsīt, yato dyāvā pṛthivī niṣṭatakṣuḥ'* –

"What was the wood (*vanam*), what is the tree from which they have shaped the heaven and earth? Brahman is the wood and Brahman is the tree from which they have shaped the heaven and the earth".

The first part of the verse raises the question as to what is the material cause of the universe and what is the material out of which it is made? The later part of the verse gives the answer in terms of Brahman as the *upādāna* denoted by the words *brahma vanaṁ* and that Brahman itself is the material denoted by the words *brahma sa vṛkṣa*. On the basis of it, the *sūtra* says: *'sākṣācca ubhaya amnāt*[10]*'*. That is, the Scriptural text speaks of Brahman itself as both the *upādāna kāraṇa* and the accessory cause (*sahakāri kāraṇa*). That it is also *nimitta* is implied in the verse.

The Muṇḍaka Upaniṣad also states that Brahman is *'yoni'* or source of the universe, implying that it is the material cause on the analogy of the spider creating the web. Based on this, Bādarāyaṇa says: *Yoniśca hi gīyate*[11].

As pointed out earlier, the Taittirīya also states that Brahman itself becomes the universe by undergoing modification (*ātmakṛteḥ pariṇāmāt*) in the sense that *prakṛti* which constitutes its body is made to evolve into the manifest universe from its unmanifest state. Taking all these facts, Vedānta Deśika contends that there is no inconsistency in admitting Brahman as both the material and instrumental cause of the universe[12]

An objection is raised against this conclusion. Whatever is regarded as *upādāna kāraṇa*, the same cannot be *nimitta kāraṇa*. That is, whatever is other than *upādāna* is to be regarded as *nimitta kāraṇa*. In the same way, if something is regarded as *nimitta kāraṇa,* it cannot be *upādāna kāraṇa* (*yadvā siddhaṁ nimittaṁ na bhajati tadupādānatām*). Vedānta Deśika refutes this argument as unsound. It is possible to regard the same one entity in two different forms with reference to the two different forms or states with which it is associated (*ākāra bhedāt nānātva vyavahāra yogitvaṁ siddhyati*). Both the Scriptural texts and also our common experience warrant such a theory.

According to the Upaniṣads, Brahman as associated with *cit* and *acit* in their subtle state (*sūkṣma cid-acid-viśiṣṭa brahma*) is the *upādāna kāraṇa,* while the same Brahman, when it manifests as the manifold universe by its will, becomes the *nimitta kāraṇa*. Hence there is no contradiction involved in conceiving Brahman as both the *upādāna* and *nimitta kāraṇa*.

One other objection is raised against the theory that *sūkṣma-cid-acid-viśiṣṭa-brahma* is *upādāna kāraṇa*. According to the Subāla Upaniṣad dealing with the dissolution of the universe, the different evolutes successively become absorbed in their respective causal substance. The *prakṛti* is dissolved in the *akṣara* (*jīvātman*), the *akṣara* in turn is dissolved in *tamas* and *tamas* finally becomes one with *Paramātman*. The Viṣṇu-purāṇa also states that both *prakṛti* and *puruṣa* are absorbed in *Paramātman* (*prakṛti-puruṣaścāpi ubahu etau līyete paramātmani*). According to these statements, both *prakṛti* and *puruṣa* are destroyed, the word *'laya'* being interpreted as *vināśa* or destruction. How then can it be claimed that Brahman which exists prior to the state of creation is associated with *cit* and *acit* in their unmanifest state?

Vedānta Deśika clarifies that the word *'laya'* or *'līyate'* does not imply total destruction. On the contrary, the *'laya'* of an entity is the assumption of its previous state after giving up the present state (*svāvasthā prahāṇena pūrvāvasthā prāptirūpam*). The statement *'pṛthivī apsu liyate'* means that *pṛthivī* assumes the state of *ap* or water after losing the state of *pṛthivī*. *Laya* is also understood in another way. It means merging of an entity into another without losing its nature and assuming an undistinguished form (*svāvasthā prahāṇamantareṇa vastvantarāvirbhāva anarha saṁsarga viśeṣa prāpti*). In the Subāla Upaniṣad the statement *'tamaḥ pare deva ekī bhavati'* implies that *prakṛti* and *puruṣa* assume in the state of dissolution, such a form that they become indistinguishable. It does not mean that they are totally destroyed because the Scriptural and *Smṛti* texts speak that they are *anādi* or having no beginning and also *nitya* or eternal. This is analogous to the melted iron rod and the water into which it is dipped (*ayastoyanīti*). When the melted rod is dipped into the water, it assumes the state of the iron rod without losing its metallic nature. In the same way, when *tamas* or *prakṛti* becomes united with *Paramātman*, *prakṛti* is not totally lost but it remains in *Paramātman* in the state of undistinguishable form. Thus the theory of Brahman as related to *cit* (souls) and *acit* (cosmic matter) can become *upādāna kāraṇa*. It is also the *nimitta kāraṇa* since the universe is created through the operation of His will (*saṁkalpāśrayāt nimitta kāraṇa*). This is a sounder theory than that of Advaita which explains *upādāna kāraṇatva* by resorting to *vivarta vāda* or the theory that Brahman illusorily appears as universe due to *avidyā*. It is also sounder than Sāṁkhya theory which explains causation of the universe by God as only *nimitta kāraṇa* (*asau bhoktṛ-bhogya-prabhṛti-kavacitāt viśva-ṣṛṣṭiḥ samīcī*)[13]

II. The Relation of Brahman to the Universe.

Brahman and Jagat are non-distinct (ananya).

A major objection is put forward by the ancient Vaiśeṣikas who maintain that cause and effect are absolutely different and as such Brahman cannot be regarded as material and instrumental cause of the universe. The *Ārambhaṇādhikaraṇa* discusses this important issue and explains the causal relationship between Brahman and the universe in terms of non-difference (*ananyatva*).

According to the Vaiśeṣikas cause and effect are two different entities. Taking the common example of the threads and the cloth as cause and effect, the cloth is brought into existence anew by the collection of various causal factors. What is accepted as a cause is known by a name different from that which is an effect. Thus for instance, the cause of the cloth is named as thread, whereas its effect is known as cloth. By number (*saṅkhyā*), the two are different. The threads are numerous, whereas the cloth is a single entity. By function (*vyavahāra*), they are not the same. Cloth covers the body, whereas the threads do not serve such a purpose. The knowledge of the thread is not the same as the knowledge of the cloth (*buddhi-bheda*). Cause and effect differ also in respect of shape (*ākāra*).There is also temporal difference between the two. Threads are first made and cloth is made later. Because of these several factors, effect is distinct from the cause (*anya*)[14].

Vedānta Deśika does not agree with this view. Threads may be different from the cloth but the two can be regarded as different states of the same substance, as in the example of the scroll of palm leaf and an earring made out of it by just rolling it into the shape of an earring. When it is flat, it is called a scroll but when it is rolled, it is known as an earring. In this instance, the two entities as cause and effect are different by virtue of the name, function, shape etc but still the two are modifications or states of the same substance. That is, the same substance is regarded as cause and effect with reference to the two different states it assumes (*dravaikye'pi astu sarvaṁ tadabhimatadaśā bhedataḥ*). In the same way, Brahman as the cause of the universe is regarded as non-distinct from the universe as its effect. Thus states Bādarāyaṇa:

Tad-ananyatvam ārambhaṇa śabdādibhyaḥ[15]. It means, as interpreted by Rāmānuja, that the universe is non-distinct from Brahman for the reason that the Upaniṣadic statement beginning with the word *'ārambhaṇa'* supports it. The fuller implication of the *Sūtra* is explained with reference to the passage of the Chāndogya Upaniṣad on the basis of which it is formulated.

The Upaniṣad states:

Yathā saumya ekena mṛtpiṇḍena sarvaṁ mṛṇmayaṁ vijñātam syāt, vācārambhaṇaṁ vikāro nāmadhyeyam mṛttiketyeva satyam[16]

"My dear, as by the knowledge of one lump of clay, all that is made of clay is known, the modification (the object made of clay) being connected with speech".

This statement is explained by Rāmānuja in the following way. The word *ārambhaṇa* is taken as a variant of *ālambana* on the basis of a grammatical rule. *Ālambana* means being touched (*spṛśyate*). The word *vāk* means speech. The combined word *vacā-ārambhaṇa* means being touched or being connected with speech. That is, the modification (*vikāra*) of clay in the form of configurations such as pot or pitcher and the names adopted to designate them are connected with speech for the purpose of bringing out appropriate transactions such as fetching water. The implication of this explanation is that the pot as an effect of clay is not an altogether different entity, as Vaiśeṣikas claim, but on the other hand, it is a modified form of the clay. Though cause and effect may be regarded as distinct, in actuality it is non-distinct in the sense that the pot is only the modified form of the same one substance, namely the clay (*mṛd-dravyameva saṁsthānāntara nāmadheyāntara bhāk*). The other important implication of this explanation is that the pot as a modification of clay, is not illusory (*mithyā*), as Śaṁkara contends. It is as real as the clay. This is the significance of the words: *mṛttikā dravyam ity-eva satyam,* mentioned in the Upaniṣad. Cause and effects are therefore, two different states (*avasthās*) of the same one substance.

On the basis of these explanations, Rāmānuja maintains that Brahman as the cause and the universe as its effect are *ananya* or non-distinct. By way of elucidation he points out that Brahman is always (*sarvadā*) integrally related to the universe comprising the sentient souls(*cit*) and non-sentient cosmic matter (*acit*), both in the state prior to dissolution, that is, prior to creation (*agre*) and also after the creation of the universe by its *saṁkalpa*. In its causal state (*kāraṇāvasthā*), Brahman is associated with *cit* and *acit* in their unmanifest form (*sūkṣma-cid-acid-viśiṣṭa*). When it wills to become many, the same Brahman assumes a state in which it is associated with *cit* and *acit* in their manifested gross form (*sthūla-cid-acid-viśiṣṭa-brahma*). The former is the causal state and the latter is the effect state. On the analogy of the clay and pot, the two states are not different, since Brahman which is the *ādhāra* for the unmanifested universe and also the manifested universe, is the same. The Chāndogya passage dealing with the causation of the universe supports this view. The statement: '*sadeva saumya idamagra asīt ekamevā*' implies that Brahman existed prior to creation (*agre*) as integrally related to *cit* and *acit* in their subtle form. This is the *ekatvā-vasthā* of Brahman, that is, Brahman as associated with *cit* and *acit* in their unmanifest form as different from *bahutvā-vasthā* assumed after it creates the universe by its will. The Bṛhadāraṇyaka clearly states that the universe existed in an unmanifest form prior to creation and the same became manifest after creation. Thus it says: *Tad-dhedaṁ tarhi avyākṛtam āsīt, tan-nāma rūpābhāyṁ vyākriyata*[17]. The Subāla Upaniṣad dealing with the dissolution of the universe affirms in clear terms that *tamas* which represents the unmanifest universe comprising of both the *prakrti* and the *jīvas* (*akṣara*) becomes united with Brahman (*tamaḥ pare deva ekī bhavati*[18]). The Chāndogya teaching *sad-vidyā* also states; '*Sanmūlāḥ somya imāḥ prajāḥ sadāyatanāḥ satpratiṣṭhāh*[19]'. Considering all these Upaniṣadic statements, it is obvious that Brahman as related to *sūkṣma cit* and *acit* is the material cause of the universe, on the analogy of the clay and pot cited by the Upaniṣad, and it is non-distinct from the universe created by it in the sense that the same Brahman as associated with *sūkṣma cit* and *acit* becomes Brahman as associated with *sthūla cit* and *acit*.

An objection can be raised against this theory. If *sat* or Brahman in the causal state exists along with *cit* and *acit* in their unmanifest state, how could it be regarded as *advitīya* or without a second as stated in the Upaniṣadic statements?

In reply, Vedānta Deśika points out that even the schools of Śaṁkara, Bhāskara and Yādava Prakāśa who also subscribe to the theory of Brahman as *upādāna kāraṇa*, admit that Brahman as associated with *māyā*, *upādhi* and *śakti* respectively is the cause of the universe. But they seek to overcome the conflict with the concept of *advītiya* by regarding *māyā*, *upādhi* and *śakti* as *apradhāna* or secondary principle since it is a quality (*viśeṣaṇa*), while Brahman which is *pradhāna* or primary principle remains *advitiya*. If this is the explanation offered by them, the same explanation holds good in respect of Viśiṣṭādvaita theory, which admits *cit* and *acit* as subordinate to Brahman. Brahman as the *Antaryāmin* of *prakṛti* and *puruṣa* (*jīva*) is the Principal Reality, while the other two entities are the *viśeṣaṇas* or dependent realities. Epistemologically, the substance as qualified by the *viśeṣaṇas* is one only. From the standpoint of Brahman as inherently related to *cit* and *acit*, it is one (*viśiṣṭa vivakṣayā ekatva*). Philosophically and also logically, this is a sounder theory of *Brahmopādānatva* than that of Advaitins and *bhedā-bheda vādins*, since this conforms better to the Scriptural teachings (*sarva śrutyaikarasya*)[20]

III. The Universe as an Integral Part of Brahman.

In the preceding section we have considered the causal relationship between Brahman and universe in terms of *ananyatva* or non-distinction. In a later *adhikaraṇa* included in the second *pāda* of the third *adhyāya*, Bādarāyaṇa discusses specifically the question of the relation of the non-sentient universe to Brahman in terms of *viśeṣaṇa* and *viśeṣya*. That is, *jagat* caused by Brahman is related to it in the same way as an attribute to the substance or the body to the soul (*śarīra-śarīrī bhāva*). As this subject has a direct bearing on the theory of the relationship between Brahman and the universe, it is considered appropriate to discuss it in this chapter.

In connection with the consideration of the two-fold character of Brahman (*ubhaya-liṅga*), Bādarāyaṇa introduces three *sūtras* in which he refers to the different views on the nature of the relation of Brahman to the universe in terms of *bhedā-bheda* or difference-cum-non-difference and *abheda* or non-difference by citing two illustrations: 1) serpent and its coils (*ahikuṇḍala*) and 2) The luminous body and its light (*prākaśāśraya* and *prakāśa*).

The *sūtra* containing the first illustration reads: *Ubhaya vyapadeśāt-tu ahikuṇḍalavat*[21]. It means, according to Rāmānuja, that the relation of Brahman to the universe is similar to that of the serpent and its coils, since Brahman is spoken of in the Upaniṣads as different and also non-different from the universe (*ubhaya vyapadeśāt*). Thus the Chāndogya says: *sarvaṁ khalu idaṁ brahma* – "All this is Brahman". The Śvetāśvatara states: *bhoktā bhogyaṁ preritāraṁ ca matvā*. This statement draws a distinction between Brahman and the universe. In order to reconcile these two conflicting statements, the non-sentient universe is regarded as a special form (*samsthāna viśeṣa*) of Brahman, as a coil is of the serpent. This represents a prima-facie view, according to Rāmānuja, which upholds non-difference between Brahman and the universe.

The second *sūtra* containing the illustration of the light and its luminous body reads: *prakāśāśrayādvā tejastvāt*[22]. It means – "Alternatively (*vā*), it is like light and its substrate, both being luminous. Its implication is, according to Rāmānuja, that light and its body are different but at the same time they are one in so far as both are of the nature of light (*tejas*).This also presents a second alternative prima facie theory, according to which there is difference and non-difference between Brahman and the universe.

The subsequent *sūtra* which simply reads: '*pūrvavad-vā*[23]', is taken to present the view of Bādarāyana, as admitted by both Śaṁkara and Rāmānuja. The word '*pūrvavad*' literally means 'as stated previously'. The word *'vā'* implies that the views contained in the present *sūtra* is different from the two prima facie theories mentioned in the preceding two *sūtras* supporting the relation of non-difference and difference-cum-non-difference respectively between Brahman and the universe.

The earlier *sūtra* to which Bādarāyaṇa refers, as interpreted by Rāmānuja, is the one relating to the nature of relation of *jīva* to Brahman in terms of *aṁśa* or an integral part of Brahman, which is mentioned in the third *pāda* of the second *adhyāya*. It reads: *aṁśo nānāvyapadeśāt anyathā ca*[24] - "The self is an integral part of Brahman on account of difference and otherwise (non-difference) also." The fuller implications of this *sūtra* will be explained in the chapter on the Doctrine of Jīva. For the present it may be noted that Bādarāyaṇa has in mind this *sūtra*, when he says *'pūrvavad-vā'* to explain the relationship between the universe and Brahman, since the principle adopted to determine the relation of *jīva* to Brahman is equally applicable to the relation of universe to Brahman. As both *jīva* and Brahman are *śarīra* of Brahman, it is relevant to refer to the *sutra* dealing with *jīva* while discussing the relation of non-sentient universe to Brahman.

The universe is also regarded as an *aṁśa* or an integral part of Brahman since it does not have a separate existence apart from Brahman as in the case of *jīva* (*jīvavat pṛthak-siddhyanarha viśeṣaṇatvena acid vastuno brahmāṁśam*[25]). This is similar to the relation of body to the soul (*śarīra sarīrī bhāva*) adopted by Rāmānuja to explain the relationship between universe and Brahman on the authority of Antaryāmī Brāhmaṇa. The non-sentient universe, like the sentient soul, is *śarīra* of Brahman in the technical sense that these are necessarily and always supported and controlled by Brahman which is their *śarīrī* or the Indwelling Self[26]. This theory accommodates both difference and non-difference from different standpoints, difference as *śarīrī* and *śarīra* and non-difference as *śarīrī* integrally related to the *śarīra*.

IV. Refutation of the objections against the theory of Brahman as upādāna kāraṇa.

As pointed out earlier, a few objections are raised against the Vedānta doctrine of Brahman as the *upādāna kāraṇa.* One major objection raised by the Vaiśeṣikas that cause and effect are absolutely different and as such Brahman cannot be regarded as the cause of the universe is already discussed in the preceding section. There are other objections raised by the Sāṁkhyas on the assumption that there cannot be any causal relationship between Brahman and the non-sentient universe since they are of different nature. If on the other hand, Brahman and *jagat* are considered to be non-different, then the defects found in the material universe and also the afflictions of the *jīvas* would be applicable to Brahman. Further, if Brahman itself as the material cause of the universe, undergoes modification, it would affect its nature as *nirvikāra* or devoid of change. In the absence of any accessories for creation of the universe and also a useful purpose to be served, Brahman cannot be conceived as the creator of the universe. All these objections are examined by Bādarāyaṇa and set aside in order to establish the causal relation of Brahman to the universe. The following *adhikaraṇas* included in the first *pāda* of the second *adhyāya* discuss these issues and bring out the relation of Brahman to the universe.

i) *Smṛtyadhikaraṇa*
ii) *Yoga-pratyukty-adhikaraṇa*
iii) *Vilakṣaṇatvādhikaraṇa*
iv) *Bhoktṛāpatty-adhikaraṇa*
v) *Ārambhaṇādhikaraṇa*
vi) *Itaravyapadeśādhikaraṇa*
vii) *Upasamhāra-darśanādhikaraṇa*
viii) *Kṛtsnaprasakty-adhikaraṇa*
ix) *Prayojanatvādhikaraṇa*

We shall present the important points of these *adhikaraṇas,* except (v) which has been discussed earlier, as pointed out by Vedānta Deśika.

a) The Smṛti texts of Sāṁkhya and Yoga are opposed to Vedānta.

At the outset, Bādarāyaṇa discusses the issue whether the *Kapila Smṛti* or the treatises of Sāṁkhya system founded by sage Kapila and *Yoga-smṛti* or the texts of Yoga system founded by Hiraṇyagarbha, are to be accepted as authoritative for determining the teachings of the Upaniṣads relating to the cause of the universe. This matter is covered in two separate *adhikaraṇas* named as *Smṛtyadhikaraṇa* and *yoga-pratyukty-adhikaraṇa*. The prima facie view advanced in this connection is that *Smṛti* texts are generally regarded as *upabrahmaṇas* or that which elucidate the teachings contained in the *śrutis* and in view of it, the doubtful Upanisadic statements teaching about Brahman as the material cause of the universe are to be interpreted with reference to what is clearly stated in *Kapila Smṛtis*. Besides, Kapila is revered in the Vedic texts as a sage, gifted with spiritual knowledge (*ṛṣi prasūtam kapilaṁ*[27]). It is therefore contended that *kapila smṛti* is to be depended upon for ascertaining the true cause of the universe. If this view is accepted, it follows that *prakṛti* or the primordial cosmic matter is the material cause of the universe and not Brahman as claimed by the Vedāntins.

This view is rejected by Bādarāyaṇa. The relevant *sūtra* reads: *Smṛty-anavakāśadoṣa prasaṅga iti cet, na anya-smṛty-anavakāśadoṣa prasaṅgāt*[28]. Its general meaning is: "If it is argued that *Kapila Smṛti* would be rendered unauthoritative by not making use of it to determine the meaning of Vedānta texts, then it would lead to the position that other *Smṛti* texts (such as *Manusmṛti*) are of no value."

The implication of this is that there are other more authoritative *Smṛtis* such as *Manu Smṛti* and these would be rendered unauthoritative if we rely on *Kapila Smṛti* for determining the meaning of the Upaniṣadic texts. Sage Manu is also reputed to be gifted with Spiritual knowledge and his treatises mention in clear terms that Brahman is the source of the universe. We cannot therefore ignore them. Further, the teachings of Kapila that *prakṛti* is the cause of the universe is opposed to the Upaniṣadic texts. *Manu Smṛti* does not also mention *prakṛti* as the cause of the universe. The same is the case with Yoga *smṛti* founded by Hiraṇyagarbha. This is also not regarded as authoritative source book for determining the true purport of the Upaniṣadic texts dealing with the causation of the universe by Brahman. Hence the theory of Brahman as the material cause of the universe is to be admitted as taught in the Upaniṣads.

b) The Cause and Effect are of different nature.

The Sāṁkhyas advance an argument on a different ground that Brahman cannot be claimed to be the cause of the universe since the two viz. Brahman as the causal substance and the universe as its effect (*kārya*) are not of the same nature. That is, Brahman is a sentient Being, whereas the cosmic universe is non-sentient in character and the two being different in nature (*vilakṣaṇa*), there cannot be any causal relationship between them. The basis for this objection is that according to the Sāṁkhyas, the universe is constituted of three *guṇas* viz. *sattva, rajas* and *tamas* and *prakṛti* which is its cause, is also of the same nature. Hence it is logical to affirm that *prakṛti* is the cause of the universe and not Brahman, which is of different nature from the universe (*na asamāt*).

Bādarāyaṇa refutes this objection. This matter is discussed in the *vilakṣaṇādhikaraṇa*. It is not necessary that the causal substance and the effect brought out of it should be of the same nature. By way of elucidating this point, Vedānta Deśika asks the question whether there should be similarity (*sāmya*) between the cause and the effect in every respect or in respect of some aspect only (*kenacit sāmya*). Such a similarity can be seen in respect of a mountain and *paramāṇu*, in so far as the two have a common feature of being *padārthas* (substances). But it does not serve the purpose of determining the causal relationship between the two.

It may be argued that the common feature should be of such a nature that would determine the causal relationship between the cause and its effect. Then the argument stands defeated in respect of the cow dung and the scorpion born out of it (*gomayāt vṛścikādau bhagna*). There is a causal relationship between cow dung and the scorpion but we do not notice any common feature between the two. Hence it is not inappropriate to admit that Brahman as associated with *sūkṣma cit* and *acit* is the cause of the manifest universe in the sense that the same Brahman by its *saṁkalpa* assumes the state of Brahman as associated with the *sthūla cit* and *acit* (*sthūlatvam yāti*).

As explained earlier, Brahman does not transform itself into the universe in which case its nature would be affected. But on the contrary, the *acit* or the cosmic matter which constitutes the *śarīra* or body of Brahman undergoes modification. The change in the cosmic matter does not affect Brahman which is its *ādhāra,* in the same way as the changes taking place in the body of a person do not affect the self within. The *Antaryāmi Brāhmana* states that all entities in the universe including the *jīvātman,* constitute the *śarīra* or the body of Brahman. The term *śarīra* employed in the Upaniṣad is not to be taken in the ordinary sense as the physical body. As explained by Rāmānuja, *śarīra* or body with reference to Brahman is that which is always supported and also wholly controlled by it. It is defined as follows: *yasya cetanasya yaddravyam sarvātmanā svārthe niyantum dhārayitum ca śakyam tachheṣataika-svarūpam ca tat tasya śarīram.*

It means: "Any substance which a sentient self can completely control and support for its own purposes and which stands to the self in an entirely dependent relation is called its *śarīra.*"[29] On the basis of this definition, Rāmānuja regards that all sentient and non-sentient beings constitute the *śarīra* or body of Brahman, as declared in the *Antaryāmi Brāhmaṇa*. The universe is *śarīra* of Brahman in the technical sense that the universe is wholly dependent on Brahman for its existence. It is completely controlled by Brahman and it also subserves the purpose of the Supreme Being. Brahman is the *Śarīrin* or Universal Self of the universe, which is its body, because Brahman is the ground (*ādhāra*) for the universe. It is the controller (*niyantā*) and it uses the universe for its own purpose. In view of these explanations, the Vedānta theory of Brahman as the *upādāna kāraṇa* of the universe is logically tenable.

c) Brahman is not subject to the experience of pleasure and pain

If Brahman associated with the universe as its body is the cause of the universe, would it not experience the *duḥkha* or suffering inherent in the universe just as the *jīva* associated with a body experiences the *sukha* and *duḥkha*?. This is an objection which is raised by the Sāṁkhyas against the Vedānta theory of Brahman as the material cause of the universe. According to them, Brahman associated with a body cannot escape the suffering of the universe (*bhoktṛāpattiḥ*). Consequently there would be no difference between *jīva* and Brahman, since both are subject to the experience of suffering (*avibhāgaḥ*). This matter is discussed in the *Bhoktṛāpatty-adhikaraṇa*.

Bādarāyana refutes this objection. The difference between *jīva* and Brahman is well established by several Upaniṣadic texts. Though both *jīva* and Brahman are associated with a body, Brahman does not experience the suffering, unlike *jīva*. The experience of pleasure and pain is not caused by the mere body, but on the contrary it is due to the *karma* of the *jīva*. Since Brahman is free from *karma* (*apahata-pāpma*), it is not subject to any affliction caused by *karma*. This is explained on the analogy of the ruler and the subjects ruled by him (*samrād-bhṛtyādinīti*). The persons who obey the command of a ruler enjoy the rewards conferred on them and those who disobey the commands are given punishment. But the ruler himself does not experience any suffering caused by punishment to others nor does he experience any happiness enjoyed by those who are rewarded for their good conduct. In the same way, Brahman who is the Supreme Ruler of the universe is not subject to suffering or joy, while the *jivas* experience the same in accordance with their *karma*. This is the implication of the expression *'lokavat'*, mentioned in the *sutra* which reads *'bhoktṛāpatteh avibhagaścet syād lokavat'*[30]. If it be said that Brahman would be subject to the experience of pleasure and pain because of non-distinction, the reply is that there is distinction as seen in the world.

d) Brahman as the Creator of the Universe is not affected by the afflictions of the Universe.

In the *Ārambhaṇādhikaraṇa* dealing with the causal relationship between Brahman and the universe, it was established that the two as cause and effect (*kārya*) are non-different. It would then follow that *jīvas* too are non-different from Brahman in so far as they are part of the universe created by Brahman. Some of the Upaniṣadic texts such as *'tat-tvamasi'*, *'sarvaṁ khalu idaṁ brahma'* also convey the idea of non-difference between the two. But the *jīvas* are afflicted with all kinds of sufferings. It would then amount to admitting that Brahman is the creator of a universe filled with suffering. Thus the theory of Brahman as the cause of the universe would be subjected to the criticism of Brahman creating a universe, which is non-beneficial to it. This is the objection raised against the Vedānta doctrine of Brahman as the cause of the universe and it is discussed in a separate *adhikaraṇa* named *Itara-vyapadeśādhikaraṇa*. The relevant sūtra reads: *Itara-vyapadéśād hitākaraṇādi-doṣa prasaktiḥ*[31]. It means – "Since Brahman is stated to be non-different from the other (*jīva*), there would follow the defects of Brahman creating a universe not beneficial to it."

Bādarāyana sets aside this objection on the ground that it is well established in the scriptural texts that *jīva* and

Brahman by virtue of their nature are absolutely different. Thus says the *sutra*: '*adhikam tu bheda nirdeśāt*[32]. By way of elucidation, Vedānta Deśika points out that the Viśiṣṭādvaitin does not admit that the *jīva* and Brahman are essentially one (*svarūpaikyam*). On the other hand, the two are regarded as non-distinct (*ananya*) in the sense that Brahman as inherently related to the *jīvas* by virtue of its abiding as *Antaryāmin* in the *jivas* (*taṭsthyena jīvātmani antarātmatayā avasthānena ananyatvasya uktatvāt*[33]). The *Vedānta-sūtra* also states: '*Avasthiteḥ iti kāśakṛtsṇaḥ*[34]'- "It is one because Brahman abides in the *jīva*, as stated by sage Kāśakṛtsna". On the authority of *Antaryāmi Brāhmaṇa*, *jīva* is regarded as *śarīra* and Brahman as its *śarīrī* or Self. Thus Brahman as inherently related to *jīva* is one but by virtue of their *svarūpa*, the two are different. Hence the defects found in the universe do not affect Brahman, even though it is the creator of the universe.

e) Brahman is not in need of Accessories for Creation of the universe.

Another minor objection is raised against the Vedānta theory of Brahman as the creator of the universe. Generally it is seen that for the production of an object, such as a pot by the potter, the requisite accessories (*upakaraṇa*) are needed besides the material (*upādāna*) and the person to produce the object. Though Brahman may be admitted as having the capacity to function as material and instrumental cause, it does not have any kind of accessories for the creation of the variegated universe. The Upaniṣadic text merely states that prior to creation, Brahman alone existed but there is no mention of the presence of the requisite accessories. Hence the theory of Brahman as the creator of the universe is not sound. This issue is discussed in the *adhikaraṇa* named *upasaṁhāradarśanadhikaraṇa*.

Bādārayaṇa rejects this objection. The relevant *sūtra* reads: *upasaṁhāra darśanāt na iti cet na kṣīravaddhi*. It means: "If it is said that the accessories are needed for the production of an object, and in the absence of it in respect of Brahman, it cannot be the cause of the universe, the reply is it is untenable as in the instance of milk which has the power of becoming curd out of its own accord without the aids. Brahman which has the power to produce anything, can also create the universe without any accessories. Vedānta Deśika explains that Brahman possesses the *śakti* or power to create the universe without any accessories out of its *saṁkalpa*. He cites several examples to substantiate this point. The milk changes itself to curds on its own accord. The magnet attracts the iron by its own presence. The spider creates the web out of its saliva. The celestial deities create the heavenly objects by their will. A human being can make his body move by his mere desire without any accessories. Hence it is not inappropriate that the all-powerful Brahman creates the universe out of its *saṁkalpa* without the aid of any accessory.

f) Brahman does not transform itself into the Universe.

One other serious objection is raised against Brahman as the material cause of the universe. If Brahman itself becomes the universe, the question is raised whether Brahman as a whole undergoes transformation into the universe or only a part of it. In either case it affects the very nature of Brahman which being indivisible should not be subject to any change. Bādarāyaṇa discusses this issue and provides an appropriate answer to it in the *Kṛtsnaprasakty-adhikaraṇa*. The relavant *sūtra* reads: *kṛtsna prsaktiḥ niravayava śabda kopo vā*[35]. Its general meaning is, according to Rāmānuja, if Brahman is wholly transformed into the universe, it would exhaust itself in becoming the universe and there would be no Brahman left other than the universe for the purpose of meditation and attainment by the seeker of *mokṣa*. If on the other hand, a part of Brahman is transformed, Brahman would be divisible. But such a position would violate the Scriptural texts which speak of Brahman as *niravaya* or devoid of parts.

Bādarāyaṇa refutes this objection by taking recourse to the *śruti* or the Revealed Scripture as the sole dependable authority to determine these issues. The relevant *sūtra* reads: *śrutestu śabda-mūlatvat*[36]. It means, according to Rāmānuja, that such criticisms are not valid because of the Scriptural support (*śruteḥ*). That is, the Scriptural texts point out that Brahman is *niravaya* and that it also creates a variegated universe. Scripture being the sole authority in matters which are super-normal, we have to accept its teaching even though it may not appear logical. But it is also pointed out in a subsequent *sūtra* that Brahman possesses *vicitra śakti* or extraordinary powers to cause the universe through its *pariṇāma* without affecting its *svarūpa*. The Vedānta Sūtra says: *ātmani caivam vicitrāśca hi*[37] - "So also it is seen in the case of Ātman (Brahman) that it possesses variegated power". The Upaniṣad also says: *parāsya śaktiḥ vividhaiva śrūyate svābhāvikī jñāna bala kriyā ca*[38] - "His knowledge and power are revealed to be manifold". Brahman is thus endowed with extra-ordinary powers and it is therefore possible for it to create the universe without affecting its *svarūpa*. To overcome this problem, Śaṁkara resorts to *vivarta vāda* or the theory of illusory appearance of Brahman on the basis of the doctrine of *avidyā*. The universe and its origination in Brahman are fabrication of mere *avidyā* or the cosmic principle of illusion, which conceals the true nature of Brahman and projects its appearance as the universe. What is caused by *avidyā* does not affect the true nature of Brahman. The universe is not really caused or created by Brahman, but it is a mere illusory appearance. But there is no mention in the *Vedānta sūtras* about *māyā* or *avidyā as conceived by Śaṁkara* or even the concept of *vivarta*. Nor is it supported by the Upaniṣads. Hence there is no inconsistency in the stand taken by Rāmānuja to explain the material causality of Brahman on the basis of *pariṇāma* stated by *Vedānta-sūtra* and explained by Rāmānuja which is in conformity with the Upaniṣadic teachings.

g) The Purpose of Creation of the Universe.

The possibility of Brahman being the creator of the universe is questioned on the ground that there is no useful purpose served by such a creation (*na prayojanatvāt*[39]). It is asked whether the creation of the universe is for the benefit of the creator himself or for someone else. It cannot be for the benefit of Brahman, since it is stated to be one whose desires are ever-fulfilled (*avāpta samastakāmaḥ*). If it is for others out of the compassion of the creator, then the creation of the universe filled with suffering is not justified (*kāruṇyat duḥkhasṛṣṭiḥ na bhavati*). Hence the theory of Brahman as the cause of the creation of the universe is not sound.

This theory is discussed in a separate *adhikaraṇa* named '*na prayojanatvādhikaraṇa*'. The above objection is ill-founded, contends Vedānta Deśika (*andhacodyam*). As stated by Bādarāyaṇa, the creation of the universe by *Īśvara* (Brahman) is a mere sport for Him (*līlāsau lokavat syāt*). This is explained on the analogy of the king. Though the king has no specific object to achieve, he indulges in the sports or gambling activities, purely out of pleasure. If God creates the universe as a divine sport for His own pleasure, how could He be regarded as '*avāptasamastakāmaḥ*'?. In reply Vedānta Deśika points out that the concept of *avāptasamastakāmah* does not mean that God has no desires at all or that His desires are already fulfilled, but on the contrary it implies that whenever He wills a thing, it is accomplished without any obstruction (*abhimata samaye siddhiḥ*).

One other objection is raised. If God is the creator of the universe which is full of suffering and also there exists wide disparities in the suffering and happiness of individuals, He would be subject to partiality (*vaiṣamya*) and cruelty (*nairghaṇya*). This is not tenable says Bādarāyaṇa because He creates the individuals on the basis of their *karma* or their past deeds (*karma sāpekṣatvāt*). God dispenses good to those who have done good deeds and evil to those who have done wicked deeds. This is also supported by the Scriptural text – *'sādhukāri sādhurbhavati pāpakāri papo bhavati'*. Hence *Īśvara* is free from the defect of being cruel. *Karma,* which is the cause of birth in different strata, is *anadi* or beginningless, just as *jīva* is *anādi* (*anāditvāt upapadyate*). That is, the *jīvas* along with the variegated *karma* transmigrate birth after birth continuously from beginningless time like the seed and sprout (*bijāṅkurādi krama viṣama bhāva anādi karmaughabhājāṁ*[40])

1. VS I-4-23
2. This is the meaning provided by the grammarian. See Pātañjali Mahābhāṣya I-4-30 – *jani kartuḥ prakṛtiḥ*. Madhva does not admit Brahman as *upādāna kāraṇa*. He interprets this word to mean Viṣṇu
3. Ch. Up. VI-1-3.
4. *Ibid* Ch. Up. VI-1-4 to 6.
5. Ch. Up. VI-2-3. See also Tait. Up. *'so'kāmayata bahusyāṁ prajāyeyeti'*. *See* also V.S. I-4-24 *'abhidhyopadesācca'*
6. Tait. Up. II-7.
7. VS I-4-26 and 27.
8. Br. Up. III-4-70.
9. *See* AS verse 144.
10. VS I-4-25.
11. VS I-4-28.
12. AS verse 146. *tasmāt kartāpi devaḥ prakṛtirapi bhavet sarvatattvāntarātmā. kartāpi* means *nimitta-bhūtopi. Prakṛtirapi bhavet* means Brahman can become *upādāna kāraṇa.*
13. *See* AS verse 148
14. *See* RB II-1-15. *See* also TMK 1-20.
15. VS II-1-15
16. Ch. Up. VI-1-1
17. Br. Up. III-4-7.
18. Sub. Up. II
19. Ch. Up. VI-3-3.
20. AS verse 167
21. VS III-2-26.
22. VS III-2-27.
23. VS III-2-28.
24. VS II-3-42
25. RB III-2-28.

26. See section III-(2) for fuller implication of *śarīra*.
27. See Svet. Up. V-2
28. VS-II-1-1.
29. For further implications of the definition, see R.B. II-1-9. Also, F.V.V. pp50-51.
30. VS. II-1-14
31. VS II-1-21
32. VS II-1-22
33. AS verse 168.
34. VS I-4-22.
35. VS II-1-26.
36. VS II-1-27
37. VS II-1-28.
38. Svet. Up. VI-8.
39. VS II-1-32.
40. AS verse 173.

Chapter Six

THE THEORY OF COSMIC CREATION

In the first *adhyāya* of *Brahma-sūtra* known as *Samanvayādhyāya*, Bādarāyaṇa establishes by a systematic and methodical examination of the important passages dealing with Brahman, that it is the sole cause of the universe (*jagatkāraṇa*). In the second *adhyāya* which is titled *Avirodhādhyāya*, he attempts to reaffirm on a solid basis this important Vedānta doctrine by a critical examination of the theories of the other schools of thought which were prevalent during his time and which were opposed to the central doctrine enunciated in the preceding *adhyāya*. The schools which come up for consideration in the order in which it is stated in the *Brahma-sūtra*, are: Sāṁkhya, Yoga, Vaiśeṣika, the four schools of Buddhism – Vaibhāṣika, Sautrāntika, Yogācāra and Mādhyamika, Jaina, Pāśupata, and Pāñcarātra. Of these, the schools of Sāṁkhya and Yoga receive special attention since the founders of these systems are Kapila, a reputed Vedic sage and Hiraṇyagarbha, a Vedic deity. The followers of these schools do not admit Brahman as the cause of the universe. They ascribe the origin of the universe to *prakṛti*, the primordial cosmic matter, which either independently or through the association of *Īśvara* (in the case of Yoga school) evolves itself into the universe. The schools of Vaiśeṣika, Buddhist and Jaina trace the origin of the universe to the *paramāṇus* or atoms which are infinitesimal and suprasensible reals. The school of Pāśupata upholds that *Īśvara*, named

Paśupati, is only the *nimitta kāraṇa* of the universe. As these views are opposed to the Vedānta doctrine of Brahman, they need to be refuted in order to prove the soundness of the Vedānta theory (*svapakṣasthāpanāya parapakāḥ pratikṣepa*). The *Pāñcarātra* school, however, is taken up for consideration for the purpose of clarifying that its teachings are not opposed to Vedānta as claimed by some critics.

The following eight *Adhikaraṇas* of the second *pāda* of the second *adhyāya* are devoted for this purpose.

1. Racanā-nupapatty-adhikaraṇa
2. Mahad-dhīrghādhikaraṇa
3. Samudāyādhikaraṇa
4. Upalabdhy-adhikaraṇa
5. Sarvathānupapatty-adhikaraṇa
6. Ekasmin-asambhavādhikaraṇa
7. Paśupatyādhikaraṇa
8. Utpatty-asambhavādhikaraṇa

The scope of the critical examination is confined to show that the philosophical theories of these schools in general and, in particular, the views advanced by some of them regarding the process of cosmic creation are logically untenable and thereby establish that the Vedānta doctrine of Brahman as the cause of the universe is free from such inconsistencies. In some of the *Adhikaraṇas* of the third and fourth *pāda*, Bādarāyaṇa also discusses the ontological status of the evolutes of *prakṛti* such as *viyat* or ether and *tejas* or the element of fire to prove that Brahman is the cause of these evolutes. In this connection the process of the formation of the physical universe by Brahman is also explained. We shall consider all these matters as presented by Vedānta Deśika in the *Adhikaraṇa sārāvalī*.

I. The Sāṁkhya Theory of Cosmic Evolution

This is discussed in the *Racanānupapatty-adhikaraṇa*. According to the Sāṁkhyas, the *mūla-prakṛti* or the primordial cosmic matter is the cause of the universe. *Prakṛti* is constituted of three *guṇas* viz. *sattva, rajas* and *tamas*. It is non-sentient in character (*acetana*), one, omnipresent (*sarvagata*) and constantly changing (*satata-vikriyā*). Prior to its evolution the three *guṇas* remain in a state of equilibrium. When this equilibrium is disturbed, it evolves itself into various modifications in a particular order. The first evolute of *prakṛti* is known as *mahat* and from *mahat* evolves *ahaṁkāra*. The *ahaṁkāra* is also characterized by the three *guṇas* and accordingly it is of three kinds: *sāttvika, rājasa* and *tāmasa*. From *sāttvika ahaṁkāra*, in which the *sattva* element is predominant, the eleven sense organs including the *manas* are evolved. From the *tāmasa ahaṁkāra*, the five *tanmātras* or subtle elements evolve. From the *tanmātras* arise the five gross elements – *ākāśa, vāyu, tejas, jala* and *pṛthivī*. *Puruṣa* which is distinct from *prakṛti*, is sentient, eternal, all-pervasive and unchanging. Besides *puruṣa* and *prakṛti* as the two fundamental ontological principles, the ancient Saṁkhyas do not admit *Īśvara* or God as a separate Being.[1]

The origin of the universe is explained on the basis of the evolution of the unmanifest *prakṛti* into manifest universe of its own accord. That is, when the equilibrium of the three *guṇas* is disturbed, it evolves itself into twenty three evolutes including the five physical elements. The physical universe is caused by the combination of the five elements.

Bādarāyaṇa does not accept this theory of cosmic creation. His criticism is mainly directed to point out that the orderly process of evolution of the *prakṛti* into the manifest universe cannot take place without the control and direction of a Sentient Being. The relevant sūtra reads: *Racanā-nupatteśca na anumānam pravṛtteśca*[2]. It means: *prakṛti* (which is established on the basis of inference) cannot be the cause of the universe because of the untenability (*anupapatty*) of cosmic creation (without it being guided by an intelligent Being) and also the need of an intelligent Being for the initiation of the evolutionary activity (*pravṛtteśca*). The implication of the *sūtra* is that *prakṛti* being a non-sentient entity, cannot evolve itself into manifold universe unless it is guided or controlled by an intelligent Being possessing the knowledge of the object. As Vedānta Deśika explains, we have seen in our ordinary experience that objects such as a piece of cloth and pots are made by persons having knowledge of the objects such as a weaver or potter. In the case of mountains, oceans etc, these are regarded as creations of God on the authority of the Scriptural texts. It is therefore inconceivable how the non-sentient *prakṛti* can evolve itself into the manifold variegated universe without the guidance of an intelligent Being.

The Sāṁkhyas cite a few illustrations in defence of their theory. The green grass consumed by a cow is converted into milk. The milk becomes curds. The water particles of the ocean are formed into thick water-bearing clouds. The magnet is found to attract iron. In these cases there seems to be no role of an intelligent person.

But this argument is not tenable, contends Vedānta Deśika. In all these cases, there is the role of a sentient Being which causes such changes (*tad akhilaṁ cetana adhiṣṭhitam*). This is proved by the Vedāntins on the strength of the Scriptural texts or on the basis of inference by the Vaiśeṣikas.

The Sāṁkhyas argue that the presence of the *Puruṣa*, the eternal sentient individual Self, with *prakṛti*, can cause the evolution of *prakṛti* into the universe. This is explained on the analogy of a blind and lame person. A blind person is enabled to move with the help of a lame person. In the same way, with the mere association or presence of the intelligent *Puruṣa*, the *prakṛti* can evolve itself into the universe. Even this explanation is unsatisfactory. *Puruṣa* in the Sāṁkhya system is present eternally and it is not possible to account for the initiation of the evolutionary process at a particular point of time on that basis.

There are other inconsistencies in the Sāṁkhya theory of cosmic creation. According to the Sāṁkhyas, the *prakṛti* comprising of the three *guṇas* is the cause of the creation of the universe, when the equilibrium of the *guṇas* is disturbed. Dissolution of the universe takes place when the same three *guṇas* remain in a state of equipoise. But *prakṛti* comprising of the three *guṇas* is *vibhu* or all-pervasive. What is *vibhu* all the time cannot admit itself the two different states of creation and dissolution (*teṣām nityam vibhutve sama-viṣama daśādi kīdṛg vadeyuḥ*[3]).

The Sāṁkhyas also account for bondage and release on the basis of the superimposition of the *prakṛti* on the *Puruṣa* (*anyonyā-adhyāsa*) and total dissociation of *puruṣa* with *prakṛti* respectively on the analogy of the white crystal and red flower placed close to it. The pure white crystal is mistaken to be red on account of the superimposition of the redness on the crystal and when the flower is taken away, the crystal remains in its pure form. In the same way, *puruṣa* who is eternally pure and free from bondage is supposed to be bound on account of its conjunction with mind or *antaḥkaraṇa* which is a product of *prakṛti*. When *puruṣa* is dissociated with *antaḥkaraṇa* and all its functions, it becomes free. This is how bondage and liberation from bondage are accounted for.

This is also an unsatisfactory theory, contends Vedānta Deśika, because both the *puruṣa* and *prakṛti* do not possess *cetanatva* or knowledge as a *dharma*. *Prakṛti* is non-sentient in character. *Puruṣa*, though it is regarded as sentient, is not admitted by the Sāṁkhyas as the subject of knowledge. It is *nirlepa* or untouched by all mental qualities such as *jñāna*, desire, capacity to function (*prayatna*). How then such a *puruṣa* can become associated with bondage and also liberated from it.

Further the Sāṁkhyas state that the main function of *prakṛti* is to cause bondage to the *puruṣa* in the form of experience of pleasure and pain and also bring liberation for it.[4]

If *puruṣa*, is *nityamukta* for the Sāṁkhyas, how can it be subject to bondage and liberation from it? All these teachings, if subjected to logical analysis are found to be inconsistent. Hence the Sāṁkhya theory of *Pradhāna* as the cause of the universe, is not sound.

II. Vaiśeṣika Theory of Cosmic Creation

This is examined in the *Mahad-dīrgādhikaraṇa*. The Vaiśeṣikas, unlike the Sāṁkhyas admit *Īśvara* but they ascribe the origin of the universe to the *paramāṇus* or the atoms which are eternal, partless, infinitesimal and suprasensuous reals. The four gross elements – earth, water, fire and air of which the universe is constituted are not derived from the *prakṛti* but from such atoms. The process of origination of these physical elements takes place as follows. When two atoms, for example, of earth, come together, they form a binary compound known as *dvyaṇuka*. Like the primary atoms, it is infinitely small in size and is therefore supersensuous. Three such binaries, suitably adjusted produce a triad known as *tryaṇuka*, which is identified with the dust particle we notice in the sun-beam through the window. This is regarded as a visible entity. Its magnitude is finite and all other finite objects are made out of such triads. The large size of an object such as a mountain or the small size of an object such as a mustard seed is due to the combination of a number of *tryaṇukas* formed out of the primary atoms. The existence of the atoms is deduced from the known divisibility of perceivable material objects. According to the Vaiśeṣikas the divisibility must terminate at some stage and cannot go on indefinitely. The terminal stage in the process of this division represents *paramāṇus* or the atoms which are the uncaused cause of all that is finite in the universe.

Bādarāyaṇa rejects this theory. The main point of criticism is directed towards the impossibility of the combination of the *paramāṇus*. The relevant sūtra reads: *Mahad-dhīrghavad-vā hṛsva parimaṇḍalābhyām*[5]. The word *hṛsva* means *dvyaṇuka* and *parimaṇḍala* means *paramāṇus*. *Mahad-dhīrgha* implies *tryaṇuka*. The general meaning of the *sūtra* is that the theory of the origination of the universe from the atoms is unsound in the same way as the formation of the *dvyaṇukas* out of the *paramāṇus*. By way of elucidation, Vedānta Deśika points out that the very formation of the *dvyaṇukas* by the combination of two primary atoms is inconceivable. Since the atoms are partless (*niravaya*), the question is asked: When two *paramāṇus* come together, do they combine as a whole or only in parts? If they combine as a whole, there would be complete interpenetration. That is, one submerges in the other and consequently the *dvyaṇukas* formed out of it is not of bigger magnitude. How then could such *dvyaṇukas* produce the things bigger than themselves? If on the contrary, the atoms combine in parts, then the atoms should be admitted to be as possessing parts or sides as in the case of physical objects. We speak of two physical objects coming together only in respect of a side. But such a possibility is ruled out in respect of the atoms which according to the Vaiśeṣikas do not possess any part or spatial property. Thus, if the combination of two *paramāṇus* cannot be explained satisfactorily, the theory of *paramāṇus* as the material cause of the universe cannot be established.

The theory of Vaiśeṣikas also suffers from another serious defect. How does the original combination or conjunction of two primary atoms take place? It needs some principle which causes the movement of the atoms to come together. For this purpose, the Vaiśesikas posit the *adṛṣṭa* or the unseen force. Where does it abide and how does it operate? If it abides in the individual soul, it cannot cause motion in the atoms which are outside it. If this be possible, then *ātman* being nitya should always cause the creation. If on the other hand, it abides in the atoms, then the *adṛṣṭa* being non-sentient cannot have the capacity of bringing about the combination of the atoms. Besides, *adṛṣṭa* caused by the deeds of the souls cannot exist in the atoms.

It may be possible to explain the operation of *adṛṣṭa* by conceiving *Īśvara* as instrumental in bringing together the atoms. That is, *Īśvara,* through His *saṁkalpa* (will) can cause the combination of atoms as *dvyaṇukas* and *tryaṇukas* and through them the formation of the universe. But the theory of *Īśvara* which is formulated on the basis of *anumāna* or inference, is defective as stated in the *Śāstra-yonitvādhikaraṇa*. If *Īśvara* is admitted as the Supreme Being endowed with omniscience and omnipotence, on the authority of the Upaniṣads, as the Vedāntins do, then it would be possible to account for the creation of the universe through His *saṁkalpa*. But such a view is not acceptable to the Vaiśeṣikas and hence the theory of *paramāṇus* as the cause of the universe is unsound (*asamañjasa*).

III. Buddhist Theories of Cosmic Origin

There are four schools of Buddhism viz. Vaibhāṣika, Sautrāntika, Yogācāra and Mādhyamika. The Vaibhāṣikas and the Sautrāntikas trace the origin of the universe to the *paramāṇus* which are regarded as momentary in character (*kṣaṇika*). The Yogācāras and the Mādhyamikas offer different views regarding the nature of physical phenomena. All these theories stand opposed to the Vedānta doctrine of Brahman and universe and hence they are taken up by Bādarāyaṇa for critical examination. The following three *adhikaraṇas* are exclusively devoted to the consideration of this matter.

1) *Samudāyādhikarana* which discusses the theories of Vaibhāṣikas and Sautrāntikas.
2) *Upalabdhy-adhikaraṇa* dealing with Yogācāra theory.
3) *Sarvathā-anupapatty adhikaraṇa* which examines the Mādhyamika theory.

a) Vaibhāṣika Theory

The origin of the universe which is traced to the *paramāṇus* is explained as follows. The four physical elements viz. *pṛthivī* or earth, *ap* or water, *vāyu* or air and *tejas* or fire which are evident to perceptual experience are regarded as constituted of atoms. Each element possesses certain qualities. The atoms of earth possess qualities of colour, taste, touch and smell. The atoms of water contain qualities of colour, taste and touch. The atoms of *tejas* possess the qualities of colour and touch while the atoms of *vāyu* contain the quality of touch only. When these atoms combine together, they become the aggregates of four physical elements (*bhūta*). The physical bodies, the sense organs (*indriyas)* and the objects of the external world are formed by the combination of the aggregates of four physical elements. The Vaibhāṣikas do not admit ātman or soul as a separate entity. The mind called *citta* and the series of mental ideas serve the purpose of the self through which the knowledge of the external objects arise. All things, both the external objects and the internal ideas are momentary (*kṣaṇika*) in character.

Bādarāyaṇa rejects this theory as most unsound. If all things exist only for a moment, the very formation of the universe cannot take place out of the aggregates of *paramāṇus* and the aggregates of physical and mental atoms of the bodies and other objects.[6] *paramāṇus*, according to the Vaibhāṣikas originate in the first moment and the same in the next moment combine themselves into an aggregate and in the third moment these become the physical elements such as *pṛthivī* out of which the formation of the universe takes place. If the *paramāṇu* perishes in the very next moment soon after it comes into existence how then can it cause the *pṛthivī* etc out of which the bodies arise? If *paramāṇus* are momentary in nature, physical elements constituted of the *paramāṇus* and the formation of the universe out of such elements is inconceivable. Even the cognition of the external objects by the *citta* or mind through sense contacts cannot also be explained if the objects and the *buddhi* do not have a permanent existence.

b) Sautrāntika Theory

The Sautrāntikas also offer a similar kind of explanation regarding the formation of the universe. The criticisms leveled against the Vaibhāṣika regarding the formation of the universe also apply to the Sautrāntikas.

They also maintain that the external object is not directly perceived but it is to be inferred on the basis of the cognition of the objects that takes place. The justification for such a view is that objects, being momentary cannot be present at the time they are seen. If they were present, they would persist for at least two moments. That is, when they served as the cause of perception and when they were actually perceived. If things have only momentary existence, then it is only a past thing that can be perceived. So what is present externally when perception takes place is only the successor in the object series of the member that served as its cause. The previous member leaves its impression on the percipient mind before it disappears and it is from impression (*ākāra*) that we infer the prior existence of the corresponding object.

This theory is subjected to severe criticism by Vedānta Deśika in the *Tattva-muktā-kalāpa*. All the arguments advanced by the Sautrāntika Buddhists are examined in detail and refuted. The main point of criticism is that it is impossible for an object to transfer its image or impression to *jñāna*. The Sautrāntika adopts the analogy of the reflection of the face in the mirror in support of its theory. Though we do not see our face, it is perceived when it is reflected in a mirror. This is what is meant by *ākāra-samarpaṇa* or transference of the image. Such an explanation does not hold good in respect of knowledge and object. Jñāna by its nature is devoid of any form (*nirākāra*). How could there be a reflection of it[7]! In the case of the mirror, reflection is possible in the glass because it is tainted with mercury. There is no such conditioning factor (*upādhi*) in respect of *jñāna*. Besides, *jñāna* as well as the object, according to the Soutrantika are momentary. By the time the object transfers its image to *jñāna*, the former would have changed. The object to be reflected and the recipient of the reflection are not of the same temporal order and hence the reflection of the objects is not possible.

It may be possible to explain the transference of the quality of one entity to the other by way of proximity as in the example of white crystal placed next to the red flower. But this explanation would not hold in respect of knowledge and the object since there is no common feature between the two (*dvayamapi ekākāroparaktam na*). Only two entities having physical form could be juxtaposed but for the Sautrāntikas both are formless (*vyaṁśe naivābhimukhyaṁ*). Besides, all objects are momentary and at the time knowledge arises, the particular momentary object ceases to exist. Hence the *ākāra* of the object cannot be passed on to knowledge.

c) The Theory of Yogācara

Unlike the Vaibhāṣika and Sautrāntika, this school of Buddhism denies even the existence of the external objects. According to it, knowledge which is described as *vijñāna* is the sole reality and its content is false. There is neither subject nor object but only a succession of ideas. The specific form which cognition at any particular instant assumes is determined not by an outside object presented to it as the realists believe but by the latent impression (*vāsanā*) left behind by past experience which in turn goes back to another impression, that again to another experience and so on, indefinitely in a beginningless series. Only these ideas (*vijñāna*) are real and the external objects have no reality of their own. The latter are just projections of the internal (mental) ideas. Hence they are called *vijñānavādin*, since apart from the series of mental ideas, nothing really exists. As this doctrine denies the very existence of the external world and also the process of knowing the external objects, it is subjected to a critical examination in a separate *adhikaraṇa* named as *Upalabdhy-adhikaraṇa*. The criticism is confined to two important points. First, it is not possible to deny the existence of external objects because our experience reveals that knowledge is always related to a subject and also to an object (*na abhāva upalabdheḥ*[8]). Secondly, the external objects experienced by us are not similar to the dream objects, that is, the objects experienced in the dream state (*vaidharmyācca na svapnādivat*[9]).

In the *Tattva-muktā-kalāpa* Vedānta Deśika presents a more detailed criticism against the theory of Yogācāra after examining all the possible arguments advanced by them. We shall take note of the important points of the criticism.

The main point of criticism is that knowledge which manifests as 'I know' is an internal phenomenon, whereas the object which manifests as 'This is an external entity', and the two which are distinct, can never be one and the same. That is 'knowing' and 'being' can never be identical as claimed by the Yogācāra.

Against this, the following argument is put forward by Yogācāra. There is an invariable association between knowledge and its content (*sahopalambha niyama*). Thought and objects always appear together and neither can appear without the other. It is not therefore correct to assume that they are distinct and they may well be regarded as different phases of one and the same factor.

Vedānta Deśika refutes this argument. The fact that knowledge and object are found together does not establish that knowledge and object are one and the same. There is invariable concomitance or association between smoke and fire but nevertheless it does not follow that they are the same. In fact the very concept of 'invariable association' is meaningful only when two separate entities exist (*sahamāti-niyamādyanyathaiva atra siddham*[10]).

Another argument is advanced by the Yogācara based on the analogy of the dream where experience takes place without corresponding objects. That is, in dream we experience the objects but the objects experienced do not actually exist. In the same way, though our ordinary experience may refer to external objects, the latter do not really exist. This is rejected on the ground that there is a difference between the dream objects and the objects seen in the waking state. Thus it is stated in the *sūtra: vaidharmyācca na svapnādivat*[11]. According to the Viśiṣṭadvaitin, even the dream objects are real for the duration of the dream since these are the creations of *Īśvara* as stated in the Upaniṣads. If these are still regarded as non-real it is because these are sublated in the waking experience. But nevertheless, they exist as long as one is dreaming as otherwise there cannot be any experience of it. But the objects of the waking state are not sublated. They do exist all the time as long as they last and as such they are real.

Vedānta Deśika further observes that knowledge which arises only in relation to objects cannot be devoid of content. In the case of perceptual knowledge, perception takes place only when there is sense contact with the objects that exist. *Smṛti* or memory also occurs with regard to an object or event already experienced. Even illusory cognition presupposes previous experience of an object. Taking the instance of illusion of shell-silver, if shell did not exist, it could not have been mistaken for silver. Thus all our knowledge depends on the existence of objects. The admission of the reality of external objects is therefore absolutely essential for the functioning of knowledge. If knowledge has no relation to any object other than itself, it ceases to be knowledge.

Further, it is a matter of common experience that knowledge is variegated and this diversity is possible because of the differences in their contents. If existence of objects is denied, the diversity of knowledge cannot be explained.

The *Vijñānavādin* tries to explain the diversity of experience on the basis of the variegated *vāsanās*, which are in the form of a continuous series like the flowing river from a beginningless time. *Vijñāna* is also a series of momentary mental processes, and the *vāsanās* which are associated with them influence *vijñāna* and thereby cause the diversity of experience.

Such an explanation does not hold good, contends Vedānta Deśika. *Vāsanā* for a Buddhist is *kṣaṇika*. That is, it changes every moment. In the series of cognitions, when the earlier cognition ceases to exist, the *vāsanā* associated with it is also erased and hence it cannot influence the next momentary cognition. If the series of cognitions is admitted as one continuous cognition, it may be possible to account for the continuation of the *vāsanā* and its influence on the cognition. Alternatively reality of external objects is to be admitted to account for diversity of experience. Neither is accepted by the *Vijñanavādin* and his theory of knowledge is therefore untenable.

d) Mādhyamika Theory

The Mādhyamika Buddhists advance an absolutely different view regarding the nature of the objects of the external world. According to them the objects of the external world do not have real existence. No entity in the universe is of the nature of sat or existent. If something is sat, it should not be sublated and should always exist everywhere in the same form. It cannot be otherwise, since any change in its *svarūpa* is not possible. Nothing in the universe is of the form of *asat*. What is *asat* should not appear to cognition. But it is not so, because at sometime or some place or in some manner it appears to cognition. It cannot be both sat and *asat* because of the defects pointed out in respect of first two alternatives. Besides, it involves self-contradiction. Nor could it be said that it is devoid of *sat* and *asat* because of the same objection stated with regard to the third alternative. These are the four possible modes of predication, and *tattva* or what is considered to be a real entity cannot be characterized by any of these predications, taken either singly or taken in combination. That is *tattva* is neither real nor unreal nor real-unreal nor different from both real and unreal but different from all the four alternatives. Thus they describe *tattva* as *'catuṣkoṭi vinirmuktam'*[12]. That is, it is *śūnya* in the words of Mādhyamika or absolutely indeterminable. If this be the nature of the *tattva*, then the universe and the objects do not exist as such.

Bādarāyaṇa rejects this doctrine. The *adhikaraṇa* named as *Sarvathā-nupapatty-adhikaraṇa* is devoted to this matter.

The relevant sūtra reads: *sarvathā-anupapatteśca*[13]. It means – "The doctrine of Mādhyamika, that everything in this universe is indeterminable (*sarvaśūnya*) is totally untenable". The implication of this, as explained by Vedānta Deśika is that it is purely a speculative theory without having any support of the *pramāṇas* (*amānataḥ sveṣṭā vāda*). He raises two alternatives. Is this theory established on the basis of admission of the generally accepted *pramāṇas*? Or is it proved without any *pramāṇas*. If *pramāṇas* are accepted, the Mādhyamika cannot prove such a theory. If it is not accepted, then the theory stands defeated and the theory of his opponent would stand justified (*tat-prahāṇe paramatam akṣobhyam*). That is, if the theory of *sarvaśūnyatva* is rejected, the reality of the universe accepted by the opponent becomes established.

The Mādhyamika attempts to prove his theory on the basis of the admission of the concept of *samvṛti*, an illusory principle which makes what is non-existent as existent. Even the postulation of such a concept would not help to prove that everything is *śūnya* (*asat samvṛtiḥ na arthasiddhyai*).

Vedānta Deśika points out that it is impossible to conceive *tattva* as absolutely indeterminable (*śūnya*). The words *śūnya* (void) and *tuccha* (non-existent) which appear to mean total negation (*sarvaśūnya*) do not imply absolute non-existence. Negation necessarily presupposes its counter correlate. It does not deny total non-existence at any time or at any place. When we say that an object does not exist, it only means that it exists at some other place or at some other time, but not that it is absolutely non-existent like the sky-flower. Absolute non-existence (*sarvathā-śūnyatva*) is not logically tenable. What does not exist here and now does exist elsewhere and some other time. It is not therefore correct to deny the reality of external objects and also the *jñāna*, *jñātā* etc on the basis of *śūnya-vāda* (*nirupādhika niṣedhaḥ adṛṭāt na kalpyaḥ*[14]).

One other argument is advanced by the Mādhyamika in support of his theory. An object such as a pot, does not exist prior to its production. Nor does it exist after it is destroyed. What does not exist, either prior to its production or after it is destroyed, ceases to exist. It does not also exist during the middle period like the sky-flower (*gagana kusumavat syānna madhye*). This argument is untenable, contends Vedānta Deśika. The very fact that the pot is perceived to exist at present, does not prove its non-existence.

An objection is also raised on the basis of the causal relation between the cause and effect. Is the effect produced from the cause that undergoes modification (*vikāra*) or from one which does not (*avikṛtiḥ*)?. If it be the former, then it is asked whether or not this modification is produced by some other modification. If this question is pursued, we are condemned to an infinite regress. If it be the latter, then the effect would abide all the time the cause continues.

This is an irrelevant objection, contends Vedānta Deśika. It is well known that the effect is caused by the association of the requisite accessories with the causal substance (*sāmagryā kārya siddheḥ*). The lump of clay undergoes modification into a pot when only the accessories such as the potter, the wheel and stick are operative. There is therefore no room for the fallacy of infinite regress in respect of *kāraṇa*.

In the absence of the admission of the valid *pramāṇas*, it is not possible to prove the theory of the Mādhyamikas viz. everything is *śūnya*. If on the basis of the concept of *samvṛti*, an illusory principle postulated by the Mādhyamika, all their theories, though not valid, appear to be valid, then on the basis of the same explanation, it is possible to assert that even the stand adopted by the opponent and also the criticisms offered by them are all valid. Thus, by resorting to the concept of *samvṛti*, which corresponds to the Advaita concept of *māyā*, the cosmic principle of illusion, it is not possible to establish the theory of *sarva-śūnyatva*.

Incidentally Vedānta Deśika briefly enumerates the various theories of error and truth. These are: *Anyathākhyāti* of Naiyāyikas or the theory of mis-apprehension of shell for silver, *akhyāti* of Mīmāṁsakas or the theory of non-discrimination between shell and silver, *viṣayarahita-dhīḥ* of some Buddhists or the erroneous knowledge without a content, the theory of cognition of something without an objective basis (*anadhiṣṭhāna dhiḥ*), held by some Buddhists, *bāhyārthākārayogaḥ* – the transference of the *ākāra* of the external object on the internal cognition (view of Sautrāntikas), error as different from sat and *asat* (*sadasat itara dhīḥ*) held by Advaitin, contentless cognition (*śūnya-dhīḥ*) of Mādhyamikas, *ātmadhīḥ* or the cognition itself projecting in a different form held by Yogācāra. These theories advanced by other schools are wrong. The sound and correct theory is that all that is perceptually seen is real including the vision of silver in shell (*yathārthakhyāti*) as this is in conformity with the Scriptural teaching and the *pañcīkaraṇa* theory. But in a few exceptional cases where *pañcīkaraṇa* is not applicable, it is *satkhyāti* combined with *akhyāti*[15]

iv) Jaina Theory of universe

The Jainas also trace the origin of the universe to the *paramāṇus* and they do not accept *Īśvara* as the cause of the universe. Bādarāyana therefore takes it up for critical examination as it is opposed to the Vedānta doctrine. This subject is considered in a separate *adhikaraṇa* named *Ekasmin-asambhavādhikaraṇa*. The main criticism is directed to prove the logical untenability of the central theory of *sapta-bhangī* or the seven-fold description of the nature of all the entities in the universe developed by the Jainas.

According to the Jainas the universe comprises of *jīvas* and *ajīvas* but there is no *Īśvara*. They admit six categories (*dravyas*) viz. *jīva, dharma, adharma, pudgala, kāla* and *ākāśa*. The term *pudgala* refers to the substance possessing the qualities of *rūpa, rasa, gandha* and *sparśa*. It is of two types, one in the form of *paramāṇus* and the other in the form of the conglomerations of *paramāṇus*. These are air, water, fire, earth and all kinds of material bodies.[16] The universe is formed out of such conglomeration of *paramāṇus*.

Regarding the nature of the objects in the universe, it is not of one uniform character but manifold (*anekānta*). When we look at a thing from different view points, we arrive at different conclusions. Thus, a jug is a *dravya* in the sense that it is of the nature of collection of atoms but it is not a *dravya* like another substance like *ākāśa*. It is a *dravya* in one sense and not a *dravya* in another sense. In the same way, an object looked at from different standpoints could be described as different in character. By adopting such a theory it is concluded that objects are different as well as non-different.

Jainas seek to justify the possibility of different views regarding the nature of an entity from different standpoints on the basis of the *syādvāda,* also named as *saptabhaṅgi* or the seven-fold formula. The word '*syād*' means maybe. The reality, in their opinion is extremely indeterminate in its nature and it is not possible to make any affirmation which is universally and absolutely valid. They conceive of seven possible alternatives in describing the nature of an entity as follows.

1. Maybe, is (*syād asti*)
2. Maybe, is not (*syād-nāsti*)
3. Maybe, is and is not (*syād asti ca nāsti ca*)
4. Maybe, is inexpressible (*syād avyaktavyam*)
5. Maybe is and is inexpressible (*syād asti ca avyaktavyam*)
6. Maybe is not and is inexpressible (*syād nāsti ca avyaktavyam*)
7. Maybe is, and is not and is inexpressible. (*syād asti ca nāsti ca avyaktavyam*)

The Jainas apply the seven-fold formula even to the substance and the qualities which are called *paryāyas* or modes. The *paryāyas* are modifications taking place in the substance and are accidental in character. Since both features – substance and modes are admitted in respect of the same identical object and at the same time, it is possible to speak of coexistence of permanence and change or unity and difference at the same time and in respect of the same object. Judged as an enduring entity, substance is permanent (*nitya*) and non-different (*abhinna*) and the same with reference to the various modifications it constantly undergoes is non-permanent and different (*bhinna*).

This theory is rejected by Bādarāyaṇa on the ground that it is impossible to speak of different characteristics in respect of the same one entity at the same time. The relevant sūtra reads: '*naikasminn-asambhavāt*'[17]. It means, as explained by Rāmānuja, that it is impossible that the contradictory characteristics such as existence and non-existence are applicable at the same time to one substance. Vedānta Deśika points out that it is a theory riddled with self-contradiction (*vyāghāta*) since two mutually opposed characteristics cannot be affirmed in respect of one and the same entity at the same time. *Sattva* means existence or being and *asattva* means non-existence or non-being. These two are mutually opposed and cannot be affirmed of the same object. It maybe possible to regard an object as being as well as non-being with reference to the limiting conditions (*upādhis*) such as change of place or change of time or change of form. For example a pot exists at the present time but it does not exist at a later time. Pot exists in a particular place but it does not exist in another place. It exists as pot but it does not exist as another object. The *asattva* or non-existence can be attributed to an object on the basis of *upādhi* and this is regarded as *sopādhika upādhi*, which is logically conceivable. But the affirmation of non-existence in respect of an object without any reference to *upādhi* (*nirupādhika asatvam*) to the same one object and at the same time, as Jainas do on the basis of *saptabhaṅgi* theory advanced by them, is logically untenable. This is the point of criticism leveled by Vedānta Deśika against the jaina theory (*na ca nirupādhikaḥ kvāpy asatvādiyogaḥ*[18]).

Some of the philosophical doctrines of the jainas also suffer from serious defects.

1) The jīva is of the size of the body.
2) The jīva in the state of *mukti* is *vibhu* though it is associated with a body.
3) *Mukti* is continuous upward movement.
4) *Dharma* and *adharma* are pervasive like *ākāśa*.
5) The earth is always moving downward.

All these theories are opposed to the Upanisadic teachings and are also logically untenable.

v) The Theory of Pāsupata

The Pāśupatas, the followers of the ancient Śaivite religious sect, account for the origin of the universe through the media of *prakṛti* presided over by *Īśvara* (*Īśvara adhiṣṭhita prakṛti*). Though *Īśvara* is admitted on the basis of inference as an instrumental cause (*nimitta kāraṇa*) of the universe, it does not, unlike the Seśvara Sāṁkhyas accept the Upaniṣadic teachings as a source of authority for proving the existence of Īśvara. Besides in matters of religious mode of life and practices (*ācāra*) it follows its own customs which are almost opposed to the accepted Vedic practices[19]. Hence Bādarāyaṇa deals with the Pāśupata theory separately and refutes it after a critical examination. This subject is covered in the *adhikaraṇa* named *Paśupatyadhikaraṇa*.

The relevant *sūtra* states: *patyuḥ asāmañjasyāt*[20]. Its general meaning, as explained by Rāmānuja, is that the theory of Paśupati (which is the name for Rudra), is not acceptable to the Vedāntins since it is full of inconsistency and also opposed to the Vedic teachings. In his commentary on the *sūtra*, Rāmānuja mentions briefly the various customs observed by the Pāśupatas for the purpose of attainment of higher spiritual goal and shows how these are opposed to the Vedic teachings on *tattva* and *upāsanā* (*Veda viruddha tattvopāsanā*). As regards the philosophical doctrines which are more important than the religious customs, it is pointed out that the postulation of *Īśvara* for the purpose of accounting for the evolution of the *prakṛti* into the manifest universe suffers from serious defect. *Īśvara* is admitted on the basis of inference as the *nimitta kāraṇa*. That is, *Īśvara*, the Ruler of the *prakṛti*, causes the evolution of the universe. If *Īśvara* is the *nimitta kāraṇa* similar to the production of the pot by the potter, He should also possess a body for creating the universe through the media of *prakṛti*. If body is admitted, then he would be subject to the *puṇya* and *pāpa* similar to the *jīvātman* who, with a body, experiences pleasure and pain. If *Īśvara* is without a body, He cannot function as the instrumental cause by presiding over *prakṛti*. Hence the very theory of cosmic creation by Paśupati as a presiding Deity over *prakṛti* is defective.

vi) The Theory of Pāñcarātra

Along with the refutation of the rival schools of thought, which are opposed to Vedānta, the theory of the *Pāñcarātra* school also comes up for consideration. Though this is considered to be in conformity with the Vedānta, yet its examination is justified for the main purpose of removing the doubt about its validity (*prāmāṇya*). As indicated in the *Vedānta-sūtra*, there is a view expressed in the *Pāñcarātra* literature that the *jīva* is brought into existence (*utpatti*) and such a theory is naturally opposed to the Upaniṣadic texts which declare that *jīva* is *nitya* or eternal. It therefore gives room for the doubt whether or not *Pāñcarātra* is authoritative. Bādarāyaṇa therefore seeks to clarify this point and affirm that *Pāñcarātra*, unlike Pāśupata and other rival schools of thought, is not opposed to the Vedānta. This matter is considered in a separate *adhikaraṇa* named *Utpatty-asambhavādhikaraṇa*.

The main objection which is raised against *Pāñcarātra* is

that we come across a stray statement in the Pāñcarātra Samhitā which appears to speak of the origin (*utpatti*) of *jīva*. Thus states the *Parama-samhitā: paramakāraṇāt parabrahma-bhūtāt vāsudevāt saṁkarṣaṇo nāma jīvo jāyate, saṁkarṣaṇāt pradyumna-saṁjñāṁ mano jāyate, tasmāt aniruddha saṁjño ahaṁkāro jāyate*. It means: "From Vāsudeva who is the Supreme Brahman and the primary cause, originates the individual soul called Saṁkarṣaṇa. From Saṁkarṣaṇa the internal organ called Pradyumna and from Pradyumna, the principle of *ahaṁkāra* called Aniruddha is born".

Prima facie, this statement conveys the idea that *jīva* originates from Brahman. But according to the Upaniṣads, the *jīva* is *nitya* or eternal and it has neither an origin nor end[21]. Hence *Pāñcarātra* cannot be authoritative (*pāñcarātram na pramāṇam*).

Bādarāyaṇa refutes this objection. The concerned statement of the *Pāñcarātra Samhitā* does not speak of the origin of the *jīva*. On the contrary, it implies, as explained by Rāmānuja that Vāsudeva, Saṁkarṣaṇa, Pradyumna and Aniruddha referred to in the statement are manifestations (*vyūhas*) of Parabrahma for the purpose of meditation by the devotees seeking to attain Brahman. Saṁkarṣaṇa is not the name for *jīva*. Nor is Pradyumna *manas*. In the same way, Aniruddha cannot be *ahaṁkāra*. The association of *jīva* with Saṁkarṣaṇa, *manas* with Pradyumna and *ahaṁkara* with Aniruddha convey the idea that these three forms of Vāsudeva are the presiding deities of these principles respectively. The term *jāyate* does not literally mean "originates" but on the other hand it implies *prādurbhāva* or manifestation in the form of *vyūha avatāra* out of the *saṁkalpa* of Vāsudeva.

Further, the very Pāñcarātra Samhitā denies the origin of *jīva*. Thus it states that *jīva* is *anādi* and also *ananta* or without end (*jīvo anādi anantaḥ kathita iti tad-utpatti pakṣo na hīṣṭaḥ*[22]). All these points are fully explained by Rāmānuja by adequate references to the Pāñcarātra treatises. Hence it is wrong to assume that Pāñcarātra is opposed to the Upaniṣads. In fact, Vyāsa, the author of Mahābhārata extols Pāñcarātra treatises as the most authoritative texts for knowing the ways and means of attainment of the Supreme Goal[23]

VII. The Ontological Status of the Evolutes of Prakṛti

In the preceding sections the theories of the rival schools of thought regarding cosmic creation were critically examined in order to prove the soundness of the Vedānta doctrine of Brahman as the cause of the universe consisting of both the sentient souls (*cit*) and non-sentient entities (*acit*). A few objections are raised against this view on the assumption that some of the evolutes such as *viyat* or ether, *vāyu* or air and *indriyas* or sense organs are *nitya* or eternal and as such Brahman cannot be the cause of them. Bādarāyana takes up this subject for consideration in the *Viyad-adhikaraṇa, Tejodhikaraṇa* and the *Prāṇotpatty-adhikaraṇa* included in the second *adhyāya*. In this connection, he also explains the process of the formation of the physical universe by Brahman. As these matters are related to the theory of Brahman as the creator of the universe we shall examine them in this chapter.

Regarding *viyat* which is termed in Vedānta as *ākāśa* or ether, the Vaiśeṣikas maintain the view that it is *nitya* or eternal and hence it cannot be regarded as *kārya* or an entity brought into existence by Brahman. The main argument in support of this view is that *ākāśa* is *niravaya dravya,* that is, an entity without any parts and hence it cannot be regarded as a product caused by something else. In other words it is *nitya*. If it were *nitya,* how can it be claimed that Brahman is the cause of it?

As regards the Upaniṣadic statements *'ātmanaḥ ākāśa sambhūtaḥ'* which speaks of the *ākāśa* as being caused by Ātman (Brahman) the Vaiśeṣikas argue that such statements are to be understood in a secondary sense (*gauṇa*) on the basis of the same explanation as offered in respect of the origin of *jīva* in the Pāñcarātra literature.

Bādarāyaṇa refutes this argument. He categorically states that *ākāśa* is caused by Brahman. The sūtra says *'asti tu'* "It (*ākāśa*) has an origin". The basis of this categorical affirmation is that several Scriptural texts clearly mention that *ākāśa* is caused by Brahman. As against strong scriptural evidence, inferential argument stands sublated.

It may be argued that the Chāndogya passage describing the process of evolution, mentions at first that *sat* (Brahman) created *tejas* (*tat tejo asṛjata*), but it does not refer to the causation of *ākāśa*, In another text of Bṛhadāraṇyaka, it is stated that both *vāyu* (air) and *antarikṣa* (ether) are eternal (*amṛta*). Hence it is appropriate to adopt a secondary meaning for the word *'utpatti'* (*sambhūta*) mentioned in respect of *ākāśa*.

This argument is unsound, contends Bādarāyaṇa for the obvious reason that the very Chāndogya Upaniṣad points out that the entire universe which covers all the elements including *ākāśa*, is ensouled by Brahman (*aitadātmyam idaṁ sarvam*). Besides, the general statement 'By the knowledge of the one, all other things become known' cannot be justified if *ākāśa* were not a product of Brahman.

The mention of the creation of *tejas* as the first element by Brahman in the Taittirīya Upaniṣad does not rule out the origination of *ākāśa*, as stated in many other texts. The description of *vāyu* and *antarikṣa* as *amṛta* is to be understood in the sense that they exist for a long duration (*cirakāla vartitva*). Hence there is no justification to regard *viyat* as eternal (*nitya*).

As Vedānta Deśika points out, the inferential argument adopted by Vaiśeṣikas on the basis of the premise *'niravaya dravya'* is fallacious. *Dravya* or substance is that which exists and is known by *pramāṇas*. According to the *satkāryavāda*, both the cause and effect are *dravyas*, since effect is only a modified state of the causal substance. What is called *'kārya'* or effect such as a pot is not a new product as Vaiśeṣikas believe. It is the same causal substance viz. clay which has assumed the modified form as pot. If all the five elements are accepted as evolutes of *prakṛti* as evidenced by the Scriptural texts speaking of the process of evolution, only *ākāśa* cannot be *nitya* for the mere reason that it is a *niravaya dravya*. The illustrations cited by the Chāndogya Upaniṣad such as clay and its products fully support the *satkāryavāda* according to which effects are the modifications of the causal substance.

On the basis of the explanations offered in respect of *ākāśa*, the view that *vāyu* is eternal (*nitya*) is rejected. *Vāyu* too is a *kārya* or product brought into existence by Brahman. If it were not an entity caused by Brahman, then the knowledge of Brahman would not lead to the knowledge of all that is created by it as stated in the Chāndogya Upaniṣad.

Another issue is raised with regard to the causation of the evolutes by Brahman. According to the Upaniṣadic passages dealing with the order of evolution, It is stated that *agni* or fire is caused by *vāyu* (*vayoḥ agniḥ*), ap or water is caused by *agni* (*agneḥ apaḥ*), *pṛthivī* is caused by *ap* (*adbhyaḥ pṛthivī*) etc.. Accordingly the cause of each element is the preceding one. It cannot therefore be said that Brahman is the cause of all such evolutes.

Bādarāyaṇa does not accept this view. In the *Tejodhikaraṇa*, which deals with this issue, the implication of these Upaniṣadic statements is explained. The text '*vayoḥ agniḥ*' does not mean that *vāyu* causes *agni*. On the other hand it implies that Paramātman as the *Antaryāmin* of *vāyu* creates *agni*. This meaning is evident from other texts which state that '*tejo aikṣata*' or fire willed to create and '*tā āpa aikṣata*' or water willed to create. Since the capacity to will (*īkṣaṇa*) cannot be attributed to a non-sentient entity, it follows that all such statements are to be interpreted in the sense that Brahman as inherent in those respective elements causes the creation of the subsequent evolute. In a more specific way, the Muṇḍaka mentions in one sweeping statement that all these things viz. *prāṇa, manas, indriyas, khaṁ* (ether), *vāyu, ap, jyotis* and *pṛthivī* originate from Brahman[24]. In this text, though the order of creation of the evolutes is not mentioned, it states that Brahman is the cause of all things. This point is to be taken note of wherever the order of evolution is mentioned. That is, the immediate preceding evolute as inherently related to *Paramātman* as its *Antaryāmin* is the cause of the succeeding evolute. It is therefore relevant to regard Brahman as the cause of all the evolutes.

Regarding the ontological status of *indriyas* (sense organs), the question is raised whether the *indriyas* designated as *prāṇas* in the Upaniṣad, are created by Brahman. This doubt arises because the Scriptural text says that *prāṇas* equated with *ṛsis* existed prior to the creation of the universe. Thus states the *Śatapatha Brāhmaṇa*: *Asadvā idam agra āsīt tadāhuḥ, kiṁ tadāsīt iti, ṛṣayo vā va te āgre āsan, tadāhuḥ ke te ṛṣayaḥ, prāṇa vā va ṛṣayaḥ*"[25]– "In the beginning (prior to creation) all this was non-being (*asat*). What was that they say? Those *ṛṣis* were indeed that non-being, thus they say. And who were those *ṛṣis*? The *prāṇas* indeed were those *ṛṣis*."

On the basis of this authority, it is contended that *prāṇas* denoted by the term *ṛṣayaḥ* in plural, are not created since they are regarded to have existed even prior to creation.

This matter is discussed in a separate *adhikaraṇa* of the fourth *pāda* named *Prāṇotpatty-adhikaraṇa*. Bādarāyaṇa straightaway rejects this view on the strength of the Upaniṣadic texts which clearly state that prior to the creation only Brahman existed. Thus states the Chāndogya: *sadeva saumya idam agra āsīt*. The Aitareya Upaniṣad also says: *ātmā vā idam eka agra āsīt*. Besides, the Muṇḍaka Upaniṣad states that from Brahman originate *prāṇa, manas* and all *indriyas* (*etasmāt jāyate prāṇo manaḥ sarvendriyāṇi ca*). There is no mention as in the case of *jīvatman* that *prāṇas* (*indriyas*) are *nitya*. The term *prāṇa* named as *ṛṣayaḥ* which is stated to have existed prior to creation in the *Śatapatha*

Brāhmaṇa, refers to the *Paramātman.* In the Upaniṣadic parlance the term *prāṇa* also stands for Brahman (*prāṇarṣitve paramatmānyapi hi sughatitā*[26]). Etymologically *prāṇa* also denotes *Paramātman* (*sarva prāṇi prāṇena hetuḥ*).

Incidentally Bādarāyaṇa also discusses the number and nature of *Indriyas* and also *prāṇa* or the vital breath. The six *adhikaraṇas* in the fourth pāda are devoted to the consideration of this matter. We shall take note of the important points.

According to the prima facie view, the number of indriyas is seven. The basis of this theory is that the Muṇḍakopaniṣad mentions that seven senses move along with the *jīva* during its exit from the body (*sapta prāṇaḥ prabhavanti*). Bādarāyaṇa does not accept this view because *Śruti* and *Smṛti* texts speak of eleven *indriyas* including *manas* (*indriyāṇi daśaikaṁ ca*). According to the theory of evolution, accepted on the basis of the Scriptural authority, eleven *indriyas* emanate from *Sāttvika Ahaṁkāra tattva*. These are five cognitive organs (*jñanendriyas*), five cognative organs (*karmendriyas*) and mind (*manas*). All these are accessories (*upakaraṇas*) for the *jīva* to function. It is also pointed out that *indriyas* are not merely external physical organs as is commonly understood but they are subtle sense faculties which are monadic in character (*aṇu*). The justification for this view is that the Upaniṣads speak of the exit of the *indriyas* from the body along with the *jīva*. If *indriyas* were *vibhu* or all-pervasive as some believe, their exit from the body along with the *jīva* is inconceivable. Even though the sense organs are atomic in character, they can cognize objects which are far from them through their *vṛttis* or outflow of energy of the sense organ generated by the respective sense data (*vṛttyā dūrastha-dhīs-syāt*).

Along with the theory of *indriyas*, the nature of *prāṇa* or vital breath is also discussed in a separate *adhikaraṇa* named *Vāyukriyādhikaraṇa*. The issue that comes up for consideration is whether the *prāṇa-vāyu* or the vital breath referred to in the Upaniṣad is an independent entity (*tattva*) or it is only a modification of the gross element of *vāyu* (*vāyukriyā*). On the strength of the Scriptural text, Bādarāyana points out that *prāṇa* is not mere *vāyu* present in the body (*na dehāntar-vāyumātra*). The Upaniṣadic text clearly says: From this arises *prāṇa, manas,* all *indriyas,* ether, *vāyu* etc.[27] As *prāṇa* and *vāyu* are mentioned separately in the same text, the two are not identical. Nor is it a function (*kriyā*) of *vāyu* because it is mentioned along with *dravyas.* Thus says Bādarāyaṇa: *na vāyukriye pṛthag upadeśāt*[28]. It is not even an independent *tattva* (*tattvāntara*) similar to *tejas* because in the enumeration of the twenty four *tattvas, prāṇa* does not figure. It is therefore assumed that *vāyu* itself assumes different modifications and *prāṇa-vāyu* is one such modified form of *vāyu.* The same *prāṇa-vāyu* assumes different names such as *prāṇa, apāna, samāna, vyāna, udāna.* Even this *prāṇa-vāyu* is monadic in character (*aṇuśca*) since it is stated in the Upaniṣad that it also moves along with the *jīva* when it exits from the body after death. Thus says the Upaniṣad: *taṁ utkrāmantaṁ prāṇo anutkrāmati*[29].

Incidentally Bādarāyaṇa clarifies that *prāṇa* or vital breath which is often designated as *indriya,* is not, strictly speaking, an *indriya* or sense organ as in the case of the ten sense organs and the mind for the reason that the Upaniṣad mentions *prāṇa* as distinct from the eleven sense organs. Thus says the Upaniṣad: *etasmāt jāyate prāṇo manaḥ sarvendriyāṇi ca.* In describing the exit of the *jīva* from the body after death, the Upaniṣad mentions separately that *prāṇa* moves along with the *jīva* and that other *indriyas* follow *prāṇa* (*prāṇam anutkrāmantaṁ sarve prāṇā anutkrāmanti*). Besides, during the state of deep sleep, the *indriyas* do not function, but *prāṇa* subsists. According to the theory of evolution of *prakṛti,* the ten sense organs and mind emanate from *sāttvika ahaṁkāra* and not *prāṇa.* In fact *indriya* is defined as that which is the modification of *ahaṁkāra* (*sāttvika ahaṁkāra vikṛtitvam*) and this definition does not apply to *prāṇa. Prāṇa* is therefore different from *indriyas.* One other important point which is brought out by Bādarāyaṇa is that the function of all *indriyas* and also *prāṇa* (vital breath) is regulated by *jīva* who is the controller of them (*adhiṣṭhātṛ*). But this power is endowed to *jīva* by *Paramātman*. Similarly the celestial deities such as *agni* which are stated to be the presiding deities of the sense organs including mind, are controlled by Brahman who is the Inner Controller (*Antaryāmin*) of all entities as stated in the *Antaryāmi Brāhmaṇa*.

VIII. The Process of Formation of the Physical Universe

In the preceding *adhikaraṇas* Bādarāyaṇa has discussed the issues concerning the ontological status of some of the evolutes of *prakṛti* such as *viyat*, *indriyas* and *prāṇa* in order to establish that these are also caused by Brahman. As allied to the subject of cosmic creation, another important matter relating to the actual formation of the variegated physical universe needs to be considered. According to the theory of evolution, as admitted by the Upaniṣads, *prakṛti* as regulated by Brahman evolves itself into the five gross elements through various stages in a particular order. This is regarded as *samaṣṭi-sṛṣṭi* or the creation of the aggregate universe. This represents the first stage of creation. After this stage is reached, the actual creation of the physical universe with all its diversity starts. This is known as *vyaṣṭi-sṛṣṭi* or the creation of the universe of space and matter with all its diversity. This represents the secondary stage of creation. As stated in the Chāndogya Upaniṣad, the formation of the physical universe is first done by the admixture of different parts of the five elements in certain proportion. This is technically called *pañcīkaraṇa* or quintuplication of the five elements.[30]

The Chāndogya speaks of the admixture of only three elements viz. *ap*, *tejas* and *pṛthivī*. This is known as *trivṛtkaraṇa*. As Vedānta Deśika states, *trivṛtkaraṇa* is not different from *pañcīkaraṇa* referred to in other Upaniṣadic texts. It is illustrative of *pañcīkaraṇa*. After completing the *pañcīkaraṇa*, the rest of the universe with all its diversity is created out of the five elements (*pañca-bhūta*) after mixing them in appropriate proportion.

The question to be considered in this connection is whether the formation of different entities in the universe by assigning them a name and form (*nāma-rūpa-vyākaraṇa*) is done by Brahman or by Hiraṇyagarbha, also known as *Caturmukha-brahmā* to whom the task of creation is specially entrusted. This doubt arises because of two reasons. First, the *Smṛti* texts state that *Caturmukha- brahmā* is the creator of the aggregate universe (*vyaṣṭi-nāmādi sṛṣṭā*). Secondly, the following statement of the Chāndogya Upaniṣad referring to the *anupraveśa* and *nāma-rūpa vyākaraṇa* gives the impression that *jīvātman* assigns the *nāma* and *rūpa* to all entities at the time of creation: *anena jīvenātmanā anupraviśya nāmarūpe vyākaravāṇi*[31]. Bādarāyaṇa therefore discusses this matter in a separate *adhikaraṇa* named as *saṁjñāmūrti-klṛpty-adhikaraṇa*.

The following *sūtra* clarifies the position: *saṁjñāmūrtiklṛptistu trivṛtkurvata upadeśāt*[32]. It means that the assignment of names and forms to the created objects is done by the same (*Paramātman*) who did the *trivṛtkaraṇa* or the admixture of these primary elements, because the Scriptural text teaches it accordingly. The passage of the Chāndogya Upaniṣad dealing with the creation of the universe clearly points out that Brahman itself which caused the evolution of *prakṛti* into twenty three evolutes including five gross elements, resolved to enter into the elements (*ap*, *tejas* and *pṛthivī*) along with the *jīvatman* (*jīvenātmanā*) and thereafter gave names and forms to them. Both these functions namely the entry into the elements and the assignment of names and forms are performed by *Paramātman*. The possibility of *Caturmukha Brahmā* performing the task of assignment of *nāma* and *rūpa* to the created objects does not arise because prior to the creation of the universe, he does not exist. According to the *Śruti* and *Smṛti* texts, *Caturmukha Brahmā* was created only after the *samaṣṭi-sṛṣṭi* or the creation of the aggregate universe upto five gross elements was completed.

Vedānta Deśika points out that the expression *'anena jīvenātmanā'* is not to be taken as the identity of *jīva* and Brahman, as Advaita assumes, because it is so well established in the Upaniṣads that *jīva* and Brahman are two separate ontological entities. Hence the statement *'anena jīvenātmanā anupraviśya'* is to be understood as Brahman along with *jīva* with which it is inseparably related enters into the created objects. The word *'praviśya'* with the prefix *'anu'* implies that *Paramātman* causes the *jīva* to enter and soon after, along with the *jīva,* He also enters[33]. In other words both *Paramātman* and *jīva* enter into the created objects and thereafter the created objects are assigned with names and forms. After this is done, the manifold universe of names and forms comes into existence. Thus, Brahman is the cause of both *samaṣṭi-sṛṣṭi* or the creation of the aggregate universe and also *vyaṣṭi-sṛṣṭi* or the creation of the diversified (variegated) universe with the manifold names and forms.

---

1. *See* RB II-2-1 for details of Sāṁkhya theory.
2. VS II-2-21.
3. AS verse 181.
4. *See* Sāṁkhyakārikā – *samsarati badhyate mucyate ca nānāśrayā prakṛtiḥ.* Also, *puruṣasya darśanārtham kaivalyārtham tathā pradhānasya*
5. VS II-2-20
6. *See* VS II-2-17. *samudāya ubhayahetuke'pi tad-aprāptiḥ.*
7. *See* TMK – IV-27. *svacche parasmin chāyā na bhavati, asau rūpásūnye na ca syāt.*
8. VS II-2-27.
9. VS II-2-28.
10. TMK – IV-27
11. VS II-2-28.
12. *See* TMK SS-IV-18. *na sannāsanna sad-asanna cāpyanubhayātmakam; catuṣkoṭi vinirmuktaṁ tattvam mādhyamikā viduḥ. See* also T.R.V Murthy – Central Philosophy of Buddhism. P 228.*See* also AS verse 198
13. VS II-2-30.
14. AS verse 198
15. *See* AS verse 201. *prāyo buddhiḥ yathārthā śrutivid-abhimatā kvāpi*

bhedāgrahādi. *See* also Cintāmaṇi: *tathā ca akhyāti-saṁvalite yathārthakhyāthiḥ trayyanta vidāṁ asmākam abhimata-ityarthaḥ*.

16. For details of Jaina theory, *see* RB II-2-31.
17. VS- II-2-31.
18. AS verse 203.
19. *See* RB II-2-35 for details.
20. VS II-2-35
21. *See* Ka. Up. I-2-18. *na jāyate mṛyate vā kadācit*. Also *nityo nityānāṁ*.
22. AS verse 214.
23. *See* Mahābhārata XII-348-61 – *idaṁ mahopaniṣadam caturveda samanvitam*. *See* also M.Bh. XII-348: *idaṁ śreyam idaṁ brahma idaṁ hitam anuttamam*.
24. *See* Mund. Up II-1-3. *Etasmāt jāyate prāṇo manaḥ sarvendriyāṇi ca. khaṁ vāyur āpaḥ pṛthivī viśvasya dhāriṇī*.
25. Śatapatha Brāhmaṇa VI-1-1.
26. AS verse 255.
27. Mund. Up. II-1-3. *See* fn.24
28. VS. II-4-8
29. Br. Up. VI-4-2
30. *See* FVV. Ch.10 p321-322 for details regarding *pañcīkaraṇa*.
31. Ch. Up. VI-3-1
32. VS II-4-17
33. *See* AS verse 264.

CHAPTER SEVEN

THE DOCTRINE OF JĪVA AND BRAHMAN

Though *Brahma-sūtra* is primarily concerned with the study of Brahman, the ultimate metaphysical Reality of the Upaniṣads, it also accords equal importance to the subject of *jīvātman*. Bādarāyaṇa acknowledges on the authority of the Upaniṣads that *jīvātman* is a separate ontological entity as distinct from Brahman. As we have observed in the chapters 2 to 4, several *adhikaraṇas* of the first *adhyāya* dealing with the nature and distinguishing characteristics (*dharmas*) of Brahman refer to the *jīvātman* as a prima facie theory and affirms that Brahman is distinct from *jīva* and that the *dharmas* refered to in the Upaniṣadic texts are not applicable to *jīvātman*. Bādarāyaṇa in one of the *sūtras* specifically states that Brahman is other than the *jīva* because of the difference between the two (*adhikaṁ tu bhedanirdeśāt*)[1]. In the second *adhyāya* while discussing the issue whether *viyat* and other evolutes of *prakṛti* are eternal, he brings up the theory of *Ātman*. In this connection, five *adhikaraṇas* are exclusively devoted to the discussion of the nature of *jīvātman* and its relation to Brahman. Again in the third *adhyāya* dealing with the *sādhana* or the means of attainment of Brahman, Bādarāyaṇa discusses the theory of transmigration of the *jīva* and also its condition in the states of waking, dream, deep sleep (*suṣupti*) and swoon (*murchā*). Six *adhikaraṇas* of *pāda* 1 and four *adhikaraṇas* of pāda 2 of this *adhyāya* cover these subjects. In the fourth *adhyāya* which deals mainly with the Supreme Goal to be attained by the *jīva*, he examines the status of the *jīva* in the state of *mokṣa* in six *adhikaraṇas*. We shall discuss all these matters except the status of *jīva* in *mokṣa*, in the present chapter. The nature of *jīva* in the state of *mukti* will be considered in the chapter on the Supreme Goal.

I. Jīva as Eternal (nitya).

This is the subject-matter of the *Ātmādhikaraṇa* which is devoted to prove that *jīvātman* is eternal on the basis of the Scriptural authority and also on rational ground. As explained by Vedānta Deśika, the need to affirm the eternality of *jīvātman* arises because of the doubts arising from a few Scriptural texts which convey the idea that *jīva* is also subject to origin. The Chāndogya Upaniṣad dealing with *sad-vidyā*, states that all beings have *sat* as their source and all that exists is ensouled by *sat* (Brahman). Prior to creation, if *sat* alone existed, and if everything in the universe is caused by *sat*, it would follow that *jīvas* as the effect (*kārya*) of Brahman are also originated. Besides, a few Scriptural texts explicitly state that *jīvas* are brought into existence. Thus says the Taittirīya Brāhmaṇa: "Prajāpati (*Caturmukha Brahmā*) created the *jīvas*"[2]. Besides, the general statement in the Chāndogya that the knowledge of the one principle (Brahman) leads to the knowledge of all else, would not be justified if *jīvas* were not the products of Brahman.

In order to refute these views, Bādarāyaṇa introduces the following *sūtra* which affirms that *jīva* is eternal: *Na ātmā śruteḥ, nityatvācca tabhyaḥ*[3]. It means, according to Rāmānuja, that *Ātman* (*jīvātman*) is not subject to origin (*utpatti*) unlike *viyat* or ether (referred to in an earlier *sūtra*) because the Scriptural texts deny the origin of *jīva* and also that very Scriptural texts declare that *jīva* is eternal (*nityavācca tābhyaḥ*). Thus says the Kaṭha Upaniṣad: *ajo nityaḥ śāśvato'yaṁ purāṇaḥ*[4] - "unborn, eternal, everlasting, existing from time immemorial". The Śvetāśvatara Upaniṣad also mentions the eternality and plurality of the *jīvas*: *nityo nityānāṁ cetanaḥ cetanānāṁ eko bahūnāṁ yo vidadhāti kāmān*[5] – "One eternal sentient being (Brahman) fulfills the desires of many eternal sentient beings (*jīvas*)".

As regards the statements which speak of the origin of the *jīva* (*janana*), these have to be understood in the sense that *jīvas* are associated with the physical body and sense organs. As explained by Rāmānuja, *jīvas* exist in Brahman in a subtle state at the time of dissolution of the universe. When the creation of the universe takes place, they are associated with the bodies and the sense organs to enable them to function and reap the benefit of *karma*. In this process the only change that takes place in the *jīva* is in respect of its *jñāna* which is its essential attribute (*dharmabhūta-jñāna*). That is, the attributive knowledge which was dormant during the state of dissolution is enabled to function by associating it with the body and the senses. This change effected in the *jñāna* does not amount to change in the *svarūpa* of the *jīva* (*svarūpānyathābhāva*), unlike in the case of non-sentient entities such as *viyat*. *Jīvātman* is therefore *nitya* as declared by the Scriptural texts.

There is also a rational justification for admitting the *nityatva* of *jīva*. If *jīva* were not eternal, then the results of the meritorious and sinful deeds performed in one's present lifetime would cease at the end of the life (*kṛta vipraṇāśa*) and there would be no scope for reaping the effects of these good or bad deeds in the next life. In the same way, the effects of good or bad deeds not done previously would have to be experienced in the present life (*akṛta abhyāgama*). But both these possibilities are opposed to the commonly accepted theory of *karma* and its influence on the life of the *jīvas*.

In this connection, Vedānta Deśika mentions briefly the theories of *jīva* advanced by rival schools of thought viz. Cārvākas, Buddhists, Advaita, Bhāskara and Yādava Prakāśa and rejects them on the ground that these are unsound and also opposed to the teachings of the Scriptural texts.[6]

According to the Cārvākas, the body itself is the soul. This is rejected because without the admission of an intelligent principle as different from the body, it is not possible to explain satisfactorily the knowledge of external objects and the recollection of the experiences of the past. The argument of the Cārvākas that consciousness (*caitanya*) is produced by the aggregation of the different organs of the body is untenable. If the element of consciousness is not found in each part of the body, it cannot arise from the aggregate of the parts of the body.

Some Buddhists maintain that the series of thoughts (*dhī-santāna*) itself is the self (*jīva*) and it lasts until the dissolution of the universe. Even this is an unsound theory because bondage and release and the attainment of a higher spiritual Goal cannot be satisfactorily explained.[7]

The followers of Advaita Vedānta admit *jīva* but it is regarded as the Self (Brahman) conditioned by the limiting adjuncts such as *antaḥkaraṇas* (internal organs) caused by *avidyā*. During the state of bondage, *jīva* is associated with *avidyā* which is beginningless (*anādi*). It persists until it is liberated (*āmokṣa*). In view of this, it may be regarded as *nitya* as declared by the Upaniṣad.

Even this theory is unsound. The persistence of jīvahood (*jivabhāva*) until the state of total liberation from bondage (*āmokṣa-sthāyī jīvabhāvaḥ*) cannot be regarded as eternal (*nitya*). Such a state of *jīva* is also considered to be *apuruṣārtha* by some Advaitins. Besides, this theory of *jīva* stands opposed to the Scriptural texts which explicitly state that *jīvas* are *nitya*.

II. Jīva as Jñātā

This is the subject-matter of the *Jñādhikaraṇa* which establishes that *jīva* is not merely of the nature of knowledge but also the knowing subject (*jñātā*). The relevant *sūtra* reads: *jño ata eva*[8]. It means, as interpreted by Rāmānuja, that this *ātman* (referred to in the earlier *sūtra*) is of the nature of *jñātṛ* (knowing subject) because it is stated so in the *Śruti* texts.[9]

By way of explaining the fuller implication of the *sūtra*, Rāmānuja points out that according to the Advaitins the *jīvātman* is essentially constituted of knowledge (*jñāna-svarūpa eva*).The Bṛhadāraṇyaka Upaniṣad employs the term *vijñāna* for *Ātman* (*yo vijñāne tiṣṭhan*).[10] The Taittirīya also uses the word *vijñāna* for *ātman* (*vijñānaṁ yajñaṁ tanute*).[11] The *Viṣṇu Purāṇa* also explicitly states that ātman is *jñānasvarūpa*.[12] On the basis of these Scriptural and *Smṛti* texts, it is contended that *ātman* which is the same as Brahman is of the nature of knowledge. Due to its association with the *antaḥkaraṇa* or internal organ, it is regarded as *jñātā* or knower. *Jñātṛtva* is therefore an adventious *dharma* of *ātman* superimposed on it due to *avidyā*.

There is another view held by the Vaiśeṣikas, according to which *jīva* which is omnipresent (*sarvagata*) cannot be of the nature of knowledge since it would amount to the admission of its becoming aware of everything, at all times and everywhere (*sarvadā sarvatra upalabdhiprasaṅgaḥ*). Besides, in the state of deep sleep, knowledge is not found to be present. It is therefore contended that *jñāna* as a *dharma* is an adventious quality of *jīva* arising as and when the mind and the sense organs are in contact with the objects (*upādhija jñātṛtva*).

The *Vedānta-sūtra*, as interpreted by Rāmānuja, rejects both these views as these are defective and not supported by the Scriptural texts. *Jīva* is stated to be '*jñaḥ*' which implies that *ātman* is only *jñātṛ-svarūpa* or of the nature of knowing subject. It is neither mere *jñāna-svarūpa*, as Buddhists and Advaitins believe nor *jaḍa-svarūpa* or non-sentient in character, as Vaiśeṣikas believe. On the other hand, *jīvātman* which is of the nature of *jñāna* is also of the nature of *jñātṛtva*. Both these aspects of *jīvātman* are fully supported by the Upaniṣadic texts.

According to the Scriptural text quoted by Rāmānuja, *jīva* only knows. Thus it is stated: '*jānātyeva ayaṁ puruṣaḥ*' "This *puruṣa* only knows". The Bṛhadāraṇyaka describes *jīvātman* as *vijñātā*[13] which means that it is of the nature of knowledge. The Praśna Upaniṣad explicitly states: *eṣa hi draṣṭā śrotā ghrātā rasayitā mantā boddhā vijñānātmā puruṣaḥ*[14] - "He verily is the one (*jīvātman*) who is the seer, the hearer, the smeller, the taster, the thinker, the knower (*boddhā*), the doer, the individual self (*puruṣa*) who is of the nature of knowledge(*vijñānātmā*)".

The words *boddhā* and *vijñānātmā* employed in this statement affirm both the *jñātṛtva* and *jñānatva* of *jīvātman*. On the authority of these texts, it is admitted that *jīvātman* is of the nature of knowledge and also possesses *jñāna* as a *dharma* (*jñānatvavat jñātṛtvamapi svābhāvikam*)

Vedānta Deśika explains the significance of the Scriptural text: '*jānāty-eva ayaṁ puruṣaḥ*' quoted by Rāmānuja. The word *eva* added to *jānāti* implies that *jīvātman* is never *ajñātā*, that is, devoid of knowledge (*ātmā kadācidapi ajñātā na bhavati*). It implies that *jñātṛtva* is a permanent *dharma* (*nitya*). In other words, its knowledge is *nitya*, as is evidenced by the statement of Bṛhadāraṇyaka Upaniṣad '*na vijñātuḥ vijñāteḥ viparilopo vidyate*[15]' – "The knowledge (*vijñāteḥ*) of *ātman*(*vijñātuḥ*) is not subject to destruction".[16] The description of *jīva* as *vijñāna* only implies that it is not non-sentient (*jaḍa*).

Thus it is affirmed that the *ātman* which is *nitya* and of *jñāna-svarūpa* also possesses *jñātṛtva* as its *dharma*.

Against this conclusion an objection is raised. According to some, *jīva* is regarded as *vibhu* or all-pervasive. Its description in the Upaniṣad as *mahān ātmā* or great self also implies its *vibhutva* character. If *ātmā* which is *vibhu* is of the nature of *jñāna* and also possesses knowledge as its essential *dharma*, then it should reveal itself always everywhere. But it is not so.

This objection is not tenable, contends Vedānta Deśika, because *jīvātman* is not *vibhu*. On the contrary, it is monadic in character (*aṇu*), as is evident from the Upaniṣads. Thus says the Muṇḍaka Upaniṣad: '*Eṣo aṇurātmā cetasā veditavyaḥ*'[17] – "This *ātman* which is *aṇu* is to be known through mind". Besides Scriptural support, Bādarāyaṇa has advanced several arguments to establish the theory that *jīva* is *aṇu* by answering the possible objections against it. Several *sūtras* are devoted to discuss the issue related to the size (*parimāṇa*) of *jīva* and affirm that *jīva* is *aṇu*. One of the arguments in support of it is that the exit of the soul from the body after death (*utkrānti*) and its movement to the higher realms and also its return to this world, as stated in the Upaniṣads[18], would not be possible if *jīva* were *vibhu* (*utkrānti gati āgatīnām*).[19] The Upaniṣads also speak of the *jīvātman* in terms of measurement (*unmāna*) by the selection of comparative instances. Thus says the Śvetāśvatara Upaniṣad: "The individual self is to be known as part of the hundredth part of the tip of a hair divided a hundred times".[20] Being *aṇu* and located in one's body, it cannot experience everything and at all places. Though it is *aṇu*, it can experience the objects nearby and also far off through its *jñāna*, just as a lamp can illuminate much larger area around it.

Jīva located in the body manifests itself as *aham* or "I" (*ahaṁ iti svenaiva siddhyati*[21]). It is self-luminous (*svayaṁ prakāśa*) as it does not require another knowledge for its manifestation. Even in the state of deep sleep (*suṣupti*) it reveals itself as 'I', as is evident from the experience which arises in the form 'I slept happily' soon after waking up. But during the state of deep sleep and swoon, the knowledge does not manifest itself fully since its function is restricted due to the absence of objects to be experienced (*dhī-saṅkocāt*).

The description of *jīva* as '*mahān ātmā*' does not mean that *jīva* is *vibhu*. On the other hand, as stated in the *Vedānta-sūtra*, this statement in the Bṛhadāraṇyaka contextually refers to *Paramātman* or Brahman who is to be meditated upon by *jīvātman*. Similarly in the statement of the Śvetāśvatara '*sa ca ānantyāya kalpate*', the term *ananta* or infinite with reference to *jīva* means that *jñāna* which is the essential attribute of *jīva* (*dharma-bhūtajñāna*) becomes infinite in the state of *mukti*. Then the *jīvātman* becomes an omniscient being totally free from *karma*. The term *'sarvagata'* used in respect of *jīva* implies that *jīva* as a spiritual monad is capable of entering into all sentient beings (*sarvacetana antaḥpraveśa sāmarthyam*[22]).

III. Jīva as Kartā

This is the subject matter of *Kartṛadhikaraṇa* which discusses whether or not *jīva* is *kartā* or the agent of action. This issue arises because a few Scriptural and *Smṛti* texts appear to deny *kartṛtva* for *jīva*. The Kaṭhopaniṣad mentions that the self (*jīvātman*) is not the killer (*nā'yam hanti*[23]) and this statement prima facie implies that it is devoid of *kartṛtva*. The *Bhagavadgītā* also ascribes the act of agency (*kartṛtva*) to the three *guṇas* of *prakṛti* and regards *jīva* as free from it.[24] The *Gītā* also describes that *jīva* is not subject to any modification and as such it cannot have the *kartṛtva* which involves change (*vikṛti virahataḥ*).[25]

Keeping in mind such possible objections which are untenable, Bādarāyaṇa introduces the following *sūtra* which affirms that *jīva* is *kartā*: *Kartā śāstrārtha-vattvāt*[26]. It means: "*jīva* is the agent of action on account of Scripture becoming meaningful". By way of elucidating the implication of this *sūtra*, Rāmānuja points out that there are several Scriptural injunctions in the form of commanding an individual to perform good deeds for attaining heaven and prohibiting him from doing evil deeds. All these Śāstraic injunctions would be rendered meaningless if an individual soul were not the agent of action. The Vedic commands have no significance in respect of a non-sentient entity such as the *guṇas* of *prakṛti* or even the *buddhi* (internal organ). They are intended only for those who can understand and follow them. In view of this, it is maintained that *jīva* is *kartā*.

This view has the support of the Scriptural texts. The Bṛhadāraṇyaka Upaniṣad states that *jīvātman* moves freely within the body by using the sense organs.[27] The Taittiriya text says that *jīvātman* designated as *vijñāna*, performs *yāga*.[28] The Praśna Upaniṣad categorically states that the self (*jīvātman*) is *kartā*. *Kartṛtva* is therefore admitted as the intrinsic dharma of *jīva*, like *jñātṛtva*.

According to some schools of thought, *kartṛtva* belongs to *buddhi* or the internal organ and that the self is regarded as *kartā* either due to its proximity to *buddhi* or due to the superimposition of *dharma* of *buddhi* on the self. This view is untenable, contends Vedānta Deśika. If the self is *kartā* because of its proximity to *buddhi*, then *buddhi* being the same for all individuals, the fruits of the actions of one individual should also be reaped by another since there is no special feature of *buddhi* which distinguishes one from the other. The theory of superimposition of *buddhi* and its mental activities on the self is also defective because superimposition cannot take place due to the absence of any similarity between *buddhi* and the self. Superimposition is possible if there is some similarity between two objects as in the case of the shell and silver. The reflection of the pure self in the *buddhi* is also ruled out since the self does not possess any form (*rūpa*) to allow for its reflection in the *buddhi*.

Further, if the self is not admitted to be the agent of action, it cannot also be the *bhoktā* or the enjoyer of the fruits of action. If this capacity to experience the pleasure and pain is ascribed to *buddhi*, it would be opposed to the theory that *jivātman* is *bhoktā*, as maintained by the Sāṁkhyas and the Viśiṣtādvaitin. If *jīvātmā* is not *bhoktā*, then the teachings of Vedānta about bondage and liberation from it would be of no value (*bandha mokṣādi śāstram vitathameva*). *Jīvātman* is therefore to be admitted as both the *kartā* and *bhoktā*.

Vedānta Deśika also points out that the admission of *jñātṛtva, kartṛtva, bhoktṛtva* for the self does not affect its immutable character. If an entity transforms itself from one state to another, as in the case of a lump of clay into a pot, then the immutable character of the self becomes affected. No such transformation takes place in respect of the self.

Whatever modification takes place, these apply to its attributive knowledge (*dharma-bhūta jñāna*) which is distinct from the self and the latter (*jīva*) remains unaffected by them. *Jīva* is regarded as *jñātā* or the knower in the sense that it is the *āśraya* or substrate for *jñāna*, which is its essential attribute. All experiences of *jīva* take place through this knowledge. By being *āśraya* to *jñāna* which is subject to modification, the *svarūpa* of the *jīva* is not subjected to any change. In the same way, *kartṛtva* and *bhoktṛtva* admitted in respect of *jīva* do not involve change in it. *Jīva* is the *kartā* in the sense that it is the *āśraya* or the substrate for *kṛti* or effort. Effort is caused by a desire (*icchā*) to do an act. It is therefore a mental modification or an *avasthā* of *jñāna*. It is not to be confused with the actual physical activity which follows subsequent to the desire to do an act. By being an *āśraya* for *kṛti* caused by a desire, which is a particular state of knowledge, *jīva* as *kartā* is not affected by the change.

Likewise, *jīva* is *bhoktā* by being the *āśraya* for *bhoga* or the experience of pleasure and pain (*sukha-duḥkhānubha-vāśraya*)[29]. Pleasure and pain are different states (*avasthās*) of *jñāna*. Pleasure is an agreeable disposition of the mind (*anukūla-jñāna*) and pain is the disagreeable disposition of the mind (*pratikūla-jñāna*). As *jīva* is the *āśraya* for such states of experience, it is regarded as *bhokta* or enjoyer of pleasure and pain. The change involved in such mental dispositions applies to the attributive knowledge (*dharma-bhūtajñāna*) and not to the *jīva*. Such an explanation is logically tenable since in the Viśiṣṭādvaita system, *jñāna* as a *dharma* is distinct from *jīvātman* and the modifications taking place in the *dharma* do not affect the *svarūpa* of the *dharmī*.[30]

In view of these explanations it is not correct to say that the physical activities related to *kartṛtva*, the mental functions related to *jñātṛtva*, the desire to enjoy the fruits of the deeds (*vāncchā*), the capacity to do an act (*praśakana*) and the effort to be made for these purposes (*yatana*) do not belong to the *jīva*[31]. All these functions are to be performed in order to fulfill the commands of the *Śāstra* or

Sacred texts. The dictates of the *Śāstra* are intended for the good of an individual. The physical body and the sense organs including the intellect are provided as accessories to the *jīva* for the purpose of observing the commands of the *Śāstra*. Even the capacity to obey the dictates of the *Śāstra* is conferred to an individual in accordance with his past *karma* (*śāstra yogyā daśā niyati niyamitā*). Vedānta Deśika concludes that the *jīvātman* is to be admitted as *jñātā*, *kartā* and also *bhoktā* as these are well established by all the *pramāṇas* (*sarvaiḥ pramāṇaiḥ jñātā kartā bhoktā ca bhāti*).[32]

IV The Dependence of Jīvātman on Paramātman.

This is the subject-matter of a separate *adhikaraṇa* named *Parāyattādhikaraṇa*. In the preceding sections, it is seen that according to Bādarāyaṇa *jīva* is *jñātā*, *kartā* and *bhoktā*. In this connection the question arises whether *jīva* acts on its own independently or its activity is dependent on *Paramātman*. This is an important issue related to the theory of free will and determinism. If the *jīva* is not free to act (*svatantra*) and is dependent on *Paramātman*, it cannot be regarded as *kartā*. According to Pāṇini also, *kartā* is one who is free (*svatantraḥ kartā*). In the absence of freedom for the *jīvas*, the Scriptural injunctions commanding to do good deeds and not to do what is prohibited would be of no significance.

To meet these objections, Bādarāyaṇa introduces the following *sūtra*: *parāttu tat śruteḥ*[33]. It means, as interpreted by Rāmānuja, that the activity of the *jīva* takes place on account of *Paramātman* (*kartṛtvam asya jīvasya paramātmana eva hetoḥ bhavati*), because it is stated so in the Scripture (*śruteḥ*). The *Antaryāmi Brāhmaṇa* explicitly states that *Paramātman* abides in the *jīvātman* and controls it from within. The Taittirīya Āraṇyaka states specifically that *Paramātman* enters into all beings and controls them (*antaḥ praviṣṭaḥ śāstā janānāṁ sarvātmā*).[34] The *Bhagavadgīta* also reiterates that the Lord (*Īśvara*) resides in the heart of all beings and thereby controls them.[35] Lord Kṛṣṇa also states in the *Gīta*: *sarvasya ca'haṁ hṛdi sanniviṣṭah mattaḥ smṛti jñānam apohanaṁ ca*[36]–"I am seated in the hearts of all. From Me, memory, knowledge and their loss arise."

On the authority of these Scriptural and *Smṛti* texts Bādarāyaṇa affirms that *kartṛtva* of *jīva* is also caused by *Paramātman*. The question is raised: If *Paramātman* controls the activity of *jīva*, can it be *kartā*? In reply, Vedānta Deśika explains that this dependence of *jīva* on *Paramātman* does not affect its *kartṛtva*. *Jīva* is dependent for all its activities on several factors such as *karma* in the form of *puṇya* and *pāpa* accruing from the deeds of the past, *indriyas*, *kāla* (time), *prakṛti* (nature), *niyati* (unseen potency). But none of these is considered to affect the *kartṛtva* of the *jīva*. In the same way, if Īśvara who is the controller of all, as stated in the Scriptural texts, prompts *jīva* to act, the *kartṛtva* of *jīva* should not be affected. There are two types of *kartṛtva*: *prayojaka kartṛtva*, that is, *Paramātman* impells the *jīva* to act and *prayojya kartṛtva* or *jīva* acts being impelled by *Īśvara*. *Jīva* is *kartā* as impelled by *Paramātman*. This does not affect the capacity of *jīva* to function as *kartā*.

As Bādarāyaṇa states, the Divine will operates in response to an effort made by an individual in accordance with his former actions (*kṛta prayatnāpekṣa*), so that the injunctions and prohibitions of the *Śāstras* are not rendered futile.[37] This also absolves God of the criticism of cruelty and partiality.

There are two kinds of causal factors which influence the actions of individuals. One is general (*sādhāraṇa kāraṇa*) which is common to all and the second is the special cause (*viśeṣa kāraṇa*). The rain water, for instance is a common cause for the sprouts, whereas the seeds are the special cause for the sprouts. In the same way, *Īśvara* serves as the common cause for all the activities of beings at all times, past, present and future. The *karma* in the form of *puṇya* and *pāpa* accruing from the deeds of the past is the special cause for one's action leading to happiness or suffering. Hence *Īśvara* being the common cause is not responsible for *sukha* or *duḥkha* of an individual. In the *Gītā*, Lord Himself says that He is equal to all (*samo'ham sarva bhuteṣu*)[38] and that none is hateful or dear to Him. But there are Scriptural statements to the effect that God alone makes one to do evil deeds and He throws them to the hell and that He alone makes one to perform good deeds and uplifts them to a higher realm.[39] These statements are applicable only to special individuals. That is, for those who are specially devoted to God and worship Him as the sole refuge, for them God showers His grace and helps them to attain the higher goal. For those who always indulge in evil deeds and do not have any devotion to God, they are being punished by throwing them down. Hence there is no room for criticism that God is cruel or partial in His dispensation of the results of one's good or bad action.

A serious objection is raised against the theory of *jīva* as *kartā*. If *Īśvara* is the main *kartā* and *jīva* is reduced to the position of a lump of clay solely dependent on the former, how can *jīva* be regarded as *kartā*? If it is not *kartā*, then it is not also *bhoktā*. This objection is not tenable, contends Vedānta Deśika. As pointed out earlier *Īśvara* is also *kartā* as He impels *jīva* to do an act (*prayojaka kartā*) and so also *jīva* is *karta* as being impelled by *Īśvara (tat prayojyatvena kartā*). That *jīva* is *kartā* is evident to our experience. In the judgements 'I know', 'I do' etc., the entity denoted by 'I' (*aham-arthaḥ*) is admitted as the agent of mental and physical activities of an individual. This entity is not mere consciousness (*cinmātra*), nor is it internal organ (*ahaṁkara*), since it is non-sentient and as such it cannot have the function of knowing. It is the *jīvātman*, which as a sentient spiritual entity, is the *kartā* even though it is dependent on *Īśvara*. The *jīva* is capable of acting as the agent of action since it is endowed with knowledge and it is therefore distinct from non-sentient *ahaṁkāra* (*svecchāpūrva pravṛtteḥ ayam acid-adhikaḥ*).[40] Even though *Īśvara* functions as *kartā* out of His will (*icchā*), He is capable of controlling everything in the universe other than Himself. The *kartṛtva* of *Īśvara* however is of a different nature than that of *jīvātman*. Both the sentient *jīva* and non-sentient beings are dependent on *Īśvara* for their very *svarūpa*, existence (*sthiti*) and activities (*pravṛtti*). Nevertheless the *jīva* is *kartā*. The *kartṛtva* of *Īśvara*, *jīva* and non-sentient entity are comparable to the charioteer (*sārathi*), the horses that pull the chariot and the chariot itself respectively. The Lord who controls everything is the charioteer. The horses which pull the chariot being controlled by the charioteer is *jīvātman* and the chariot which moves being pulled by the horses which are controlled by the charioteer is the non-sentient being. Thus the *kartṛtva* is of a different nature in each case though the process of action (*pravṛtti*) is common to all the three (*sārathyādi krameṇa pratiniyatagatiḥ syāt trayāṇām pravṛttiḥ*[41]).

Vedānta Deśika further points out that it is not correct to assume that *jīva* is totally dependent on *Īśvara* for its action, similar to a non-sentient entity. It has some freedom to act on its own. As Rāmānuja explains in his comment on the *Vedānta-sūtra*[42], a distinction is drawn between the initial action of the individual and the subsequent activity. In all human effort, the individual initially wills to do a thing. To this extent he is free to do what he desires. Based on this initial action, the subsequent activity which follows is approved by *Īśvara*. By according such an approval, *Īśvara* prompts the individual to proceed further (*Paramātmā tadanumatidānena pravartayati)*.[43] If it were not so, injunctions in this regard would become futile. Even though *Īśvara* gives His approval to the activity initiated by an individual, He does not become the *kartā*. The actual *kartā* is the individual himself. To this extent *jīva* possesses the freedom and *Īśvara* also remains as the controller of all human action. Thus the *jīva's* freedom is reconciled with the power of *Īśvara* as the controller of all actions.

It may be asked whether *Īśvara*, by according His approval to the subsequent activity of the individual, can escape the moral responsibility for the consequences of the act which may either be good or evil. Thus for instance, if an individual indulges in a sinful act, does not God become a participant in it in so far as He remains neutral and does not prevent the person from doing so? The answer to this is in the negative. In all these cases, the initial action is important and that alone determines the moral responsibility of the individual. God has endowed to each individual the mental faculty to think and act rightly. He has also given the ethical code (*Śāstra*) as a guide to act in the right way and avoid what is considered to be sinful. To this extent, God is the general cause (*sādhāraṇa-hetu*) for the activities of all human beings, in the same way as the rain water is a common cause for the growth of plants. An individual is expected to exercise his thinking power and make use of the guidelines in initiating his activity. In this respect he becomes the special cause (*viśeṣa kāraṇa*) for the results accruing from them, like the special effort made by one to cultivate the land with the help of rain water for better yield. Neglecting the common factors, if one indulges in sinful activities, God cannot be responsible for the consequences. If God remains neutral by merely according His approval to an act already initiated by an individual, it is due to the fact that the individual who initially acts under the influence of the past *karma*, should be allowed to reap the consequences of the *karma*.

V. The Relation of Jīva to Brahman

This is an important subject in Vedānta and it is discussed in a separate *adhikaraṇa* titled *Aṁśādhikaraṇa*. The issue involved is whether *jīva* is different from Brahman or is it non-different from Brahman. This question arises because several Upaniṣadic texts state that *jīva* and Brahman are different since the two ontological entities are of different nature. Thus the Kaṭha Upanisad states: *jñā jñau dvau ajau īśa anisau* [44] - "There are two unborn ones, the omniscient and the ignorant, the one all-powerful and the other powerless". There are also Upaniṣadic texts which convey the idea that *jīva* and Brahman are non-different. Thus says the Chāndogya: *tat-tvamasi* – "Thou art that". The Bṛhadāraṇyaka states: *ayamātmā Brahmā* – "This *Ātman* is Brahman"[45]. In view of these apparently conflicting statements the relation of *jīvātman* to Brahman needs to be discussed and the correct position explained. Though in connection with the theory of universe in relation to Brahman which is discussed in the *Ārambhaṇādhikaraṇa,* it is pointed out that the universe which comprises both non-sentient *prakṛti* and the sentient *jīvas,* is non-distinct from Brahman (*ananya*), Bādarāyaṇa takes up separately the subject of *jīva's* relation to Brahman to remove the doubts arising from the conflicting views advanced by different schools of Vedānta regarding this matter (*bahu kumati mata kṣiptaye*).[46]

Bādarāyaṇa explains the relation of *jīva* to Brahman in terms of '*aṁśa*'. The relevant *sūtra* reads: *Aṁśo nānā vyapadeśāt anyathā cā Pi dāśakitavāditvam adhīyata eke.*[47] It means: "*Jīva* is the *aṁśa* of Brahman on account of difference and otherwise (non-difference) also; in some (recensions of Vedas) it is spoken of as being of the nature of slaves, fishermen etc.".

Though the term '*aṁśa*' used in the *sūtra* is intended to explain the nature of the relation of *jīva* to Brahman and uphold the validity of the texts speaking of both difference and non-difference between *jīva* and Brahman, its fuller implication has become a subject of controversy among the commentators. *Aṁśa* literally means "part" but Brahman being *niravaya* or partless, it is difficult to conceive how *jīva* can be a part of Brahman. The Scriptural and *Smṛti* texts also employ the terms such as *pāda, aṁśa, śakti, tanu* or body to describe *jīva's* relation to Brahman. It is therefore necessary to clarify in what sense the term *aṁśa* is used by Bādarāyaṇa. The following are the theories advanced by the other schools of Vedānta to explain how the *jīva* is an *aṁśa* of Brahman. Vedānta Deśika examines them critically and proves that they are defective.

It may be possible

to say that *jīva* is an *aṁśa* of Brahman in the same way as the incarnated divine beings like Rāma, Kṛṣṇa etc. are the *aṁśas* of Paravāsudeva. But this explanation is not applicable to *jīva* since Brahman being *niravaya*, does not admit in it any *aṁśa*. To overcome this difficulty Brahman may be conceived as an aggregate of numerous *jīvas* (*cit samaṣṭiḥ*) similar to the jungle of numerous trees, and that each *jīva* in it is a part similar to each tree in the jungle being a separate tree. But this explanation would go against the Upaniṣadic statement that Brahman wills to become many. What is an aggregate of multiple *jīvas* cannot be one unitary entity which can become many.

According to another theory, *jīva* is an *aṁśa* of Brahman being conditioned by limiting adjuncts such as the bodies and the *antaḥkaraṇas* in the same way as the one all-pervasive ether becomes many when conditioned by several receptacles such as pots. That is, the very Brahman assumes the form of *jīvas* when conditioned by the physical bodies. With the removal of the limiting condition (*upādhi*), *jīva* becomes Brahman. This theory known as *upādhibrahmavāda* is upheld by Bhāskara. This view is also unsound, contends Vedānta Désika. If Brahman is aware that the conditioned self is non-different from it, it would not like to assume the form of *jīva* since it would result in its own destruction. It cannot be said that Brahman is unaware of it, because as an omniscient Being, it should know the happiness and suffering experienced by each body on account of the past *karma*, similar to a yogi assuming several bodies is able to know the experiences of each body. But such a possibility cannot be admitted in respect of *Īśvara*. This theory also suffers from other limitations. Does Brahman as associated with *upādhis* experience pleasure and pain everywhere in the form of *jīva*? Or the same Brahman as different from *jīvas* associated with *upādhis* experiences pleasure and pain? Or Brahman as undifferentiated, experiences pleasure and pain whenever it is conditioned? Or the very limiting condition (*upādhi*) such as the body associated with some other limiting condition experiences pleasure and pain? None of these alternatives is tenable. The first alternative is most unsound since it would amount to the admission of Brahman as associated with *upādhi* at all the time. Regarding the second, Brahman which is undivided would be subjected to divisibility. If Brahman experiences *sukha* and *duḥkha* as and when associated with *upādhi*, there would be, at every moment, liberation and bondage. The last option would end up with the admission of *Cārvāka* theory of physical body itself as *jīva*. Further the Upaniṣadic texts teaching the attainment of the status of similarity by the *jīva* with Brahman in the state of *mukti*, would become meaningless.

Some Advaitins maintain that *jīvas* are reflections of Brahman in the internal organs caused by *māyā*, similar to the reflections of the moon in waves of water (*chāyāṁśa jīvaḥ*). As reflections of Brahman in the internal organs, *jīvas* are regarded as *aṁśas* of Brahman. Vedānta Deśika subjects this theory to a critical examination. He raises the following objections. The reflections of the moon in water is to be seen by somebody. In the case of *jīvas* as reflections of Brahman, who is the seer (*draṣṭā*)? Is it Brahman itself? Or is it some other non-sentient entity other than Brahman? Is it the very *jīva*? Is it someone other than these three? It cannot be Brahman because according to the Advaitin, it is not the cogniser. Nor can it be a non-sentient entity since it is also devoid of the capacity to see. Regarding the third alternative, *jīva* itself cannot be the seer because prior to the existence of *jīva* as reflection of Brahman, *jīva* does not exist (*klṛpteḥ prāk svātma hāneḥ*). That is, unless Brahman is reflected in the *antaḥkaraṇa*, *jīva* does not come into existence and how can *jīva* cognize itself? The last alternative is also not tenable since other than Brahman, *jīva* and *avidyā*, nothing else is admitted by the Advaitins.[48]

Yādava Prakāśa advances a different theory of *jīva* as a part of Brahman. According to him, Brahman which is *sanmātra* or of the nature of consciousness, is associated with three-fold *śakti* viz. *Īśvara-śakti, cit-śakti* and *acit-śakti*. *Sat* or consciousness is present in all the three. Brahman itself, through the three-fold power it possesses, undergoes changes as God, individual souls and cosmic matter, just as water of the sea turns into waves, foam and bubbles. The individual souls are the transformed principles of *cit-śakti* of Brahman. Though they are different from Brahman, they are essentially Brahman, as the waves in actuality are non-different from water of the sea.

This theory is also considered defective. Other than the *sat*, which is the very Brahman, there are no separate entities as *jīvas*. But the Upaniṣadic texts acknowledge Brahman as different from *jīvas* and non-sentient *acit* and that Brahman as the *Antaryāmin* or Inner controller, is immanent in all.

There is one other theory referred to by Vedānta Deśika which is stated to be advocated by some Vedāntins. This theory is similar to the view of the Madhvas. According to this theory, *jīva* is considered as an *aṁśa* of Brahman in respect of certain common characteristics such as *jñāna* and *ānanda*, in the same way as the crown of the Meru mountain which is an *aṁśa* of Meru (*meroḥ aṁśaḥ kirīṭa prabhṛtiḥ*)[49]. This view is also considered defective because the crown (*kirīṭa*) cannot be the *aṁśa* or part of the *svarūpa* of meru mountain in the proper sense of the term. The *jīvas* and *Paramātman* are absolutely different and remain so always. In view of it, *jīvas* cannot be regarded as *aṁśa* of Paramātman on the limited basis of some similarity between the two.

What then is the meaning of the term *aṁśa*? It is not to be taken as a divisible part of a whole entity since Brahman is indivisible. Nor can it be regarded as an *aṁśa* of *Paramātman* on the analogy of the moon and its reflections in the waves. Nor can it be an *aṁśa* in the sense of ether being conditioned by *upādhi*. Nor is it part of *sanmātra* Brahman similar to the waves of the ocean. It is to be understood as the integral part of one entity (*ekavastu eka deśatva*). To be more specific, it means, as Rāmānuja explains that *aṁśa* is an essential attribute (*viśeṣana*) of a qualified substance (*viśiṣṭasya ekavastunaḥ viśeṣaṇāṁśam aṁśa eva*)[50]. A substance which is a qualified entity is inseparably related to its essential attribute, just as the sun is related to its rays. The essential attribute which is inseparably related to the substance is an *aṁśa* of that substance. Such a relationship between the two is known as *aṁśa-aṁśi bhāva* or *viśeṣaṇa-viśeṣya bhāva*. In the ontological sense it is called *śarīra-śarīri bhāva* or the relation of the body to the soul. In the same way *jīva* is related to Brahman as *aṁśa* is to *aṁśī* (Brahman). It is in this sense that Bādarāyaṇa employs the term *aṁśa* in explaining the relation of *jīva* to Brahman. This is evident from the fact that *aṁśatva* understood in this sense viz. *jīva* as inseperably related to Brahman, accords validity to the Scriptural texts speaking of both difference (*nānā vyapadeśa*) and non-difference (*anyathā ca*) between *jīva* and Brahman. The individual soul and Brahman are different by virtue of their intrinsic nature like substance and its essential attribute. They can also be non-different or one as Brahman integrally related to the soul, similar to the substance as inherently related to the attribute is one qualified entity (*viśiṣṭa dravya*). The *Antaryāmi Brāhmaṇa* fully supports the view that *jīvātman* in which *Paramātman* abides as *Antaryāmin*, is its *śarīra* or body in the technical sense that it is always supported and controlled by *Paramātman*. This view is also expressed in the *Vedānta-sūtra 'Avasthiteḥ iti kāśakṛtsnaḥ'*, which means that *Paramātman* abides in *jīva*. Hence *jīva* can be taken as *aṁśa* of Brahman (*tasmāt jīvo viśiṣṭe bhagavati guṇavat tatprakārāṁśa uktaḥ*)[51].

One possible objection that can be raised against this conclusion is that *jīvas* being part of Brahman, the defects found in the *jīvas* particularly the experience of happiness and suffering would also be applicable to *Paramātman*. This possibility is ruled out on the ground that *jīvas* and *Paramātman* being different in nature, the defects found in the *jīvas* do not apply to Paramätman, just as the changes taking place in the physical body do not affect the *jīva*. This is also logically justified. According to the epistemology of *Viśiṣṭādvaita*, the substance and attribute are different and the changes of the attribute do not affect the substance which is only the *āśraya* or substrate for the attributes.

Nor is there any possibility of all *jīvas* having the same kind of experience on account of *aṁśatva* or the characteristic of being a part of Brahman being common to all. This is due to the fact that *jīvas* are many and also abide in each body and are different from one another. Besides it is monadic (*aṇu*) in nature. The experience of happiness and suffering of one individual which is due to its past *karma*, is not experienced by the *jīva* of another individual.

All these difficulties arise in respect of the theories of *jīva* advanced by Bhāskara, Yādava Prakāśa and the Advaitins, since *jīva* in respect of its intrinsic nature (*svarūpa*) is essentially Brahman. As pointed out earlier, it is not possible to account for the variation in the experiences on the basis of *upādhis* or the limiting adjuncts such as *antaḥkaraṇas*, either caused by the illusory *avidyā* in the case of Advaitins or the real factors as in the case of Bhāskara and Yādava Prakāśa. Hence the theory of *jīva* as *aṁśa* of Brahman, as explained by Rāmānuja on the basis of the Scriptural authority and the relevant *Vedānta-sūtra*, is sound.

VI. The Theory of Transmigration of Jīva

After discussing the nature of *jīva* as *nitya*, *jñātā*, *kartā*, *bhoktā* and *aṁśa* of Brahman, Bādarāyaṇa deals with another important aspect of *jīva* entangled with bondage (*baddha jīva*). The subjects which come up for consideration are : movement of the *jīva* after the death of a person to the higher realms to enjoy the fruits of *karma* (deeds), manner of its rebirth, the conditions of *jīva* during the states of waking, dream, deep sleep (*suṣupti*) and swoon (*mūrchā*). The main purpose of considering this matter is to make an individual seeking *mokṣa* aware of the afflictions to which a *jīva* is subjected during the state of bondage and thereby develop a sense of detachment towards transient worldly pleasures (*vairāgya*) and consequently a craving for the attainment of the eternal Spiritual Goal. This is the reason for including this subject in the first *pāda* of the third *adhyāya,* though it is mainly concerned with the *sādhana* or the ways and means of attaining Brahman. We shall however discuss this matter in the present chapter as it has a direct bearing on the doctrine of *jīva*.

The theory of the *jīva* as *nitya* or devoid of either birth or death implies that it exists even after the death of a person in some form or other and also either in this universe or in some other realms. An important question which arises in this connection is: Does the *jīva,* which has performed meritorious deeds (*iṣṭādhikāri*) , after it departs from the body, move on to the realm of the moon (*candra-loka*) along with its subtle body (*bhūta-sūkṣma)* which comprises five subtle elements, *indriyas* and *prāṇa*? The question is relevant because the passage of Chāndogya Upaniṣad dealing with the *Pañcāgni-vidyā* describes the process of rebirth of the soul by adopting the metaphors of five fires into which the *jīva,* conceived as *ap* or water is offered as oblation. It is not clear from the passage whether or not the *jīva* departs from the body along with the *bhūta-sūkṣma or the subtle elements* to enable it to assume a different body in the realm of the moon.

According to the prima facie view, the disembodied soul does not carry with it the subtle elements. The argument in support of this view is that the soul can assume a body and organs in the realm to which it goes due to the influence of the merit acquired by it in the past life. As it is monadic in size (*aṇu*), it is possible for the *jīva* to move into another realm even without a subtle body (*jīvasya aṇor-gatiḥ*). *Īśvara* can also cause the movement for it as in the case of *prāṇa* which is made to move upward at the time of death. It is therefore unnecessary to postulate that the *jīva,* when it moves to a higher realm after death, carries with it the *bhūta-sūkṣma*.

Bādarāyaṇa does not accept this theory and affirms on the basis of the proper interpretation of the concerned Upaniṣadic passage that the *jīvātman* moves to the higher realm along with the subtle elements in order to assume a different body in the other region. The relevant *sūtra* reads: *Tadantara pratipattau raṁhati saṁ-pariṣvaktaḥ praśnanirū-paṇābhyām*[52]. It means: *Jīva* moves, fully enveloped with the subtle elements when it enters into another body as this is evident from the Upaniṣadic statements containing the question and answer given to it.

The fuller implication of the *sūtra* can be understood with reference to the Chāndogya-passage dealing with the rebirth of the soul. In this passage containing a dialogue between Śvetaketu (son of Āruṇi) and Pravāhana Jābāli (king of Pāñcāla), the following five questions are raised:

1. How these persons, when they die, go to the different places?
2. How they come back to the world?
3. How the *svargaloka* (heaven) is not filled by the people going there again and again after death?
4. What is the means of access to the divine path (*Devayāna*) and the path leading to the fathers (*Pitṛyāna*)?
5. After which round of offering of the libation, the jīva conceived as water (*ap*), attains the name of *puruṣa* (*vettha yathā pañcamyām āhutyau āpaḥ puruṣa-vacaso bhavanti*)?[53]

Of these, the last question is important as it relates to the manner of the *jīva's* rebirth after death. In reply to these questions the Upaniṣad describes the process of rebirth in five stages by using the metaphors of five fires (*pañcāgni*).

At the first stage, the disembodied soul, designated as *śraddhā*, soon after it reaches the realm of the moon, is offered as oblation to the fire designated as heaven (*dyuloka*) by the celestial deities. It then assumes a divine and beautiful body (*amṛtamayaṁ dehaṁ*) named as Somarāja to enable it to enjoy the heavenly pleasures in the realm of the moon. In the second stage, the soul is offered to the fire designated as *parjanya* (the God of rains) and it then takes the form of rain water. In the third stage, it is made to enter into the physical world which is also metaphorically described as *agni*. It then becomes mixed up with the food grains. In the fourth stage, the soul is made to enter the body of a man which is also described as *agni*, through the food consumed by him. It then takes the form of semen. In the fifth and final stage, the soul is made to enter into the womb of a woman, which is described as *agni*, through the sexual intercourse. It then assumes the designation of *puruṣa* or human body (*puruṣa vacaso bhavanti*).[54]

Thus, according to this passage, the soul described as *ap* or water and also as *śraddhā* is offered as oblation successively to the sacrificial fires of heaven, the rain-God, the physical world and the man and at each stage it assumes the respective gross forms as that of the moon (that is, a lustrous body similar to the moon), rain (*parjanya*), food (*anna*), semen (*retas*). The fifth oblation in the form of semen which is offered to the fire conceived as the woman, takes the form of human body (*puruṣa*). This is the implication of the statement of the Upaniṣad: *pañcamyāṁ āhutau āpaḥ puruṣa vacaso bhavanti*. This is the direct reply to the fifth question viz. *'vettha yatha pancamyāṁ āpaḥ puruṣa-vacaso bhavanti'*[55].

Taking into consideration this question and the reply given to it in the passage, it is obvious that according to the Upaniṣad, the *jīva* designated as *āpaḥ* and also *śraddhā* assumes a new body after it enters into the womb of a woman which is metaphorically described as *agni* by passing through the four earlier stages described as *dyuloka* or the heaven, *parjanya-loka* or the realm of the rain-Gods, the physical universe (*pṛthivī*) as the food (*anna*) and as the semen of a man through the food consumed by him, and finally into the womb of the woman through sexual intercourse. On the basis of this description, the term *'ap'* mentioned in the Upaniṣad to denote the *jīva*, implies that *jīva* is associated with all five subtle elements and also *indriyas* including *prāṇa*. According to the *Pañcīkaraṇa* theory, all objects in the universe are constituted of all five elements and hence the mention of *'ap'* is illustrative of the other four elements.

Separately, the Upaniṣad states that when the *jīva* exits from the body at the time of death, the *prāṇa* along with the *indriyas* follow it (*prāṇam anutkrāmantaṁ sarve prāṇā anutkrāmanti*).[56] The term *śraddhā* employed in the Upaniṣad in place of *āpa* as oblation to be offered to the fire (designated as *parjanya*), also denotes *jīva* along with its subtle elements. Hence Bādarāyaṇa affirms that *jīva* when it leaves the body moves into the realm of the moon along with the *bhūta-sūkṣma* (*raṁhati sampariṣvaktaḥ*).[57]

In connection with the movement of the *jīva* into the realm of the moon and its return to the physical world to be reborn as *puruṣa*, the following issues are raised:

1) Does the *jīva* return to the earth after it has fully experienced the effects of all the good deeds performed earlier or does it have the residue of the *puṇya karmas* yet to be experienced?
2) Do all persons, that is, those who have performed the prescribed deeds and also those who do not observe the prescribed deeds go to the realm of the moon?
3) When the soul descends from the realm of the moon to the earth through the *ākāśa* or ether, does it assume the form of *ākāśa* or mere semblance of it?
4) How long do the souls remain in *ākāśa*?
5) In what form does the soul abide in the food grains, plants, trees etc before it enters the human body?

As these questions have a bearing on the theory of transmigration of the soul, Bādarāyaṇa attempts to clarify them in the following four *adhikaraṇas*. 1. *Kṛtātyādhikaraṇa*

2. *Aniṣṭādikāryadhikaraṇa* 3. *Tatsvābhāvyāpattyadhikaraṇa* 4. *Nāticirādy-adhikaraṇa*. We shall take note of the important points without going into the details.

Regarding the first question, it is stated in the Chāndogya Upaniṣad that only the householders who have performed the meritorious deeds such as *yajña* and other humanitarian services go to the realm of the moon to reap the benefits of their deeds.[58] It is also pointed out that after having enjoyed them completely (*yāvat saṁpātaṁ uṣitvā*), they return to the earth through the same path as they traversed to the higher realm. Thus says the Upaniṣad: *Tasmin yāvat saṁpātam uṣitvā athaitam-eva adhvānaṁ punaḥ nivartante*[59] - "They remain in the realm of moon till the merit of their *karma* lasts and after having enjoyed it, they return through the same path they ascended." On the basis of these teachings it is maintained that *jīva* would have enjoyed the fruits of good *karma* in the realm of the moon and returned to the earth without any residual *karma*, to be reborn. This view is also corroborated by the statement of Bṛhadāraṇyaka Upaniṣad which says that after having experienced all *karma*, the soul returns to the mundane existence (*prāpyāntaṁ karmaṇaḥ tasya yatkiñcit iha karoti ayam; tasmāt lokāt punar-etyasmai lokāya karmaṇe*[60]). This is the prima facie view.

Bādarāyaṇa does not accept this view. The relevant *sūtra* reads: *Kṛtātyaye anuśayavān-dṛṣṭa-smṛtibhyāṁ yathā etam-anevaṁ ca* [61].

It means: "After having experienced the fruits of the good deeds, *jīva* returns to the earth with a residue of *karma*. It is stated so in the Scriptural and *Smṛti* texts. When it returns, it traverses either through the same pathway or some other pathway also."

In elucidating the implication of this *sūtra*, Vedānta Deśika points out that if the soul in the realm of the moon would have exhausted all the effects of the past deeds, then its rebirth as individuals with good or bad life and higher or lower status cannot be explained. The Scriptural text also says: *tadya iha ramaṇīya caraṇa abhyāśo ha yatte ramaṇīyam yoniṁ āpadyeran brāhmaṇa yoniṁ kṣatriya yoniṁ vaiśya yoniṁ vā atha ya iha kapūya caraṇa abhyāśo ha yatte kapūyam yoniṁ āpadyeran svayoniṁ vā sūkara yoniṁ vā caṇḍāla yoniṁ vā.*[62]

"Those whose conduct has been good here will soon get birth such as a *Brāhmaṇa, Kṣatriya* or *Vaiśya*. But those whose conduct is evil, will be born in evil births such as the birth of a dog or a pig or the birth of a lowest caste. "

Hence it is concluded that the souls which have gone to the realm of the moon do return to the earth with residual *karma* to be yet experienced in the next life.

The author of the *sūtra* clarifies by quoting Bādari's view that the term *caraṇa* used in the Upaniṣad does not merely mean *ācāra* or conduct but it also implies both *puṇya* or merit and *pāpa* or evil (*sukṛta duṣkṛte eva iti tu Bādari).*[63]

ii) Regarding the second question - whether the individuals who have not performed the meritorious deeds go to the realm of the moon – the prima facie view is that those who have not done good deeds also go to the realm of the moon. In support of it, a few Scriptural and *Smṛti* texts are quoted. The Kauṣītikī Upaniṣad says: *ye vai ca asmāt lokāt prayānti candramasameva te sarve gacchanti*[64] - "All those who depart from this world after death go only to the realm of the moon". The word *'sarve'* or 'all' would cover even the sinners who first go to the world of Yama. After undergoing punishment there, they will go to the realm of the moon.

Bādarāyaṇa does not accept this view. The Upaniṣads have laid down two separate paths viz *arcirādi mārga* and *dhūmra-mārga* intended for two different categories of persons viz., those who have observed prescribed meditation on Brahman for attainment of *mokṣa* and those who have performed prescribed deeds for other higher benefits. The former category of persons do not go to the realm of the moon. It is only the latter category of persons who aspire for heaven and other material benefits, go to the *candraloka*. It is not therefore correct to say that even the persons who have not performed the good deeds (*aniṣṭādhikārī*), go to the realm of the moon after death.

Further it is also stated that the persons other than the two categories – those who observe prescribed meditation (*vidyā*) and those who perform good *karma*, do not have to go to the realm of the moon. These are the sinners who take rebirth even without going through the process of five stages, as pointed out in the *Pañcāgni-vidyā*. They are born in other forms such as animals, birds, insects, plants etc. The Chāndogya text states that there are three other ways in which living beings come into existence: *Teṣāṁ khalu eṣāṁ bhūtānāṁ trīṇyeva bījam bhavanti aṇḍajam jīvajaṁ udbhijjaṁ*[65] "There are only three origins for all beings: those born of eggs, those born of creatures (womb) and those born of seeds (plants). Birds and reptiles are born of eggs. Animals and human beings are born through wombs. Plants and trees are born of seeds. In all these cases there is no need for the souls to pass through the five stages, as stated in the *Pañcāgni-vidyā*. It is only the individuals who have performed the meritorious deeds (*iṣṭādhikārī*) that go to the realm of the moon and they are reborn through the media of clouds, rain, food grains and semen of *puruṣa* and finally through the entry into the womb of a woman.

iii) We now come to the third question. During the descent of the soul from the realm of the moon, the soul is stated to go to *ākāśa* (ether). From *ākāśa* to *vāyu*, then it becomes *dhūma* or smoke, then it becomes cloud and thereafter it falls on earth as rain. After having fallen on earth, they enter paddy, corn, plants, seeds etc. It is indeed very difficult and may even take a long time to come out of it. It takes birth in the form of human being only through one who has eaten that food grain and whenever he ejects it through his semen into the generative organ of the woman.

The relevant passage reads:

Tasmin yāvat saṁpātam uṣitvā athaitam eva adhvānaṁ punar-nivartante, yathaitam ākāśaṁ, ākāśād vāyuṁ, vāyur-

bhūtvā dhumo bhavati, dhumo bhūtva abhraṁ bhavati.[66]

Abhram bhūtvā megho bhavati megho bhūtvā pravarṣati, tai ha vrīhi yavā oṣadhi-vanaspatayaḥ tila māṣa iti jāyante; ato vai khalu durniṣprapataram, yo yo hy-annam atto yo retaḥ siñcati tad bhūya eva bhavati.[67]

With reference to this passage, third question is asked: When the *jīva* on its descent to earth enters *ākāśa* does it become *ākāśa* or does it become similar to it? The answer given by Bādarāyaṇa is that it assumes similarity to *ākāśa* (*sādṛśya*). That is, it gets united with *ākāśa* and hence it is regarded as similar to *ākāśa* (*tat-saṁsarga-kṛta tad-sādṛśyāpatty abhiprāyam*).

The next question is: How long the *jīva* stays in *ākāśa*? The answer is that it does not stay there for too long (*nāticireṇa*) because in the subsequent sentence referring to its entry into the food grains, it is said that it is indeed very difficult to get out of them (*dur-niṣprapataram*).

Regarding the question relating to the manner in which the soul remains in the food grains before it enters into the human body in the form of *retas* (semen), Bādarāyaṇa states that it becomes stuck to (associated with) the *jīva* which is already inherent in the grain (*anyādhiṣṭhite*)[68], in the same way as it becomes closely associated with (*saṁsthita*) *ākāśa*, clouds etc. Its implication is that it is born as the food grain (assume the form of grain), since it does not have to experience any *sukha* and *duḥkha* at this stage. When the food grain associated with the *jīva* is consumed by a human being and transformed into semen, and subsequently when the semen is transmitted to the sexual organ of a woman, it does not have the scope to experience the effects of *karma*. As stated earlier, the purpose of mentioning all these details of the process of rebirth is to create a sense of detachment towards the life of a *jīva* during the state of bondage and develop in the individual the craving for escape from bondage and also aspiration for the attainment of the eternal Spiritual Goal.

VII. Four States of Jīva in Bondage

After discussing the issues relating to the rebirth of the soul, Bādarāyaṇa presents the conditions of jiva during the states of dream, deep sleep and swoon. The following *adhikaraṇas* in the second *pāda* of the third *adhyāya* deal with this subject:1. *Sandhyādhikaraṇa* 2. *Tadabhāvādhikaraṇa* 3. *Karmānusmṛtyādhikaraṇa* 4. *Mugdhādhikaraṇa*. As pointed out earlier, the objective of taking up this matter in the *Sādhana pāda* is to bring to light how the *jīva* during the state of bondage is subject to various afflictions, whereas *Paramātman* is free from all such defects (*nirdoṣa*). This knowledge would be useful to the aspirant for *mokṣa*, for cultivating *vairāgya* or non-attachment to worldly life and develop a deep craving (*tṛṣṇā*) for the attainment of *Paramātman* who is the Supreme Goal.[69] As will be seen presently, in all these states *Paramātman* causes for the *jīva* the experience of the dream objects, the sound sleep and the unconscious condition respectively because *jīva*, though it is *kartā* and *bhoktā*, is dependent on *Paramātman*. This awareness of *jīva's* dependence on *Paramātman* is also useful to realize the greatness (*māhātmya*) of Brahman who is the sole object of *upāsanā*. This is the justification for discussing the different conditions (*avasthās*) of *jīva* in the second *pāda* of *Sādhanādhyāya* prior to the discussion of the twofold nature of Brahman as free from defects and also endowed with numerous auspicious attributes (*nirasta nikhila doṣah ananta kalyāṇa guṇa viśiṣṭaḥ*).

a) State of dream

This subject is considered in the *Sandhyādhikaraṇa*. The word *sandhyā* refers to the state of dream since it occurs in between the waking state and the dreamless state. The question which comes up for consideration is whether the objects experienced in dream are created by *jīva* or *Paramātman*. The prima facie view is that these are created by the *jīva* because it is so stated in the Upaniṣad. The Bṛhadāraṇyaka

Upaniṣad states: *na tatra rathayogāḥ na panthāno bhavati...atha ratha rathayogaṁ panthāḥ sṛjate...sa hi kartā*[70] "There are no chariots in the state of dream, no horses, no roads ; then he creates chariots, horses and roads He is the creator". In the statement *'sa hi sṛjate'* the word *'sa'* is taken as *jīva* since it experiences the dream objects. Since *jīva* is stated to possess the power to create objects at its will (*satyasaṁkalpa*), as in the case of *Īśvara,* it is possible to explain the creation of dream objects by *jīva*. The Kaṭhopaniṣad mentions that *puruṣa* (*jīva*) can create objects in accordance with its desire.[71]

Bādarāyaṇa does not accept this view. *Jīva* does not have the capacity to create dream objects by its will. Though *satya-saṁkalpatva* is the intrinsic nature of *jīva,* according to the Upaniṣad, this capacity is eclipsed by the *karma* during the state of bondage and it becomes manifest only when it is fully liberated from bondage. Hence *jīva* cannot create the dream objects. Only *Paramātman,* who is endowed with unchecked freedom and power to create anything by will, causes the various dream objects to be experienced by the individuals concerned. These are regarded as mere *māyā* (*māyāmātra*) in the sense that these are wondrous creations (*āścaryarūpa sṛṣṭi*) of *Paramātman. Māyā* does not imply, as Advaitins claim, the illusory appearance. If *jīva* did possess this capacity then it would not have created for itself undesirable objects or events (*anabhimate samutpādanādeḥ ayogāt*). Besides, it is believed on the strength of Scriptural texts that the dreams are portenders (*sūcaka*) of auspicious and inauspicious events for a person. Hence it is appropriate to admit that the dream experiences of *jīva* are caused by *Paramātman.*

b) State of suṣupti

Suṣupti is a state of deep sleep in which there is no experience of dream (*svapnānubhavaḥ*). In other words, it is dreamless deep sleep. According to the Upaniṣads, this occurs when the *jīva* is resting in the subtle arteries named *hitā nāḍi* radiating from the heart and also in the *nāḍi* called the *purītat*. It also happens when jīva is resting in *Paramātman* who abides in the heart (*hārdam brahma*). The Upaniṣadic texts refer to three places as the resting ground for the *jīva* during the state of *suṣupti*. Thus says the Chāndogya: *Tad yatraitat suptaḥ samastaḥ samprasannaḥ svapnam na vijānāti, āsu tadā nāḍiṣu sṛpto bhavati. ...tejasā hi tadā saṁpanno bhavati*[72] "The jīva during deep sleep withdraws all the senses and in a state of tranquility it does not see any dream and it then becomes united with *tejas* (Brahman)".

The Bṛhadāraṇyaka describes *suṣupti* as follows: *atha yadā suṣupto bhavati yadā na kasyacana veda, hitā nāma nāḍyo dvāsaptati-sahasrāṇi hṛdayāt purītat abhipratiṣṭhante; tābhiḥ pratyavasṛpya purītati śete.*[73]

"When the *jiva* is in deep sleep and is not aware of anything, there are 72000 *nāḍis* called *hitā* which radiate from the heart towards the *purītat*. Through them it moves forth and rests in the *purīta nāḍi*". The Chāndogya elsewhere states that when a person goes to deep sleep, the *jīva* is united with *sat* (Brahman) (*yatra etat puruṣaḥ svapiti nāma, satā somya tadā sampanno bhavati.*[74]

Thus three different places are mentioned in the Upaniṣads. The question arises: Where does the *jīva* rest during the state of *suṣupti*? According to the prima facie view it has to be one of the three since *jīva* cannot repose in all three places at the same time. Bādarāyaṇa clarifies the position. If any one of the three places is accepted as the reposing ground, then the other two mentioned in the Upaniṣad stand rejected. This is not appropriate as it would amount to the rejection of what is stated in the Upaniṣad. Hence all the three places together have to be accepted as the resting place for jīva during *suṣupti*. Such an explanation is plausible on the analogy of a person sleeping on a bed spread over a cot which is located in a mansion (*prāsāda khaṭva paryaṅka-nyāya*). The *nāḍis* and the *purītat* correspond to the mansion and the cot respectively, whereas the bed corresponds to the *Paramātman*. Though the mansion, cot and bed are different, the three together serve the common purpose of providing the resting place. On the basis of this explanation, it is affirmed by Bādarāyaṇa that *sat* or Brahman is the actual resting place for *jīva*. That is, during deep sleep, *jīva* reposes in Brahman abiding in the heart and it does not therefore experience any dream at this time (*ato brahmaiva sākṣāt suṣupti sthānam*). This conclusion becomes confirmed by the Chāndogya text which states that *jīva* having come back from sat (Brahman) does not know that it has returned from it (*satā āgamya na viduḥ satā āgacchāmahe*[75]). This fact that the *jīva* returns to its normal state reveals that the state of *suṣupti* is a transitory state for *jīva* when it is temporarily united with Brahman and it does not imply that *jīva* becomes identical with Brahman, as Advaitins claim.

Further the same *jīva* which enjoyed the sound dreamless sleep comes back to its normal waking state (*yaḥ suptaḥ sa eva uttiṣṭhati*). This is evident from the fact that the same person recollects that he slept well. The *jīva* has yet to experience the *puṇya* and *pāpa* of the previous life prior to its attaining *mokṣa*. The Upanisadic texts also state with reference to the *jīva* experiencing *suṣupti*: "Whatever creatures they were here, whether a lion, or tiger or wolf etc, they become the same again." Further if one who experiences *suṣupti* is liberated, the Vedānta enjoining the observation of prescribed *sādhana* for attaining liberation would be rendered futile. The statement that *jīva* is united with Brahman is only intended to convey that *jīva* which is subjected to afflictions during waking state gets fully rested in *suṣupti* for a while.

c) State of swoon

This is also a state to which *jīva* is subjected. It is described in the *Vedānta-sūtra* as '*ardha saṁpatti*' which means "half dead". That is, it is neither a state of waking nor dream, since there is no consciousness in this state. It is not even *suṣupti* because the state of *mūrcchā* can also be caused by a head injury. Nor is it total death since there is life in the body and there is also the possibility of one waking up from the state of unconsciousness. Death is total cessation of the functioning of all organs and *prāṇa*. Hence it is regarded as a state of half-death (*mugdhāvasthā*) to which a *jīva* is sometimes liable.

---

1. *See* VS II-1-22. *See* also VS. I-1-17 *na itaro anupapatteḥ*. Also, VS I-1-18 *bheda vyapadeśācca*
2. Tait. Br. I-1-10. *Prajāpatiḥ prajā asṛjata*
3. VS II-3-18
4. Ka. Up. I-2-18
5. Śvet. Up. VI-13
6. *See* AS verse 228
7. *See* FVV. pp196-7
8. VS II-3-19
9. The word *jna* in the *sutra* is interpreted as knowing subject on the authority of *Pāṇini-sūtra*. *See Pāṇini- sūtra* III-1-35. *Igupadhjñaprikara jānātiti jñaḥ jīvaḥ*.
10. Br. Up. V-7-22
11. Tait. Up. II-5-1
12. VP. I-2-6 *jñānasvarūpam atyatanirmalaṁ paramārthataḥ*
13. Br. Up. *VI-3-30*
14. Praśna Up. IV-9.
15. Br. Up. VI-3-30
16. *See* AS verse 231. *Jñāna alopādi vākyānuguṇa viṣayatāṁ yāti asau evakāraḥ*
17. Muṇḍ. Up – II-1-9
18. Br. Up IV-4-2 *Eṣa ātmā niṣkrāmati śarīra deśebhyaḥ*. Also Kau. Up. *Asmāt lokāt prayānti candramasa eva te sarve gacchanti , tasmāt lokāt punareti.*
19. VS II-2-20
20. *See* Śvet. Up. V-9
21. *See* TMK II-5. See also FVV pp193-94
22. AS verse 232
23. Kaṭha. Up. I-2-19
24. *See* BG. III-27. *Prakṛteḥ kriyamāṇāni guṇaih. karmāṇi sarvaśaḥ, ahaṁkāra vimūḍhātmā kartā'ham ity manyate. See* also BG. XIII-20. *Kārya kāraṇa kartṛtve hetuḥ prakṛtirucyate*
25. BG. II-24. *Acchedyo'yaṁ adahyo'yaṁ*
26. VS II-3-33 *See* also AS.verse 233
27. Br. Up. IV-1-18 *Evamaiveṣa etān prāṇān grahītvā sve śarire yathā kāmān parivartate*

28. Tait. Up. II-5 *Vijñānaṁ yajñaṁ kurute*
29. *See* RB on BG. XIII-20
30. *See* FVV Chapter 6. pp198-99
31. *See* AS verse 235. *Vyāpāra jñāna vāncchā praśakana yatana ayogayuktistu mandā*
32. *See* AS verse 235
33. VS II-3-41
34. Tait. Āraṇyaka. III-11-10
35. BG. XVIII-61
36. BG. XV-15
37. *See* VS I-3-41. *Kṛta prayatnāpekṣastu vihita-pratiṣiddha avaiyarthyādibhyaḥ*
38. BG. IX-29
39. *See* Kau. Up. III-6. *Eṣa eva asādhu karma kārayati taṁ yam-adho ninīṣati, esa eva sādhu karma kārayati taṁ yamebhyo lokebhya unninīṣati*
40. *See* AS verse 240
41. *See* AS verse 240.
42. VS II-3-41. *Kṛta prayatnāpekṣastu vihita-pratiṣiddhavaiyarthyādibhyaḥ*
43. RB. II-3-41
44. Ka. Up. I-9
45. Br. Up.II-4-6
46. *See* AS. Verse 244
47. VS II-3-42
48. *See* AS. Verse 247
49. *See* AS. Verse 249
50. RB. II-3-42
51. *See* AS verse 249
52. VS III-1-1
53. *See* Ch. Up. V-3-3
54. *Ibid*
55. Ch. Up. V-9-1
56. Br. Up. VI-4-2
57. VS III-1-1
58. Ch. Up. V-1-3
59. Ch. Up. V-10-5
60. Br. Up. VI-4-6
61. VS III-1-8
62. Ch. Up. V-10-7
63. VS III-1-11
64. Kau. Up. I-3
65. Ch. Up. VI-3-1
66. *Ibid* V-10-5
67. Ch. Up. V-10-8
68. VS III-1-24. *Anyādhiṣtite pūrvavad abhilāpāt*

69. *See* AS verse 289
70. Br. Up. VI-3-10
71. Katha Up. II-5-8. *Ya eṣu supteṣu jāgrati kāmaṁ kāmaṁ puruṣo nirmimāṇaḥ*
72. Ch. Up. VIII-6-3
73. Br. Up. IV-1-19
74. Ch. Up. VI-8-1
75. Ch. Up. VI-10-2

Chapter Eight

THE DOCTRINE OF SĀDHANĀ

The Vedānta is regarded as *mokṣa-śāstra* since its main objective is to teach the ways and means of attainment of Brahman which is the Supreme Goal (*Parama-puruṣārtha*). Thus says the *Taittirīya* Upaniṣad: "The knower of Brahman (*brahmavit*) attains the highest Goal (*āpnoti Paraṁ*). Bādarāyaṇa, therefore, accords special attention to this subject. The entire third *adhyāya* of *Brahma-sūtra*, which is titled *Sādhanādhyāya*, is devoted to the discussion of the *sādhana*. Nearly fifty-five *adhikaraṇas* included in the four *pādas* of this *adhyāya* and also six *adhikaraṇas* of the first *pāda* of the fourth *adhyāya* deal with different aspects of *sādhana* viz., 1) Brahman as the worthy object of meditation, 2) the nature of *sādhana*, 3) different types of *vidyā* or *upāsanā*, 4) *karma* as subordinate means to *vidyā*, 5) the components and other pre-requisites of *upāsanā*. We shall discuss all these matters in the present chapter as presented in the *Adhikaraṇa-sārāvalī*.

I. Brahman as the Object of Meditation

a. Brahman as Ubhayaliṅga

According to Bādarāyaṇa, *vidyā*, also named as *upāsanā* or unceasing meditation on Brahman, is the direct means for the attainment of the Supreme Goal. Thus it is stated in the *sūtra*: *Puruṣārtho ataḥ śabdāt iti Bādarāyaṇah*[1]. It means that in the opinion of Bādarāyaṇa, the Supreme Goal is attained only by means of *vidyā* (the word *ataḥ* in the *sūtra* being read as *vidyātaḥ* in the context of the earlier *pāda* dealing with *vidyā*), because it is so declared by the *Scriptural* texts (*śabdāt*). The fuller implications of the *sūtra* as well as the nature and other details about *vidyā* are discussed later. Prior to it, Bādarāyaṇa takes up an important subject dealing with the two-fold character of Brahman described as *ubhayaliṅga*, that is, Brahman as totally free from all defects (*nirasta-nikhila doṣatva*) and Brahman as endowed with numerous auspicious attributes (*samasta-kalyāṇa-guṇākaratva*). Though he has presented in the first *adhyāya*, the nature and distinguishing characteristics of Brahman by methodically examining all the relevant Upaniṣadic texts, he brings up the subject of two-fold character of Brahman separately in the *Sādhanādhyāya* for two reasons. First, it was pointed out in the preceding *adhikaraṇas* of *pāda* 1 and 2 that *jīva* abiding in the physical body is subject to various afflictions. In this connection, the question arises: whether *Paramātman* who also abides in the bodies of individuals and also in the non-sentient material entities as their *Antaryāmin* would be affected by the defects found in them? If He is affected, would such a *Paramātman* be the worthy object of meditation for the attainment of the Supreme Goal? In order to remove this doubt and establish that *Paramātman* is the worthy object of meditation, it becomes necessary to prove on the basis of the Scriptural texts that Brahman is untouched by afflictions and other defects (*nirdoṣa*) and also that it is endowed with numerous auspicious attributes (*kalyāṇa guṇas*). This knowledge about Brahman as *ubhayaliñga* is essential for meditation since it generates in the *upāsaka* a craving to attain it (*prāpya tṛṣṇā*).

The second important reason for bringing up this subject of Brahman as *ubhayaliṅga*, is to refute the theory of Brahman as *nirguṇa* or devoid of all attributes as conceived by Advaita Vedānta. According to Vedānta Deśika, the concept of Brahman as *nirguṇa* is itself defective. Such a

Brahman cannot be the object of meditation for attaining the *puruṣārtha*[2].

Keeping all these points in mind, Bādarāyaṇa introduces the following *sūtra* in the *Sādhanādhyāya*: *Na sthānato'pi parasya ubhayaliṅgam sarvatra hi*[3].

The word *sthānataḥ* along with the negative particle *na* means, in the context of preceding *adhikaraṇas* dealing with the different states of *jīva*, that *Paramātman* (*Para*) is not touched by the defects found in the bodies of *jīvas* in spite of its immanence in the *jīvas* and other entities as *Antaryāmin*. The reason for this is provided in the next two words of the *sūtra* "*ubhayaliṅgam sarvatra hi*" which mean that in all *Scriptural* and *Smṛti* texts (*sarvatra*), Brahman is described as possessing two-fold character (*ubhayaliṅgam*), that is, as essentially free from all defects (*nirasta-nikhila-doṣah*) and also endowed with auspicious attributes (*kalyāṇa-gunātmaka*). Thus says the *Chāndogya* Upaniṣad: *Eṣa ātmā apahatapāpmā vijaro vimṛtyuḥ viśoko vijighatso apipāsaḥ satyakāmaḥ satyasaṁkalpaḥ*[4] - "Brahman is free from evil, free from old age, free from death, free from grief, free from hunger, free from thirst, whose desires are self-fulfilled, and whose desires are not obstructed". In the above statement the two-fold character of Brahman is explicitly mentioned. There are many other Upaniṣadic texts referring to either of these aspects of Brahman and these are quoted by Rāmānuja in his commentary on subsequent *sūtras* of this *adhikaraṇa*. The *Visṇupurāṇa* also reiterates the same truth[5].

By way of elucidation, it is pointed out that *karma* of an individual self is the cause for experiencing either *sukha* or happiness or *duḥkha* or suffering by *jīva*. Hence *jīva* during the state of its bondage is subjected to afflictions. In the case of *Paramātman*, He is free from *karma* and hence in spite of His immanence in *jīvas*, He remains unaffected by the afflictions. The description of Brahman as *apahatapāpmā* implies that it is free from both *puṇya* and *pāpa*. The *Muṇḍaka* Upaniṣad [6] by citing the classic illustration of two birds sitting on the same tree, one eating the fruit and the other sitting passively, clearly conveys that *jīva* experiences the fruit of *karma*, whereas *Paramātman* remains passive without experiencing the effects of *karma*. More importantly the *Antaryāmī Brāhmaṇa*, while describing how *Paramātman* abides in non-sentient entities such as *pṛthivī*, *ap*, etc., and also in the *jīvātman*, states that He is your Self, the *Antaryāmin* (Inner controller) and also *amṛta* (*sa ta ātmā antaryāmyamṛtaḥ*). The word *amṛta* which is repeated in each statement implies that *Paramātman*, though abiding in the body of an individual and other material entities, is totally untouched by the defects.

An objection may be raised against this view. If *Paramātman* by virtue of His being *apahatapāpmā* is not affected by the afflictions of the physical bodies in which He is immanent, how then *jīva*, which is also described as *apahatapāpmā* by the *Chāndogya* Upaniṣad becomes affected by afflictions by abiding in the physical body? The answer to this is that though *jīva* in respect of its essential nature is free from evil (*apahatapāpmā*), this quality of *jīva* is eclipsed during the state of bondage due to *karma*. Only when it is totally liberated from bondage and attains the state of *mukti*, its *apahatapāpmatva* becomes fully manifest. But *Paramātman*, unlike *jīvātman* remains all the time free from evil as He is not subject to *karma*. Hence He remains untouched by defects at all time despite His immanence in the *jīvas* and other material objects.

A major objection is raised against the theory of Brahman as *ubhayaliṅga*. The Upaniṣads describe Brahman in two ways. Some texts speak of Brahman as possessing qualities. On the contrary, some texts state that Brahman is devoid of qualities. As these two kinds of statements are mutually opposed, Brahman cannot be conceived as devoid of qualities and also possessing qualities. To overcome this conflict, Brahman is to be admitted as *nirviśeṣa* or devoid of all characteristics (*samasta-viśeṣarahitam nirvikalpakameva brahma pratipattavyam*).[7] The reason advanced in support of it is that a large number of Upaniṣadic texts describe Brahman as devoid of all determinations. This is the argument advanced by Śaṁkara. There is also a logical justification for adopting this explanation. According to the *Apaccheda-nyāya*[8] or the principle of what is later being of greater force than the earlier, *nirguṇa śrutis* are more valid than the *saguṇa śrutis.* That is, the texts which deny all qualities are of greater validity than the texts which refer to qualities because denial presupposes that which is to be denied.

This objection is ruled out by Vedānta Deśika. It is true that there is apparent conflict between *saguṇa śrutis* and *nirguṇa śrutis.* But it is possible to reconcile this apparent conflict by adopting the *Mīmāṁsā* principle known as *utsarga-apavāda nyāya.* According to this principle, the negative texts can be interpreted in accordance with the affirmative texts. Thus for instance, there is a general Scriptural statement which enjoins that animals should not be injured, while another statement points out that a particular animal named *chāga* or goat is to be offered for a specific sacrifice. The conflict between these two statements is overcome by interpreting the general statement to mean that the animal other than those enjoined in the Scriptural text for sacrificial purposes should not be injured. The same logic holds good in respect of *saguṇa* and *nirguṇa* texts. If some texts affirm that Brahman possesses qualities, while others deny the same such as *niṣkalaṁ, niṣkriyaṁ, śāntaṁ niravadyaṁ* and *nirañjanaṁ*[9], the latter (*nirguṇa śrutis*) should be understood to mean the denial of the qualities other than those mentioned in the *saguṇa śrutis.* (*vihita vyatirikta guṇa niṣedhaḥ*). In other words, the implication of the negative texts is that Brahman is devoid of such inauspicious attributes as *vikāra* (change), *karma* etc., but not that it is devoid of all characteristics. Such an interpretation, though it restricts the import of the negative texts to some extent, maintains the validity of both the *saguṇa* and *nirguṇa* texts. Further, the *apaccheda nyāya* is applicable where the two texts which are not always opposed to each other follow as the earlier and later (*aniyata virodha paurvāparyehy-apaccheda nyāyaḥ*).[10] In the case of *saguṇa* and *nirguṇa śrutis*, these are always opposed to each other (*nitya virodha*). Hence it is not appropriate to overcome the conflict by resorting to this principle. On the other hand it is more relevant to take recourse to the principle adopted in the *upakrama adhikaraṇa* of *Mīmāṁsā*, that is, the principle of what is stated at the commencement of the passage stands valid rather than what is said later. Thus, when the apparent conflict between the *saguṇa vākyas* and *nirguṇa vākyas* can be easily resolved without according lesser validity to the *saguṇa śrutis*, it is not appropriate to maintain that the *nirguṇa śrutis* alone are authoritative and on that basis, maintain that Brahman is to be conceived only as devoid of all attributes[11].

It is argued that Brahman, according to the Upaniṣad, is of the nature of knowledge (*jñāna-svarūpa*). Thus states the *Taittirīya*: "*Satyaṁ jñānaṁ anantaṁ brahma*"- "Brahman is truth, knowledge and infinite". Brahman as *jñāna-svarūpa* cannot also be the substrate for *jñāna* as its *dharma*. In view of it, the description of Brahman as qualified with attributes such as *sarvajñatva, satyasaṁkalpatva* etc., is not valid.

This argument is also untenable, contends Vedānta Deśika. Just as the statement which describes Brahman as *jñāna* is valid, the texts which speak of the *guṇas* of Brahman are also equally valid. The fact that Brahman is *jñāna-svarūpa* does not rule out that Brahman is also endowed with *sarvajñatva* or other attributes. In fact, the Upaniṣad explicitly points out that the knowledge and power possessed by Brahman are manifold and constitutes its intrinsic nature (*parāsya śaktiḥ vividhaiva śrūyate, svābhāvikī jñāna-bala-kriyā ca*).[12] We have to admit the validity of both the texts.

The *Smṛti* texts also affirm that Brahman is free from all defects and also possesses infinite auspicious attributes. They cite the example of the sun and its reflection in the water in support of the theory that Brahman, though is immanent in all entities in the universe, is untouched by the defects found in them. Just as the defects found in the waves of the water do not affect the sun, in the same way defects found in the objects in which Brahman is immanent, do not affect it. One other illustration is cited by the author of the *sūtra* to defend the theory of Brahman remaining unaffected by the defects. *Ākāśa* or ether is one and is also all-pervasive. It is found to be present in several receptacles such as pots of different sizes. The defects caused to the *ākāśa* due to its being conditioned by the pots of small or large sizes do not affect in any way the all-pervasive *ākāśa*. In this example, unlike the sun and its reflection in the waves, *ākāśa* is physically present in the conditioning entities. In the same way, Brahman which is in all the entities in the universe is not touched by the defects found in the objects.

A serious objection is raised against the theory of Brahman as *ubhayaliṅga*. According to an important passage of *Bṛhadāraṇyaka*[13] describing Brahman as having two forms, viz., *mūrta* and *amūrta* or gross and subtle, and the negation of the same by the words '*neti neti;* or 'not this not this', implies that Brahman is *nirviśeṣa,* that is, devoid of all forms. How then Brahman be regarded as qualified with attributes? This is the view advanced by Śaṁkara in interpreting the *Vedānta sūtra* which reads: *prakṛtaitāvattvaṁ hi pratiṣedhati tato bravīti ca bhūyaḥ*[14]. It means, according to Śaṁkara, that the Upaniṣadic text, '*neti neti*' (not this, not this) negates in respect of Brahman the predication of the two forms mentioned in the earlier part of the passage and this is supported by what is said later on about Brahman.

The *sūtra* relating to this matter is regarded as a separate *adhikaraṇa* by Śaṁkara named *Prakṛtaitāvattvādhikaraṇa*. But according to Rāmānuja, it is part of the *Ubhayaliṅgādhikaraṇa* since it supports the theory of Brahman as *ubhayaliṅga*. The argument advanced by Śaṁkara is refuted by Rāmānuja. The wording of the *sūtra*, as properly understood, does not deny the distinctive characteristics of the two modes (*mūrta* and *amūrta* forms) declared previously because that would be senseless to teach them first and finally deny the same. There is no indication in the Upaniṣadic passage dealing with this matter to suggest that these are falsely imposed on Brahman. On the contrary, it merely denies the *prakṛtaitāvattvam* or the limited nature of Brahman as previously stated. In other words, it denies that Brahman possesses only this much of qualification as described previously. The word *'iti'* or 'so' which refers to that limited nature of the phrase *'na iti'* (not so), therefore, means that Brahman is not to be distinguished only by the previously stated modes (*na iti na iti – naivam naivam, ukta prakāra mātram na bhavati brahma*). This explanation is confirmed by the fact that subsequent to the expression *'neti neti'*, significant positive statements are made about Brahman. Thus states the Upaniṣad: *na hy etasmāt iti nety-anyat param asti: atha nāmadheyaṁ, satyasya satyaṁ*[15]. It means, according to Rāmānuja, there is nothing higher or greater than Brahman referred to earlier as implied by the words *anyat* or *para* in the text. In other words, no other Being which is more glorious both in respect of *svarūpa* and *guṇas*, ever exists. This is indicated by the designation (*nāmadheya*) of Brahman as *satyasya satyaṁ*, which means the Reality of the reals. *Satya*, according to the Upaniṣad, is *prāṇa* which denotes the *jīva*. Brahman is more real than the *jīvas* since the former is never subject to any change, while the *jīva* becomes subject to change during the state of bondage to the extent that its *jñāna* undergoes modification. The positive statement made in the Upaniṣad subsequent to the negation as *neti neti*, emphasizes this glory of Brahman. This is conveyed by the words in the *sūtra* *'tato bravīti bhūyaḥ'*[16]. Thus it follows that this particular *sūtra* does not prove that Brahman is *nirviśeṣa* but on the contrary, it affirms that it is *saviśeṣa* or endowed with characteristics. Vedānta Deśika concludes that Brahman is *ubhayaliṅga* that is, it is free from all defects and that it is also qualified by numerous auspicious attributes and that this is the well established theory of Vedānta. (*tasmāt brahma dviliṅgaṁ dvividhā vibhavam ityeva Vedānta pakṣaḥ*)[17]. Brahman is therefore the worthy object of meditation or *vidyā* which is the direct means to attain the Supreme Goal, as stated by Bādarāyaṇa in the *Vedānta-sūtra* (*vidyātaḥ puruṣārthaḥ*).

b) Brahman as the Supreme Reality

Bādarāyaṇa provides two additional reasons for establishing that Brahman is the worthy object of meditation and attainment (*prāpya*). These are: 1) Brahman is the Supreme Reality (*para-tattva*) which implies that there is no higher Reality than Brahman. 2) Brahman bestows all the desired goals (*puruṣārtha*) including *mokṣa* to those who worship Him. Both these points are important to justify the need of seeking Brahman only as the object meditation. Two separate *adhikaraṇas* named *Parādhikaraṇa* and *Phalādhikaraṇa* are devoted to the discussion of these matters.

The need to prove that Brahman is the highest Reality arises because there is a theory, which seems to have existed during the time of Bādarāyaṇa named *Vyomātīta-vāda*, which claims that there is a Reality which is higher than Brahman. The basis for this theory is that a few stray Scriptural texts which describe Brahman in terms such as *setu* or bridge *unmāna* or having dimension, *saṁbandha* or connection to something else to be attained and *bheda* or existence of a different higher entity. Bādarāyaṇa mentions these points, as prima facic view, in the following *sūtra*: *Param ataḥ setu unmāna saṁbandha bheda vyapadeśebhyaḥ*[18].

The word *setu* generally means bridge intended to cross from one side to the other side of the river (*kulāntara prāpti hetuḥ*). Thus says the *Chāndogya*: *atha ya ātmā sa setuḥ vidhṛtiḥ eṣām lokānāṁ asaṁbhedāya*[19]. It also states that after crossing this, one becomes free from bondage. These statements convey the idea that there is something higher than Brahman to be attained. The word *unmāna* means that which is limited by dimension. The *Chāndogya* describes Brahman as having four parts (*catuṣpād-brahma*).[20] Such a description of Brahman implies that there exists a higher Reality devoid of all limitations. *Saṁbandha* means connection or relationship. The description of Brahman by the *Muṇḍaka* that it is the bridge to immortality (*amṛtasya eṣa setuḥ*)[21] indicates that Brahman serves as the means to attain something higher. The word *bheda* mentioned in the *sūtra* means difference, that is, the distinction is drawn between two entities described as *para* (high) and *parāt para* (higher than *para*). Thus states the *Muṇḍaka*: *parāt paraṁ puruṣam upaiti*[22]. The *Śvetāśvatara* also says: *tato yaduttarataraṁ tad arūpam anāmayaṁ*[23]. Considering all these statements, it is contended that there is a higher Reality to be attained other than Brahman. Hence it is contended that Brahman cannot be regarded as the only object of meditation for the attainment of the Supreme Goal.

Bādarāyaṇa rejects all these arguments. The description of Brahman as *setu* does not imply that it is the causeway like a bridge to reach the other shore. The word *setu* derived from the root verb *sinoti* or that which holds together, means with reference to Brahman that it has the capacity to hold together all the sentient and non-sentient entities in the universe under its control in their respective places without their becoming mixed up (*badhnāti svasmin sarvaṁ cid-acid-vastujātam asaṁkīrṇam*).[24] The same Upaniṣadic text describing Brahman as *setu* uses the expression '*eṣāṁ lokānāṁ asaṁbhedāya*'[25] which means that Brahman as *setu* prevents the various entities of the universe getting mixed up.

The description of Brahman as *catuṣpāt* implying the dimensional limitation, is intended to provide a concrete form for Brahman for the purpose of easy comprehension to enable the *upāsaka* to meditate upon it (*budhyarthaḥ pādavat*).[26] Though Brahman is *vibhu* or all-pervasive and infinite, it is conceived as limited by associating it with a limiting adjunct (*upādhi*) for purposes of easy meditation (*upāsanārtham*).

The description of Brahman as the bridge to *amṛta* or *mokṣa,* is not inappropriate since Brahman, according to Vedānta, is both *prāpaka* or means and also *prāpya* or goal to be attained (*upapatteśca*).[27] The *Muṇḍakopaniṣad* states that whomsoever He (*Paramātma*) chooses, only that individual can attain *Paramātmā* (*yamaiva eṣa vṛṇute tena labhyaḥ*). This statement, as we have explained earlier, conveys the idea that *Paramātman* serves as the means (*upāya*) for attaining Him. Even though meditation (*upāsanā*) is laid down as the *sādhana* to attain *Paramātman, mokṣa* is conferred on the individual by the grace of God in response to the observance of devoted meditation upon Him. *Paramātman* is therefore regarded as *Siddhopāya;* that is, the ever-existing God is Himself the principal cause for attaining Him out of His grace. *Bhakti-yoga* or *upāsanā* is the *Sādhyopāya,* since this serves as means to earn His grace.

Regarding the Scriptural statements which appear to indicate the exstence of a principle other than what is regarded as *para,* it is pointed out that these very texts deny the existence of Reality other than Brahman (*tathā anyapratiṣedhāt*)[28]. Since everything is pervaded by Brahman, the question of the existence of a Reality other than Brahman does not arise. The *Śvetāśvatara* says: *Tenedaṁ pūrṇaṁ puruṣeṇa sarvaṁ*[29] - "All this is fully pervaded by that *puruṣa* (Brahman). The *Muṇḍaka* states: *nityaṁ vibhuṁ sarvagataṁ susūkṣmaṁ yat bhūtayoniṁ paripaśyanti dhīrāḥ*[30] - "It is eternal, all-pervasive, omnipresent, very subtle, the cause of the universe". It is therefore affirmed that Brahman is the highest Reality and it is to be sought for by the aspirant for *mokṣa* through the means of unceasing meditation.

c) Brahman as the Bestower of Mokṣa

Brahman is not only the highest Reality to be sought for but it is also the bestower of the fruit of the *upāsanā* (*phala*) which in the context of the *Brahma-vidyā* stands for *mokṣa.* Thus states the *sūtra*: *phalam ataḥ upapatteḥ*[31]. It means: It stands to reason that the desired goals are obtained from Brahman. The need to emphasise this point arises because *Paramātman* (Brahman) who is to be meditated upon should be capable of conferring the desired fruit. That is, *puruṣārtha* or the Supreme Goal for which *vidyā* or meditation is enjoined in the Upaniṣad is to be bestowed directly by *Paramātman*. If some one else or some other principle were to confer the fruit, there would be no justification for meditating on Brahman.

There is a view which is advanced by Jaimini that *karma* or the deeds such as *yāga* performed by an individual for the attainment of heaven etc., confer the fruits. According to the Mīmāṁsaka though the *yāga* does not give the desired fruit soon after it is performed, it confers the result later on at the appropriate time through an unseen potency named *apūrva* in the form of *puṇya* or merit secured by the performance of the *yāga*.

Bādarāyaṇa rejects this theory. Neither the *yāga* nor this *apūrva* generated by it can directly confer the fruit, since these are non-sentient in character. It is therefore appropriate to admit that *Paramātman* Himself who is worshipped through the sacrifice and who is meditated upon with devotion by the *upāsaka* for attainment of *mokṣa*, bestows the desired results. According to the Vedānta, even if other celestial deities are worshipped by means of prescribed rituals, the one who bestows the desired fruit is *Paramātman* who is the indwelling Self (*antarātmā*) of these deities. The Scriptural texts explicitly state that *Paramātman* is the bestower of the desired fruit. The *Taittirīya* text says: *eṣa eva ānandayāti*. This very *Ānandamaya ātmā* (Brahman) confers bliss (*ānanda*) to the seekers of *mokṣa*. Thus, it is concluded that Brahman being the Supreme Reality and also the sole benefactor (*phalaprada*) is worthy of meditation.

II. The Theory of *Brahma-vidyā*

As pointed out earlier, *vidyā* is the direct *sādhana* for the attainment of the Supreme Goal (*vidyātaḥ puruṣārthaḥ*). The term *vidyā* employed in the Upaniṣads and the *Brahmasūtra*, stands for *upāsanā* or unceasing meditation on Brahman. The Upaniṣads refer to several *vidyās* as the *sādhana* for the attainment of Brahman. These are described differently, that is, with different names and different attributes (*guṇas*) with which Brahman is to be meditated upon. Thus for instance, the meditation on *Sat* (Brahman) conceived as the source of the universe, which is imparted by Uddālaka to Śvetaketu in the *Chāndogya* Upaniṣad, is named *sad-vidyā*. The meditation on Brahman as *daharākāśa* or the subtle space abiding within the heart of an individual along with the eight attributes viz., *apahatapāpmā, vijaraḥ, vimṛtyuḥ, viśokaḥ, vijighatsaḥ, apīpāsaḥ, satyakāmaḥ, satyasaṅkalpaḥ*, is titled *Dahara-vidyā*. The meditation on Brahman as infinitely great (*bhūmā*) is known as *Bhūmā-vidyā*. The meditation on Brahman conceived as the cause of the creation, sustenance and dissolution of the universe (*tajjalān*) which is taught by sage Śāṇḍilya in the *Chāndogya* Upaniṣad, is named *Śāṇḍilya-vidyā*. Brahman as *ānandamaya* or infinitely blissful, which is to be meditated upon, is known by the name of *Ānandamaya vidyā*. The commentators on the *Brahma-sūtras* have acknowledged thirty-two such *vidyās* which are taught in different Upaniṣads for attaining Brahman. Hence these are called *Brahma-vidyās*. A list of these as acknowledged by Vedānta Deśika in the *Adhikaraṇa-sārāvalī* is given in the appendix II along with the references to the respective passages of the Upaniṣads and also the names of the *adhikaraṇas* in which these are dealt with.

Bādarāyaṇa does not present the details of these *vidyās*. However the *sūtras* imply the Upaniṣadic texts dealing with them, as is evident from the *viṣaya-vākyas* or the Upaniṣadic texts concerned with the subject-matter of the *sūtras*. He, however, discusses certain issues relating to the different *vidyās*. The following are some of the important issues which are related to the *vidyās*:

1) Are these various *vidyās* different (*nānā*) or non-different?

2) If they are different, do the *vidyās* taken together are to be observed as *sādhana* for attaining Brahman? Or do they serve as alternative means to attain the same Goal?

3) If the same *vidyā* is mentioned in two different Upaniṣads such as *Dahara-vidyā* and *Vaiśvānara-vidyā* with varying description in terms of the *guṇas* with which Brahman is to be meditated, do they constitute different *vidyās*?

4) If Brahman which is qualified with numerous *guṇas* is to be meditated upon along with its *guṇas*, which are the *gunas* to be included (*upasamhārya*) and which are the *guṇas* to be excluded (*anupasaṁhārya*) for the purpose of meditation?

5) If only limited number of *guṇas* are to be contemplated along with Brahman, as laid down in the Upaniṣadic passages dealing with a particular *vidyā*, would Brahman which is the object of attainment be realized in its complete form?

6) In respect of some *vidyās* certain religious observances such as *śirovṛta, udgīthopāsanā* etc., are also prescribed as part of the observance of *upāsanā*. Are these religious observances to be followed in respect of all the *Brahma-vidyās*?

Bādarāyaṇa attempts to clarify these questions since it is necessary to know precisely the nature (*svarūpa*) of the *vidyās* to be pursued for the attainment of the spiritual Goal. The entire third *pāda* of the *Sādhanādhyāya*, which is titled *Guṇopasaṁhāra pāda*, comprising as many as 26 *adhikaraṇas*, is devoted to this matter. Some of the details of these discussions do not have much philosophical importance. It is also difficult to comprehend them since the observance of these *vidyās* are not in vogue. We shall therefore leave out the details and take note of the important points which are relevant for understanding the nature of the *sādhana*.

The first and most important question to be considered is whether the *vidyās* such as *Sadvidyā, Dahara-vidyā, Upakosala-vidyā, Sāṇḍilya-vidyā* etc., are different (*nānā*)? Bādarāyaṇa states that they are different.[32]

According to the prima facie view, the *vidyās* are not different because they are all intended to attain the same Brahman as the goal and they are all designated as *Brahma-vidyā*. Even the terms used for enjoining the meditation such as *dhyāyīta, upāsīta*, etc., have the same import.

This view is not accepted by Bādarāyaṇa. Thus it is stated in the *sūtra*: *Nānā śabdādibhedāt*.[33] The various *vidyās* enjoined in the Upaniṣads are different (*nānā*) because the *śabda* or the Scriptural statements in the form of injunctions and *rūpa* or description of each *vidyā* in terms of the *guṇas* with which Brahman is to be meditated upon vary. The word *ādi* in the *sūtra* implies, *rūpa* or description, *ākhyā* or designation and other factors. The Mīmāṁsakas have adopted four principles to determine the difference or non-difference between ritualistic deeds mentioned in the different *śākhās* of the Vedas. These are: a) *codanā* or the injunctive statement enjoining the performance of a sacrifice; b) *saṁyoga* or the connection of the sacrifice with the goal to be attained; c) *rūpa* or the detailed description of the sacrifice and d) *ākhyā* or the name adopted for the sacrifice.[34] On the basis of these principles, Bādarāyaṇa also maintains the view that the various *vidyās* enjoined in the Upaniṣads are different (*nānā*). The reason for adopting this view is contained in the words '*śabdādi bhedāt*' in the *sūtra*. *Śabdabheda* means Scriptural statements in the form of injunctions (*codanā*) such as *vidyāt, dhyāyīta, upāsīta* etc. which are different. The names adopted for the *vidyās* (*ākhyā*) such as *Dahara-vidyā, Sadvidyā* are different. *Rūpa* or description of these *vidyās* in terms of the *guṇas* with which Brahman is to be meditated also differs. The *śabda-bheda* along with *rūpa-bheda* mainly differentiate one *vidyā* from the other.

As Vedānta Deśika explains, though Bādarāyaṇa has mentioned *śabda-bheda* as the main criterion for regarding the *vidyās* as different, *rūpa-bheda* is to be accorded greater importance (*Śabdasya bhedastu ayam upacarito rūpa-bheda drāḍhamne*).[35] Another reason for mentioning *śabda-bheda* in the *sūtra* is to emphasise that *vidyā* or *upāsanā* is enjoined as the means to attain Brahman and thereby refute the wrong view of Advaitin, that *jñāna* or direct realization of Brahman as means to *mokṣa* is not enjoined (*avidheya jñāna*).

If all *vidyās* are different, the next question arises whether these *vidyās* taken together (*samuccaya*) are to be observed for attaining Brahman or do they serve as alternative means for this purpose? This doubt arises because in the case of *svarga* or heaven as the goal of attainment, the same individual is found to observe several rituals for the purpose of enjoying greater benefits in heaven. In the same way, it is possible that one can practise several *vidyās* together to enjoy the bliss of Brahman in greater measure. (*Brahmānubhave-bhūyastvāpekṣayā samuccayopi sambhavati*).

Bādarāyaṇa does not accept this view. The relevant *sūtra* reads: *vikalpa aviśiṣṭa phalatvāt*.[36] The different *vidyās* are regarded as the alternative means to attain Brahman (*vikalpaḥ*) because the nature of the attainment is the same for all the *vidyās* (*aviśiṣṭa phalatvāt*). That is, the enjoyment of the infinite bliss of Brahman (*atiśaya brahmānand-ānubhava*) is the Supreme Goal of the *vidyās*. The Upaniṣadic texts support it. The *Taittirīya* says: *sa eko brahmaṇa ānandaḥ śrotriyasya ca akāmahatasya*) - "The liberated *jīva* who is steadfast in Brahman enjoys that infinite *ānanda* of Brahman." *Muṇḍaka* says: *nirañjanaḥ paramaṁ sāmyam upaiti*. - "The *jīva*, soon after it is liberated from bondage attains equal status with Brahman." The *sāmyatva* or equality is in respect of enjoyment of bliss both by Brahman and *jīva*, as stated by Bādarāyaṇa (*bhogamātra sāmyāt*). Hence it is justified to regard these *vidyās* as alternative means to attain Brahman.

The third question to be considered is: whether the same *vidyā* mentioned in different *śākhās* of the Upaniṣads with some varying description in terms of *guṇas* with which

Brahman is to be meditated upon, is to be treated as different or as one? The *Dahara-vidyā*, for instance, is mentioned both in the *Chāndogya* and *Taittirīya* Upaṇiṣad. In the *Chāndogya*, it is enjoined that the meditation on Brahman is to be observed along with eight attributes such as *apahata pāpmatva, satyakāmatva, satyasaṁkalpatva* etc. The same *vidyā* is also mentioned in a general way in the *Taittirīya* by briefly stating that the *dahara-ākāśa* or the subtle space (denoting Brahman) is to be meditated upon along with what it contains (*tasmin yadantaḥ tad-upāsitavyam*). The *Taittirīya* text does not mention the eight *guṇas* referred to in the *Chāndogya*. In the same way, the *Vaiśvānara vidyā* is referred to in two Upaniṣads belonging to different *śākhas*. In both these places, meditation on *Vaiśvānara* as Brahman is enjoined for attaining the same goal. The question arises whether the *vidyā* referred to in more than one place is the same or different. Bādarāyaṇa replies that they constitute the same *upāsanā*.The relevant *sūtra* reads; *sarva vedānta pratyayam codanadyaviśeṣāt*.[37] It means that the *vidyas* taught in all the Upaniṣads is one. The reason advanced in support of it is that there is no difference in the *codanā* or the words enjoining it (*vidhāyaka-vākya*). The word *ādi* implies that there is also no difference in respect of the designation of the *vidyā* (*nāmadheya*), the nature of the goal to be attained (*phala*) and the description of the object of meditation (*rūpa*). Another point which is brought out in this connection is that the *guṇas* which are mentioned in respect of a *vidyā* in one place are to be included in respect of the *vidyā* enjoined in another Upaniṣad, if both the *vidyās* are the same. Taking the example of *Dahara-vidyā*, the eight *guṇas* mentioned in the *Chāndogya* in respect of *Dahara-vidyā* are also to be included in respect of the *Dahara-vidyā* mentioned in the *Taittirīya* Upaniṣad. This principle holds good in respect of other *vidyās* such as *Vaiśvānara-vidyā* which is referred to in more than one Upaniṣad. The inclusion of the *guṇas* enumerated at one place in respect of a *vidyā* stated in another Upaniṣad, where these are not mentioned, is called *guṇopasaṁhāra*. In the third *pāda* of *Sādhanādhyāya*, Bādarāyaṇa discusses a few other *vidyās* such as *Prāṇa-vidyā, Puruṣa-vidyā, Śāṇḍilya-vidyā, Uṣastikahola-vidyā* and *Udgītha-vidyā*. These are some of the *vidyās* which are mentioned in more than one Upaniṣad and it therefore becomes necessary to clarify whether they are separate or not. Wherever they are found to be not different *vidyās*, the *guṇas* with which Brahman is to be meditated have to be included in respect of the same *vidyā* enjoined elsewhere (*upasaṁhāra*).

The next important question which is considered by Bādarāyaṇa in the *Guṇopasaṁhāra pāda* is: Which are the *guṇas* to be contemplated along with Brahman while observing the meditation upon it? The question is relevant because the *guṇas* of Brahman are numerically infinite (*ananta*). It is impossible for a *upāsaka* to contemplate on all of them. It is only practicable to meditate on Brahman as qualified with a limited number of *guṇas*. If only a limited number of *guṇas* are to be contemplated along with Brahman, would Brahman which is the object of attainment be realized in its complete form? According to the *tatkratu nyāya*[38], in whatever form an individual observes meditation, the object of attainment is also in the same form. If Brahman is meditated as qualified with a few attributes, then the Brahman realized through such a meditation cannot be regarded as Brahman in its comprehensive form (*prāptiḥ aṁśataḥ syāt*).

Vedānta Deśika does not accept this argument. He contends that the *tatkratu-nyāya* is not applicable in the case of meditation on Brahman, because the Upaniṣadic texts categorically state that an individual who resorts to meditation on Brahman as qualified with attributes as stated in the passage dealing with *Brahma-vidyā*, attains a status equal to that of Brahman soon after he is liberated from bondage. Thus says the *Muṇḍaka*: *Nirañjanaḥ paramaṁ sāmyam upaiti*. On the authority of the Scriptural texts, it is maintained that a person who meditates on Brahman attains Brahman in its full form, that is, as qualified with all the attributes including those which are not contemplated during the meditation. Whatever be the mode of meditation (*vidyā*), the attainment of the goal by means of it is the same for all the *vidyās* enjoined in the Upaniṣads. The *tatkratu-nyāya* is to be understood in this restricted sense in respect of *vidyā*[39].

Regarding the *gunas* with which Brahman is to be meditated upon, Bādarāyaṇa states that the distinguishing *guṇas* of Brahman such as *ānanda* which are inseparably related to Brahman and which are essential for comprehending Brahman are to be necessarily contemplated along with Brahman in respect of all *vidyās*. These are *ānanda, satya, jñāna* and *ananta*. As will be pointed out presently, *amalatva* is also to be added to these four attributes. The relevant *sūtra* reads: *Ānandādayaḥ pradhānasya.*[40] Its meaning, as interpreted by Rāmānuja, is that the *guṇas* such as *ānanda* is non-different (inseparable) from the *pradhāna*, that is, Brahman which is the *guṇī* and hence these are to be contemplated along with Brahman in all the *vidyās*.

By way of elucidation, Vedānta Deśika points out that there are two types of *dharmas* or attributes belonging to an object. One is called *svarūpa-nirūpaka dharma* or essential attributes by means of which alone the nature of an object is comprehended. The second type of *dharmas* is known as *nirūpita svarūpa viśeṣaṇas*, that is, the secondary qualities which become evident only after the *svarūpa* of the object is known. Taking the instance of a cow, *gotva* is an essential attribute of cow through which the cow as different from other animals is identified. The qualities such as its form, colour, etc., are secondary qualities through which we come to know more about the cow. In the same way, *Brahma-svarūpa* can only be comprehended through its distinguishing characteristics such as *satyatva, jñānatva, anantatva* and *ānandatva*, as stated in the Upaniṣad. The *guṇas* such as omniscience, omnipotence, compassionate etc., are the secondary qualities which can be known only after *Brahma-svarūpa* is comprehended. For the purpose of meditation on Brahman, the essential qualities which are inseparable from Brahman and which are useful to know what Brahman is, have to be necessarily contemplated at the time of meditation. Along with these, such other *guṇas* as are mentioned separately in respect of each *vidyā* are to be contemplated. Thus, for instance, while observing the *Daharavidyā,* which is enjoined in the *Taittirīya* Upaniṣad, Brahman is to be meditated upon as qualified with eight *guṇas* such as *apahatapāpmā, satyasaṁkalpa,* etc. In addition to it, the five essential attributes such as *ānanda* have also to be contemplated during meditation on Brahman. The description of Brahman in the *Taittirīya* passage enjoining meditation on Brahman as *ānandamaya,* we come across description of Brahman as possessing qualities such as *priya* or joy, *modaḥ* or happiness, *pramoda* or enjoyment etc., which are metaphorically stated as *śiras* or head, *pakṣah* or sides and *puccha* or tail respectively for the purpose of easy comprehension of Brahman in physical form. But these do not constitute the essential qualities of Brahman and hence they are to be excluded from the purview of the meditation.

We come across two *vidyās* taught in the *Bṛhadāraṇyaka* and *Muṇḍakopaniṣad* which are designated as *Gārgi-akṣaravidyā* and *Akṣara-paravidyā* respectively. Both these *vidyās* enjoin the meditation on *akṣara* as Brahman. *Akṣara* is described in negative terms. Thus says the *Bṛhadāraṇyaka*: "It is neither gross nor subtle, neither short nor long, neither red nor adhesive. It is neither shadow nor darkness, neither air nor space, It is unattached, without taste, without smell, without eyes, without ears, without organ of speech, without mind, without radiance, without breath, without mouth, without measure, having no interior or exterior. It does not eat anything, nor is it eaten by anyone".[41] The *Muṇḍaka* Upaniṣad describes *akṣara* as follows: "That which is imperceivable, ungraspable, without hands or feet, which is eternal, all-pervading, omnipresent, exceedingly subtle, that is the imperishable (*avyayam*) which the wise perceive as the source of beings (*bhūtayoni*).[42] The question to be considered is: Whether the meditation on Brahman as *akṣara* (*Akṣara-vidyā*) requires the contemplation of these negative qualities (*niṣedha guṇas*), along with four essential attributes referred to in the *Ānandādyadhikaraṇa*? Bādarāyaṇa categorically states that the negative qualities such as *asthūlatva* attributed to *akṣara* should be necessarily included among the other essential attributes such as *ānanda* with which Brahman is to be meditated upon. The relevant *sūtra* reads: *akṣara dhiyāṁ tu avarodhaḥ sāmānya tadbhāvābhyāṁ aupasadavat taduktam*.[43] It means: The negative qualities attributed to Brahman are to be included in the meditation on it, since Brahman is the object of meditation in all *vidyās* and so also these negative qualities which are useful to know its nature exist in it. (*sarveṣu upāsaneṣu upāsyasya akṣarasya brahmaṇah samānatvāt asthūlatvādīnāṁ tatsvarūpa pratītau bhāvācca*).[44] According to Rāmānuja, description of Brahman with the negative qualities conveys the essential nature of Brahman as devoid of all physical qualities. In other words, the negation of such physical qualities as found in material objects in respect of Brahman establishes that Brahman is absolutely free from all defilements (*heyapratyanīka*). *Heyapratyanīkatva* itself therefore constitutes the essential nature of Brahman similar to *satyatva, jñānatva* and *anantatva*. Hence Bādarāyaṇa takes the view that Brahman is to be meditated upon in all *vidyās* as qualified by *amalatva,* which is synonymous with *heyapratyanīkatva,* along with other four essential attributes viz., *satyatva, jñānatva, anantatva* and *ānandatva*. These five qualities establish that Brahman is different both from all the sentient beings and also non-sentient entities (*sakala cid-acid vilakṣaṇa*).

A few other allied issues also come up for discussion in the *Guṇopasaṁhāra pāda*. One of them is whether the meditation on Brahman also involves the contemplation of *jīvātman*. If so, in what form *jīvātman* is to be meditated upon? Is *jīvātman* to be meditated in its embodied state as *kartā, bhoktā,* etc., or in its true form as qualified with its essential attributes such as *apahatapāpmā, satyasaṁkalpa* etc. Bādarāyaṇa states that the meditation on *jīvātman* which is part of the meditation on Brahman is to be contemplated in its true form. The relevant *sūtra* reads: *vyatirekas-tadbhāva-bhāvitvāt na tu upalabdhivat.*[45] *Jīvātman* is to be meditated in that form as different from that form in the state of bondage (*vyatirekaḥ*), since the attainment is in accordance with the form of meditation, just as in the case of meditation upon Brahman.

Other minor issues relate to the observance of certain religious ceremonies such as *śirovratra* or carrying a pot of fire on the head, recitation of certain prayers at the commencement of the Upaniṣad dealing with *vidyā*.

The question arises whether these constitute the subsidiary means to main *upāsanā* and if so, would it have to be observed in respect of the practice of all the *upāsanās* for *mokṣa*. Bādarāyaṇa clarifies that these requirements are not the *aṅga* or subsidiary means to the *upāsanā* and hence they need not be observed in respect of any *Brahma-vidyā*.

III. Karma as Subsidiary Means to *Vidyā*

In the preceding section we have discussed the general issues relating to the *Brahma-vidyā* or the meditation on Brahman. As the Upaniṣads mention several *vidyās* each with varying description of the *guṇas* to be associated with Brahman, it became necessary for Bādarāyaṇa to discuss these issues and establish that all *vidyās* enjoined in the Upaniṣads, though they are different (*nānā*), serve as alternative *sādhanas* for attaining the same Goal viz., Brahman.

Before explaining the nature of vidyā (*vidyā-svarūpa*), Bādarāyaṇa takes up another important matter concerning the role of *karma* or the observance of the prescribed deeds in relation to the *vidyā* or *upasanā*. This subject has assumed special importance in Vedānta since according to Jaimini, the exponent of Pūrva-mīmāṁsā, *vidyā* is subordinate aid (*aṅga*) to *karma* or the performance of prescribed deeds. Bādarāyaṇa therefore discusses in detail the place of *karma* in the *sādhana* for *mokṣa*. The major part of the fourth *pāda* of *Sādhanādhyāya* which is called *Aṅgapāda* is devoted to this matter. It establishes after critically examining the views of the Pūrva-mīmāṁsaka, that the performance of the prescribed deeds is a necessary aid (*aṅga*) to *vidyā*.

The *Puruṣārthādhikaraṇa* mainly deals with this subject. The main *sūtra* reads: *Puruṣārtho ataḥ śabdāt iti Bādarāyaṇaḥ*[46]. The word *ataḥ* in the *sūtra* in the context of the earlier *pāda* dealing with the *vidyās*, is to be read as *vidyātaḥ*, that is, through *vidyā*. The total meaning of the *sūtra* is that in the opinion of Bādarāyaṇa, the Supreme Goal is attained only through the means of *vidyā*, since it is so declared in the Scriptural texts (*śabdāt*). As is evident from the subsequent *sūtras* of this *adhikaraṇa*, the implication of the *sūtra* is that *karma* cannot be direct *sādhana* to *mokṣa* but it is *vidyā* aided by *karma* that constitutes the *sādhana*. This view is fully supported by the Upaniṣads. Thus says the *Taittirīya* Upaniṣad: "The knower of Brahman attains the highest." The *Muṇḍaka* states: "He who knows Brahman becomes (similar to) Brahman."[47] The *Śvetāśvatara* says: "There is no other means than knowing Brahman to overcome bondage."[48] In all such statements, *vedana* which denotes *vidyā*, is the direct means to *mokṣa*. The fact that Bādarāyaṇa mentions his own name in the *sūtra* confirms that this is the correct theory according to Vedānta.

The Mīmāṁsakas maintain that *karma* is the means to liberation whereas *vidyā* enjoined in the Upaniṣads is a subsidiary aid to it. The main reason advanced in support of it is that *jīvā* is *kartā* or the agent of *karma* and it is therefore more important to know about the nature of *jīvātman*. The Upaniṣadic texts which speak of the knowledge of Brahman as the means to attain the Supreme Goal are intended to provide the knowledge of *jīvātman*. Such a knowledge serves as a purificatory act (*saṁskāra*) for the *jīvā* which is actually the *kartā* of the rites. (*kratuṣu kartuḥ jīvātmā*). According to this view, *jīva* and Brahman are non-different and the references made to Brahman in the Upaniṣads imply *jīvātman*. The texts which speak about *jñāna* as the means to *puruṣārtha* are to be treated as *arthavādas* or the glorificatory statements about the goal to be attained. Hence *vidyā* is *aṅga* or subsidiary aid to *karma*.

Bādarāyaṇa rejects this theory because *vidyā* referred to in the Upaniṣads is not concerned with *jīvātman*, in which case its knowledge would have been useful to *karma*. But on the other hand, it relates to Brahman which is different from *jīvā*, as stated in several Upaniṣadic texts and also *Vedānta-sūtras*. Bādarāyaṇa, therefore reaffirms that *puruṣārtha* is attained only by means of *vidyā*.

A few other arguments are advanced in support of the view that *vidyā* is *aṅga* to *karma*. In the *Īśāvāsya* Upaniṣad, it is stated that one should live for hundred years (till the end of life) by performing *karma*.[49] This is taken to imply that performance of *karma* is of greater significance and that *vidyā* is subordinate to *karma*.

This is not correct, contends Vedānta Deśika. What is implied by this statement is that the person observing *Brahma-vidyā* should also perform the prescribed deeds as an aid to *vidyā*.

Another argument against the theory of Bādarāyaṇa is that in the *Bṛhadāraṇyaka* Upaniṣad it is stated that both *vidyā* and *karma* follow the *upāsaka*. (*Vidyā-karmaṇī samanvārabhete*[50]). The mention of both *vidyā* and *karma* is taken to imply that *vidyā* is *anga* to *karma*.

This argument is also untenable. The mere mention of both *vidyā* and *karma* together does not determine that *karma* is the principal means (*aṅgī*) whereas *vidyā* is subordinate means (*aṅga*). If we go by other Scriptural texts, it is obvious that *karma* is the *aṅga*, whereas *vidyā* is the angī or principal means to the Supreme Goal. Thus says the *Bṛhadāraṇyaka* Upaniṣad: *tametaṁ vedānuvacanena brāhmaṇā vividiṣanti yajñena dānena tapasā anāśakena*[51] - "Brahmins desire to know Brahman by means of recitation of Vedas, *yajña*, *dāna*, *tapas*, fasting etc." Another text says: *kaṣāye karmabhiḥ pakve tato jñānam pravartate*[52] - "*Brahmajñāna* arises only after the afflictions which cause bondage are eradicated by the performance of *karma*". The *Gītā* also points out that even *jñānīs* such as Janaka attained perfection through the performance of deeds (*karmaṇaiva hi saṁsiddhiṁ āsthitāḥ janakādayaḥ*).[53] Considering all these statements, it is concluded that *Brahma-vidyā* cannot serve as an aid to *karma* (*vidyā makhādeḥ aṅgam na*)[54]. On the contrary, *karma* is the subsidiary aid to *vidyā*.

In this connection an important issue is raised. According to the *Chāndogya* Upaniṣad, there are three categories of persons: a) the *gṛhastha* or the householders who perform *yajña, dāna* and *adhyayana;* b) the *sannyāsīns* or those who have renounced the life of a *gṛhastha* and engaged in *tapas* and also the *parivrājakas* living in the forest who also perform *tapas;* c) the *brahmacārins* or those who live in the hermit of a preceptor for learning Vedas. The three categories of persons are described by the *Chāndogya* as *trayo-dharma-skandhas* or persons belonging to three *āśramas* or stages of life[55]. All of them are stated to observe strict celibacy (*ūrdhvaretas*). Of these the *sannyāsīns* and *brahmacārins* are not eligible for the performance of the rites which need the lighting of the sacrificial fire (*agnīndhana*). In respect of these individuals *karma* cannot be the *aṅga* to *vidyā*. In the absence of *karma* as *aṅga*, even *Brahma-vidyā* cannot be pursued by them.

Bādarāyaṇa does not accept this view. The *Chāndogya* Upaniṣad mentions that these individuals are engaged in the meditation on Brahman and that they also attain immortality (*brahmasaṁstho amṛtatvameti*). Those who pursue meditation on Brahman are required to do the prescribed *karma*. It is true that they may not be eligible for performing the rituals which need the litting of the sacrificial fire (*agnīndhanādy-anapekṣā*)[56].However, they are required to do only such *karmas* as are laid down for that particular *āśrama;* as subsidiary aid to *vidyā* (*kevala svāśrama vihita karmāpekṣā*).

But this exceptional condition does not apply to the *gṛhasthas* since they are eligible to perform the rites by litting the sacrificial fire. They are therefore required to observe *yajña, dāna, tapas* etc., as aid to *vidyā*. The relevant *sūtra* reads: *sarvāpekṣā ca yajñādi śruteḥ aśvavat.*[57] It means that there is need of all rituals on account of the Scriptural statement regarding the performance of sacrifice and the rest, as in the example of a horse. The *Śruti* referred to in the *sūtra* is the *Bṛhadāraṇyaka* text which states: *Tametaṁ vedānuvacanena brāhmaṇā vividiṣanti yajñena dānena tapasā anāśakena.*[58] "The seekers of Brahman desire to know Him (Brahman) by the study of the Veda, by sacrifice, by charity and fasting." Though the word *'vividiṣanti'* in the Upaniṣad literally means 'desire to know', it is generally understood as *vedana* or knowledge of Brahman. *Yajña, dāna, tapas* etc., which are prescribed by the Upaniṣad constitute the prerequisites for knowing Brahman. As will be explained later, the term *vedana* stands for *vidyā* or *upāsanā* (unceasing meditation on Brahman culminating in clear vision of Brahman). *Karma* such as *yajña, dāna,* tapas etc., prescribed by the Upaniṣads serve as aid to *vidyā* and these have to be necessarily observed by the *upāsaka* until he attains liberation. This is explained by the analogy of the horse. A horse which is intended for the purpose of going from one place to another is to be used along with the requisite accessories such as saddle, bridle etc., until one reaches the destination. In the same way, performance of the prescribed rituals are to be observed as accessories to *vidyā* until one attains the *mokṣa*.

Besides the performance of the prescribed rituals, Bādarāyaṇa lays down another set of accessories for the householders as aid to *vidyā*. These are in the form of development of virtues such as *śama* or tranquility, *dama* or control of senses, *uparati* or inner satisfaction, *titikṣu* or patience and *samāhitatva* or equanimity. The relevant *sūtra* reads: *Śamadamādy-upetas-syāt-tathāpi tu tadvidheḥ tadaṅgataya teṣām-api avaśyānuṣṭheyatvāt.*[59] It means: A householder should be equipped with *śama, dama* etc., because they are enjoined and that they should be practised as auxiliaries to *vidyā*. It is not correct to argue that the observance of the *yajña* etc., involves the use of the mind and *indriyas* and as such they would be a hindrance to the development of calmness for the person engaged in *upāsanā*. The operation of mind and sense organs for the purpose of performing the prescribed deeds does not affect the mental equanimity since the prescribed ritualistic activities are undertaken as worship of *Paramātman* (*paramapuruṣa ārādhanā*). It therefore helps to acquire *śama, dama* etc., by the *upāsaka*.

Incidentally, Bādarāyaṇa points out that the control of the food (*āhāra niyama*) is also equally important for the *upāsaka*. He is not required to accept all kinds of food except in special circumstance such as at the time of losing one's *prāṇa* (*prāṇātyaye*). This is evident from the episode of Uṣasti in the *Chāndogya* Upaniṣad, who is stated to have accepted the cooked beans meant for the horses offered by the horseman for the sake of sustaining his *prāṇa*.[60]

In addition to the development of virtues such as *śama, dama* etc., Bādarāyaṇa prescribes other mental qualities such as *pāṇḍitya, mauna, bālya,* as accessories to *vidyā* on the authority of the *Bṛhadāraṇyaka* Upaniṣad. Thus it states: *tasmāt brahmaṇaḥ pāṇḍityaṁ nirvidya bālyena tisṭhāset. bālyaṁ ca pāṇḍityaṁ ca nirvidya atha muniḥ*.[61] This subject is discussed in two separate *adhikaraṇas: Sahakāryantaravidhyadhikaraṇa* and *Anāviṣkārādhikaraṇa*. The important point to be noted is the implication of the terms *pāṇḍitya, mauna* and *bālyatva*. Mauna signifies the acquisition of the capacity to reflect repeatedly the object of meditation (*upāsanā ālambanasya punaḥ punaḥ saṁsīlanam*). *Bālyatva* refers to childlike innocence without manifesting externally his greatness as a *Brahma-jñānī* (*anāviṣkurvan*). *Pāṇḍitya* means deep knowledge about Brahman.

It was pointed out earlier that the performance of *karma* such as *yajña, dāna*, etc., is an aid to *Brahma-vidyā*. That is, these have to be *observed* by those who undertake meditation on Brahman. The question arises whether these have also to be observed by others such as the *gṛhasthas* who are not the seekers of *mokṣa*? Bādarāyaṇa replies that these have to be observed even by the persons belonging to the *gṛhasthāśrama* or the stage of householders, since these *karmas* are also enjoined for them. The relevant *sūtra* reads: *vihitatvācca āśrama karmāpi.*[62] It means: The performance of *Agnihotra* and other *nitya* and *naimittika karmas* is applicable even to persons belonging to that stage of life (*gṛhasthāśrama*) because these are enjoined by Scripture for them also. The same type of *karma* can serve the purpose of attaining other desired results such as *svarga* and also *mokṣa,* depending on the motive with which it is performed. (*viniyoga pṛthaktva*). In the case of the *mumukṣu* or the aspirant for *mokṣa, yajña, dāna,* etc., serve as accessories (*sahakāri*) to *vidyā*. In the case of *non-mumukṣu* who is leading the life of a *gṛhastha,* these serve as *āśrama karma,* that is, as obligatory deeds to be observed by the *gṛhastha.*

There are certain types of individuals who do not fall under the categories of the four *āśramas*. These are the persons who are not either married or those who after marriage have become widowers. These are regarded as *nirāśramī* or one not belonging to any of the four stages of life. They are not eligible, according to the *Dharmaśāstra,* for the performance of rituals prescribed for the four *āśramas*. The question arises whether these persons are permitted to observe *Brahma-vidyā*. Bādarāyaṇa states that such persons are also eligible for *Brahma-vidyā* as this is evident from the episodes of Vedic and *purāṇic* personalities such as Raikva, Bhīṣma, Saṁvartaka, etc. However, persons who have thrown out of a particular *āśrama* for having committed sinful acts are forbidden from pursuing *Brahma-vidyā* since the observance of *vidyā* by such persons is prohibited by the *śāstra.*

Before concluding the discussion about the nature of *karma* as *aṅga* or subsidiary means to *upāsanā* and also other accessories needed for it, Bādarāyaṇa considers the question whether or not *upāsanā* observed either for achieving desired goals such as heavenly bliss or *mokṣa*, leads to the attainment of it. Two separate *adhikaraṇas* named *Aihikādhikaraṇa* and *Muktiphalādhikaraṇa* are devoted for this purpose. There are two types of *Brahmopāsanā* - one observed for the purpose of attaining benefits other than *mokṣa* such as heavenly bliss, wealth etc., and the other done purely for attaining *mokṣa.* Bādarāyaṇa states that in either case, if there are no obstacles in the form of strong *prārabdha karma,* the goal is attained soon after completing meditation. Otherwise, there would be delay.

IV. The Nature of *Vidyā* (*Upāsanā*)

In the *Sādhanādhyāya* Bādarāyaṇa has discussed the following three important matters relating to the *Brahma-vidyā* or *upāsanā* on Brahman which is the direct *sādhana* to *mokṣa*. 1) Brahman is the worthy object of meditation as it is free from all defects and also endowed with infinite auspicious attributes. Brahman is also the highest Reality and the bestower of the desired goal. 2) For the purpose of attainment of Brahman, which is the Supreme Goal, one of the thirty-two *vidyās* or modes of meditation as laid down by the Upasniṣads is to be adopted. In the observance of the *upāsanā* on Brahman, the *upāsaka* has to contemplate on such attributes (*guṇas*) as are prescribed by the Upaniṣads in respect of the *vidyās* along with five essential attributes viz., *satya, jñāna, ananta, ānanda* and *amala*. 3) The *upāsanā* as aided by *karma* or the performance of the prescribed rituals according to one's *āśrama* is mandatory. After having dealt with all these matters in the *adhikaraṇas* of third and fourth *pāda* of *Sādhanādhyāya,* Bādarāyaṇa proceeds to discuss the *svarūpa* or the nature of *vidyā*. This topic is covered in the first *pāda* of the fourth *adhyāya,* which is titled *Phalādhyāya*. In the earlier *adhikaraṇa* named *Puruṣārthādhikaraṇa* Bādarāyaṇa merely mentions that the Supreme Goal is attained only by means of *vidyā* (*vidyātaḥ puruṣārthaḥ*). But the nature of the *vidyā* was not fully explained. The details about the nature of the *vidyā* are therefore presented in the first *pāda* of *Phalādhyāya*. Another reason for presenting this matter in the *Phalādhyāya* is that the *vidyā* or *upāsanā* as enunciated in the Upaniṣad is invariably connected with the goal to be attained. (*Brahmopāsanāya mukty-avinābhūtam*). As will be explained presently, the observance of *upāsanā* or the unceasing meditation on Brahman as the direct *sādhana* to *mokṣa* till the end of own's life (*yāvadāyuṣam*) is sure to culminate in the attainment of Brahman.

The first question to be considered is whether *vidyā* stands for mere knowledge (*jñāna*) of Brahman, that is, the direct realization of Brahman (*sākṣātkāra*), as Śaṁkara interprets, or does it refer to *upāsanā* or unceasing meditation culminating in the clear vision of Brahman (*upāsanātmaka jñāna*), as Rāmānuja maintains?

Prima facie, the Upaniṣadic texts lend support to the view that *vedana* or knowledge is the direct means to attain Brahman. Thus says the *Taittirīya*: *Brahmavid āpnoti paraṁ*- "The knower of Brahman attains the highest". The *Muṇḍaka* states: '*Brahmaveda brahmaiva bhavati*' - "He who knows Brahman becomes (similar to) Brahman". The Upaniṣads also mention *dhyāna, upāsanā, nididhyāsana* and *dhruvāsmṛti* as the means to attain Brahman. These terms convey the idea that *upāsanā* or unceasing meditation on Brahman is the direct means to *mokṣa*. If *vidyā* stands for *jñāna* as the *sādhana* for *mokṣa,* it does not have to be repeatedly practised. There is also no mention in the Upaniṣad that it is to be observed repeatedly. When once *jñāna* arises, *jīva* is liberated from bondage. If on the other hand, *vidyā* means *upāsanā* it is to be repeatedly practised until the goal is attained.

Bādarāyaṇa therefore first discusses this issue before enunciating the nature of the *sādhana* in the *Āvṛtyadhikaraṇa*. The relevant *sūtra* reads: *āvṛttih asakṛt upadeśāt.*[63] *Āvṛttiḥ* means repeated observance and *asakṛt* means more than once. From this it follows that whatever be the *sādhana* for *mokṣa*, it is to be observed repeatedly and continuously until the goal is achieved.

Now comes the main question whether *vedana* and *upāsanā* mean the same or do they refer to different disciplines? The answer is that the two terms are synonyms and refer to the same *sādhana* as this is evident from the Upaniṣadic teachings. This is what is meant by the word *'upadeśāt'* in the *sūtra*.

By way of elucidating this point, Rāmānuja points out that the Upaniṣads employ the terms *vedana* and *upāsanā* as interchangeable words. In the *Chāndogya* Upaniṣad discussing the manner of doing *upāsanā* on Brahman, the passage commences with the statement *'mano brahmeti upāsīta'* using the expression *upāsīta*. While concluding this passage it is stated: *'ya evaṁ veda'* [64]. The term *veda* is used here in place of *upāsīta* mentioned at the commencement. Taking into consideration the context of the passage, *veda* mentioned in the concluding statement means the same as *upāsīta* used at the beginning. In another passage of the *Chāndogya* referring to the greatness of sage Raikva, the opening sentence states *'yastad-veda yat sa veda'*, meaning what Raikva knew, that is to be known. While concluding this narration, it is stated 'whatever *devatā* you meditate upon (*tvaṁ upāsate*)[65], tell me in detail about the same deity'. In this passage, unlike the previous one, the term *veda* is used at the beginning and at the end the word *upāsīta* is employed. If we take into consideration both the passages it is obvious that according to the Upaniṣads, *vedana* and *upāsanā* bear the same meaning.[66] Veda or *vedana* employed in the Upaniṣad therefore denotes *upāsanā*.

The Upaniṣads also employ the terms *dhyāna* and *nididhyāsana* as means to *mokṣa*. Thus says the *Muṇḍaka*: *tatastu tam paśyati niṣkalaṁ dhyāyamānaḥ* [67] - "He who engages himself in meditation sees Him (*Paramātman*) who is free from parts". The *Bṛhadāraṇyaka* states: *'ātmā va are draṣṭavyaḥ śrotavyo mantavyo nididhyāsitayah'* -"Verily the self (Brahman) is to be seen, to be heard, to be reflected and to be meditated upon". As the terms *dhyāna* and *nididhyāsana* are used in the same context as *vedana,* suggesting that these are the direct means to attain Brahman, these terms should bear the same meaning as *vedana.* Otherwise it would amount to the admission of different means to *mokṣa,* which is not philosophically acceptable. The term *dhyāna* is derived from the root word *'dhyai cintāyāṁ'*. *Cintana* means concentrated contemplation in the form of uninterrupted remembrance of the object of meditation similar to the unbroken flow of oil poured out of a vessel (*tailadhārāvat avicchinna smṛti-santati*). This idea is conveyed in the expression *'dhruvānusmṛti* or unceasing meditation which is mentioned in the same *Chāndogya,* as the means to *mokṣa.* Thus says the Upaniṣad: *Sattva śuddhau dhruvāsmṛtiḥ, smṛti lambhe sarvagranthīnāṁ vipramokṣaḥ.*[68] The Upaniṣad also uses the expression *darśana* or *sākṣātkāra* as the means to *mokṣa.* The term *darśana* bears the same meaning as *vedana.* Thus it is stated in the Kaṭhopaniṣad. *'Nicāyya taṁ mṛtyumukhād pramucyate'.*[69] The term *nicāyya* derived from the root word *cāyṛ darśane* means *darśana* or *sākṣātkāra.* Thus it follows that the terms *vedana, dhyāna, upāsanā, dhruvāsmṛti* and *darśana* are synonymous.

Rāmānuja further points out that the term *bhakti* or *bhakti-yoga* employed in the *Gītā* is also synonymous with *upāsanā.* Though the term *bhakti* is not used in the Upaniṣad, it is implied in the statement of *Muṇḍaka* Upaniṣad, which is further elucidated in the *Bhagavad-gītā.* Thus says the *Muṇḍaka*: *Nāyam ātmā pravacanena labhyo na medhayā na bahunā śrutena; yamaiva eṣa vṛṇute tena labhyaḥ tasyaiṣa ātmā vivṛṇute tanūṁ svāṁ*[70] - "This Self (Brahman) cannot be attained by the study of Vedas, nor by meditation nor through much hearing. He is to be attained only by one whom the Self (*Paramātman*) chooses. To such a person, the Self (*Paramātman*) reveals His true form". The implication of this statement, as explained by Rāmānuja, is that one who is dearest to God is chosen by Him (*priyatama eva hi varaṇīyo bhavati*). Who is the dearest to God? The *Bhagavad-*

gītā provides the answer as to who is regarded as the dearest. Thus says the *Gītā*: "To those who crave for eternal union with Me and meditate on Me, I bestow to them with love, that clear vision (of *Paramātman*) by which they attain Me."[71] It also says: "One who is most devoted to God is the one who is dearest to Me". By way of elucidating the statement of the *Muṇḍaka* Upaniṣad, the Gītā points out that there is no other way of attaining God except by *ananya bhakti* or intense loving meditation on God. Thus it is stated: "*Nāhaṁ vedair na tapasā na dānena na ce'jyayā...bhaktyā tu ananyayā śakya aham evam vidho Arjuna: jñātuṁ draṣṭuṁ ca tattvena praveṣṭuṁ ca parantapa.*[72] The term *bhakti* is derived from the root word *bhaj* which means *sevā* or meditation (*bhaj sevāyām*). In common usage, it is understood in the sense of love towards the respected or elderly person (*mahanīya viṣaye prītiḥ*). *Prīti* or love is a state of knowledge, a mental disposition. *Bhakti* with reference to God, therefore means unceasing meditation with intense love for the Supreme Being (*snehapūrvam anudhyānaṁ bhaktiritya-bhidhīyate*).[73] According to *Nighaṇṭu* (glossary of Vedic terms), the terms *sevā*, *bhakti* and *upāsti* bear the same meaning.[74] *Bhakti* is therefore synonymous with *upāsanā*, *dhyāna* and *dhruvāsmṛti*. As pointed out earlier, when several terms are employed in the same context as the means to *mokṣa*, these cannot be taken as different means since the Goal to be attained is the same. Nor can they be regarded as alternative *sādhanas*. *Nididhyāsana* which denotes *upāsanā* or the steadfast meditation is a rigorous discipline, whereas *jñāna* or *darśana* which denotes direct realization is an easy path to *mokṣa*. The option between these two disciplines is therefore untenable. In such a circumstance, the Mīmāṁsā principle of interpretation is to be adopted to resolve the apparent conflicting statements regarding *sādhana* to *mokṣa*. According to this principle, when two or more terms are used in the Vedic texts in the same context, the general terms are understood in the sense of the specific term, as in the case of *chāga* and *paśu*. *Paśu* is a general term which refers to any kind of animal. But it is ascertained by subsequent specification that it bears the meaning of *chāga* or goat, which is a specific term. Accordingly, in the present context, *jñāna, vedana, darśana, dhyāna, upāsanā* and *dhruvāsmṛti* are treated as general terms and they all denote *Bhakti* or *Bhakti-yoga* which is a specific term. Rāmānuja therefore comes to the conclusion that *upāsanā* or *bhakti* as denoted by the word *vidyā* used in the *Vedānta-sūtra* is the direct means to *mokṣa*. The *vedana* implied in the *sūtra* which is the same as *upāsanā* in the Upaniṣad and *bhakti*-yoga in the *Gītā* is to be observed repeatedly and continuously until the goal is achieved, as stated in the *sūtra 'asakṛt āvṛttiḥ'*.

This view is also supported by the *Smṛti* texts as stated in the subsequent *sūtra* reading *'Liṅgācca'*[75]. *Liṅga* denotes *Smṛti* texts. It means that even *Smṛti* texts support the view that *vedana* or *upāsanā* is to be repeatedly and continuously practised. While commenting on this *sūtra*, Rāmānuja quotes the following verse from *Viṣṇupurāṇa*. *Tadrūpapratyaye caikā santatiśca anyanispṛhā; tad-dhyānaṁ prathamaiḥ ṣaḍbhiḥ angaiḥ niṣpādyate tathā.*[76] It means that *dhyāna* on *Paramātman* is the concentrated and uninterrupted series of recollection of the object of meditation and it is to be accomplished with the aid of first six *yogāṅgas*. That is, before embarking on *dhyāna, dhāraṇa* or concentration on the object of contemplation is needed. This is the sixth limb of *Yoga* discipline laid down by Pātañjali. *Dhāraṇa* invariably presupposes the mental purity by way of cultivation of ethical virtues (*yama*) and observance of religious duties (*niyamas*); a steady posture (*āsana*), control of breath (*prāṇāyāma*) and control of sense organs (*pratyāhāra*). Thus according to the *Vedānta-sūtra*, as interpreted by Rāmānuja, *dhyāna* or *upāsanā* on Brahman involves the observance of the *yogāṅgas*. Thus it is a rigorous religious discipline. It is not mere *bhakti* or loving devotion to God as is generally understood. *Bhakti* or devotion to God is no doubt needed to undertake *upāsanā*, but when *bhakti* is adopted as *sādhana* to *mokṣa*, it involves the eight-fold psycho-religious discipline. Though Bādarāyaṇa does not employ the term *aṣṭāṅga-yoga*, some of the components of the yoga-discipline are mentioned by him in the *sūtras*. The *sūtra 'dhyānācca'*[77] implies that unceasing meditation requires the concentration of mind. Bādarāyaṇa also specifically states that steadiness of mind and body (*acalatvam ca*)[78] and the selection of suitable place and proper environment[79] are very important for the practice of *dhyāna*-yoga. The *sutra* reading: *'Smaranti ca'*[80] refers to the other details about the *yogāṅgas* mentioned in the *Bhagavad-gīta*[81].

As stated in the earlier section dealing with *karma* in relation to *vidyā*, the scrupulous observance of the prescribed *karmas* according to one's *āśrama* or the stage of life and the cultivation of *śama, dama*, etc. as ethical virtues are equally important since these constitute the subsidiary aid to *upāsanā*.

More important than the compliance with the yoga-discipline, the *upāsanā* is to be practised until the end of one's life. Thus says the *sūtra*: *āprayāṇāt tatrāpi hi dṛṣṭam.*[82] This confirms that *vedana* or *vidyā* is not merely the direct knowledge of Brahman, as Advaitin maintains, but, on the contrary, it denotes *upāsanā* as a rigorous discipline to be practised continuously until one attains the Supreme Goal.

Bādarāyaṇa also discusses another important issue relating to the *upāsanā* viz., the manner in which the individual who is the *upāsaka* should meditate on Brahman, which is the *upāsya* or the object of meditation. The question to be considered is whether the *upāsaka* should meditate on Brahman as different from him or as non-different from him, that is, as his *Ātman* (Inner Self). This issue is examined in a separate *adhikaraṇa* named *Ātmatvopāsanādhikaraṇa*. The relevant *sūtra* reads: *'Ātmeti-tu-upagacchanti grāhayanti ca'*[83]. It means, as explained by Rāmānuja, that the *upāsaka* should meditate on Brahman as its Inner Self (*Ātmetyeva*). By way of elucidation, he points out that just as *jīva* of *upāsaka* stands as the self for the body, in the same way,

Brahman is the *Ātman* for his *jīva*. Why should he meditate in this way? The reason is that the Sacred texts teach that Brahman is the *Ātman* in the sense that it is the Inner Self or *Antaryāmin* of *jīva*. Thus says the Upanisad: *'tvaṁ vā ahamasmi bhagavo devate ahaṁ vai tvamasi'* - "O worshipful Deity, I am indeed Thou and Thou art indeed I". The term "I" ultimately denotes the Paramatman and hence the two terms 'I' and 'Thou' mean the same.

An objection is raised against this view. In the earlier *adhyāyas* it is specifically stated that *jīva* is absolutely different from Brahman (*atyanta bhinnah*) and that Brahman is *vibhu* or all-pervasive whereas *jīva* is *aṇu* or monodic in nature. It would not therefore be appropriate to meditate on Brahman as non-different from Brahman. Besides the *upāsanā* is intended for the attainment of *mokṣa* and meditation on *jīva* as Brahman in a wrong manner would not help to achieve the desired goal.

In reply to this objection Vedānta Deśika points out that Bādarāyaṇa does not advocate that *jīva* and Brahman are essentially identical (*svarūpaikya*). Nor does he suggest that *jīva* is to be meditated upon (conceived as Brahman), similar to the *upāsanā* on *udgītha* or the syllable *'aum'* conceived as Brahman. If he accepted either of these views, the objection raised above would be valid. But it is not so. What is actually required for the purpose of meditation on Brahman is that *upāsaka* should contemplate during *upāsanā* that Brahman is his *Antaryāmin* in the form *'Ahaṁ brahmāsmi'* – "I am Brahman". The primary import of the term *'ahaṁ'* is *Paramātman* who is the *antarātmā* of *jīva* (*svātmāntarātmani ahaṁ-iti vacaso'pi atra mukhya pravṛtteḥ*).[84] This interpretation is justified both logically and philosophically. In the judgements 'I am *manuṣya* (human being), I am *deva* (celestial being), the terms *manuṣyatva, devatva*, etc., refer to the physical body (*dehavācī*) and yet they are applicable in the primary sense to the *jīvātman* to which the body actually belongs. In the same way, the term *ahaṁ* denoting the *jīva* is applicable to *Paramātman*, who is its *antarātmā*.

Hence it is not inappropriate to meditate on Brahman in the form '*Ahaṁ brahmāsmi*', that is: 'I' as *jīvātman* is having Brahman as my *Antaryāmin* (*ahaṁ brahmātmakosmi*). This does not amount to the contemplation of Brahman as identical with *jīva*, as contended by Advaitin, for the reason that *jīva* and Brahman by virtue of their intrinsic nature are of different character, as evidenced by numerous Scriptural texts and also the *Vedanta-sūtras*. The Scriptural texts also declare that Brahman is immanent in the *jīvas* as *Antaryāmin*. Thus says the *Bṛhadāraṇyaka*: *ya ātmani tiṣṭhan, ātmano antaro yam ātmā na veda, yasyātmā śarīram, ya ātmānam antaro yamayati, sa ta ātmā antaryāmy amṛtaḥ.*[85] The *Chāndogya* states: *Sanmūlāḥ somya, imāḥ sarvāḥ prajāḥ sadāyatanāḥ sat-pratiṣṭhitāḥ, aitadatmyam idam sarvaṁ.*[86] All these texts convey that Brahman is the *Ātman* of all entities in the universe including the *jīvas*. It is therefore fully justified to say, as the Upaniṣad states, that I (*jīva*) am Thou (*Paramātman*) and that Thou art I (*jīva*).

In all such statements where two terms are expressed in the same *vibhakti* (*samāna adhikaraṇa*) by equating two entities such as Brahman and *jīva*, as in the texts '*tat-tvam-asi*' '*ahaṁ-brahmāsmi*', these have to be taken in the sense that Brahman is the *Antaryāmin* of *jīva* and as such the two are one as inherently related as body to the soul. This explanation is fully justified on the basis of the principle of *sāmānādhikaraṇya* adopted by the grammarian.[87]

---

1. VS III–4–1
2. *See* AS verse 304
3. VS III-2-II
4. Ch. Up VIII–1–5
5. V.P VI–5–84 & 85 *Samasta kalyāṇa guṇātmakośau... Tejobalaiśvarya mahāvabodha suvīrya śaktyādi guṇaikarāśiḥ; Paraḥ parāṇaṁ sakalā na yatra kleśadayaḥ santi parāvareśe*
6. *Muṇḍ Up.* III–1–1 *Dvā suparṇā sayujā sakhāya samānaṁ vṛkṣam pariṣasvājate; tayor-anyaḥ pippalaṁ svādvatti anaśnan anyo abhicakāśiti*
7. *See* S.B.III-2-11
8. *Apaccheda-nyāya* is the principle of the later substating the earlier. It is so called since it is formulated in the *pūrva-mīmāṁsā* in

connection with the expiatory rites consequent on different priests letting go (*apaccheda*) their hold of the tucked up waist cloth of the priest in front while going round the sacrificial fire.

9. Śvet.Up. VI-19
10. *See* Śatadūṣaṇī, vāda.52. *See* also FVV pp230-31.
11. *See* AS verse 307
12. Śvet. Up. VI-8
13. Br. Up. IV-3-1 *See Philosophy of the Upaniṣads.* pp 61-62
14. VS III-2-21
15. *See* Br. Up. IV - 3 - 6
16. *See* RB. III-2-21. *See* also the *Philosophy of the Vedānta-sūtra.* pp 63-64.
17. *See* ASverse 309
18. VS III-2-30
19. Ch. Up. VIII-4-1
20. Ch. Up. III-8-2
21. Mu. Up. II-2-5
22. Mu. Up. III-2-8
23. Śvet. Up. III-10
24. *See* RB.III-2-31
25. Ch. Up. VIII-4-1
26. VS III-2-32
27. VS III-2-34
28. VS III-2-35
29. Śvet. Up. III-9
30. Mu. Up. I-1-6
31. VS III-3-37
32. VS III-3-56
33. VS III-3-56
34. *See Mīmāṁsā sūtra* II-4-9 *ekam vā saṁyoga rūpa codanākhyā viśeṣāt*
35. *See* AS verse 384
36. VS III-3-57
37. VS III-3-1
38. *See*.Ch. Up. III-14-1 *Yathākratuḥ asmin loke puruṣo bhavati tathetaḥ pretya bhavati.*
39. AS verse 325 *Taireva dharmaiḥ tad-itara sahitaiḥ pūrṇakāmasya param prāpyam brahmaiva na anyat kimapi phalam*
40. VS III-3-11
41. Br. Up. V-8-8. *See* also chapter 3, section IX
42. Mu. Up. I-I-5 *See* also chapter 3, section V
43. VS III-3-33
44. *See* RB. III-3-33
45. VS III-3-52
46. VS III-4-1
47. Mu. Up. .. *Brahma veda brahmaiva bhavati*

48. Śvet. Up. *Tamevā viditvā atimṛtyum-eti nānyah panthā vidyate ayanāya*
49. Iśa. Up. 2 *Kurvannevaha karmāṇi jijīviṣet śatam samaḥ*
50. Br. Up. VI-4-2
51. Br. Up. VI-4-22
52. B.G. III-20
53. AS verse 399
54. *See* Ch. Up. II-23-1
55. *See* VS. III-4-25
56. VS III-4-26
57. Br. Up. VI-4-22
58. VS III-4-27
59. *See* Ch. Up. I-10-3
60. Br. Up. V-5-1
61. VS III-4-32
62. VS IV -1-1
63. *See* Ch. Up. III-18-1 to 3
64. *Ibid* IV-1-4 & IV-1-2
65. *See* RB I-1-1 *vidyupāsyayoḥ vyatirekeṇa upakrama upasamhārāt. See also SB.IV-I-I*
66. Mu. Up. III-1-8
67. Ch. Up. VII-26-2
68. Katha Up. III-15
69. Mu. Up. V-2-3
70. BG X-10 *Teṣāṁ satatayuktānāṁ bhajatāṁ prītipūrvakam dadāmi buddhi-yogaṁ taṁ yena māṁ upayānti te*
71. *Ibid* XI-53 & 54
72. *See* Śrutaprakāśikā on RB I-1-1
73. *Ibid, Sevā bhaktirupāsti iti naighaṇṭukokteḥ*
74. VS IV-1-2
75. VP VI-7-91
76. VS IV-1-8
77. VS IV-1-9
78. VS IV-1-11 *Yatraikāgratā tatra aviśṣāt*
79. VS IV-1-10
80. BG VI -11 & 12
81. VS IV-1-12
82. VS IV-1-3
83. AS verse 441
84. Br. Up. V-7-22
85. Ch. Up. VI-8-6
86. *See* Mahābhāṣyā on Pāṇini *sūtra: Bhinnapravṛtti nimittānāṁ śabdānāṁ ekasmin arthe sāmānadhikaraṇyam. See* also AV. Chapter 1

CHAPTER NINE

THE DOCTRINE OF PARAMA PURUṢĀRTHA

The fourth *adhyāya* of the *Brahma-Sūtra* which is titled *Phalādhyāya* is devoted to the discussion of the nature of the Supreme Goal (*Parama Puruṣārtha*) which is to be attained by the aspirant for *mokṣa* after duly observing the prescribed *upāsanā* or meditation on Brahman. In the previous chapter, we have discussed in detail, all aspects of the *sādhana* as enunciated by Bādarāyaṇa on the authority of the Upaniṣads. In the present chapter we shall deal with the nature of *phala* or the goal to be attained by *upāsanā*. This will comprise the following four theories, which have a bearing on *mokṣa*, the Supreme Goal. i) The liberation of *jīva* from bondage caused by *karma* in the form of *puṇya* and *pāpa*. ii) *Utkrānti* or the exit of the jīva from the body after liberation. iii) *Arcirādi-mārga* or the path through which the liberated jīva marches to the abode of Brahman and iv) The status of *jīva* in the state of *mukti*. These are the topics which are covered in the last five *adhikaraṇas* of first *pāda* named *Āvṛttipāda*, eleven *adhikaraṇas* of second *pāda* named *Utkrāntipāda*, the five *adhikaraṇas* of third *pāda* named *Gatipāda* and six *adhikaraṇas* of the fourth *pāda* named *Muktipāda*. As *mokṣa* is attained only after the death of the *upāsaka*, it is considered relevant to discuss these subjects in the *Phalādhyāya*.

I. The Nature of Liberation of the Jīva from bondage

As will be explained later, *mokṣa* or liberation of the jīva from bondage leading to the attainment of a status equal to that of Brahman, constitutes the Supreme Goal. *Mukti* is possible when the individual becomes totally free from *karma* in the form of both *puṇya* and *pāpa*. Bādarāyaṇa first discusses how the *upāsanā* or the unceasing meditation on Brahman observed by the aspirant for *mokṣa* until the end of the life, helps to liberate the soul from bondage. Bondage is caused by *karma* in the form of *puṇya* and *pāpa*. The *karma* which is also known as *avidyā* is beginningless (*anādi*). Normally it is to be overcome only by experiencing it fully. A *Smṛti* text also says that *karma* cannot be totally eradicated until it is fully experienced through several epochs (*nābhuktam kṣīyate karma kalpakoṭi śatairapi*[1]). If this is the case, how is it possible to get rid of it by the mere observance of *upāsanā*.

Bādarāyaṇa states that the *Brahma-vidyā* has the power to put an end to all the sins (*pāpa*) committed prior to the embarkation on *upāsanā* and also the sins committed subsequent to the commencement of the *upāsanā*. The relevant *sūtra* reads: *Tad-adhigame uttara-pūrvāghayor aśleṣa vināśau; tadvyapadeśāt*[2]. The word *tad-adhigame* means according to Rāmānuja, after the *upāsaka* has reached a state of perfection in the practice of *upāsanā*, resulting in a clearer vision of Brahman (*darśana-samānākāra jñāna*). *Uttarāgha* means the sins committed after the commencement of the *upāsanā*. *Purvāgha* refers to the sins committed prior to the commencement of the meditation. *Aśleṣa* means non-attachment, that is, not being affected (This applies to *uttarāgha*). *Vināśa* means destruction (This applies to *purvāgha)*. The total meaning of the *sūtra* is: "When the meditation on Brahman is completed by an individual, the sins committed by him in the past (prior to it) are destroyed and the sins committed subsequent to its commencement do not cling to him. The reason for advancing this view is that the Upaniṣadic texts state accordingly (*tad-vyapadeśāt*). Thus says the Chāndogya: *Tad-yathā puṣkara-palāśa āpo na śliṣyante evaṁ vidi pāpaṁ karma na śliṣyate*[3]–"Just as the water on the lotus leaf does not stick to it, so also the evil deeds do not touch the Brahman-knower". Another text says: *Tad yathā-iṣīka tūlam agnau protaṁ pradūyeta evaṁ hāsya sarve pāpmānaḥ pradūyante* [4] – "Just as the cotton-like fibre thrown into the fire, gets totally burnt, in the same way, all the sins of the *upāsaka* are burnt". On the authority of these Scriptural texts, it is maintained that the *upāsaka* who has had the clearer vision of Brahman through the unceasing and devoted meditation on Brahman is not touched by the effects of the past deeds and so also by the sinful deeds committed subsequent to the commencement of the *upāsanā*.

By way of clarification, Vedānta Deśika points out that the Scriptural texts convey that *Brahmopāsanā* is efficacious enough to remove the effects of the past deeds and also those arising subsequent to the *upāsanā*. This is possible because the meditation on *Paramātman* (*Brahman*) itself constitutes the *prāyaścitta* or expiatory rites for the removal of all the sins committed by the *upāsaka* (*tādṛg vidyaiva tanniṣkṛtiḥ*[5]). The devoted meditation on Brahman is prescribed as a *prāyaścitta* in order to overcome all *karmas* (*prāyaścitta-krameṇa parabhajanaṁ coditam karma-śāntyai*[6]). In so far as it is capable of removing all obstacles including *karma* in the form of *puṇya* and *pāpa*, *Brahma-vidyā* is regarded as a *prāyaścitta* for all sins. The *Gītā* also says that self-knowledge in the form of fire (*jñānāgni*) burns all the *karmas* (*jñānāgniḥ sarvakarmāṇi bhasmasāt kurute*).

Regarding the *Smṛti* text which states that the effects of the sinful deeds have to be overcome only by experiencing them, it is intended to emphasize the need of observing appropriate expiatory rites (*prāyaścitta*) to overcome their strong ill-effects. This is the general rule and it does not apply to *upāsanā* which has the power to eradicate the sins of the past. The Scriptural texts speaking of the eradication of the sins by *Brahmopāsanā* are not therefore to be taken as glorifactory statements, as the critic observes.

The Upaniṣadic text says that *Brahma-vidyā* takes away all sins (*sarve pāpmānaḥ pradūyante*[7]). The word *pāpmānaḥ* expressed in plural is intended to mean both sin as well as merit (*puṇya*). Though the word *puṇya* is not mentioned in the *Śruti*, it becomes included in the word *pāpma*, because for an aspirant to *mokṣa*, even *puṇya* has the same effect as *pāpa*, in so far as it stands in the way of attainment of *mokṣa*. The Upaniṣad itself mentions specifically both *sukṛta* and *duṣkṛta* are to be cast off. After mentioning both *sukṛta* and *duṣkṛta*, the text says in one sweeping statement '*na sukṛtam na duṣkrtam sarve pāpmānaḥ*'. Therefore *Brahma-vidyā* destroys not only all the sins but all the *puṇyas* too accumulated by the *upāsaka*. On the basis of this text, the author of the *sūtra* says: *itarasyāpi evam asaṁśleṣaḥ pāte tu*[8]. It means: "Regarding the others (*puṇya*) there is likewise non-clinging and destruction of (previous *puṇya*), soon after the fall of the body".

Vedānta Deśika explains the fuller implication of the term *agha-vināśa* or the destruction of the sins. The Kaṭha Upaniṣad says that unless one is free from all sins, one will not be able to achieve *mokṣa* (*nā virato duśçaritāt*[9]). If *puṇya* and *pāpa* do not affect the *Brahma-jñanī*, why should he get rid of them totally for attaining *mokṣa*? In reply, it is pointed out that *pāpa* is of two kinds. One which is committed intentionally and the other which is committed unintentionally. What is done intentionally needs to be overcome by suitable expiatory rituals. Only that which is committed unintentionally does not affect the *Brahma-jñānī* because his *upāsanā* on Brahman is capable of counteracting it. The Kaṭha Upaniṣad refers to the need of overcoming the sins committed intentionally.[10] In the same way it is to be understood that only *puṇya* acquired by a *Brahma-jñānī* unintentionally, will not bear any result for him. This is the significance of the statement that *Brahma-jñānī* is not affected by *puṇya* and *pāpa*.

As regards the *agha aśleṣa* or the non-clinging of the sins committed after the commencement of the *upāsanā*, Vedānta Deśika clarifies that the power of the *karma* to bear its fruit is arrested by *Paramātman* (*karmaśakteḥ anudaya aśleṣaḥ*). If it gives the result, it is prevented from doing so (*uadaye tannivṛttiḥ vināśaḥ*). This explanation is justified because according to the Viśiṣṭādvaita, the pleasure and displeasure of the Supreme Lord stand for *puṇya* and *pāpa* respectively (*śaktiḥ sa ca praṇetuḥ taducita phalakṛt nigraha anugrāhatmā*)[11].

Vedānta Deśika also points out that a *Brahma-vit* does not generally commit any sins intentionally since he is always cautious in his actions and avoids sinful acts (*sarvadā sāvadhānā brahmavid-dhīpūrvam uttarāghaṁ na sṛjati*). If by accident he commits a sin, he gets rid of it by appropriate expiatory rite. Alternatively he will overcome it by experiencing the ill-effects of it by undergoing the light punishment inflicted on him by God as a remedy for the sin committed by the *upāsaka*. In any case, a *brahma-niṣṭha* is sure to attain *mokṣa* at the end of the life when his *prārabdha karma* comes to an end. The Chāndogya states: *Tasya tāvadeva ciram yāvan na vimokṣye atha sampatsye*[12]– "For him, there is delay only so long as he is not released from the body. Thereafter he attains *mokṣa*". As long as the *jīva* is embodied due to the *karma*, he cannot attain *mokṣa*. Whenever the *prārabdha-karma*, that is the *karma* which has begun to bear its effect ceases, the *upāsaka* attains *mokṣa* soon after he is freed from the association of the body caused by the *karma*. This may take place either at the end of the present life or in a subsequent life as and when the *prārabdha karma* comes to an end[13].

II. The Theory of Exit of the Jīva from the Body (utkrānti)

In the preceding section we have considered how the individual who embarks on *upāsanā* for the attainment of *mokṣa* becomes free from *karma* in the form of both *puṅya* and *pāpa* acquired prior to the *upāsanā* and also subsequent to its commencement, because the *upāsanā* itself, being a *prāyaścitta*, has the efficacy to eradicate it. In the second *pada* of the *Phalādhyāya* named *utkrānti-pāda*, Bādarāyaṇa explains how the *jīva* of the *upāsaka,* soon after the death, exits from the body. This is called *utkrānti* and it also constitutes another important aspect of the *phala* or fruit of the *upāsanā*. It is therefore considered relevant to deal with this subject in the *Phalādhyāya*. Another important reason for taking up this matter in this context is to set aside the wrong theories of the Sāṁkhyas that the *jīva* is *nitya-mukta* or eternally free and also of the *Māyāvādins* who advocate the theory of *jīvan-mukti* or that the *Brahma-vit* is *mukta* even though he is embodied. The eleven *adhikaraṇas* included in the second *pāda* of this *adhyāya* discuss how the *jīva* along with the *indriyas, manas* and *prāṇa* exit from the body through the *mūrdhanya nāḍi* and move to the higher abode through the *arcirādi mārga*. We shall take note of the important points as presented in the *Adhikaraṇa-sārāvalī*.

The Chāndogya Upaniṣad dealing with the exit of the soul at the time of death states: *Asya somya puruṣasya prayato vāk manasi saṁpadyate, manaḥ prāṇe, prāṇaḥ tejasi, tejaḥ parasyāṁ devatāyāṁ*[14].

"When a person (*puruṣa*) dies, his speech merges in the mind, the mind in the vital breath (*prāṇa*), the *prāṇa* in the fire (*tejas)* and *tejas* in the Supreme Being."

With regard to the statement '*vāk manasi saṁpadyate*' in the above passage, the question arises whether the very sense organ of speech itself (*vāg-indriya*) merges in the mind or only the function of speech (*vāg-vṛtti*) merges in it. According to the prima facie view, only the function of the *vāg-indriya* becomes merged in the mind. The reason for taking this view is that the absorption of the cognitive organs in the mind is not at all possible (*asambhavaḥ*). Besides, in the process of dissolution, the effect is absorbed in its causal substance and since the sense organ of speech is not caused by the mind, it cannot merge in the mind. Hence it is to be admitted that only its function of speech is absorbed in the mind. This is possible because the function of speech is dependent on the mind.

Bādarāyaṇa does not accept this view. The very sense organ of speech (*vāg-indriya*) becomes merged in the mind at the time of the death of a person. The relevant *sūtra* reads: *Vāg-manasi darśanāt śabdācca.*[15] It means that the organ of speech gets merged in the mind, because it is evident to our perceptual experience and also supported by the Scriptural text. We find that when the *vāg-indriya* ceases to function, the mind is found to be still working. Besides, the Upaniṣadic text speaks of the merging of the *vāg-indriya* in the mind. It does not specifically mention that the function of *vāg-indriya* gets absorbed in the mind. It is also not known that with the cessation of the function of speech, the *vāg-indriya* ceases to exist. It is therefore to be admitted that the sense-organ of speech itself becomes merged in the mind. The word '*saṁpadyate*' is to be understood as becoming united with the mind (*saṁ-yujyate*) and not that it is dissolved in the mind (*līyate*). As Vedānta Deśika explains, *saṁpattiḥ* is to be interpreted as *saṁśleṣa*. The word *vāk* mentioned in the *sūtra* also includes all other sense organs. That is, as in the case of *vāg-indriya*, all other senses are also united with the mind. This is made evident from the following statement of the Praśna Upaniṣad: *Tasmāt upaśānta tejaḥ punarbhavam indriyaiḥ manasi saṁpadyamānaiḥ*[16] – " When the heat of the body is extinguished (soon after death), the soul along with the mind with which all sense organs are united, gets into the vital breath for taking another birth. In this statement, it is specifically mentioned that all *indriyas* are united with the mind (*indriyaiḥ manasi saṁpadyamānaiḥ*).

In the next stage, the mind, with which all *indriyas* are united, gets merged in the *prāṇa* or the vital breath. Thus says the Upaniṣad: *manaḥ prāṇe*. Accordingly, Bādarāyaṇa states: *Tan-manaḥ prāṇa uttarāt.*[17] It means – "The mind is united with the vital breath because of the Upaniṣadic statement to this effect".

Here also the question arises whether *manas* is merged in *prāṇa* or it becomes merely united with *prāṇa*? The reason for this doubt is that the Upaniṣad describes *prāṇa* as constituted of *ap* or water (*āpomayaḥ prāṇaḥ*). It implies that *ap* is the cause of *prāṇa*. In view of it, it is relevant to regard that manas is dissolved in *prāṇa,* which is its causal substance. *Manas* is also described in the Upaniṣad as *annamaya* which signifies that it is caused by *pṛthivī,* the word *anna* or food being taken as *pṛthivī.* Hence it is appropriate to accept that mind as associated with *indriyas* gets absorbed in the *prāna.*

Bādarāyaṇa does not accept this argument. The expressions *āpomayaḥ* and *annamayah* in respect of *prāṇa* and *manas* respectively do not imply that *prāṇa* is caused by *ap* and mind by anna or *pṛthivī.* The affix *'mayaṭ'* added to these words signify that *prāṇa* and *manas* are nourished by water and food respectively. It does not mean that water is the cause of *prāṇa* and so also *pṛthivī* (food) is the cause of the mind. The word *saṁpadyate* employed in the statement cannot therefore be taken to mean as *līyate* but on the contrary, as in the case of *vāk* and *manas,* it means they become united (*saṁbandha or saṁsleṣa*[18]).

In the next stage the *prāṇa* which is associated with the mind and the sense organs, becomes united with *tejas.* Thus says the Upaniṣad: *Prāṇaḥ tejasi.* The question to be considered is, what does the term *tejas* stand for? Does it refer to the mere element of *tejas* (fire) or does it denote the *jīvātman* associated with the five other elements? If we go by the text of the Upaniṣad, *prāṇa* becomes united with *tejas* or element of fire. It would not be appropriate to introduce the principle of *jīva* and interpret the text to mean *'prāṇa* as associated with the *jīva* becomes united with *tejas'.* This is the prima facie view.

Bādarāyaṇa does not accept it. According to him, *prāṇa* as associated with *jīva* becomes united with *tejas.* The relevant *sūtra* reads: *So adhyakṣe tad-upagamādibhyaḥ*[19]. It means that *prāṇa* becomes united with *jīva* (*adhyakṣe*) which is the Lord of all sense organs (*karaṇādhipa*) because it is stated in the Upaniṣad that the *prāṇa* follows the *jīva* (*prāṇasya jivopagama*). Thus says the Bṛhadāraṇyaka Upaniṣad: *Evam eva imam ātmānaṁ antakāle sarve prāṇā abhisamāyanti* [20] – "In the same way, all the *prāṇas* proceed towards the *jīvātman* at the time of death." The Upaniṣad also describes that all the *prāṇas* move with the *jīva* at the time of death as the faithful followers of the king follow him during his return after victory even though they are not ordered to do so". In another text of Bṛhadāraṇyaka, it is clearly stated that *prāṇa* follows the *jīva* when it exits from the body *(tam utkrāmantaṁ prāṇo anutkrāmati* [21] *)*. There are sufficient number of Upaniṣadic statements which point out that there is close connection between *prāṇa* and *jīva*. It is therefore appropriate to say that *prāṇa* is first united with *jīva* and then *jīva* along with *prāṇa* becomes united with *tejas*. Even though *jīva* is not mentioned in the Upaniṣad, it is to be admitted as related to *prāṇa*. This is justified on the analogy of the statement : "The river Yamunā enters the ocean". The river Yamunā first joins the river Gaṅgā and Gaṅgā united with Yamunā reaches the ocean. Nevertheless we say that Yamunā enters the ocean. In the same way it is not inappropriate to say that *prāṇa* as associated with *jīva* is united with *tejas*.

The word *tejas* mentioned in the Upaniṣadic text (*prāṇaḥ tejasi*) refers not merely to *tejas* but all other elements because the physical body with which *jīva* is associated consists of all the five elements. In view of it, *jīva* is described in the Upaniṣad as *pṛthivīmaya, āpomaya, tejomaya* etc. Bādarāyaṇa therefore states that *prāṇa* along with *jīva* is united with all the five elements. The relevant *sūtra* reads: *Bhūteṣu tat śruteḥ*[22]. Another reason for this view is that no single element by itself is capable of producing an effect. Only when all the five elements are combined together in different proportion, they are capable of producing the effect. This is supported by the theory of *pañcīkaraṇa* or quintuplication taught in the Upaniṣads. As explained in Chapter 6, the creation of the manifold universe (*vyaṣṭi-sṛṣṭi*) takes place only when all the five elements are mixed in certain proportion. Thus it is maintained that during the time of exit of the soul from the body, *jīva* as associated with the subtle body which comprises the five subtle elements, *indriyas* including *manas* and *prāṇa* moves out on its onward march to higher realms.

In connection with the theory of *utkrānti*, an important issue comes up for consideration. The question is raised whether the *utkrānti* described in the Upaniṣads is applicable to both kinds of persons – those who have realized Brahman through meditation (*viduṣa*) and those who have not undertaken the *upāsanā* to attain Brahman (*aviduṣa*). The reason for this doubt is the following statement of the Kaṭha Upaniṣad which conveys the impression that the knower of Brahman attains Brahman here itself: *Yadā sarve pramucyante kāmā ye asya hṛdi sthitāh; atha martyo amṛto bhavati atra Brahma samaśnute*[23] – "When all the desires that persist in the heart have been abandoned by an individual, that mortal becomes immortal and enjoys Brahman here". Another text says: *Tamevam vidvān amṛta iha bhavati* – "He who knows Brahman becomes immortal here itself". On the basis of such statements it is argued that *utkrānti* is not required for the persons who have realized Brahman[24]. Bādarāyaṇa clarifies this doubt. He points out that the *utkrānti* is common for both the *upāsaka* and non-*upāsaka* upto the point of entering into the *mūrdhanya-nāḍi*, also called the *suṣumnā nādi* or the main artery leading from the heart to the crown of the head. The relevant *sūtra* reads: *Samānā ca āsṛtyupakramād-amṛtatvam ca anupoṣya*[25]. The word *sṛtiḥ* means the path named as *arcirādi mārga* through which the *jīva* traverses to the higher abode. *Upakrama* means the entry into the *mūrdhanya-nāḍi* through which the *jīva* exits from the body. *Āsṛtyupakramāt* therefore means prior to the entry into the *mūrdhanya-nāḍi*. The meaning of the *sūtra* is that prior to the entry into the *mūrdhanya-nāḍi* , the *utkrānti* is common to both the *upāsaka* and the non-*upāsaka*. Regarding the attainment of immortality and enjoyment of Brahman here itself stated in the Upaniṣad, it is pointed out that this refers to the enjoyment of Brahman during the observance of the *upāsanā*. The word *amṛtatva* does not mean the attainment of *mokṣa,* because the *upāsaka* is still embodied. The Chāndogya clearly states that as long as one is associated with the body, *mokṣa* is not attained (*tasya tāvadeva ciram yāvan na vimokṣye*[26]). As will be pointed out later, the attainment of *mokṣa* takes place only after the *jīva* traverses through the *arcirādi mārga* and gets rid of the *sūkṣma śarīra* or the subtle body with which it exits from the body and moves to the higher abode. Hence the word *amṛtatva* referred to in the Upaniṣadic text is to be taken in a figurative sense (*upacāra*). It is to be understood in the sense that the sins committed by the *upāsaka* in the past are eradicated while the sins committed after the commencement of the *upāsanā* do not affect him due to the efficacy of the *upāsanā*.. This is what is implied by the words *'amṛtatvam anupoṣya'* in the *sūtra*. It means that the *upāsaka* enjoys *amṛtatva* without getting rid of the body and the sense organs.

It may be argued that the *utkrānti* mentioned in the Upaniṣad is to be taken as applicable to the person who meditates on *Saguṇa* Brahman, while those who have had direct realization of Brahman (*ātmaikya jñāna)* do not need *utkrānti* since they have become *mukta* or free from bondage soon after the cessation of *avidyā*. Even though he is embodied, he is regarded as *mukta*. This state of the *Brahmavit* is regarded as *jīvan-mukti.*

This theory is unsound, contends Vedānta Deśika. In the first place, the concept of *Nirguṇa* Brahman as distinct from *Saguṇa* Brahman is not warranted by the *pramāṇas* including the Scriptural texts (*kutracit mānahāneḥ*). Secondly, the theory of *jīvan-mukti* which upholds that *Brahmavit* is a *mukta* even though he is embodied, is a self-contradiction, similar to the concept of a barren woman's son (*mātā-vandhyā*). If one becomes totally liberated from bondage due to the removal of *avidyā* after attaining direct knowledge of Brahman, he should not again experience any afflictions but in actual life we find that even the *Brahmavit* who is associated with the body is subjected to physical suffering. It may be argued that with the cessation of *avidyā,* which is the cause of bondage, the *jīva* is totally liberated from bondage soon after separation from the body consequent to the death and there would be no need for it to assume a subtle body for the purpose of movement to the higher abodes, since it is possible to explain the movement of the *jīva* on the basis of its being monadic in size (*aṇutva*). If jīva needs a body to hold conversation with the celestial deities in the realm of the moon as stated in the Upaniṣad, even this can be made possible for the *jīva* by its assuming a different body by its will for this purpose. Hence the need of *utkrānti* for the *jīva* and also the necessity of a subtle body for the purpose of movement to higher realms are unjustified.

Vedānta Deśika refutes this argument. The total eradication of *avidyā*, which is the cause of bondage requires the exit of the *jīva* from the body and also its movement through the *arcirādi mārga* to the higher abode (*kṛtsnāvidyā nivṛttiḥ parapada gamana āpekṣiṇi*[27]). Though soon after the death, the gross physical body is cast off, the *jīva* is still associated with the subtle body with which it exits through the *suṣumnā nāḍi* and then moves forward through the *arcirādi-mārga* to the *Brahma-loka* as evidenced by the Upaniṣadic texts. It casts off the subtle body only after it attains the *Brahma-loka*. As long as the subtle body exists, *avidyā* also persists. Hence the *mukti* or the *mokṣa* proper is attained by the *jīva* only after it traverses through the *arcirādi mārga* and reaches *Brahma-loka*. This point is also implied in the *sūtra* which reads: *Tad āpīteḥ saṁsāru vyapdeśāt*[28]– "The saṁsāra or bondage continues till the final dissolution of the subtle body and the attainment of Brahman."[29] As will be pointed out later, the *jīva* being enveloped with the subtle body exits from the body and attains Brahman only after reaching *Brahma-loka* through the *arcirādi-mārga*, as evidenced by the Upaniṣads.

In the final stage of *utkrānti*, the *jīva* associated with the subtle sense organs, mind, *prāṇa* as well as the subtle elements becomes united with the Supreme Deity (*paradevatā*). Thus says the Chāndogya Upaniṣad: *Vāk manasi saṁpadyate, manaḥ prāṇe, prāṇaḥ tejasi, tejaḥ parasyāṁ devatāyāṁ*.[30] As explained earlier, the implication of the merging of *jīva* with *paradevatā* is that the *jīva* becomes united with *paradevatā*. In this connection the question arises: Do the subtle elements with which the *jīva* is associated, become united with the Supreme Deity who exists in His own Abode or the *Paramātman* who abides in the body as the *Antaryāmin*? What is the purpose of the *jīva* associated with the subtle elements being united with the Supreme Deity? Regarding the first question it is answered that *jīva* associated with the elements is united with the *Paramātman* who is immanent in the body as the *Antaryāmin*, since the attainment of *Paramātman* in the higher Abode cannot take place while *jīva* is still associated with the body. Hence the union of *jīva* with *Paramātman* at this stage is with the *Paramātman* abiding in one's body as Antaryāmin. The purpose of this union with *Paramātman* within the body is for securing some temporary relief from the afflictions to which the *jīva* was subjected during the state of bondage. This temporary union with *paradevatā* is not intended for the *jīva* to reap the benefits of the *upāsanā*. The Upaniṣadic text merely states that *tejas* implying *jīva* with elements, is united with the *paradevatā*. The *sūtra* also says: *Tāni pare tathā hy āha*.[31] It means - "These subtle elements associated with the *jīva* become united with the Supreme Deity. The Scripture also says so".

The word *saṁpadyate* is to be added to the statement '*tejaḥ parasyām devatāyāṁ*'. The meaning offered earlier for the word *saṁpadyate* is to be adopted here also. It means that the *jīva* associated with *tejas* (subtle elements) gets absorbed in the Supreme Deity in such a way that the two entities cannot be differentiated (*avibhāga*). Thus states the *sūtra: Avibhāgo vacanāt*.[32] It means – "When the *jīva* is united with *Paramātman* at the time of death, the two cannot be differentiated". It does not imply, that it is dissolved in its causal substance but on the contrary, it means that it becomes united with it in such a way that the two entities become indistinguishable.

After describing the process of dissolution of the body, Bādarāyaṇa explains on the authority of the Upanisads how the *jīva* is enabled to move out of the body along with its *sūkṣma śarīra* through the *mūrdhanya-nāḍi* or the main artery radiating from the heart to the crown of the head. It is pointed out that *Paramātman* who is propitiated by the devoted *upāsanā*, out of His grace illumines the *nāḍi* in front of the heart to enable the *jīva* to come out of the heart and enter the *mūrdhanya-nāḍi*. The relevant *sūtra* reads: *Tadokogra jvalanaṁ tat prakāśita-dvāro vidyā-sāmarthyāt tat-seṣagaty-anusmṛti-yogācca hārdā-nugṛhītaḥ śatādhikāyā*[33]. The word *'oka'* means the heart in which the *jīva* is present. *Agre* means front part of the heart. *Jvalana* means illumination. This illumination is caused by *Paramātman* in response to the devoted *upāsanā* performed by the *upāsaka* and also his constant contemplation on the *arcirādi mārga* as part of an aid to *upāsanā* (*tat-seṣagati anusmṛti yogāt*). The Upaniṣad states that there are 101 *nāḍis* radiating from the heart (*śatādhikāyā*). The particular *nādi* which radiates to the crown of the head, which is called *suṣumnā-nāḍi*, is illumined by *Paramātman* abiding in the heart out of His grace (*hārdānugṛhīta*). The *jīva* is then enabled to exit through this *nādi* and take its onward march to the higher abode through the *arcirādi mārga*.

The reason for offering this detailed explanation in the *sūtra* is to meet the objection that it may not be possible for the *jīva* to locate the main artery going upward to the crown of the head, amongst several other subtle arteries (*na bhavati suśaka mukti nādi vivektum*). This is made possible, says Bādarāyaṇa, because of the special grace showered on the *upāsaka* by *Paramātman* in response to the devoted meditation on Him. *Paramātman* illumines the main artery to enable the *jīva* to know it (*vidyā samprīta hārda prāsadana mahasā*). This point is supported by the Bṛhadāraṇyaka Upaniṣad: *Tasya ha etasya hṛdayam pradyotate, tena pradyotena eṣa ātmā niṣkrāmati*[34] – "The opening of the main artery of the heart of the *upāsaka* is illumined; through this opening which is illumined the *jīva* moves out of the heart to the *suṣumnā-nāḍi* also named *mūrdhanya-nāḍi*. From this description it is obvious that the entry to the *mūrdhanya-nāḍi* is possible only for the *viduṣa*, that is, for the one who observes *upāsanā* for the attainment of *Paramātman*. Those who do not observe *upāsanā*, will exit from the body through the other arteries.

Vedānta Deśika presents an apt description of the exit of *mumukṣu* from the body after death in the following words: "The Supreme Lord associated with Goddess Lakṣmī, who is the protector of all the seven worlds, who resides in the center of the heart (*hārdā*), reveals to the *upāsaka* at the time of departure from the body, the opening of the *suṣumnā nāḍi* which radiates from the bottom of the navel to the crown of the head and pushes out the *jīva* through it to reach the highest abode, similar to the shooting of an arrow[35].

After the *jīva* of the *upāsaka* exits from the body through the *suṣumnā-nāḍi*, it proceeds to the realm of the sun following the course of its rays. Thus states the Chāndogya Upaniṣad: *Atha yatra etasmāt śarīrāt utkrāmati, atha etaireva raṣmibhiḥ ūrdhvam ākramate*[36]. Generally the rays of the sun are present during the day time. The question arises: What would happen to the *jīva* of the *upāsaka* who dies in the night since the rays of the sun are not found in the night? It is pointed out in reply that during the night, the sun's rays are present, even though they are not visible to us due to darkness. The presence of the rays is inferred on the basis of the fact that heat radiated by the sun persists even in the night. Even during autumn season or on cloudy days, we do not see either the sun or its rays, yet we admit the presence of the sun. The statement of the Upaniṣad regarding the onward march of the *jīva* through the rays of the sun is justified. On the basis of this, the *sūtra* also states: *Raṣmy-anusārī*[37]– "The *jīva* proceeds upward following the course of the rays of the sun".

Incidentally the question arises whether the *upāsaka* who dies in the night attains Brahman because a *Smṛti* text condemns death in the night and speaks highly about death in the day time.[38] This gives the impression that the *upāsaka* who dies in the night does not go to the higher Abode. Bādarāyaṇa does not accept this argument. It is not correct to say that the *upāsaka* who dies in the night does not attain Brahman. What holds the *upāsaka* from the attainment of *mokṣa* is the association of the soul with the body caused by the *prārabdha-karma*. This is evidenced by the Chāndogya Upaniṣad: *Tasya tāvadeva ciram yāvan na vimokṣye, atha saṁpatsyate* [39] – "For the *vidvān*, there is delay only as long as the body (caused by *prārabdha-karma*) lasts; thereafter he attains *mokṣa*." Once the *upāsaka* becomes free from the *karma*, as a result of the *upāsanā*, he is sure to attain *mokṣa*. Hence the death of the *vidvān* even in the night does not affect his attainment of Brahman. This is the implication of the *Vedānta-sūtra*: *Niśi na iti cet, na, sambandhasya yāvad deha bhāvitāt, darśayati ca.*[40]

"If it is contended that the person who dies in the night does not attain *mokṣa*, it is replied that it is not correct, because the connection of the *upāsaka* with *karma* lasts as long as the body remains. The Scripture also says so."

For the same reason as advanced in respect of death during the night, the *upāsaka* attains Brahman even if he dies during the half-period when the sun moves southward (*dakṣiṇāyana*). There is a stray statement in the Upaniṣad that a person who dies in *dakṣiṇāyana* goes to the realm of the moon: *atha yo dakṣiṇe pramīyate pitṛṇāmeva mahimānam gatvā, candramasa sāyujyam gacchati*[41] . This view is set aside. The period of death is immaterial. What is needed for the attainment of *mokṣa* is the total cessation of *karma* which includes the body of the *jīva*. When once the *upāsaka* is totally liberated from it, he is sure to attain *mokṣa*.

III. The Theory of Arcirādi Mārga

In the previous section, we have considered the theory of *utkrānti* or the exit of the *jīva* from the body. It is seen how Bādarāyaṇa explains on the basis of the Chāndogya Upaniṣad that the *jīva* withdraws itself from the gross state of the physical body to the subtle state and ascends to the highest realm through the path of *arcirādi*. The *saṁpatti* or dissolution of the body is not conceived as its destruction (*laya*) but a gradual process of involution which is effected by the indwelling *Paramātman*. The final exit of the *jīva* from the body takes place through the *suṣumnā-nāḍi*, the main artery that radiates from the heart to the crown of the head.

After the *utkrānti* the ascent of the *jīvātman* commences through the different realms (*lokas*) ruled by the celestial beings. This pathway through which the *jīva* traverses to the highest abode of *Paramātman* is called *arcirādi-mārga*, since *arcis* or light (fire) is the first realm to which the *jīva* goes through the rays of the sun soon after its exit from the body. The Upaniṣads give an account of this pathway ruled by various celestial deities. There are a few conflicting statements regarding the pathway to *mokṣa*. Bādarāyaṇa therefore discusses this matter and presents the correct theory of *arcirādi-mārga* in the five *adhikaraṇas* included in the third *pāda* named *gatipāda* of the fourth *adhyāya*. As pointed out earlier, the subject of *gati* or the pathway to *mokṣa* is another aspect of the *phala* or the goal to be attained by means of *upāsanā* and hence it is included in this *adhyāya*.

The first question which comes up for consideration is whether there is only one pathway for the liberated *jīva* to attain *Brahma-loka* or there are other routes. The Chāndogya states: *Atha...arciṣameva abhisaṁbhavanti arciṣo ahaḥ, ahnā āpūryamāṇapakṣam, āpūryamāṇa pakṣāt yān ṣadudangeti māsāṁstān, māsebhyaḥ saṁvatsaraṁ, saṁvatsarāt ādityaṁ, ādityāt candramasaṁ, candramaso vidyutaṁ, tatpuruṣo amānavaḥ, sa etān brahma gamayati eṣa devapatho brahmapathaḥ.*[42]

"They (the Brahman-knowers) attain the light or fire (*arcis*), from the light the day, from the day the bright fortnight of lunar month (*śuklapakṣa*), from the bright fortnight to the bright half of the year when the sun travels northward (*uttarāyaṇa*), from the half-year period to the year (*saṁvatsara*), from the year to the sun, from the sun to the moon, from the moon to the lightning, (from there) to the celestial *puruṣa* (*amānavaḥ*), who leads them to Brahman". This is the *devapatha* or Divine path and this is also the *Brahmapatha* or the *path* that leads to Brahman."

The Kauṣītikī Upaniṣad, on the other hand, describes the path in a different way: *Sa etaṁ devayānaṁ panthānam āpadya agnilokaṁ āgacchati, sa vāyulokaṁ, sa varuṇalokaṁ, sa ādityalokaṁ, sa indralokaṁ, sa prajāpatilokam, sa brahmalokaṁ*[43]–"After attaining the Divine path, the man of *vidyā* comes to the realm of *agni*, then he comes to the realm of *vāyu*, he comes to the realm of *varuṇa*, he comes to the realm of the sun, he comes to the realm of *Indra*, he comes to the realm of *Prajāpati* (Brahmā); he then comes to the world of Brahman."

The Bṛhadāraṇyaka Upaniṣad describes the pathway in a different manner. It mentions only the following areas in this order: *arcis, ahas, śukla-pakṣa, uttarāyaṇa, devaloka, Āditya* and *Vaidyuta* (*amānava puruṣa*)[44].

In view of these varying accounts of the pathway to *Brahma-loka*, it cannot be conclusively established that there is only one pathway to *mokṣa (na vyavasthā arcirādeḥ)*. These may also be regarded as alternative paths.

Bādarāyaṇa does not accept this view. He states that the liberated *jīvas* attain Brahman only through the same pathway which commences with *arcis* because this is well established in the Upaniṣads. The *sūtra* reads: *Arcirādinā tatprathīteḥ*[45]. It means that all Upaniṣads state that the path to *mokṣa* is one and it begins with *arcis* or the light. The *upāsaka* therefore goes to *Brahma-loka* only through this pathway. The names of the celestial deities ruling these areas such as *agni, āditya* etc are common in respect of the descriptions offered by different Upaniṣads. If there are a few omissions as is found in the statements of the different Upaniṣads, these have to be added on the basis of the Mīmāṁsa principle of *upasaṁhāra* or inclusion of the *guṇas* of Brahman adopted in connection with the meditation on Brahman along with the *guṇas* in the *guṇopasaṁhāra pāda* of the third *adhyāya*[46].

Regarding the order in which the celestial deities are mentioned in the Upaniṣads, there are a few points of difference. Bādarāyaṇa clarifies these. In the Chāndogya it is stated that *jīva* proceeds from the half-year to *saṁvatsara* (year) and from the year to the sun (*āditya*). In the Bṛhadāraṇyaka Upaniṣad it is mentioned that from the half-year it goes to *devaloka* and from *devaloka* to the sun. In another text, *vāyu* is introduced between the year and the sun. *Vāyu* is thus an additional principle. The question is whether *vāyuloka* is different from *devaloka* mentioned in the Bṛhadāraṇyaka Upaniṣad. Bādarāyaṇa points out that the *devaloka* itself refers to *vāyu* without any specification. Therefore *vāyu* is taken to imply *devaloka* and it is to be included between *saṁvatsara* and *āditya*. The *sūtra* reads: '*Vāyum abdād-aviśeṣa viśeṣābhyāṁ*'[47] – "From the year to *vāyu*, on account of non-specification and specification".

That *vāyu* in one place is mentioned as a general term and in another place with specific description in terms of its function. But both the terms refer to one entity viz. *vāyuloka* and this is included in between *saṁvatsara* and *āditya*.

Similarly the word *varuṇa* who is the deity ruling the rains (*parjanya*) is to be added after *vidyut* or lightning since the two are connected together. Thus it is stated in the *sūtra*: *Taṭito adhi varuṇaḥ sambandhāt* [48] – "*Varuṇa* is to be placed after lightning because of the connection between the two". That is, it is to be associated with *vidyut* (lightning) because *varuṇa* is the presiding deity of water contained in the clouds.

After reconciling all these conflicting statements, Vedānta Deśika enunciates the path of the celestial deities in the following order: *jyotis* or fire, *ahas* or the day, *śuklapakṣa* or the bright fortnight of the lunar month, *uttarāyaṇa* or the bright half of the year when the sun travels northward, *saṁvatsara* or the year, *vāyu* or air, *āditya* or sun, *candra* or moon and *vidyut* or lightning accompanied by *Varuṇa, Indra* and *Prajāpati.*

It is also pointed out that the light (fire), day, month, year etc do not refer to the physical entities but they refer to the deities presiding over them. They are known as *ativahikas* or those who serve as guides enroute to the Abode of *Paramātman,* known as *paramapada.*

These deities are commanded by *Paramātman* to serve as guides to the jīva proceeding to *mokṣa.* Thus states the *sūtra*: *Ātivahikas-talliṅgāt.*[49] *Ātivāhanam* means leading or guiding the persons who are going in the pathway (*ativahanaṁ ganṭṛṇāṁ gamayitṛttvam*). These are therefore, not places of enjoyment (*bhoga-sthāna*) nor do they serve as identity marks enroute. They are the escorting deities similar to the *Amānava-puruṣa* or the presiding deity of *vidyut* (lightning) who leads the *jīvas* to the abode of Brahman. The Chāndogya specifically states that the *Amānava-puruṣa* leads the *jīva* to *Brahma-loka* (*puruṣo amānavaḥ sa enām brahma gamayati*). The same function of guiding the *jivas* is also performed by other celestial deities.

IV. The Goal of Attainment by Jīva

In the preceding section it was pointed out that the liberated *jīva* after its exit from the body traverses through the Divine pathway being guided by the celestial deities. In its final stage of the march, the *jīva* is escorted to the *Brahma-loka* by the *Amānava-puruṣa.* Thus it is stated in the Chāndogya: *Tat puruṣo amānavaḥ sa enāṅ brahma gamayati*[50]. "The *amānava-puruṣa* leads the *jīva* to Brahma". The proper implication of this statement which indicates the final goal of attainment needs to be understood. The issue involved here is whether the term Brahma mentioned in the statement denotes the Brahman who is the Supreme Being or the *Caturmukha-Brahmā*, also named as *Hiraṇyagarbha*, a lower deity entrusted with the task of actual creation of the universe.

With reference to the *jīvas* who are led by the celestial deities, the question assumes the following form: Do the escorting deities (*ātivahikas*) lead those *jīvas* who meditate upon Brahman or those who meditate on the *Caturmukha-Brahmā* or those who meditate on the Individual self itself (*jīvātmā*) conceived as inherently related to Brahman (*Brahmātmakatā*)? The third alternative is relevant because, according to the Chāndogya Upaniṣad dealing with *Pañcāgni-vidyā*, those who meditate on the pure *jīvātman* as inherently related to Brahman also traverse through *arcirādi-mārga*. This is an important issue relating to the nature of the Supreme Goal and it is therefore discussed by Bādarāyaṇa in a separate *adhikaraṇa* titled *Kāryādhikaraṇa*. There are two conflicting views regarding this matter advanced by ancient *ācāryas*, Bādari and Jaimini. Bādarāyaṇa critically examines them and presents his own view which is in conformity with the Upaniṣadic teachings.

According to Bādari, the *ātivahikas* lead only those who meditate on *Hiraṇyagarbha* who is designated as Brahmā. This view with supporting arguments is expressed by Bādarāyaṇa himself in five *sūtras*. The main *sūtra* in which the name of Bādari is mentioned, reads: *Kāryam bādari asya gaty-upapatteḥ*[51]. The term *kārya* in this *sūtra* is taken to mean *Hiraṇyagarbha*, a lower deity, also named as *Caturmukha-Brahmā*. The *sūtra*, as interpreted by both Śaṁkara and Rāmānuja, means that those who meditate on *kārya-brahma* (*Hiraṇyagarbha*) are led by the *ātivahikas* because the movement of the liberated *jīva* through the *arcirādi mārga* (*asya gatiḥ*) is conceivable only in respect of them. By way of elucidation, it is pointed out that the Supreme Brahman is infinite (*vibhu*) and also all-pervasive and it does not therefore stand to reason that the individual who meditates upon it is required to go to another realm to attain it. That is, Brahman being omnipresent, is already realized in this world by means of meditation and there is no need to traverse through the *arcirādi mārga* to attain it in a higher realm. The same view is also held by Śaṁkara who holds the theory of two Brahmans – *saguṇa* and *nirguṇa*. According to him, *nirguṇa Brahman* which is the higher Brahman, is infinite and all-pervasive (*sarvagata*) and it cannot be regarded to have a location (*pradeśa*) or an abode of its own. Hence the *kāryam* in the *sūtra* is taken as the lower Brahman or *Saguṇa Brahman* designated as *Hiraṇyagarbha*. He has a realm of his own known as *Brahmaloka* to which the liberated souls are led through the *arcirādi-mārga* by the *ātivahikas*.

An objection is raised against this explanation. The word Brahma in the neuter gender generally signifies the higher Brahman. If Brahman is to mean *Hiraṇyagarbha*, the text should have stated *'brahmāṇam gamayati'*. But it is not so. Hence the term Brahma cannot be taken as *Hiraṇyagarbha*. In reply to this objection, it is pointed out that there is close proximity of *Brahmā* as *Hiraṇyagarbha* to the Supreme Brahman, since the former, according to the Upaniṣads was the very first principle created by Brahman (*yo brahmāṇam vidadhāti pūrvam*). In view of it, Brahma in a secondary sense can be taken as *Caturmukha-Brahmā* (*sāmīpyāt tu tad vyapadeśaḥ*).[52]

There is another objection against the theory of Bādari. According to the Upaniṣads, those liberated souls which traverse through the *arcirādi-mārga* do not return to the mundane existence to be reborn. The realm of *Caturmukha-Brahmā* along with its ruler is subjected to dissolution at the end of certain number of *yugas*. The *jīvas* which have gone to that realm would also be subject to dissolution and as such the immortality (*amṛtatva*) attained by meditation on *Hiraṇyagarbha* would also be affected.

Bādari himself replies to this objection. As and when dissolution of this realm takes place, *Caturmukha-Brahma* along with all the *jīvas* residing in that realm attains Brahman as a result of the meditation observed by

Caturmukha-Brahmā and the *jīvas*. The relevant *sūtra* reads: *Kāryātyaye tad adhyakṣeṇa saha ataḥ paraṁ abhidhānāt*[53]– "When the destruction of the realm of *Caturmukha-Brahmā* takes place, the *jīvas* along with the ruler of *Brahma-loka* attains the Supreme Brahman. This is supported by the *Śruti* as well as the *Smṛti* texts". The Taittirīya Nārāyaṇa Upaniṣad states: *Te brahmaloke tu parāntakāle parāmṛtāt parimucyanti sarve* [54]–"All of them who reside in the world of the four-faced Brahmā are released at the end of the life of Brahmā by virtue of their meditation on Brahman".

This is also supported by the following *Smṛti* text: *Brahmaṇā saha te sarve samprāpte prati-saṁcare; parasya ante kṛtātmānaḥ praviśanti paraṁ padam.*[55]

"When the time of dissolution of all the worlds comes at the end of the life of Brahmā, all those who had observed *bhakti-yoga* and those who were living in his world, attain *Para-Brahman* which is the Supreme Goal, along with the four-faced *Brahmā*".

The above explanation would amount to the admission of *mukti* in two stages. This is called *krama-mukti* which is also accepted by Śaṁkara. Those who meditate on *saguṇa Brahman* attain first the *Brahma-loka*, the realm of *Hiraṇyagarabha* through the *arcirādi mārga*, as stated in the Upaniṣad. But the attainment of this realm does not represent the proper *mokṣa*. The *mokṣa* proper, according to Śaṁkara, is the realization of the identity of *jīva* with *nirguṇa Brahman*. This can be attained as and when an individual obtains the *ātmaikya-jñāna*. Such an individual does not have to pass through *arcirādi mārga*, nor does he have the *utkrānti* or exit of the *jīva* from the body. With the direct realization of the absolute identity of *jīvātman* and Brahman, he becomes liberated from bondage straightaway. Those individuals who are not qualified to attain direct realization of Brahman are required to observe the *upāsanā* on *Saguṇa Brahman* and obtain the *mokṣa* proper after attaining the *Brahma-loka* of *Caturmukha-Brahmā*.[56]

Vedānta Deśika summarily rejects this theory on the ground that several Scriptural texts establish that there is a

Supreme Abode of Visṇu (Brahman) and that the *upāsaka* who meditates on Brahman attains it by traversing through the *arcirādi-mārga* and enjoys the bliss of Brahman. The Kaṭha Upaniṣad explicitly states: *So'dhvanaḥ param āpnoti tad-viṣṇoḥ paramaṁ padam'*. Against such a strong Scriptural authority, the theory of Bādari cannot be sustained. As will be seen presently, Jaimini also rejects it.

According to sage Jaimini, only those who have meditated upon Brahman are led by the *ātivahakas* direct to the Supreme Brahman. The main reason for holding this view is that in the Upaniṣadic statement *'Tat puruṣo amānavaḥ enān brahma gamayati'*, the term *brahma* denotes the Supreme Brahman. Thus it is stated by Bādarāyaṇa in the *sūtra*: *Param jaiminiḥ mukhyatvāt.*[57] By way of elucidation, Vedānta Deśika points out that the Scriptural texts reveal that the *arcirādi mārga* through which the liberated *jīva* is escorted by the *ātivāhakas* leads to the Divine Abode designated as *paramapada* or *paramaṁdhāma* (*asau arcirādi mārgaḥ paramaṁ dhāma gamayati*). The word *dhāma* also means the *Paramapuruṣa* or the Supreme Being as implied by the statement *'tad-viṣṇoḥ paramaṁ padam'*. Further, only after the *jīva* attains Brahman by traversing through the *arcirādi mārga*, it becomes totally liberated from *karma* and manifests itself in its true nature. This is made evident by the Chāndogya Upaniṣad which states: *Eṣa saṁprasādaḥ asmāt śarīrāt samutthāya paraṁjyotir upasaṁpadya svena rūpeṇa abhiniṣpadyate*[58] "This serene being (*jīvātman*) having risen from the body and having attained the Supreme Light (Brahman) manifests itself in its own nature". The implication of this statement is that the *jīva*, after it has traversed through the *arcirādi-mārga* and reached Brahman in its higher abode, gets rid of the *karma* which had eclipsed its true nature and then manifests itself in its true nature. Keeping in mind this Scriptural text, Bādarāyaṇa states in the *sūtra*: *Darśanācca*[59] which supports the view advanced by Jaimini. The Chāndogya also specifically states that the *jīva* obtains the realm of Brahman after it gets rid of *karma* totally (*dhūtvā śarīraṁ akṛtam kṛtātmā brahmalokam abhisambhavāmi*)[60]–"I, the jīva, cast off the body and then as well-blessed soul, attain the realm of Brahman".

Bādarāyaṇa does not accept both the theories of Bādari and Jaimini, since he considers them as defective. He offers his own view on this subject. The crucial *sūtra* relating to it reads: *Apratīkālambanān nayati iti bādarāyaṇa ubhayathā ca doṣāt tatkratuśca*[61]. The word *pratīka* in the context of *upāsanā* means the sentient and non-sentient entities which are caused by Brahman. *Tad-ālambana* means making use of them as objects of meditation by conceiving the same as symbol of Brahman. *Apratīka ālambanān* therefore means those individuals who do not meditate on such symbols. The total meaning of the *sūtra* is: "In the opinion of Bādarāyaṇa, persons other than those who meditate upon the symbols as Brahman are led by the celestial deities to Brahman, because the two views (advanced by Bādari and Jaimini) are defective. Besides, this view (of Bādarāyaṇa) conforms to the principle of *tat-kratu nyāya*.

The fuller implications of the *sūtra* are brought out by Rāmānuja. He explains how the theories of Bādari and Jaimini are defective and how Bādarāyaṇa's view is different from that of Jaimini. It is not correct to say that the celestial deities lead only those who have meditated upon *kārya-brahmā* (*Hiraṇya-garbha*), as Bādari believes. Nor can it be said, as Jaimini contends, that those who meditate only upon *Para-Brahma* are led by the *ātivahikas*. It is also not correct to maintain that those who meditate on symbols of Brahman are escorted by the celestial deities. On the contrary, the *ātivahikas* escort those who have meditated upon the *Para-Brahman* and also those who have meditated on their own *ātmā* (*jīvātmā*) as dissociated with the body (that is, in its natural form) but as inherently related to Brahman (*Brahmātmaka*). This is the significance of the statement of Bādarāyaṇa in the *sūtra*.

The reason for upholding this view is contained in the words of the *sūtra*: *Ubhayathā ca doṣāt*. The view of Bādari which restricts it to *upāsakas* on *kārya-brahmā* stands opposed to the Upaniṣadic texts which explicitly state that soon after the *jīva* departs from the body, it reaches Brahman (and not *Hiraṇyagarbha*). The text reads: *Eṣa samprasādaḥ asmāt śarīrāt samutthāya paraṁ jyotir upasaṁpadya.*[62] *Paraṁ jyotis* means Brahman, whom the *jīva* attains after departing from the body. If on the other hand, the movement of the *jīva* escorted by the celestial deities is restricted to those who meditate only upon Brahman, as Jaimini believes, then it would militate against the Chāndogya text, dealing with the *Pañcāgni-vidyā,* which states that even those who meditate on *jīvātman* as inherently related to Brahman also traverse to the higher realm through the *arcirādi mārga.* The relevant text reads: *Tad ya ittham viduḥ ye ce'me araṇye śraddhā tapa iti upāsate, te arciṣam abhisaṁbhavanti.*[63] This text, as interpreted by Rāmānuja, refers to the *upāsanā* on *jīvātman* as the body of Brahman, that is, as inherently related to Brahman.

Further this theory conforms to the principle of *tat-kratu-nyāya.* According to this principle, in whatever form a person meditates, the goal attained should be of the same form. Regarding the meditation upon the pure form of *jīvātman* as inherently related to Brahman, the object of meditation is Brahman which is the *śarīrī* (*Ātman*) of *jīva* and hence the attainment of Brahman through the *arcirādi mārga* is justifiable in accordance with the *tat-kratu-nyāya.*

The meditation on the non-sentient entities such as *prakṛti* and its effects, *prāṇa* or vital breath etc as *pratīkas,* that is, these being conceived as Brahman would not lead to the attainment of Brahman through the *arcirādi mārga.* Such meditations confer other material benefits as described in the passage dealing with *Bhūmā-vidyā.* In this passge fifteen entities commencing with *nāma* and ending with *prāṇa* are suggested for meditation by Sanatkumāra to Nārada but all of them are rejected as not suitable for attaining the Supreme Brahman designated as *bhūmā.* The *upāsakas* on symbols of Brahman (*pratīkas*) who are categorized as *pratīkālambanān* are not eligible to traverse through the *arcirādi mārga* and attain Brahman. Other than these, who are categorized as *apratīkālambanān* by Bādarāyaṇa, are led by the *ātivāhikas* or celestial deities to the *Brahma-loka*.

V. The Nature of the Supreme Goal

After discussing the theory of *utrkrānti* or exit of the *jīva* from the body and also the theory of *arcirādi-gati* or the movement of the *jīva* into the *Brahma-loka* through the Divine path guided by the celestial deities, Bādarāyaṇa presents the theory of *mokṣa* which is the Supreme Goal attained by the liberated *jīva* (*muktātmā*). Two important subjects come up for consideration in this regard: 1) The nature of the attainment by the *jīva* in the state of *mukti* and 2) The status of the *jīva* in relation to Brahman in terms of equality and enjoyment of infinite bliss. Both these theories are important since they provide a positive significance for the concept of *mokṣa* rather than its description as cessation of *avidyā* (*avidyā nivṛttiḥ*) or as total liberation from bondage caused by karma. Bādarāyaṇa therefore discusses these matters in the fourth *pāda,* titled *Muktipāda*, of the *Phalādhyāya* in the following six *adhikaraṇas*.

i) *Sampadyāvirbhāvādhikaraṇa*
ii) *Avibhāga-dṛṣṭatvādhikaraṇa*
iii) *Brāhmādhikaraṇa*
iv) *Saṁkalpādhikaraṇa*
v) *Abhāvādhikaraṇa*
vi) *Jagad-vyāpāravarjādhikaraṇa*

We shall present the important points related to these *adhikaraṇas*.

a) The Nature of Attainment by Jīva in the State of Mukti.

The first issue which needs to be considered is whether the *jīva* which attains Brahman acquires any new form in the state of *mukti* or does it remain in its own form (*svena rūpeṇa*).

This question is relevant because it determines whether the state of attainment by the *jīva* can be treated as a goal in the proper sense. That is, unless what is attained is something different from what it was before, it cannot be a goal. The Chāndogya Upaniṣad dealing with this matter merely states: *Eṣa samprasādaḥ asmāt śarīrāt samutthāya paraṁjyotir upasaṁpadya svena rūpeṇa abhiniṣpadyate*[64]– "This serene being (*jīvātman*) having risen from the body and having attained the Supreme Light (Brahman), manifests itself in its own form". Based on this passage, the *sūtra* states: *Sampadya āvirbhāvaḥ svena śabdāt*[65]. It means that (the *jīva*) after reaching Brahman manifests itself in its own natural form because of the word *svena* or "its own" used in the Upaniṣad.

The crucial word in the *sūtra* is *āvirbhāva* or the manifestation of the *jīva* in its own form (*svena rūpeṇa*). The *jīva* by its nature always exists in its own form, even during the state of bondage. So also in the state of *mukti* it manifests itself in its own form. How can that state be regarded as a goal achieved by it?. In the state of *suṣupti* or deep sleep, the mind and the sense organs do not function and the *jīva* exists in its own form. But that state is not treated as *mokṣa* for *jīva*. Hence it is necessary to admit that *jīva* in the state of *mokṣa* assumes a new body or form, similar to the individuals who attain *svarga* by performing *yāga* (*tasmāt muktaḥ sva-anyat bhajati vapuḥ asau devavat*). This is the prima facie view advanced regarding this matter.

Vedānta Deśika refutes this argument. The word *svena* used in the Upaniṣad along with *rūpeṇa* does not imply that *jīva* assumes a new form. If it means the new form or body, as the critic contends, then the word *svena* would be meaningless (*svena iti śabdo aphalaḥ bhavet*). Hence it is to be admitted that *jīva* manifests itself in the state of *mukti* in its own form. The word *sva* signifies the natural form of *jīva* (*svābhāvika rūpa*). That is, *jīva* manifests itself in the state of *mukti* in its natural form.

If the *jīva* manifests itself in its natural form in the state of *mukti*, can this state be regarded as a Goal of attainment? In reply, it is explained by Rāmānuja that the liberated *jīva* abides in its essential nature only after it becomes totally liberated from *karma* and its effect in the form of body. Though the essential nature of the *jīva* is eternally accomplished, it can still be regarded as a goal. During the state of bondage, the true nature of the *jīva* was obscured by *avidyā* in the form of *karma* and with the removal of this obscuration (*tirodhāna nivṛtti*), the *jīva* is now made to manifest itself in its true nature. This is what is meant by the term *abhiniṣpadyate* used in the Upaniṣad which has the same meaning as *āvirbhāva* used in the *sūtra*. This *āvirbhāva* of the true nature of the *jīva* is treated as a goal attained.

By way of further elucidation, Rāmānuja points out on the basis of the subsequent *sūtra* (*Ātmā prakaraṇāt*[66]) and also on the authority of the Chāndogya Upaniṣad, that *jīvātman* possesses eight attributes.[67] During the state of bondage, these attributes are obscured by *karma*. But these essential characteristics become manifested during the state of *mukti*. These are not newly brought into existence, but are only made to manifest after the removal of *karma*. This is illustrated on the analogy of the gem and its luster. When the dirt on the gem is removed, its luster is restored but not newly produced. In the same way, the essential characteristics of the *jīva* are not produced but are made to manifest by getting rid of *karma* which had obscured them during the state of bondage. This is the proper implication of the term *abhiniṣpadyate* used in the Upaniṣad and '*āvirbhāva*' used in the *sūtra*. Such an *āvirbhāva* can be treated as a goal of attainment. As Vedānta Deśika explains, *āvirbhāva* taken in the sense of manifestation of the inherent qualities of the *jīva* and which were eclipsed during the state of bondage, by the removal of *karma* (*avidyā nivṛtti*) is itself a goal attained by the *jīva*. This explanation is logically tenable in the Viśiṣṭādvaita because *jīvātman* is *saguṇa*, that is, endowed with qualities and as such it is possible to speak of two states (*avasthās*) for it. In the state of bondage the *jīva* exists with its *guṇas* eclipsed and in the state of *mukti*, it manifests itself with the *guṇas*. Such an explanation cannot be offered in respect of Advaita theory, since *jīvasvarūpa* being always the same cannot admit any change in the state of *mukti*. What is *nitya-siddha* or that which exists always in the same form, cannot be regarded as *sādhya* or something attained. Mere *avidyā nivṛtti* cannot also be regarded as *mokṣa* because the Upaniṣads also speak of the enjoyment of bliss of Brahman by the *jīva* in the state of *mukti*[68]. Hence the concept of *mokṣa* is meaningful if it is conceived as *avidyā-nivṛtti* leading to the enjoyment of bliss of Brahman.

b) The manner in which the Jīva enjoys Brahman

The next important issue to be considered is the manner in which the *jīva* enjoys Brahman in the state of *mukti*. The Taittirīya Upaniṣad states: *So'śnute sarvān kāmān saha brahmaṇa vipaścitā*"[69] – "The *jīva* enjoys all desirable qualities (*guṇas*) of Brahman along with the omniscient Brahman". The question which arises in this connection is: Whether the *jīvātman* enjoys the guṇas of Brahman as being separate from Brahman (*pṛthag-bhūtam*) or whether it experiences the same as being non-distinct (*avibhaktam*) since it is inseparably related to Brahman. According to the prima facie view, *jīva* experiences the *guṇas* as separate from Brahman. The reason for advancing this view is that the Scriptural as well as the *Smṛti* texts speak of *sāmya* or equality and *sādharmya* or similarity in respect of attributes between Brahman and the *mukta jīva*. Thus says the Muṇḍaka Upaniṣad: *Yadā paśyaḥ paśyate rukmavarṇam kartāram īśaṁ puruṣaṁ brahmayoniṁ, tadā vidvān puṇya pāpe vidhūya nirañjanaḥ paramaṁ sāmyam upaiti* [70] – "When the seer of Brahman (*jīva*) sees the *Puruṣa* (*Paramātman*) who possesses a divine lustrous body, who is the Ruler of the universe, who is the cause of the unmanifest *prakṛti*, then the knower of Brahman, casting off good and evil, and becoming free from all blemishes, attains Supreme equality with the Lord (*paramaṁ sāmyam upaiti*). The *Bhagavad-gīta* says: *Idaṁ jñānam upāśritya mama sādharmyam āgatāḥ; sarge'pi nopajāyante pralaye na vyathayanti ca* [71] – "Those who have acquired the knowledge of Brahman attain a status similar to Mine (Lord), thereafter they are neither born at the time of creation nor do they suffer at the time of dissolution". These texts which speak of *sāmya* and *sādharmya* between *jīvātman* and *Paramātman*, imply difference between the two. The Upanisads also mention that *jīva* and Brahman are different. The Śvetāśvatara clearly states: *Pṛthagātmānam preritāraṁ ca matvā*–"The individual self is to be known as distinct from the Controller (Brahman). On the basis of these teachings it is contended that *jīva* experiences Brahman in the state of *mukti* as distinct from it *(tasmāt parasmāt sa pṛthag-bhāseta)*.

This view is rejected by Bādarāyaṇa. The relevant *sūtra* reads: *Avibhāgena dṛṣṭātvat*.[72] It means, as interpreted by Rāmānuja, that the *mukta-jīva* enjoys himself as non-distinct from it because it is so realized by the *jīva* in the state of *mukti*. By way of elucidation, Rāmānuja points out that *jīva* and Brahman, though they are distinct real entities, are integrally related (*apṛthag-bhūta*) as substance and attribute (*prakāri* and *prakāra*). In view of it, the two are *avibhāga* or non-distinct in the sense that *jīva* as a *prakāra* or a mode of Brahman is inseparable from Brahman, similar to the soul and body or substance and its attribute. This is the actual fact (*tattva*) as evidenced by the Scriptural texts. The *Antaryāmi Brāhmaṇa* clearly states that Brahman indwells within the *jīvātman* and the latter is its *śarīra* or body in the technical sense. The author of the *Brahma-sūtra* also affirms that *Paramātman* abides in the *jīva*. The relevant *sūtra* says: *avasthiteḥ iti kāśa-kṛtsnaḥ*.[73] When the *jīva* attains Brahman after it is liberated from bondage, it realizes that it is integrally related to Brahman (*parasmāt brahmaṇaḥ svātmānam anubhavati muktaḥ* [74]). This is the implication of the word '*dṛṣṭatvāt*' mentioned in the *sūtra*. Though *jīva* by virtue of its intrinsic nature is inseparable from Brahman, this fact is actually visualized only in the state of *mukti* by the *jīva*, because it has now become free from *avidyā* in the form of *karma* which obscured the true knowledge of the *jīvātman* in relation to *Paramātman*. It is therefore appropriate to state that *jīva* enjoys itself as inseparably related to Brahman (*avibhāgena*).

If Brahman and the *jīva* are non-distinct, how is it possible to say that the *jīva* along with Brahman, enjoys all the desirable qualities (*guṇas*) of Brahman as stated in the Taittirīya? Similary, if the two are non-distinct, it is inconceivable how there could be *paramaṁ sāmya* or perfect similarity between the two in the state of *mokṣa*? It is therefore contended that the enjoyment of Brahman in the state of *mukti* by the *jīva* as *avibhāga* is opposed to the Scriptural teaching. This objection is based on the assumption that Brahman and *jīva* are identical (*svarūpaikya*).

This argument is untenable, contends Vedānta Deśika, because Brahman and *jīva* are different by nature, though they are non-distinct in the sense that Brahman as inherently related to the *jīva* is one. The Taittirīya text referring to the nature of the goal states: *So'śnute sarvān kāmān saha; brahmaṇā vipaścitā iti'*. It means "He (*mukta jīva*) enjoys all desirable *guṇas* of Brahman along with (*saha*) the omniscient Brahman". The word *saha* combined with Brahman means that jīva enjoys both *guṇas* and Brahman. This is called *Bhoktṛ-sāhitya,* that is, the object of enjoyment for the *jīva* is both Brahman and its qualities. This interpretation gives greater importance to jīva than to Brahman since jiva is the *bhoktā* or the one who enjoys both Brahman and *guṇas*. This is not appropriate since Brahman is the Lord and *jīva* is its subordinate (*Śeṣa*). It is therefore considered more proper to interpret the text to mean that both Brahman and *jīva* together (*saha*) enjoy all the desirable *guṇas*. This is called *bhogya-sāhitya*. That is, the object of enjoyment is the same for Brahman and *jīva,* similar to the father and son together enjoying the same delicious food. This interpretation is also justified with reference to the passage in which the nature of the goal attained by the *brahma-vit* is being explained by the Upaniṣadic passage (*tasmāt tad-bhogya bhāve bhavatu taducitaṁ brahmaṇā-vyākṛteśca*[75]). In either case the distinction between *jīva* and Brahman stands established. When the difference between the two is proved, the word *avibhāga* employed by Bādarāyaṇa in the *sūtra* is intended to convey the idea that *jīva* is not an independent Reality (*svatantra abrahmātmaka*) but it exists as a dependent Reality, being inherently related to *Paramātman* (*bhede siddhe svaniṣthasthiti pariharaṇam hy-atra sūtropapādyam*).

Vedānta Deśika also explains the implication of *parama sāmyatva* between *jīva* and Brahman referred to in the Muṇḍaka Upaniṣad (*nirañjanaḥ paramaṁ sāmyam upaiti*). In this statement the word *'paramaṁ sāmyam'* does not imply perfect equality in every respect since the Upaniṣad does not contain any teaching to this effect. It is therefore to be taken as similarity only in respect of certain attributes such as *jñāna, ānanda, amalatva* etc. When a piece of stone and a piece of gold are weighed and found to be of equal weight, it does not mean that the two are equal in every respect. In the same way the equality of *jīva* and Brahman in the state of *mokṣa* is to be understood as similarity in respect of certain aspects only. As will be explained later, *jīva* does not have the divine functions of creation of the universe, unlike *Paramātman*. Since it is well established by several Upaniṣadic texts that *jīvātman* stands in relation to Brahman as the body to the soul, the statement such as *'brahmavit brahmaiva bhavati'* are to be understood in the sense that *mukta-jīva* attains the status of Brahman (*sādharmya*) or equality in respect of certain aspects and not absolute identity (*brahmaiva ityādi vākyam prathayati samatām*).[76]

c) The Specific Form in which Jīva manifests in the State of Mukti

The specific *svarūpa* or the intrinsic nature of the *jīva* that manifests itself after attaining Brahman is discussed in detail by Bādarāyaṇa in a separate *adhikaraṇa* named *Brāhmādhikaraṇa*. The need for discussing this matter arises because there are conflicting views in this regard as conveyed by the Upaniṣadic texts and also by the two ancient *ācāryas*, Jaimini and Auḍulomi. Bādarāyaṇa therefore examines their views and presents his own view on the subject.

According to the view held by Jaimini, the *jīva* manifests itself with all the eight attributes described by the Chāndogya Upaniṣad in respect of Brahman. The *sūtra* in which this view is expressed reads: *Brāhmeṇa jaimini upanyāsādibhyaḥ*[77]. The word *Brāhmeṇa* means the attributes described in respect of Brahman. The word *upanyāsa* means that which is stated in the Upaniṣad. In the earlier part of the passage of Chāndogya dealing with the nature of the Supreme Goal to be attained by the *jīva* after liberation from bondage, Brahman is described as *apahata-pāpma, vijaraḥ, vimṛtyuḥ, viśokaḥ, vijighatsuḥ, apipāsaḥ, satyakāmaḥ* and *satyasaṁkalpaḥ*. In the later part of the passage dealing with the subject of *jīvātmā*, all these eight attributes are ascribed to *jīvātman*. It is therefore maintained by Jaimini that *jīvātman* also possesses all these qualities as part of its intrinsic nature. These were however, not manifest in the state of bondage, but when the *jīvātman* is freed from bondage, these become manifest. This theory rules out the possibility of conceiving *jīvātman* as constituted of consciousness only (*cin-mātra svarūpa*) as held by some (Auḍulomi) because what is only consciousness without having knowledge as its attribute cannot experience Brahman.

According to Auḍulomi, *jīva* manifests itself in its true nature which is pure consciousness only. The relevant *sūtra* reads: *Cititanmātreṇa tadātmakatvāt iti Auḍulomih.*[78] *Cit* means consciousness or knowledge. *Cin-mātra* means that the self is constituted of only consciousness. Hence it is said that *jīvātman* manifests itself in the state of *mukti* as consciousness only and not with the attributes. There are Upaniṣadic statements which describe the Self as a mass of consciousness. Thus says the Bṛhadāraṇyaka: *Vijñāna ghana eva*[79] – "Consciousness only is its essential nature". Another text describes that *ātman* is entirely of the nature of consciousness, both inside and outside, similar to the lump of salt being entirely saltish both in the interior and exterior.[80] The word *'eva'* in the text excludes the attribution of any *guṇas* to the *jīvātman*. The statement which refers to the *guṇas* such as *apahatapāpma, satyasaṁkalpa* etc. do not really belong to the Self as these are falsely attributed to it on account of *upādhis* or adjuncts, as explained by Śaṁkara.

Bādarāyaṇa examines both these theories. He offers his own view which reconciles both these views. The relevant *sūtra* reads: *Evamapi upanyāsāt pūrvabhāvāt avirodhaṁ Bādarāyaṇah*[81]. The *sūtra*, as explained by Rāmānuja, means that Bādarāyaṇa is of the opinion that although the *jīva* is described essentially of the nature of consciousness (*evam-api*), there is no contradiction in admitting the attributes in respect of *jīva*. These are taught in the Upaniṣad (*upanyāsāt*) and these are present in the *jīva* (*purva-bhāvāt*). In other words, according to Bādarāyaṇa, *jīva* which is essentially of the nature of consciousness can also possess other attributes mentioned in the Upaniṣads because both these points are admitted by the Upaniṣads. In the absence of any conflict, there is no justification to resort to the explanation that the attributes are superimposed on the *jīvātman* due to *avidyā* for the purpose of reconciling the two conflicting Upaniṣadic statements. Nor is it appropriate to accord greater validity to the text describing *jīva* as *prajñāna-ghana eva* and lesser validity to the text ascribing *guṇas* to the *jīva*. The validity of both the texts can be maintained on the basis of the explanation offered by Bādarāyaṇa. As regards the expression *'eva'* added to *prajñāna-ghana*, it does not preclude the admission of other *guṇas*. It only implies that *jīva* is essentially constituted of consciousness but this does not rule out the possession of other attributes which are warranted by the Upaniṣadic texts. Taking the illustration of the lump of salt, cited by the Upaniṣads in support of Auḍulomi's view, what is meant is that there is no part of it which is devoid of salt element, but it does not rule out other qualities such as its shape, hardness, colour etc. In the same way when the Upaniṣad says that *Ātman* is only a mass of *vijñāna* or consciousness, it signifies that it is entirely of the nature of consciousness and that there is no non-sentient element in it. The other qualities are also to be admitted as these are mentioned by the Upaniṣad.

VI. The Status of Jīva with Brahman in the State of Mukti

The Chāndogya Upaniṣad states that the *jīvātman* in the state of *mukti* is capable of fulfilling whatever it desires. Such a capacity is described as *satya-saṁkalpa*. Though this quality is inherent in the *jīva*, it becomes manifest after the *jīvātman* gets rid of the *karma* and attains Brahman. This is substantiated by the Upaniṣad with the description of the free activities of the *jīva* in the state of *mukti*. Thus it says: *Sa tatra paryeti jakṣat krīḍan ramamāṇaḥ strībhirvā yānairvā jñātibhirvā* [82] – "He moves about there laughing, playing, rejoicing, be it with women, chariots or relatives." Another text says: *Sa yadi pitṛlokakāmo bhavati saṁkalpād eva asya pitaraḥ samupatiṣṭhanti*[83] – "If he desires the world of fathers, by his mere will the fathers rise to receive him". Two questions arise in this connection. First, does the *jīva* fulfill all its desires out of its own will or with some effort as in the case of ordinary individuals? Secondly does the liberated *jīva* possess a body and the sense organs to perform the activities?

Bādarāyaṇa answers these questions. The two

adhikaraṇas titled *Saṁkalpādhikaraṇa* and *Abhāvādhikaraṇa* are exclusively devoted to the discussion of these issues. Regarding the first question, Bādarāyaṇa states that the *jīva* fulfills its desires purely out of its will and no additional effort is needed for the purpose. The relevant *sūtra* reads: *Samkalpād eva tat śruteḥ.*[84] The reason for holding this view is that this fact is established by the Scriptural texts.

The Chāndogya Upaniṣad itself explicitly mentions the word '*Saṁkalpād eva*' which means 'by the mere will'. The word *eva* added to *saṁkalpa* rules out the need of any additional factor. This is the significance of the concept of *satyasaṁkalpatva* which is an essential attribute ascribed to the *jīvātman* in the state of *mukti*. Its other implication, as pointed out by the author of the *Vedānta-sūtra*[85], is that *jīva* is *ananyādhipati* which means that it is not under the command of anyone else for operating its will. One who is commanded by somebody else and one who is subjected to *karma* cannot function freely. The *jīva* is not subjected to the influence of *karma*. The Upaniṣad therefore states that it becomes totally free (*sa svarāṭ bhavati*[86]). The term *svarāṭ* in respect of *mukta-jīva* signifies that *jīva* in the state of *mukti* is no longer subject to the influence of *karma* in the form of *puṇya* and *pāpa* (*akarmavaśya*). Vedānta Deśika also points out that the operation of the free will of the jīva (*saṁkalpa*) is not obstructed in any manner (*icchāvighāta na syāt*), since *jīvātman* is totally free from the influence of *karma* in the form of *puṅya* and *pāpa*.

It may be noted in this connection that the description of the activities of the *mukta* such as playing, rejoicing etc are not to be taken literally. These are not the creations of the *jīva* for its own selfish purposes. Since the *jīva* has no desires other than the enjoyment of the bliss of Brahman, being totally subservient to *Paramātman* even in the state of mukti, whatever the *jīva* desires to do are in accordance with the command of the *Paramātman* and also purely for His pleasure. As the Chāndogya states in connection with the *bhūmavidyā*, the *mukta-jīva* is *ātma-ratiḥ* or enjoys himself, *ātma-krīḍaḥ* or sports himself, *ātma-mithunaḥ* or he is his own consort and *ātma-ānandaḥ* or he is his own bliss.[87]

Regarding the second question whether the *jīva* possesses a body and the sense organs to undertake physical activities, Bādarāyaṇa first mentions the views of Bādari and Jaimini and later on presents his own view. According to Badari, the liberated *jīva* does not possess any body. Thus it is stated in the *sūtra*: *Abhāvam bādariḥ āha hi evam*.[88] The word *abhāva* in the *sūtra* means contextually the absence of a body. According to sage Bādari, the *muktātmā* does not have the body and the sense organs because the Scriptural text clearly states that as long as there is a body, one cannot escape the experience of pleasure and pain and only when one is free from the association of the body, pleasure and pain do not affect him.[89]

Jaimini on the other hand holds the view that the *mukta jīva* possesses a body and sense organs. Thus it is stated in the *sūtra*: *Bhāvaṁ jaiminiḥ vikalpa āmananāt*.[90] The reason given in support of it is contained in the word *'vikalpa āmananāt'*. *Vikalpa* means different forms (*vividhaḥ kalpaḥ or vaividhyam*). *Āmananāt* means that it is so described in the *Śruti* text. That is, the Upaniṣad describes that the mukta-jīva assumes manifold forms. Thus it states: Sa *ekadhā bhavati, tridhā bhavati, pañcadhā, saptadhā*...[91] – "He (the *mukta*) is in one form, he becomes three-fold, five-fold and seven-fold etc". The *jīva* can assume manifold forms only through its body since the *ātman* itself is aṇu and indivisible. Hence it is admitted by Jaimini that *muktātmā* possesses a body.

Bādarāyaṇa offers his own theory which attempts to reconcile the view of Bādari and Jaimini. The relevant *sūtra* reads: *Dvādaśahavat ubhayavidhaṁ Bādarāyaṇo ataḥ*.[92] It means that Bādarāyaṇa is of the opinion that the *mukta* is of both kinds (*ubhayavidhaṁ*) on account of its own will (*ataḥ*) as in the case of a twelve-day sacrifice named as *dvādaśāha*. That is, according to Bādarāyaṇa, the *mukta jīva* can assume a body if he so wills and can also remain without a body if he so wills. This is similar to the *dvādaśāha yāga* or the sacrifice which is performed for twelve days. The Scriptural texts enjoin the performance of this *yāga* in two different ways, depending on the purpose for which it is undertaken. If a person desires to acquire wealth, prosperity etc, he himself should perform it. It is then named *ahina*. If a person desires to perform a *yāga* for the welfare of humanity, then it is to be performed with the help of several other priests. In that case it is called *satra*.

On the authority of these Scriptural texts, the same *dvādaśāha yāga* is admitted as of two kinds. In the same way, it is to be admitted on the basis of the Upaniṣadic texts that a *mukta* can assume a body to render service to *Paramātman* and enjoy Him in that way, if he so wills and he can also remain without a body and enjoy *Paramātman* if he so wills.

Bādarāyaṇa further clarifies that the enjoyment of *Paramātman* by the *mukta jīva* without a body is similar to the experience of Brahman by *jīvātman* during the state of dream (*tanvabhāve sandhyāvat upapatteḥ*).[93] *Sandhyā* is the state of dream. During this state, the *jīva* experiences good objects and events such as riding on a chariot drawn by horses. The chariot, horses etc do not actually exist during the state of sleep. But these are created by *Paramātman* to enable *jīva* to experience them in the dream state in accordance with its past *karma*. In the same way, if *jīva* remains without a body, he can still experience Brahman through the body and sense organs created by *Paramātman* for this purpose.

Just as a person in the state of dream enjoys the chariots and other objects created by *Paramātman*, the *mukta* enjoys the world of fathers and other things created by *Paramātman* as part of His *leela* or sport. But such creations by *Paramātman* which are enjoyed by the *mukta jīva* without a body are not intended for the pleasure of the *jīva*, since the *jīva* in the state of *mukti* being totally free from *karma*, does not have any desire to enjoy them. All such creations are therefore intended for the pleasure of *Paramātman*.

When a *mukta-jīva* assumes a body out of his free will in the state of *mukti*, his experiences with the body are similar to the experience in the state of waking. The relevant *sūtra* reads: *Bhāve jāgradavat*.[94] The implication of this *sūtra* is that when the *mukta* creates objects and events out of his will, he experiences them in the same manner as a person in the waking state actually experiences them with body and sense organs. Even in this case, such experiences of the mukta *jīva* are intended only for the pleasure of *Paramātman* since he does not have any selfish motive for himself. Whatever the *jīva* does in the state of *mukti* is meant for the purpose of *Paramātman*.

In this connection, the question arises: How can the *jīva* which is atomic in size (*aṇu*), take on several bodies? In reply, Bādarāyaṇa states that this is possible because the attributive knowledge of the *jīvātman* in the state of *mukti* becomes infinite. This is evidenced by the Upaniṣadic text. The Śvetāśvatara states: *Sa ca ānantyāya kalpate*.[95] Though the *jīva* is atomic and also located in one small place of the body viz. heart, it has the power to pervade itself in other bodies assumed by it through its attributive knowledge. This is explained on the analogy of the lamp and its light radiated by it (*pradīpa*). The lamp is located only in one corner of a room but its light radiates all over the room. In the same way, mukta *jīva* can create several bodies by its *saṁkalpa* and activate them through the pervasion of its attributive knowledge.

Another minor objection is raised. There is a statement in the Bṛhadāraṇyaka Upaniṣad, according to which when the *jīvatman* in the state of *suṣupti*, is united with *Paramātman*, it does not know anything outside it and anything within it. It reads: *Prājñena ātmanā saṁpariṣvaktaḥ na bāhyam kiñcana veda na āntaram*.[96] If this be so, how does *muktātmā* pervade all other bodies through its attributive knowledge? Bādarāyaṇa replies to this objection by pointing out that the Upaniṣadic statement in question is not applicable to *muktātmā*. It only refers to the condition of *jīva* either in the state of deep sleep (*suṣupti*) or in the state of death when the knowledge is not functioning. In *suṣuspti*, the knowledge of the *jīva*, though present, is not functioning. But in the state of *mukti*, *jīva* becomes omniscient as stated by the Upaniṣad: *Sarvaṁ ha paśyaḥ paśyati sarvam āpnoti sarvaśaḥ*.[97]

If the *mukta jīva* is capable of creating anything desired by it, out of its *saṁkalpa*, and if it also enjoys equal status with Brahman *(paramaṁ sāmya)*, the question arises whether the *jīva* is also capable of creating the universe by its *saṁkalpa*. This is an important issue related to the status of the *jīva* in the state of *mokṣa* and it is discussed in the final *adhikaraṇa* of the *Brahma-sūtras* named *Jagad-vyāpār-avarjādhikaraṇa*.

Bādarāyaṇa states explicitly that the *mukta jīva*, though it enjoys equal status with Brahman, does not have the power to create and rule the universe since this function belongs exclusively to *Paramātman*. The relevant *sūtra* reads: *Jagadvyāpāravarjam prakaraṇāt asannihitatvācca*.[98] The word *'jagad-vyāpāra'* means the cosmic functions such as the creation of the universe and also controlling all beings in the universe (*nikhila niyamana*). The *mukta jīva* is denied of this function (*tad-varjam*), for two reasons. First, the Scriptural texts speak of this function only in respect of Brahman (*prakaraṇāt*). Secondly, while describing the process of creation of the universe by Brahman, the presence of *muktātmā* is not mentioned (*asannihitatvāt*). Thus the Taittirīya Upaniṣad dealing with the nature of Brahman defines it as that which is the cause of creation, sustenance and dissolution of the universe. Similarly the passages which deal with the creation of the universe, state that Brahman alone existed prior to creation and that by its *saṁkalpa* the universe was brought into existence. Therefore the function of creation of the universe and the power to control all sentient beings and non-sentient entities belong exclusively to Brahman. Infact this constitutes the distinguishing characteristic of Brahman and it is not applicable to *muktātmā*. The *parama-sāmya* or equal status of the *jīva* with *Paramātman* therefore excludes the function of *jagat-sṛṣṭi* and its *niyamana* for *muktātma*.

In what respect does *jīvātmā* enjoy equal status with Brahman? Bādarāyaṇa answers that it is with regard to the *bhoga* only or the experience of Brahman (*Brahmānubhava*). Thus it is stated in the *sūtra*: *Bhogamātra sāmya liṅgāt*[99]. The word *bhoga* means experience. In the context of Brahman it refers to the experience of Brahman in its true form, that is, as blissful. The *sāmya* or equality between the *mukta jīva* and Brahman is only in the matter of experience of bliss of Brahman. That is, the *mukta jīva* enjoys all the asuspicious qualities of Brahman. This is made evident by the Taittirīya text which states: *So'śnute sarvān kāmān saha brahmaṇā vipaścitā iti'* – "The *mukta jīva* enjoys all the auspicious qualities along with the omniscient Brahman". In this statement the word *kāmān* is taken to mean the 'auspicious attributes' of Brahman (*kāmyante iti kāmāḥ kalyāṇaguṇāḥ*).

The implication of the expression *'bhoga mātra sāmya'* is that the object of experience is common to both *jīva* and Brahman. In what sense is it common? As Vedānta Deśika explains, Brahman is essentially of the nature of *Ānanda* or bliss, as stated in the Taittīrya Upaniṣad. If the *svarūpa* of Brahman is blissful, it is also to be admitted that all that belongs to Brahman – its attributes as well as *vibhutis*, are also blissful in the sense that it is joyful (*sukharūpa*) for Brahman. In view of it Brahman is described in the Upaniṣad as *Bhūmā*, which is interpreted as infinite joy.[100] *Paramātman* experiences Himself as well as His own glory as blissful. *Jīva* too in the state of *mokṣa* experiences Brahman as well as its glory as blissful in full measure. This is the implication of the words *'bhogamātrasāmya'* mentioned in the *Vedānta-sūtra*. The word *mātra* rules out the *jagadvyāpāra* for *jīva*. The *mukta jīva* is regarded as having an equal status (*sāmya*) with Brahman only in respect of the enjoyment of bliss and not with regard to the cosmic functions of Brahman. In view of this, Viśiṣṭādvaita Vedānta describes mokṣa as *sāyujya*. *Sāyujya* means the state of experiencing the same object of enjoyment by two individuals together (*sayujo-bhāvaḥ*), like two persons – father and son, eating together the same delicious food. The state of *sāyujya* or the attainment of equal status with Brahman by *jīva* with regard to the enjoyment of bliss of Brahman and also its glory (*kalyāṇa guṇas*) along with Brahman constitutes the *mokṣa* proper in Viśiṣṭādvaita.

Another important feature of *mokṣa* is that the attainment of Brahman by *jīva* after it is totally liberated from bondage, is permanent (*nitya*). That is, when once the *jīva* attains Brahman, there is no return to the mundane world of bondage. Thus states the Chāndogya Upaniṣad in its concluding passage dealing with mokṣa: *Sa khalu evaṁ vartayan yāvadāyuṣam brahmalokam abhisaṁpadyate, na ca punarāvartate na ca punarāvartate*[101] – "The individual self who has lived such a disciplined life (*upāsanā* along with its accessories) all through his life, attains *Brahma-loka* from which he does not return hither again." The same truth is reiterated by Lord Kṛṣṇa in the *Bhagavad-gīta*: *Māmupetya punarjanma duḥkhālayam aśāśvatam; na'pnuvanti mahātmānaḥ saṁsiddhiṁ paramaṁ gatim*[102] – "Those who have attained Me (*Paramātman*) will not have rebirth again which is unending and which is the abode of suffering".

Based on such authoritative Scriptural and *Smṛti* texts, Bādarāyaṇa affirms in the concluding *sūtra* that there is no return for the *jīva* to mundane existence. The relevant *sūtra* reads: *Anāvṛttiḥ śabdāt*[103] – "There is no return because the Scriptural texts state so". The fuller implication of this *sūtra* is brought out by Rāmānuja. Philosophically the concept of *mokṣa* would be meaningless if the soul were to be caught up again in bondage. Theoretically there are two possibilities of return of the soul to the world of bondage. An individual out of ignorance may of his own choice desire to come back. Alternatively *Paramātman* who possesses unchecked freedom and to whom the *jīvātmā* is absolutely subordinate may command it to go back. Rāmānuja, while commenting on this *sūtra,* rules out both these possibilities. The individual who has totally become free from *karma* after realizing that other than the enjoyment of Brahman nothing else is of value and who has also become omniscient after attaining *mokṣa* is most unlikely to desire anything other than the bliss of Brahman. *Paramātman* who has abundant love and compassion for the individual self and whom he considers as His dearest (*atyartha priyaḥ*) as *Gītā* states, will never think of sending the *mukta* back. Thus under no circumstances the *jīva* which has attained the state of *mokṣa* will ever return to the world of bondage. Such a state of eternal existence for *jīva* constitutes *mokṣa,* which is the Supreme Goal, according to Viśiṣṭādvaita Vedānta.

---

1. Brahmavaivarta Purāṇa XXVI-70
2. VS IV-1-13
3. Ch. Up. IV-14-3
4. Ch. Up. V-24-3
5. *See* TMK. II-54
6. *See* AS verse 460
7. Ch. Up. V-24-3
8. VS IV-1-14.
9. Kaṭha. Up. II-24
10. *See* TMK. II-56
11. AS verse 462
12. Ch. Up. VI-14-2
13. AS verse 463. *Yukta adyaiva anyada va muniḥ* (Bādarāyaṇa) *iha manute brahmaniṣṭhasya muktim*
14. Ch. Up. VI-8-6
15. VS IV-2-1
16. Praśna. Up. III-9
17. VS IV-2-3
18. *See* AS verse 481. *prāgvat saṃśleṣa mātram tata iha hi manaḥ prāṇa ity-āmananti*
19. VS IV-2-4
20. Br. Up. VI-3-38
21. Br. Up. VI-4-2
22. VS IV-2-5
23. Kaṭha. Up. II-6-14

24. *See* AS verse 484
25. VS IV-2-7
26. Ch. Up. VI-14-2
27. *See* AS verse 485
28. VS IV-2-8
29. *See* Śrutaprakāśikā, RB IV-2-8. *utkrāntasya api gacchataḥ sūkṣma śarīra sambandhāt āpīteḥ saṁsāra iti abhiprāyaḥ*
30. Ch. Up. VI-8-6
31. VS IV-2-14
32. VS IV-2-15
33. VS IV-2-16
34. Br. Up. VI-4-2
35. *See* AS verse 493. *Svādhino hārdā-saṁjñaḥ svayam avikalayā; sampadā sākam ekaḥ sthitvā hṛtpadmamādhye sthagita nijatanuḥ saptaloka gṛhasthaḥ; nadi cakre suṣumnam nikhila dhṛtikarīm nābhi mū rdhantarūpam bhītvā tanmadhyā- randhra prahitam iṣumiva utkṣipya netā mumukṣum*
36. Ch. Up. VIII-6-5
37. VS IV-2-17
38. The following is the statement quoted by Rāmānuja. *Divā ca śuklapakṣaśca uttarāyaṇameva ca, mumūrṣtām praśastāni viparitam tu garhitam*
39. Ch. Up. VI-14-2
40. VS IV-2-18
41. Tait. Nārāyaṇa Up.
42. Ch. Up. VI-15-5
43. Kau. Up. I-29
44. Br. Up. VIII-2-15
45. VS IV-3-1
46. *See* As verse 501
47. VS IV-3-2
48. VS IV-3-3
49. VS IV-3-4
50. Ch. Up. IV-15-5
51. VS IV-3-6
52. VS IV-3-8
53. VS IV-3-9
54. Tait. Nārāyaṇa. Up. 10-14
55. Kūrma Purāṇa XII-269
56. *See* SB on VS IV-3-7
57. VS IV-3-11
58. Ch. Up. VIII-3-4
59. VS IV-3-12
60. Ch. Up. VIII-13-1
61. VS IV-3-14

62. Ch. Up. VIII-3-4
63. Ch. Up. V-10-1
64. Ch. Up. VIII-12-2
65. VS IV-4-1
66. VS IV-4-3
67. *See* Ch. Up. VIII-7-1. *Ya ātmā aphatapāpma vijāro vimṛtyuḥ viśoko vijighatso apipasaḥ satyakāmaḥ satyasaṁkalpaḥ*
68. *See* Tait. Up. II-1. *So'snute sarvān kāmān saha brāhmaṇa vipaścita.* *See* also AS verse 520
69. Tait. Up. II-1
70. Muṇḍ. Up. III-1-3
71. BG XIV-2
72. VS IV-4-4
73. VS I-4-22
74. *See* RB IV-4-4
75. AS verse 526
76. *See* AS verse 527
77. VS IV-4-5
78. VS IV-4-6
79. Br. Up. II-4-2
80. *See* Br. Up. VI-5-13
81. VS IV-4-7
82. Ch. Up. VIII-12-3
83. Ch. Up. VIII-2-1
84. VS IV-4-8
85. VS IV-4-9 *ata eva ca ananyādhīpatiḥ*
86. Ch. Up. VIII-25-2
87. Ch. Up. VII-25-2
88. VS IV-4-10
89. Ch. Up. II-12-2. *Na ha vai sasārirasya śataḥ priya-priyayoḥ apahatirasti; aśarīram vava santam na priyāpriye spṛṣaṭaḥ*
90. VS IV-4-11
91. Ch. Up. VII-26-2
92. VS IV-4-12
93. VS IV-4-13
94. VS IV-4-14
95. Śvet. Up. V-9
96. Br. Up. VI-3-21
97. Ch. Up. VII-26-2
98. VS IV-4-17
99. VS IV-4-21
100. *See* Ch. Up. VII-24-1. See also RB I-3-7. *Yo vai bhūma tat sukham (niratiśaya sukharupam)*
101. Ch. Up. VIII-15-1
102. BG. VIII-15
103. VS IV-4-22

Chapter Ten

GENERAL EVALUATION AND CONCLUSION

In the preceding chapters we have presented the philosophical doctrines of the Viśiṣṭādvaita Vedānta as enunciated by Vedānta Deśika in the *Adhikaraṇa-sārāvalī* on the basis of *Śrī-bhāṣya* of Rāmānuja. The details of the doctrines are mainly drawn from the *Vedānta-sūtras* and the connected Upaniṣadic texts, which constitute the basic source material for Vedānta. Several theories are discussed in the *adhikaraṇas* but these have been consolidated and presented as a coherent system of philosophy or *Darśana* under the following broad headings representing five major doctrines of Vedānta.

1. The doctrine of Brahman
2. The doctrine of the Universe and Brahman.
3. The doctrine of *Jīvātman* and Brahman.
4. The doctrine of *Sādhana*.
5. The doctrine of *Parama-puruṣārtha*.

In chapter 2 we have discussed the nature (*svarūpa*) of Brahman as outlined in the *adhikaraṇas* covered in the first *pāda* of first *adhyāya*. It is shown that Brahman as the Ultimate metaphysical Reality (*para-tattva*) is the primary cause of the creation, sustenance and dissolution of the universe (*jagat-kāraṇa*). As a sentient Being, it is distinct from the non-sentient cosmic matter. As a Supreme Being constituted of infinite bliss (*ānandamaya*), it is distinct from the sentient individual self (*jīvātman*). As a Spiritual Being possessing Divine body, it is also distinct from higher celestial deities such as *Akṣi-puruṣa, Āditya-puruṣa,* Indra etc, regarded as exalted individual souls. It is also distinct from non-sentient ontological entities such as *ākāśa* or cosmic ether, *prāṇa* or vital breath and *jyotis* or cosmic light.

In chapter 3, we have outlined the distinguishing characteristics (*dharmas*) of Brahman, as revealed by the *adhikaraṇas* included in *pādas* 2 and 3 of first *adhyāya*. Some of the important ones are:

Brahman is the *Sarvātmā* or the Universal Self; it is the *Antaryāmin* or the Inner Controller of all; it is the *Akṣara* or the imperishable Reality qualified with attributes; it is the *Ādhāra* or the Supporter of the universe; it is the *Vaiśvānara* or the Ruler of all souls; it is *Bhūmā* or infinitely great; it is the *Daharākāśa* or the subtle space within one's heart; it is the *Mukta-bhogya* or the object of enjoyment by the liberated souls. More importantly it is pointed out that Brahman is *Ubhayaliṅga,* that is, it is free from all defects (*heya-pratyanīka*) and also endowed with numerous auspicious attributes (*samasta-kalyāṇaguṇātmaka*).

In chapter 4 we have separately discussed one other important characteristic of Brahman viz. that it is the sole cause of the universe as revealed by a critical examination of the Upaniṣadic passages. These passages prima facie lend support to the claims of the Sāṁkhya and Yoga schools according to which *pradhāna* or the primordial cosmic matter and the *puruṣa* or the individual self is the cause of the universe.

In chapter 5 we have dealt with the doctrine of the universe and its relation to Brahman. The *adhikaraṇas* covering this subject in *pāda* 4 of first *adhyāya* attempt to establish that Brahman is the *upādāna-kāraṇa* or the material cause of the universe and that it is also *nimitta-kāraṇa* or the instrumental cause of the universe, since by its mere *saṁkapla* or will, it creates the universe. It is explained how Brahman can be admitted as the material cause of the universe without its *svarupa* as *nirvikāra* being affected through the process of *pariṇāma* or modification of the *prakṛti* from its unmanifest state to the manifest state. The several objections raised against the theory of Brahman as *upādāna-kāraṇa* are also answered. It is also pointed out how the universe as the *kārya* or the product brought into existence and Brahman, which is its *kāraṇa* or causal substance are non-distinct (*ananya*) in the sense that what is considered as *kārya* is a modified form (*avasthāntara*) of the causal substance. It is also explained that the universe which constitutes the *śarīra* or the body of Brahman, since it is wholly and always supported and controlled by Brahman, is real and is related to Brahman in the same way as the physical body is related to the soul (*śarīra-śarīrī-bhāva*).

In chapter 6, we have discussed the theory of cosmic creation as taught in the Upaniṣads and the *Vedānta-sūtras* and established the soundness of the Vedānta theory as against the defective views of the rival schools of thought such as the Śāṁkhyas, Vaiśeṣikas, Buddhists, Jainas and Pāśupata. We have also explained how the creation of the universe is caused by Brahman in two stages –the first stage through the process of evolution of *prakṛti* in a particular order upto the five gross elements (*pañca-bhūtas*) and the second stage by the admixture of the five elements (*pañcīkaraṇa*) in appropriate proportion by the *Caturmukha-brahmā,* the celestial deity created by Brahman to perform the function of the creation of the variegated physical universe.

In chapter 7, we have presented the doctrine of the *jīvātman* and its relation to Brahman. It is noted that the *adhikaraṇas* dealing with this subject in the third *pāda* of second *adhyāya* reveal without any shadow of doubt that *jīvātman* is a distinct spiritual entity as different from Brahman. It is eternal in character (*nitya*), *jñātā* or the subject of knowledge, *kartā* or the agent of action. Brahman abides in it (*avasthitiḥ*) as its Inner Controller (*Antaryāmin*). It is therefore regarded as the *aṁśa* or an integral part of Brahman in the sense that it is inherently related to

Brahman, similar to an essential attribute is inseparably related to its substrate. Though *jīva* and Brahman are different by virtue of their intrinsic nature, they are non-distinct as the two, being inseparably related, constitute one qualified entity (*viśiṣṭa*). It is also pointed out how *jīva*, entangled with bondage caused by *karma* or the deeds of the past lives, passes through the cycle of births and deaths continuously until it is liberated from bondage after duly observing the prescribed *sādhana*.

In chapter 8, we have considered the doctrine of *sādhana* or the means of attainment of Brahman. We have brought out on the basis of a large number of *adhikaraṇas* included in the third *adhyāya*, the various aspects of *sādhana*: *vidyā* or *upāsanā* as the direct means to the Supreme Goal (*puruṣārtha*), the different modes of *vidyā* or meditation, the *guṇas* with which Brahman is to be meditated upon, the nature and components of *upāsanā*, the *karma* or the performance of the prescribed rituals as a necessary aid to *vidyā* and other prerequisites for *upāsanā*. It is noted that both the object of meditation and also the goal to be attained is Brahman as endowed with attributes (*saguṇa Brahman*).

In chapter 9, we have examined the Supreme Goal (*parama-puruṣārtha*). It is observed that the *adhikaraṇas* related to this subject explain the manner of observing meditation and how the *jīva* is liberated from the *karma* in the form of *puṇya* and *pāpa*, the manner of its exit (*utkrānti*) from the body after death, the onward march of the liberated soul through the divine pathway presided over by the celestial deities and how the *jīva* finally reaches the *Brahma-loka* or the Abode of Brahman, when it attains a status equal to that of Brahman (*sāmya*) and enjoys infinite bliss. It is also pointed out that *jīva* retains its individuality even in the state of *mukti* and it does not become one with Brahman but remains in its natural form (*svena rūpa*) ever enjoying the bliss of Brahman, without any possibility of its return to mundane existence (*anāvṛttiḥ*).

The above brief resume of the contents of the book based on the *Adhikaraṇa-sārāvalī* indicates the main tenets of

Viśiṣṭādvaita Vedānta, as expounded by Rāmānuja in the *Śrī-Bhāṣya* and further elucidated by Vedānta Deśika in the *Adhikaraṇa-sārāvalī*. As will be pointed out presently, all these doctrines are reflected in the *Brahma-sūtras* and the Upaniṣads. In other words, the doctrines as presented by Vedānta Deśika fully conform to the teachings of Bādarāyaṇa as enshrined in the *sūtras* and also the connected Upaniṣadic passages. This claim can be substantiated by a comparative and critical study of the corresponding *adhikaraṇas* enunciated by the exponents of two major schools of Vedānta, Śaṁkara and Madhva. Both of them have accepted *Brahma-sūtras* as the fundamental source book of Vedānta and have also grouped the *sūtras* into *adhikaraṇas*, even though the number of *adhikaraṇas* reckoned by them varies. The total number of *adhikaraṇas*, according to Śaṁkara, is 196, whereas it is 222 for Madhva, as against 156 formulated by Rāmānuja. In the case of Madhva, some of the names adopted for the *adhikaraṇas* differ from those mentioned by Rāmānuja and Śaṁkara. Thus for instance, the *Ubhayaliṅgādhikaraṇa* included in the third *adhyāya*, which is an important topic dealing with the two-fold character of Brahman, both for Śaṁkara and Rāmānuja, is named *Sthānabhedādhikaraṇa*, without any consideration to the context in which it is introduced by Bādarāyaṇa. The *Vākyānvayādhikaraṇa* included in the fourth *pāda* of first *adhyāya*, dealing with the important subject of the relation of *jīva* to Brahman, which is acknowledged both by Rāmānuja and Śaṁkara, is named by Madhva as *Samākarṣādhikaraṇa*, overlooking the theory of *jīvātman*, referred to in the *sūtras*. However, the subject matter discussed and the *siddhānta* or the conclusive theory established in an *adhikaraṇa* is far more important than the title adopted for it. We should therefore give greater importance, for the purpose of evaluation of the soundness of the doctrines, to the consideration of the issue viz. to what extent the doctrines of Advaita Vedānta and also of Dvaita Vedānta, as compared to those advanced by the

Viśiṣṭādvaita, are philosophically and logically tenable. It may be observed on the basis of the proper interpretation of the *sūtras* and the concerned Upaniṣadic texts, in accordance with the commonly accepted principles of interpretation as laid down by the Mīmāṁsakas, without imposing on them the accepted doctrines or the preconceived postulates of a particular school of Vedānta, that a large number of *adhikaraṇas* as enunciated by Advaita Vedānta, do not strictly conform to the views of Bādarāyaṇa as enshrined in the *sūtras*. This point has been amply demonstrated by Rāmānuja in the *Śrī-Bhāṣya* and by Vedānta Deśika in the *Adhikaraṇa-sārāvalī* and also in the *Śatadūṣaṇī* which is a polemic work devoted primarily to the refutation of the doctrines of Advaita Vedānta in a systematic manner by adopting dialectical method. In the concluding *vāda* of this work which is named *'paramate sūtra svārasya-bhaṅga vāda'* (*vāda* 66), Vedānta Deśika has specifically pointed out that most of the *Vedānta-sūtras* and so also the *adhikaraṇas* do not support the tenets of Advaita Vedānta. Similarly, in the *Adhikaraṇa-sārāvalī*, he states that all the four *adhyāyas* of the Brahma-sūtras are opposed to the Advaita Vedānta since it upholds that Brahman as the Supreme Reality (*para-tattva*) is devoid of all determinations (*nirviśeṣa*) and that everything other than Brahman including the *jīvas* and the universe are phenomenal in character caused by *māyā* or cosmic ignorance[1].

Regarding the Dvaita Vedānta of Madhva, Vedānta Deśika does not mention any specific criticisms against it in the *Adhikaraṇa-sārāvalī*.[2] This may be due to the reason that the main tenets of the Vedānta advocated by Madhva regarding Brahman, *jīvātman, jagat, sādhana* and *puruṣārtha* are not basically different from those advanced by Rāmānuja. He regards this school of Vedānta as a system having close affinity to *Viśiṣṭādvaita* (*tat-sannikṛṣṭamata*).[3] However there are five important theories advanced by Madhva which are at variance with the theories advocated by Rāmānuja on the basis of the Vedānta-sūtras and also the Upanisads. These are a) Brahman is only the *nimitta-kāraṇa*. b) *jīva* is absolutely different from Brahman and the relation of *jīva* to Brahman is one of *bimba* and *pratibimba*. c) *jagat* (universe) is also absolutely different from Brahman and the two are not *ananya* or non-distinct as held by Rāmānuja on the basis of the *sūtra*. d) the direct *sādhana* to *mokṣa* is *aparokṣa-jñāna* or direct vision of Brahman generated by *nididhyāsana*. e) In the state of *mokṣa*, there is *ānanda-tāratamya* or differences in enjoyment of the *ānanda* or bliss due to the intrinsic differences of the *mukta-jīvas*.

Some criticisms are also leveled against the views of Rāmānuja expressed in the *Śrī-bhāṣya* both by the Advaitins of later period and also the followers of Madhva and in particular by Vyāsatīrtha (1460-1539) in their commentaries on Madhva's *sūtra-bhāṣya*.

Soon after the publication of the *Śatadūṣaṇī* in the 14th century by Vedānta Deśika, in which all the important doctrines of Advaita have been refuted in a systematic way, closely following the criticisms offered by Rāmānuja, in the section of *Śrī-Bhāṣya* named as *Mahāpūrvapakṣa* and *Mahāsiddhānta* included in the *Jijñāsādhikaraṇa*, no attempt seems to have been made until the 19th century by any traditional Advaita scholar to write a rejoinder to the *Śatadūṣaṇī*. The *Advaitasiddhi* of Madhusūdana Saraswatī (1540-1647) was however a rejoinder to *Vādāvalī* of Vyāsatīrtha in which the Advaita theory of *mithyātva* of *jagat* is mainly taken up for critical examination. This work was not directed towards Rāmānuja's theories. The polemical literature that developed later in the form of replies and counter-replies by the followers of Madhusūdana Saraswati were mainly directed more towards Dvaita Vedānta than to the Viśiṣṭādvaita Vedānta. Only in the recent years, Mm. AnantaKrishna Sastriar seems to have been encouraged to write a rejoinder to the *Śatadūṣaṇī*. The book titled '*Śatabhūṣaṇī*' is the outcome of this new venture. Soon after its publication, it was controverted by a contemporary Viśiṣṭādvaita scholar, Sri. Uttamur

Veeraraghavacharya in his book titled *'Paramārtha-bhūṣaṇa'*. On a dispassionate study of the *Śatabhūṣaṇī* it may be observed that this book does not offer any direct reply to the main points of criticisms leveled against Advaita doctrines either by Rāmānuja or Vedānta Deśika. On the other hand, it is in the form of defending the stand taken by the Advaita Vedānta by merely reiterating the elaborate statements drawn from the Advaita classics in support of it. This matter has been examined in my book *"Advaita and Viśiṣṭādvaita – A study based on Vedānta Deśika's Śatadūṣaṇī"* (III Edition 1999) and it is pointed in the concluding chapter that the defence put up by Sastriar is not a satisfactory reply to Vedānta Deśika's criticisms of Advaita. However in recent year, a traditional Advaita scholar, Sri Rāmāryakavi from Andhra Pradesh has published a book titled *'Śaṁkarāśaṁkara Bhāṣya Vimarśaḥ* (1953) in which an attempt is made to criticize the views of Rāmānuja against the Advaitins stated in the *Śrī-Bhāṣya*. An objective study of this work also reveals that even these criticisms of Rāmāryakavi are of superficial nature and these are more in the form of defending the Advaita position than offering any criticisms against the fundamental theories of the Viśiṣṭādvaita Vedānta.

Regarding the criticisms of Vyāsatīrtha in his *Tātparya-candrikā*, a learned commentary on Jayatirtha's Tattvaprakasa, against the views of Rāmānuja, it is found that these are mostly in the form of critical comments on the interpretation of the *sūtras* such as the meaning offered by Rāmānuja for the *sūtras* is not correct, the *pūrva-pakṣa* formulated by him is inappropriate and the *viṣayavākya* quoted in support of the *sūtra* is not relevant. These are all of exegetical nature and do not contain any solid constructive criticisms of the main theories (*prameyas*) advanced by Rāmānuja. However the criticisms of Vyāsatīrtha are also adequately replied to by a traditional Viśiṣṭādvaita scholar of the 18th century, Surapuram Srinivasacharya in the book titled *Tattvamārtaṇḍa* which covers the first two *adhyāyas* of the *Brahma-sūtra*.

We do not propose to take up the examination of the doctrinal differences that arise due to the different interpretations adopted by Śaṁkara, Rāmānuja and Madhva on the several crucial *sūtras* and also the concerned Upaniṣadic texts. This needs an independent study and falls outside the scope of the present book which is confined to the presentation of the Viśiṣṭādvaita Vedānta as expounded in the *Adhikaraṇa-sārāvalī*. This task has already been accomplished to some extent in my two books: 1) *The Philosophy of the Vedānta-sūtra – A study based on the comments of Śaṁkara, Rāmānuja and Madhva* and 2) *The Philosophy of the Upaniṣads – A study based on the comments of Śaṁkara, Rāmānuja and Madhva*. On the basis of a dispassionate study of the *Vedānta Sūtras* and the Upaniṣads, it is shown in these books that the following main tenets of Advaita Vedānta do not find any support either in the *sūtras* of Bādarāyaṇa or in the Upaniṣads, if the same are correctly interpreted with reference to the contexts and also on the basis of accepted principles of interpretation laid down by the Mīmāṁsakas.

1) *Nirviśeṣa Brahma-vāda* or the theory that Para Brahman is undifferentiated Being devoid of all determinations.
2) *Jīva* is essentially non-different from Brahman.
3) *Jagat* is illusory (mithyā).
4) *Māyā* is the cosmic principle of illusion.
5) *Ātmaikya-jñāna* is the direct means to *mokṣa*.
6) Realization of the identity of *jīva* and Brahman by the total eradication of *avidyā* is the Supreme Goal.

It is also brought out in these books that the following theories of Madhva are not reflected in the *Brahma-sūtras* and the Upaniṣads.

1) Brahman is only the *nimitta-kāraṇa* of the universe.
2) *Jīva* is absolutely different from Brahman and its relation to Brahman is that of *pratibimba* to

bimba in the sense of *sādṛśya* (similarity between the two) and dependence of *jīva* on Brahman (*tad-adhīna*).

3) The *jagat* is also absolutely different from Brahman and the two are not non-distinct (*ananya*), as stated by Bādarāyaṇa.

4) *Aparokṣa-jñāna* understood as *bimba-darśana* or direct vision of Brahman is the direct means to *mokṣa*.

We do not question these theories advanced by Śaṁkara and Madhva. These can be defended, as is done by the followers of these schools, on the basis of certain accepted premises. If we concede to the doctrine of *māya* or *avidyā*, as enunciated by the Advaitins, and the conception of two forms of Brahman as *saguṇa* and *nirguṇa* and also two grades of reality as *vyāvahārika* and *pāramārthika*, all the tenets of Advaita could be justified. Similarly if we accept the premises advanced by Dvaita Vedānta, such as the absolute difference between the three ontological entities without any unity (*abheda*) and also the differences in respect of the intrinsic nature of the *jīvas*, the tenets of Madhva could also be justified. For the purpose of general evaluation of the teachings of the *Adhikaraṇa-sārāvalī*, we should be mainly concerned to find out whether these doctrines advanced by Śaṁkara and Madhva, are philosophically sustainable, by taking into consideration the selected *adhikaraṇas* bearing on these theories as enunciated in the *Adhikaraṇa-sārāvalī*.

For this purpose, we shall confine our attention to examine three fundamental ontological theories of Vedānta (*prameyas*) viz. Brahman, *jīvātman* and *jagat* together with the controversial issues connected with them and find out which school of Vedānta offers satisfactory explanations, which can be regarded as philosophically sound. This would help us to determine the merit of the Viśiṣṭādvaita as compared to the Advaita and Dvaita.

The issues to be considered are:

1. Brahman – whether it is *nirviśeṣa* or *saviśeṣa*.
2. Whether Brahman as the primary cause of the universe is both *upādāna-kāraṇa* and *nimitta-kāraṇa*? Or is it only *nimitta-kāraṇa*.
3. *Jīvātman* – whether it is essentially non-different from Brahman or different from Brahman and how it is related to it.
4. *Jagat* (universe) - whether it is illusory (*mithyā*) or real (*satya*) and in what way it is related to Brahman.

We have selected these issues for consideration because these are not only fundamental in Vedānta but the answers provided to them determine the nature of the system either as Advaita (*kevala-abhedavāda*) or Viśiṣṭādvaita (*viśiṣṭa-abhedavāda*) or Dvaita (*kevala-bheda vāda*), the three principal schools of Vedānta and also their relative merit from the philosophical standpoint.

I. Nature of Brahman

Regarding the nature of Brahman, the main issue is whether it is *nirviśeṣa* or undifferentiated transcendental Reality devoid of all attributes (*guṇas*) or is it *saviśeṣa* or the Supreme Being endowed with numerous attributes. According to Śaṁkara, Brahman as the ultimate metaphysical Reality (*para tattva*) is *nirviśeṣa*. The Brahman described in the Upaniṣads as endowed with attributes is *apara-Brahma* or lower Brahman associated with *māyā*. Rāmānuja and Madhva do not admit two concepts of Brahman. It is only one Brahman which is the ultimate Reality, which is the same as the personal God of Religion (*sarveśvara*). It is designated as Viṣṇu or Nārāyaṇa and is endowed with infinite number of attributes. Śaṁkara seeks to justify his thesis both on the authority of the Upaniṣads and the *Vedānta-sūtras*. Both Rāmānuja and Madhva refute the view of Śaṁkara on the same authority of the Upaniṣads and *Vedānta-sūtras*.

The theory of two Brahmans, which is a major controversial issue in Vedānta, is fully discussed in the book *'The Philosophy of the Vedānta-sūtra'* (*vide* chapter 4). As pointed out therein, it is not sustainable both according to the Upaniṣads and the *Vedānta-sūtras*. The Upaniṣads no doubt, describe Brahman in two ways. That is Brahman as qualified with negative attributes (*niṣedharūpa viśeṣaṇas*) such as *adreśya, agrāhya, arūpa, niṣkriya, nirguṇa, niravayava etc.* and also with positive attributes such as *sarvajñaḥ, satyasaṁkalpaḥ, satyakāmaḥ* etc. This does not mean that Brahman is devoid of all attributes and that we have to admit two forms of Brahman as *nirguṇa* and *saguṇa*, as stated by Śaṁkara. As pointed out by Vedānta Deśika, it is possible to reconcile this apparent conflict between the *nirguṇa śrutis* and *saguṇa śrutis*, by adopting the Mīmāṁsā principle of interpretation, according to which the negative statements are to be understood in accordance with the affirmative statements. That is, *nirguṇa śrutis* are to be interpreted to mean the denial of qualities other than those mentioned in the *saguṇa śrutis* (*vihita-vyatirikta guṇaniṣedhaḥ*). Accordingly the terms such as *nirguṇa, niravaya* etc. imply that Brahman is devoid of *heya guṇas* such as *vikāra (change), karma* and physical qualities such as *sthūlatva, aṇutva, hṛsavatva* etc.[4] As Vedānta Deśika states in the *Adhikaraṇa-sārāvalī*, the very concept of Brahman as *nirguṇa* is defective because such a Brahman can neither be the object of philosophic investigation (*jijñāsā*) nor the object of meditation[5]. This point is discussed in detail in a separate *vāda* in the *Śatadūṣaṇī* under the title *'Jijñāsa-anupapatti-vādaḥ'*[6]

The second *sūtra* which defines Brahman as the cause of the three cosmic functions – *sṛṣṭi, sthiti* and *laya (janmādy asya yataḥ)* does not hold good in respect of *nirviśeṣa* Brahman. *Jagat-kāraṇatva* is an important *dharma* of Brahman and what is *nirviśeṣa* cannot possess the *dharma* of *īkṣaṇa* or the function of resolving to create the universe by its *saṁkalpa* as stated in the 5th *sūtra*. The Chāndogya text mentions explicitly that Brahman 'willed to become many' (*tad-aikṣata bahusyāṁ prajāyeyeti*). If Brahman is devoid of knowledge (*īkṣaṇa*) or the function to cause the universe in the primary sense of the term, how can it be distinguished from the non-sentient *pradhāna*, which according to the Sāṁkhyas is the primary cause of the universe?[7]

As pointed out in chapters 2 and 3, the *adhikaraṇas* of the first three *pādas* of the first *adhyāya* bring out several distinguishing characteristics of Brahman.[8] In fact the main objective of these *adhikaraṇas*, according to Vedānta Deśika, is to highlight the *gunas* of Brahman (*sarveṣām api adhikaraṇānāṁ tattat bhagavat guṇa prādhānya kṛtyam*).[9] If Brahman is *nirviśeṣa*, none of these can be ascribed to it. Śaṁkara gets over this objection by postulating two concepts of Brahman – *saguṇa* and *nirguṇa*. That the Brahman described with attributes is the *saguṇa Brahman* or the lower Brahman intended for the purpose of meditation, whereas *nirviśeṣa* Brahman which is *jñeya* or to be directly realized, is devoid of attributes. But neither the Upanisads nor the *Vedānta-sūtras* acknowledge two Brahmans – *para* and *apara*. Besides, the concept of *māyā* or *avidyā* on the basis of which such a distinction of *para* and *apara* Brahman can be sustained has also no basis either in the Upaniṣads or in the *sūtras*.

However, the following four *adhikaraṇas* are claimed by the Advaitins to support the theory of *nirguṇa Brahman*.

1. *Adṛśyatvādhikaraṇa* based on the Muṇḍaka text in which *akṣara* denoting Brahman is described as qualified with negative attributes such as *adreśyam, agrāhyam, agotram, avarṇam, acakṣuḥ śrotram, nityam, vibhum, sarvagatam, susūkṣmam, avyayam and bhūta-yonim.*[10]
2. *Dyubhvādyadhikaraṇa* based on the Muṇḍaka Upaniṣad in which Brahman is regarded as *āyatana* or support for *dyau, pṛthivī, prāṇa, antarikṣa, manas* etc. which are woven in it (*otam*)

and that alone is to be known as Atman.[11]

3. *Akṣarādhikaraṇa* based on the Bṛhadāraṇyaka text in which the same *akṣara* denoting Brahman is described purely in negative terms such as *asthūla, anaṇu, ahrasva* etc.[12]
4. *Ubhayaliṅgādhikaraṇa* which describes Brahman as of two-fold character, along with *Prakṛtaitāvattvā-dhikaraṇa* (treated as a separate adhikaraṇa by Śaṁkara), based on the Bṛhadāraṇyaka text, which negates the *mūrta* and *amūrta* forms in respect of Brahman by the words *'neti neti'*.[13]

An objective study of these *adhikaraṇas* reveals that none of these supports the theory of *nirviśeṣa* Brahman. The *sūtras* related to these topics explicitly refer to *saviśeṣa* Brahman.

In the *Adṛśyatvādiguṇakādhikaraṇa* the main *sūtra* reads: *Adṛśyatvādi guṇakaḥ dharmokteḥ.*[14] It means that the ontological entity denoted by *Akṣara* in the Muṇḍaka Upaniṣad qualified with attributes such as imperceptibility (*adṛśyatva*), is Brahman since the *dharmas* mentioned in the Upanisadic passage such as *sarvajña* and *sarvavit* exclusively belong to it. According to the Upanisad, the ultimate principle, is to be comprehended by *parā vidyā,* or higher knowledge *(atha parā yayā tadakṣaram adhigamyate)* and this statement, prima facie, may lend support to Śaṁkara's claim that it is *nirviśeṣa* Brahman, being the subject of *parā vidyā*. But Bādarāyaṇa does not acknowledge it, since he uses the terms *guṇakaḥ* and *dharmokteḥ* in the *sūtra,* which explicitly convey that *akṣara* is qualified with attributes. It is obvious that according to Bādarāyaṇa, Brahman designated as *akṣara* in the Muṇḍaka Upaniṣad, is *saviśesa* and not *nirviśeṣa,* as claimed by Śaṁkara.

Similarly in the *Dyubhvādyadhikaraṇa, Ātman* which is regarded as *āyatana* or the support for the heaven, earth, sky etc which are woven in it (*dyūbhyādyāyatanam*), cannot be regarded as *nirviśeṣa* Brahman. The word *āyatana* is interpreted by Śaṁkara as substratum for heaven, earth etc which are illusory and are therefore superimposed on Brahman *(otam)* due to avidyā. But, according to Bādarāyaṇa, the heaven, earth etc. are real since they actually exist, being the creation of Brahman and hence an undifferentiated Brahman cannot serve as *āyatana* or the substratum for that which really exists.

Regarding the *Akṣarādhikaraṇa* based on the Bṛhadāraṇyaka Upaniṣad in which *akṣara* is described purely in negative terms such as *asthūla, anaṇu* etc[15], Brahman denoted by the term *akṣara* is not *nirviśeṣa* inspite of its description in negative terms because Bādarāyaṇa in the two *sūtras*[16] bearing on this subject describes it as the supporter of the entire universe (*ambarānta dhṛteḥ*) by virtue of its possessing the power to command everything in the universe (*praśāsanāt*). That which possesses the capacity to command everything in the Universe (*praśāsanatva*) cannot be *nirviśeṣa.*

The *Ubhayaliṅgādhikaraṇa* and the *Prakṛtaitāvatt-vādhikaraṇa* are of special significance for Śaṁkara since these two topics are claimed to support strongly the theory of *nirviśeṣa* Brahman. The two main *sūtras* dealing with this matter are: *Na sthānato'pi parasya ubhayaliṅgam*[17] and *Prakṛtaitāvattvam hi pratiṣedhati tato bravītica bhūyaḥ*[18]. The first *sūtra* is construed by Śaṁkara in such a way as to convey the view that Brahman is *nrivikalpaka* or devoid of all characteristics, because everywhere (*sarvatra*) in the Upaniṣads it is described so (*samasta viśeṣa rahitam nirvikalpakameva brahma pratipattavyam)*[19]. The justification for adopting this interpretation is that the two ways of description of Brahman (*ubhayaliṅga*) viz. as possessing attributes and as devoid of attributes cannot be reconciled even by means of its association with *upādhis* or limiting adjuncts (*sthānataḥ*). If one of the two forms is to be admitted to reconcile the conflicting statements, it is to be taken as *nirviśeṣa* or Brahman as devoid of attributes, since all the Upaniṣads describe it so (*sarvatra hi*).

As we have pointed out in the chapter 8,[20] this is not a satisfactory explanation. Contextually the word *'sthānataḥ'* used in the *sūtra* means that though Brahman like *jīva*, abides in all beings as *Antaryāmin*, it is untouched by defects found in the bodies, since by nature Brahman is *apahatapāpmā* or free from defects (*nirdoṣa*). As Vedānta Deśika states, Bādarāyaṇa introduces this *sūtra* in the *Sādhanādhyāya* for the main purpose of proving that Brahman is free from defects (*nirdoṣa*) unlike *jīvātman*, so that it is sought for by aspirants to *mokṣa* as worthy object of meditation. Another important reason for bringing up this matter is to refute the theory of *nirguṇa Brahman*, because the concept of Brahman as *nirguṇa* is defective.[21] Hence the *ubhayaliṅgatva* of Brahman, if properly understood, does not support the theory of *nirviśeṣa* Brahman.

The other *sūtra* (III-2-22) which is based on the famous *mūrtā-murta Brāhmaṇa* of the Bṛhadāraṇyaka Upaniṣad, in which two forms of Brahman viz. *mūrta* and *amūrta* are negated by the expression *'neti neti'*, is taken as concrete proof for admission of Brahman as *nirviśeṣa*. This matter is fully discussed in the book *'The Philosophy of the Vedānta Sūtra'*[22] and also in the book *'The Philosophy of the Upaniṣads'*.[23] It is conclusively established by Rāmānuja that this explanation of Śaṁkara is far from satisfactory. The *sūtra* clearly states that what is negated is only the limited nature of Brahman (*prakṛtaitāvattvam*) and what is stated in the later part of the passage (*tato braviti ca bhūyaḥ*) asserts that Brahman is *satyasya satya* which refers to the glorious character of Brahman. Hence, Brahman according to this *sūtra*, is *saviśeṣa* or endowed with abundant auspicious *guṇas*.

II. Brahman as the *upādāna-kāraṇa*

The next important issue relating to Brahman is whether Brahman which is the primary cause of the three cosmic functions as defined in the Taittirīya Upaniṣad and the second aphorism of Vedānta, is the *upādāna-kāraṇa* (material cause) of the universe or is it only the *nimitta-kāraṇa* (instrumental cause). According to the *Vedānta-sūtra,* as interpreted both by Śaṁkara and Rāmānuja, Brahman is both the *upādāna* and *nimitta kāraṇa.* The relevant *sūtra* reads: *Prakṛtiśca pratijñādṛṣṭānta anuparodhāt.*[24] The word *prakṛti* on the basis of the *Pāṇini sūtra* is understood as material cause (*jani kartuḥ prakṛtiḥ*).[25] The *pratijñā* and *dṛṣṭānta* mentioned in the *sūtra* refer to the Chāndogya passage dealing with the causation of the universe where the general statement and the illustration of the lump of clay and the products made out of it to elucidate the general statement, are mentioned. On the basis of this passage, the author of the *sūtra* states that Brahman is the *upādāna-kāraṇa.* The word *'ca'* means that it is also the *nimitta-kāraṇa.* As we have explained in chapter 5, this *sūtra* is introduced in the context of the refutation of the theory of *Seśvara Sāṁkhya* (Yoga school) which admits that *prakṛti* is the material cause of the universe and *Īśvara* is the *nimitta-kāraṇa.* While refuting this theory, Bādarāyaṇa affirms that Īśvara or Brahman is also the *upādāna-kāraṇa* on the unquestionable authority of the Upaniṣadic texts. In connection with the causation of the universe, the Taittirīya Upaniṣad states that Brahman itself becomes the universe (*tad-ātmānaṁ svayam akuruta*). The Chāndogya passage dealing with the causation of the universe mentions that *Sat* (Brahman) which alone existed prior to creation willed to become many (*tad aikṣata bahuṣyāṁ prajāyeya).* In another passage of the Muṇḍaka, Brahman is regarded as the *Bhūta-yoni* which implies that it is the material cause of the universe. Considering all these facts, Bādarāyaṇa regards Brahman as the *upādāna-kāraṇa* on the analogy of the spider and the web created by it. The *sūtras* also state: *Ātmakṛteḥ, pariṇāmāt*[26]. It means that Brahman itself becomes the universe through modification. Both Śaṁkara and Rāmānuja, therefore admit that Brahman is *upādāna-kāraṇa* though they offer different explanations regarding the *pariṇāma* of Brahman without affecting its *svarūpa* as *nirvikāra.*

But Madhva does not admit that Brahman is the *upādāna-kāraṇa*. The *sūtra* which is so specific regarding this matter, is interpreted in a different way. The term *prakṛti* is interpreted to mean Viṣṇu. The justification for adopting this meaning is that all terms occurring in the *sūtras* included in the *Samanvayādhyāya* are to be interpreted in favour of *Viṣṇu*, the Supreme Being. Madhva ignores the Chāndogya passage in which the *pratijñā* and *dṛṣṭānta* are so explicitly mentioned and adopts a different *viṣaya vākya* drawn from another *vedic* text which has a reference to a different general statement and also an illustration of the rivers flowing into the ocean, which has no bearing on the subject of causality of Brahman.

Whatever justification is offered by Madhva and his followers in support of the theory of Brahman as only *nimitta-kāraṇa*, it does not conform either to the *Vedānta-sūtra* or the Chāndogya Upaniṣadic teaching which emphasizes the causal relationship between Brahman and *jagat*. The Upaniṣadic texts dealing with the causation of the universe clearly convey the view that Brahman is the material cause, though the word *upādāna* is not specifically mentioned in them. According to the definition of Brahman offered in the Taittirīya Upaniṣad and the *Vedānta-sūtra* framed on it (*janmādy asya yataḥ*), Brahman, as the primary cause of the universe is to be admitted as the material cause on the analogy of the clay and pot made out of it. Otherwise there would be no causal relationship between Brahman and jagat. In the case of the pot brought out of clay, clay is the material cause, whereas the potter, who is instrumental in making the pot, is only the *nimitta-kāraṇa*. The potter cannot be the primary cause of the pot since he needs the clay for the production of the pot. On the same analogy, if *Īśvara* is only the *nimitta-kāraṇa*, He cannot be the primary cause of the universe. It would be the *prakṛti*, since that is the material cause of the universe, according to Madhva's position. Such a view is not acceptable to Bādarāyana as is evident from the refutation of Seśvara Sāṁkhya theory of

Īśvara as *nimittakārana*. In order to establish the causal relationship between Brahman and *jagat*, Bādārayaṇa also refutes the Vaiśeṣika theory of causality, according to which cause and effect are different and affirms that Brahman as a cause and *Jagat* as its *kārya* are *ananya* or non-distinct in the sense that the effect is a modified state of the causal substance (*avasthāntara*) and as such the two are causally related[27]. Among the causal factors required for the production of a product, greater importance is to be given to the causal substance, since that is the primary cause of the effect (*kārya*). In the same way *Īśvara* or Brahman is to be admitted as the *upādāna-kāraṇa*. This is the important logical justification for ascribing the *upādāna-kāraṇatva* to Brahman. Another reason for the admission of Brahman as *upādāna kāraṇa* is that Brahman is also the cause of dissolution of the universe (*saṁhartā*). During dissolution, the universe becomes submerged in the causal substance which is *Īśvara*. The Subāla Upaniṣad clearly states that during the process of dissolution, *tamas* or the unmanifest universe becomes one with *paradevatā* (*tamaḥ pare deva ekī bhavati*)[28]. If Brahman is not the material cause, the universe should dissolve in *prakṛti* which is the material cause and not Brahman. But the Taittirīya states that the universe enters Brahman at the time of its dissolution (*yat prayanti abhisaṁviśanti*)[29].

Regarding the objection that the admission of material causality would affect the nature of Brahman as *nirvikāra*, Bādarāyaṇa himself has anticipated it and offered a suitable reply to it in two ways. First he states that we have to accept what is taught in the *Śruti* since *Śruti* is final authority in this matter. Since the Scriptural text says that Brahman is the *upādāna-kāraṇa*, we have to admit it. The relevant *sūtra* reads: *Śrutestu śabdamūlatvāt*[30]. A more rational explanation is also offered by pointing out that Brahman possesses variegated powers (*vicitra śakti*)[31] and it is therefore possible for it to undergo modification without affecting its *nirvikāratva*. Rāmānuja elucidates this point by stating that what actually undergoes modification is *prakṛti,* which is its *śarīra* according to the *Antaryāmi Brāhmaṇa* and that the changes taking place in the *śarīra* should not affect the Indwelling *Self* which is its *ādhāra.* This is logically justifiable in the Viśiṣṭādvaita system since it admits substance as different from attribute, though the two, as inseparably related, is one complex entity. The analogy cited by Rāmānuja in support of this is that the self of an individual who passes through the states of boyhood, youth, manhood and old age, is not affected by the changes taking place in the body. The same principle holds good in respect of Brahman which is inherently related to *cit* and *acit* at all times. If this explanation is not accepted, it would not be possible to justify the Upaniṣadic statement which affirms that Brahman itself becomes the manifold universe. It may be possible to resolve this problem by resorting to *vivarta vāda,* that is, Brahman itself appears illusorily as the universe due to Māyā, but the doctrine of Māyā on the basis of which, *vivarta-vāda* can be sustained is not found in the *vedānta-sūtra.*

The first *pāda* of second *adhyāya* is primarily devoted to examine all possible objections against the theory of Brahman as the *upādāna-kāraṇa.* The major one is raised by the Vaiśeṣikas to whom cause and effect are absolutely different and hence the causal relationship between Brahman and the universe cannot be admitted. The rest of the objections are raised by the Sāṁkhyas against the Vedānta theory of Brahman as *upādāna-kāraṇa*[32]. If Brahman were not the *upādāna-kāraṇa,* as enunciated in the *Prakṛtyādhikaraṇa* of the previous *pāda* (I-4), then there would be no need for all these *sūtras* mentioned in the first *pada* of Second *adhyāya.*

It therefore becomes obvious that Bādarāyaṇa admits that Brahman is the *upādāna-kāraṇa.* Further, if it were acceptable to Bādarāyaṇa that Brahman is only *nimitta-kāraṇa,* as Madhva maintains, then there would be no justification for refuting the theory of Seśvara-Sāṁkhya and the school of Pāśupata which only accept *Īśvara* as *nimitta-kāraṇa* as Madhva does. It therefore follows that according to Bādarāyaṇa, Brahman is both the *upādāna-kāraṇa* and *nimitta-kāraṇa* of the universe. In this respect, Madhva's Dvaita Vedānta suffers from a major drawback by refuting *Brahmopādānatva*. Even the schools of Yādava and Bhāskara coming after Śaṁkara and prior to Madhva accept *Brahmopādānatva*, though the explanations offered by them for *upādānatva* of Brahman is different as in the case of Śaṁkara.

III. The Theory of Jīvātman

Coming to the theory of *jīva*, the major issue to be considered is whether *jīvātman* or the individual self is non-different from Brahman or different from it. According to Śaṁkara, the *jīva* is essentially Brahman and it is regarded as many and different from Brahman due to the fact that the same Brahman being conditioned by limiting adjuncts such as bodies and *antaḥkaraṇas* appear to be different, similar to the one all-pervasive *ākāśa*, which appears to be many when the same is conditioned by several receptacles. According to another view of Advaita, the *jīvas* are reflections of the Brahman in the several *antaḥkaraṇas*, similar to the reflections of the single moon in the waves of the water. According to Rāmānuja and Madhva, *jīvātman* is a distinct, real ontological entity different from Brahman.

Both the schools attempt to establish their theories on the strength of the Upaniṣads. There are, no doubt, a few statements in the Upaniṣad which prima facie speak of non-difference between *jīva* and Brahman such as '*tat-tvamasi*', '*ayam ātmā brahma*', '*ahaṁ brahmāsmi*'. But there are also a large number of Upaniṣadic statements which affirm that *jīva* and Brahman are different. The Śvetāśvatara Upaniṣad states: *Jña jñau dvau ajau, īsa anīśa* which emphasise difference between the two in terms of one as omniscient and the other ignorant, one as Ruler and the other as that which is ruled.

The students of Vedānta are familiar with the arguments advanced by the two schools in support of their theories and there is no need to reiterate them. What we are concerned here is, whether the *Vedānta-sūtras* support the view of Advaita. As we have pointed out in the chapter 7 dealing with the *adhikaraṇas* relating to the doctrine of *jīva,* Bādarāyaṇa upholds the theory of *jiva* as different from Brahman. There are several *sutras* in the first *adhyāya* and also other *adhyāyas* which point out that *jīva* is different from Brahman. The *sūtra 'Adhikaṁ tu bhedanirdeśāt'*[33], is a categorical statement emphasizing that Brahman is different and even higher than *jīvātman.* If *jīva* were not really different from Brahman, the attainment of Brahman in a higher realm known as *Brahmaloka,* the pursuit of the prescribed *upāsanā* or any other spiritual discipline for this purpose would be of no value. The Vedānta as a *mokṣa śāstra* would be futile. The Advaitin no doubt seeks to justify all these theories of Vedānta – the difference between *jīva* and *Paramātmā,* the observance of meditation for the attainment of Brahman and the attainment of a higher spiritual goal – on the basis of empirical reality (*vyāvahārika satyatva*). That is, all that has been taught in the Vedānta has empirical value intended for the practical purposes but from a transcendental standpoint of Ultimate Reality, they are not real. By postulating the concept of *māyā,* the cosmic principle of illusion, he seeks to justify all these theories of Vedānta including the theory of *jagat* as *mithyā* (illusory).

Is the theory of *māyā* sustainable? According to the critics of Advaita, it is not. This theory is not explicitly mentioned in the Upanisads nor is it supported by the *Vedānta-sūtras.* As Vedānta Deśika observes, the concept of *avidyā* as an indeterminable principle (*anirvacanīya)* is similar to the concept of *samvṛti* admitted by the Mādhyamika Buddhists as a postulate to explain how one becomes many[34]. It is not sanctioned by the Upaniṣads, but yet it is admitted in order to uphold the absolute *Monism* or absolute-oneness of Reality. The plurality is accounted for on the basis of cosmic ignorance. This is the main reason why Rāmānuja and so also Madhva have vehemently attacked the *māyā-vāda* as it is against the spirit of Upaniṣadic teachings. It is therefore an undeniable fact that Advaita Vedānta deviates from Bādarāyaṇa in respect of the theory of *jīva,* as a real ontological entity different from Brahman, whereas Madhva and Rāmānuja conform to the *sūtras.*

IV. The Relation of Jīva and Universe to Brahman

The Upaniṣads acknowledge three ontological principles. These are *Īśvara* or Brahman who is the Ruler and controller of all, the *jīvātman,* which experiences the objects and the universe with which we are surrounded. All the three are important principles to be known in Vedānta. Thus states the Śvetāśvatara: *Bhoktā bhogyam preritāraṁ ca matvā.* All the schools of Vedānta have to admit them. There may be differences of opinion with regard to their relative ontological status in terms of the grades of reality as *paramārthika* and *vyāvahārika* or as higher and lower (*paratattva* and *aparatattva*) or as independent and dependent (*svatantra* and *paratantra*). The admission of only one principle like Brahman as absolutely real and the other two principles *jīva* and the *jagat,* as illusory, is not therefore justified. All the three have to be accepted as real ontological entities in order to formulate an acceptable and sound system of philosophy. With the admission of all the three principles, we are confronted with the question of finding a proper relationship between the three, Brahman, *jīva* and *jagat.* The question to be considered is: What is the nature of the relation between Brahman and *jīva* and also Brahman and *jagat*? These are the two major ontological problems in Vedānta. The Upaniṣads have provided an answer to these questions. Based on these Upaniṣadic passages, Bādarāyaṇa has attempted to explain the relationship between the ontological entities. All the three commentators on the *Vedānta-sūtra* have also offered different explanations on these issues. We have to examine which one is a satisfactory theory. The merit of a school of Vedānta can be determined on the basis of the philosophical soundness of the theory of relationship between the ontological entities.

Bādarāyana who acknowledges the importance of the relationship between the three ontological entities, discusses this matter in the following *adhikaraṇas:*

1) Vākyānvayādhikaraṇa
2) Aṁśādhikaraṇa
3) Prakṛtyadhikaraṇa
4) Ārambhaṇādhikaraṇa
5) Ahikuṇḍalādhikaraṇa

The topics 1 and 2 deal with the relation of *jīva* to Brahman, whereas topics 3 to 5 deal with the relation of the universe to Brahman. The details of these *adhikaraṇas* are given in the respective chapters dealing with them. The *Vedānta sūtras* covered in these *adhikaraṇas* have a direct bearing on the nature of relationship between the three ontological principles, though these *sūtras* are interpreted differently by the commentators, more specifically by Madhva.

We shall first consider the relation of *jīva* to Brahman. The topic *Vākyānvayādhikaraṇa*[35], according to Śaṁkara and Rāmānuja, deals with this subject. This is obvious from the fact that Bādarāyaṇa, while discussing the import of the term '*Ātman*' employed in the passage of *Maitreyī Brāhmaṇa*, mentions in three *sūtras*[36] the names of three sages, Āśmarathya, Auḍulomi and Kāśakṛtsna who held different views regarding the relation of Brahman to *jīva*. The *sūtras* containing the views of Āśmrathya and Auḍulomi, as interpreted by Śaṁkara and Rāmānuja, convey that the relation of *jīva* to Brahman is either non-difference (*abheda)* or difference cum non-difference (*bhedābheda*). The view expressed by Kāṣakṛtsna is regarded as the view of Bādarāyaṇa both by Śaṁkara and Rāmānuja. According to this view Brahman abides in *jīva* (*avasthiti)* and as such the two being inherently related is regarded as non-different.

Madhva offers an altogether different interpretation for these *sūtras*. These *sūtras* are taken as part of an *adhikaraṇa* named *Samākarṣādhikarṇa* and they are concerned with establishing the *samanvyaya* of the terms used in the *Karmakāṇḍa* (ritualistic portion of the Vedas). It does not appear to be relevant to bring up the subject of *karma* in the context of discussion of Brahman as the cause of the universe, particularly when the question of how the terms *ātman (jīvātman)* and *Paramātman* are employed in the Upaniṣadic passages of *Maitreyī Brāhmaṇa* as interchangeable terms. If it were *karma* and its bearing on Brahman, as Madhva contends, it does not appear relevant to discuss the question of the relation of *jīvātman* to Brahman and refer to the views of three sages regarding this matter. Obviously Madhva avoids the subject of the relation of *jīva* and Brahman, particularly, the crucial *sūtra* ascribed to Kāśakṛtsna which emphasizes the intimate relationship between *jīva* and Brahman.

The *Aṁśadhikarana* in which *jīva* is stated to be *aṁśa* of Brahman specifically deals with the relation of *jīva* to Brahman. The relevant *sūtra* of this *adhikaraṇa* reads '*Aṁśo nānāvyapadeśāt anyathā ca* etc.,[37] is introduced by Bādarāyaṇa in connection with the discussion of the nature of *jīva* as *nitya, jñātā, kartā* and *parāyatta* and it is therefore intended to explain its relation to Brahman. From the wording of the *sūtra*, it is so obvious that there are two conflicting views regarding the relation of *jīva* to Brahman, as different (*nānā*) and also non-different (*anyathā ca)* and that for the purpose of reconciling this apparent conflict, *jīva* is to be regarded as *aṁśa* of Brahman. In interpreting the term *aṁśa* or part with reference to Brahman, three different explanations are advanced by the commentators. Śaṁkara who advocates the theory of *abheda (tādātmya)* between *jīva* and Brahman, interprets *aṁśa* as '*aṁśa iva*' that is, *jīva* which is essentially Brahman appears as *aṁśa* or part of Brahman in the sense of being different from Brahman due to *avidyā*, just as the single moon appears as many when reflected in the waves of water. This theory of relation in terms of non-difference (*abheda*) is not tenable for two reasons. First, it conflicts with the several Upaniṣadic texts which categorically state *jīva* is different from Brahman by virtue of the difference in their intrinsic nature. *Jīva* is *ajña* (ignorant) while *Paramātman* is *Sarvajña*, as the Upaniṣad states. *Paramātman* is *Īśa*, while *jīva* is one ruled by Him. This is what is implied in the word *'nānāvyapadeśāt'* used in the *sūtra*. It is no doubt true that some Upanisadic texts speak of non-difference between the two. This is implied in the words *'anyathā ca'* in the *sūtra*. It is not appropriate to accord greater validity to the texts speaking non-difference (*abheda Śrutis*) and less validity to the texts emphasizing difference between *jīva* and Brahman (*bheda Śrutis*). Both are to be accepted as equally valid. In order to reconcile the two conflicting views, Bādārayaṇa employs the concept of *aṁśa*, which if correctly understood, means an integral part of *Viśiṣṭa* Reality, as Rāmānuja correctly interprets. This explanation is in full accord with the *sūtra* in which it is stated that according to Kāśakṛtsna, *Paramātman* abides in *jīva* (*Avasthiteḥ iti Kāśakṛtsnaḥ*). Both Śaṁkara and Rāmānuja acknowledge that this is the view of Bādarāyaṇa. The *Antaryāmi Brāhmaṇa* also supports it. According to this, Brahman abides in the *jīvātman* as its *Antaryāmin (ya ātmani tiṣṭhan)*. In view of it there is intimate relationship between *jīva* and *Brahman* and the two as inherently related is regarded as one.

Madhva offers an altogether different interpretation for this *sūtra*. The *jīva*, according to him, is an *aṁśa* of Brahman in the sense that it has close resemblance to Brahman in respect of its essential characteristics of knowledge (*jñāna)* and bliss (*ānanda)* and that its very existence is sustained by Brahman. It is not a physical part but it is a reflection (*pratibimba)* in the sense of likeness (*tat-sadṛśa)* to Brahman and also dependence on it (*tad-adhīnatva)*. Adopting this meaning for *aṁśa,* Madhva interprets *nānāvyapadeśa* to mean that *jīva* is described in the Scriptural texts in different ways such as father, son, brother, friend etc. The other word *'anyathā'* is interpreted to mean that *jīva* is not the source of sustenance but on the contrary, it is the one which derives its sustenance from Brahman. While there is nothing wrong in offering a different meaning for the *sūtra,* the explanation offered by Madhva does not appear relevant in the context of explaining the nature of *jīva's* relation to Brahman by Bādarāyaṇa in terms of *aṁśa* for the purpose of reconciling *abheda* and *bheda Śrutis* which explicitly state that *jīva* is different from Brahman and also non-different from it. Besides, this *sūtra* mentioning *jīva* as *aṁśa* of Brahman, according to the explanation of Madhva, would have no bearing on the *sūtra 'avasthiteḥ iti Kāśakṛtsnaḥ'* in which the relation of Brahman to *jīva* is explained by Kāśakṛtsna in terms of permanent *avasthiti* of *Paramātman* in *jīva* on the authority of the *Antaryāmi Brāhmaṇa.* The *aṁśa* and *aṁśī* relationship in the sense explained by Madhva as *bimba* and *pratibimba* does not explain in the strict logical sense the intimate relation between *jīva* and Brahman. The term *pratibimba* normally denotes a reflection of an object in another media, like the moon in the waves of water or the face in a mirror. Such a concept of *pratibimba* which is adopted by Śaṁkara affects the eternal character (*nityatva)* of *jīva,* which goes against the Upaniṣadic text and the *Vedānta-sūtra* affirming that *jīvātman* is *nitya. Sādṛśya* or similarity between two objects such as the moon and the face does not denote a relation. The dependence of one on the other (*tadadhīna*) like the jar on the floor also does not convey an inherent relation because such a relation is separable. The word *avasthiti* employed by *Vedānta-sūtra* on the basis of *Antaryāmi Brāhmaṇa* refers to a permanent and inseparable relationship between *jīva* and Brahman, as explained by Rāmānuja. The Scriptural texts speak both difference and non-difference between *jīva* and Brahman in the primary sense as pointed out by Bādarāyaṇa in the *sūtra* by using the term *'vyapadeśa'*. Śaṁkara also has to admit it. But Śaṁkara attempts to reconcile the conflict by according lesser validity to the *bheda Śrutis* and affirms that *abheda Śrutis* are more valid and as such the *jīva* and Brahman are identical. Madhva, on the contrary, gives greater importance to the *bheda Śrutis* and lesser importance to the *abheda Śrutis* and interprets the *abheda* suggested in these texts in a figurative sense. Further, Madhva has to acknowledge that the word *vyapadeśa* used by the *sūtrakāra* clearly indicates that the difference and non-difference mentioned in the Upaniṣadic texts are to be taken in their primary sense. The only way of reconciling these two concepts in respect of *jīva* and Brahman in the primary sense is to regard *jīva* as *aṁśa* of Brahman. The term *aṁśa* can be understood in several senses, as pointed out by Vedānta Deśika in the *Adhikaraṇa-sārāvalī*.[38] But none of these including what is stated by Madhva is hardly satisfactory. The only explanation which is philosophically and epistemologically justified is the one offered by Rāmānuja viz., an integral part in the sense of an essential characteristic of a *viśiṣṭa dravya* or qualified entity (*viśiṣṭa vastunaḥ ekadeśatvam)*. The implication of this explanation is that *jīva* is an integral part of Brahman since Brahman is inseparably related to *jīva,* similar to the physical body is inseparably related to its soul. Brahman, according to Viśiṣṭādvaita Vedānta, is *ajaḍa dravya* or spiritual *viśiṣṭa tattva.* It is always associated with *cit (jīvas)* and *acit* (cosmic matter) both in the state prior to creation and also in the state after creation of the universe by the *Saṁkalpa* of *Paramātman.*[39] This is evident from the Upaniṣadic texts teaching the causation of the universe. In the Chāndogya text *'Sadeva saumya idam agra āsīt – ekameva advitīyam'*, the term *sat* implies that Brahman is the material cause of the universe, since in the passage it is stated that the same *Sat* wills to become many. What serves as the material cause, should be a *viśiṣṭa tattva,* that is, it is to be associated with *cit* and *acit* in its subtle form. Otherwise, it cannot become many by its will. The Reality as pure *Viśeṣya*, as Advaitin conceives, cannot serve as *upādāna kāraṇa*, unless the cosmic principle of *māyā* is introduced to explain the evolution of the universe as an illusory manifestation of Brahman (*Vivarta*). But the doctrine of *māyā* is not supported by the Upaniṣad and the *Vedānta-sūtras*. It is therefore more appropriate and logically justified to accept Brahman as a *Viśiṣṭa tattva* and account for the causation of universe, as taught in the Upaniṣads. Hence the relation of *jīva* to Brahman as explained in the *Aṁśādhikaraṇa* by Vedānta Deśika is philosophically more sound than that offered by Śaṁkara and Madhva. As will be seen presently, the *aṁśa-aṁśī bhāva* admitted by Rāmānuja on the basis of the *Vedānta-sūtra* is the same as the *śarīra-śarīrī* relation advanced by Rāmānuja in respect of Brahman and universe in the *Ahikuṇḍalādhikaraṇa*. Such a relation accommodates both difference and non-difference between Brahman and the other two ontological entities – *jīva* and *jagat*. There is also difference between Brahman and *jīva* because the two by virtue of their intrinsic nature are of different character. The two are also non-different in the sense that Brahman as inherently related to *jīva* since it abides in *jīva*, as declared in the *Antaryāmī Brahmana*, is one as a *viśiṣṭa* entity. This kind of relation is also logically justified. A substance as a complex entity having two aspects – substrate and the quality which inheres in it, is one but the substrate and quality by their very nature are different. The essential quality of a substance is inseparably related to it. The mere substrate (*viśeṣya*) without quality is inconceivable. Brahman as a qualified spiritual substance (*ajaḍa dravya*) is one but the qualities and the substrate in which they inhere are different. A pure substance devoid of any qualities is non-existent, like the sky flower according to Vedānta Deśika.[40]

V. The Causal Relation of Universe to Brahman

Now we come to the examination of the causal relationship

between Brahman and *jagat*. This subject has received special attention in the *Vedānta-sūtras*, since the main objective of the first and second *adhyāya* of *Brahma-sūtra* is to establish the central thesis of Vedānta viz., Brahman is the sole cause of the universe (*jagatkāraṇa*). Bādarāyaṇa at the outset defines Brahman as that which is the Cause of the creation, sustenance and dissolution of the universe. It is regarded as the material cause (*upādāna-kāraṇa*) of the universe on the analogy of the lump of clay and the products made out of it, which is cited in the Chāndogya Upaniṣad in connection with the causation of the universe. The *Prakṛtyadhikaraṇa* deals with this subject. This is discussed fully in chapter 5. As we have pointed out earlier, it is important to admit that Brahman is not merely the *nimitta-kāraṇa* of the universe as the Seśvara Sāṁkhya (*yoga* school) and Madhva maintains but it is also the *upādāna-kāraṇa* of the universe. All possible objections raised against this theory by the Sāṁkhyas and in particular the Vaiśeṣikas for whom *kāraṇa* and *kārya* are absolutely different, have been fully answered by Bādarāyaṇa in the *adhikaraṇas* of first *pāda* of the second *adhyāya*. The *Ārambhaṇādhikaraṇa* is of special significance since it proves that *jagat* as *kārya* and Brahman as the causal substance are non-distinct (*ananya*) in the sense that what is regarded as *kārya* such as pot is only a modified form of the clay which is the causal substance. These two *adhikaraṇas* – *Prakṛtyadhikaraṇa* and *Ārambhaṇādhikaraṇa* establish not only the causal relationship between Brahman and *jagat* but also that *jagat* as the effect is non-distinct (*ananya*) from Brahman. The *sūtra* on this subject reads: '*Tad-ananyatvam ārambhaṇa śabdādibhyaḥ*'[41]. Thus according to Bādarāyaṇa, though Brahman and *jagat* as cause and effect are distinct, they are also non-distinct in the sense that it is the same Brahman as associated with *cit* and *acit* in their subtle form prior to creation becomes Brahman as associated with *cit* and *acit* in their gross form after the creation of the universe by the *saṁkalpa* of Brahman. This is the considered view of

Bādarāyaṇa, if the *sūtras* of *Prakṛtyādhikaraṇa* and *Ārambhaṇadhikaraṇa* are interpreted correctly without imposing the accepted doctrines or pre-conceived postulates, as Śaṁkara and Madhva have done. By introducing the *vivarta-vāda* or the theory of illusory manifestation of an object due to *avidyā*, similar to the shell appearing as silver due to ignorance of the shell, Śaṁkara does not offer a satisfactory explanation of the causal relationship between Brahman and the *jagat*. The *vivarta-vāda* would be sustainable if the theory of *avidyā* as conceived by Śaṁkara is proved. But the doctrine of *avidyā* has no basis either in the Upaniṣads or the *Vedānta-sūtra*. It is also riddled with contradictions when subjected to logical analysis as pointed out both by Rāmānuja and Madhva. Besides, *jagat* as an illusory manifestation of Brahman would be reduced to the position of an illusory entity. But according to the Upanisads and the *Vedānta-sūtra*, *jagat* is a real ontological entity and is different from Brahman, as it has been brought into existence by Brahman.

The *Ahikuṇḍalādhikaraṇa* included in the second *pāda* of third *adhyāya* specifically discusses, according to Rāmānuja, the question of relation of the universe to Brahman in terms of *viśeṣaṇa* (attribute) and *viśeṣya* (substance). That is, *jagat* which is caused by Brahman is related to it in the same way as an attribute to the substance or the body to the soul (*śarīra-śarīrī bhāva*). We have presented the details of this *adhikaraṇa* in the chapter 5 on the universe and Brahman[42]. Bādarāyaṇa introduces three *sūtras*[43] in which he refers to the different views on the nature of the relation of Brahman to the universe in terms of *bheda-abheda* or difference-cum-non-difference and *abheda* or non-difference, by citing two illustrations: a) serpent and its coil (*ahikuṇḍala*) and b) the luminous body and its light (*prakāśāśraya* and *prakāśa*). According to the first view, the universe is regarded as a special form (*samsthāna viśeṣa)* of Brahman, as coil is of the serpent. The implication of it, as explained by Rāmānuja, is that Brahman is non-different from the universe, just as the coil is non-different from the serpent. This is a prima facie theory. The second view is that there is difference and non-difference between Brahman and the universe, just as the light and its substrate (the luminous body) are both different and also non-different since both are of the same nature. This is also regarded as a prima facie theory. The third view upheld by Bādarāyaṇa is that Brahman is related to the universe in the same way as an attribute is related to its substance or the body to the soul. This is the explanation offered in connection with the relation of *jīva* to Brahman in terms of *aṁśa* and *aṁsī* in the *Aṁśādhikaraṇa*. That is, the universe is also regarded as an *aṁśa* or an integral part of Brahman since it does not have a separate existence apart from Brahman as in the case of the *jīva* (*jīvavat pṛthaksiddhy-anarha viśeṣaṇatvena acid vastuno brahmāṁśam)*[44]. This explanation is logically justified and also supported by the Upaniṣad. According to the *Antaryāmi Brahmana,* the universe is the *śarīra* of Brahman in the technical sense viz., that it is necessarily and always supported and controlled by Brahman. This theory accommodates both difference and non-difference from different stand points, difference as *śarīra* and *śarīrī* and non-difference as *śarirī* (Brahman) being integrally related to the *śarīra* (universe and also *jīva*).

The above explanation is justified because Brahman as a *Viśiṣṭa* Reality (*viśiṣṭa tattva)* is inherently related to both *cit* and *acit* at all times. As a *viśiṣṭa tattva* it is one (*eka*) but at the same time it is also different from *cit* and *acit,* since the latter are different in nature from the former. Such a kind of relation between Brahman and universe and also Brahman and *jīva* cannot be admitted either by Śaṁkara or Madhva. For Śaṁkara Brahman is absolutely one Reality devoid of all differences both external and internal with the denial of the real existence of *jīvas* and *jagat*. If three ontological real entities are not accepted, the question of the relation of Brahman and *jīva* or Brahman and *jagat* in the proper sense does not arise. This teaching is against the Upaniṣad and also the *Vedānta-sūtras.* Absolute Monism suffers from this drawback. The term *ananyatva* employed by Bādarāyaṇa to account for the causal relation of Brahman and *jagat* is interpreted by Śaṁkara as non-difference in the sense that Brahman alone exists and the *jagat* does not really exist. This is not the intention of Bādarāyaṇa. The Chāndogya Upaniṣad equates Brahman with *jagat* in the statement *'sarvaṁ khalu idaṁ Brahma'*. This equation by negating the second principle (*jagat*) is not philosophically sound. Similarly, the *aṁśa* and *aṁśī bhāva* mentioned by Bādarāyaṇa in connection with *jīva's* relation to Brahman cannot be sustained logically unless the reality of the two ontological principles is accepted.

In the case of Madhva, though he admits all the three ontological entities as real, he regards that all the three are absolutely different. He cannot therefore explain a satisfactory relationship between Brahman and *jīva* as well as Brahman and *jagat*. As pointed out earlier, the *aṁśa* and *aṁśī bhāva* as *bimba* and *pratibimba* in a technical sense as *sādṛśya* and *tadadhīnatva* does not provide a satisfactory relationship between *jīva* and Brahman. Similarly, the non-difference between Brahman and *jagat* taken in a secondary and figurative sense is also not a satisfactory logical relationship. He does not also acknowledge that the *Vakyānvayādhikaraṇa* and *Ahikuṇḍalādhikaraṇa* deal with the subject of relationship between *jīva* and Brahman and *jagat* and Brahman respectively. Both these *adhikaraṇas* are named as *Samākarṣādhikaraṇa* and *Ubhayavyapadeśādhikaraṇa* respectively and interpreted in favour of different theories which do not seem to be relevant to the context in which the *sūtras* are introduced by Bādarāyaṇa.

From the foregoing discussion of three major ontological theories and connected issues regarding Brahman as *saviśeṣa* or *nirviśeṣa*, Brahman as *upādāna* or *nimitta-kāraṇa*, the relation of *jīva* to Brahman as *bheda* or *abheda* and the status of *jagat* as *satya* or *mithyā* and also the nature of its relation to Brahman, the explanations provided by the Viśiṣṭādvaita Vedānta, as stated in the *Adhikaraṇa-sārāvalī*, are philosophically sounder than those offered by Advaita Vedānta and the Dvaita Vedānta. Vedānta Deśika is therefore justified in claiming that among the schools of Vedānta, the Viśiṣṭādvaita Vedānta as expounded by Rāmānuja deserves to be regarded as a sound system of philosophy or *Darśana*. As stated by him in the *Tattva-muktā-kalāpa*[45], the merit of this system lies in respect of following points: 1) It does not question, unlike the Advaita, the validity of what is proved by perception (*pratyakṣa*) as an important *pramāṇa (dṛṣṭe apahnatyabhāvāt)*. 2) It adopts logic or reasoning to a limited extent as supplemental to what is said in *Śruti*, unlike Naiyāyikas and Madhvas (*anumiti viṣaye lāghavasyānurodhāt*). 3) In matters which have to be proved only on the authority of the Scriptural texts, it accords equal validity to all the texts, by reconciling the apparent conflicts, as in the case of *abheda* Śrutis and *bheda Śrutis* without denial of either texts (*sastreṇaiva avaseye vihativirahite nāstikatva prahāṇāt)*. This system of Vedānta which is developed on the basis of an ancient tradition[46] is therefore unassailable to the criticisms of other schools of thought and can be regarded as philosophically sound. (*akhilatamaḥ karṣaṇam darśanam naḥ)*.

---

1. *See* AS verses 153, 268,290, 430 and 552
2. The only direct criticism made by Vedānta Deśika against Madhva is regarding the theory of *ānanda-tāratamya*. He states in the *Rahasyatrayasāra* that Ānanda Tīrtha (Madhva) overlooked the *sāmya śruti* or the Upaniṣadic text speaking of equal status of *jīva* with Brahman in the state of mukti by advocating the theory of the gradation in respect of the experience of *ānanda* by *mukta jīva*. See RTS – chapter-22.
3. *See Śatadūṣaṇī*, opening verse.
4. *See* AS. Verse 307. Also chapter 8 p 205
5. AS verse 153. *adau jijñāsatā āstām bahuvihatihatā*
6. SD vada 2
7. AS verse 153. *nirviśeṣaikya pakṣe mukhyaikṣādyaih svadharmaiḥ prakṛti-puruṣato bheda vādaḥ katham syāt*
8. *See* AS verses 78, 129. *See* also chapter 2 pp.58-59. and chapter 3, pp.60-61
9. *See* Padayojana on verse 78

10. *See* chapter 3 section V
11. *Ibid* section VII
12. *Ibid* section IX
13. *See* chapter 8, section 1
14. VS 1-2-22
15. *See* chapter 3 section IX
16. V.S I-3-9 *akṣaramambarāntadhṛteḥ*. V.S 1-3-10 *sā ca praśāsanāt*
17. VS III-2-11
18. III-2-22 acc. to SB
19. *See* SB III-2-11
20. *See* chapter 8 section 1
21. *See* AS. Verse 290
22. *See* Philosopy of Vedāntasūtra : Chapter 4 , pp 60-64
23. *See* Philosopy of the Upaniṣads : pp.11-12
24. VS I-4-23 acc. to RB and I-4-24 acc. to SB. *See* also chapter 5, section 1
25. Pāṇini Mahābhāṣya I-4-30
26. VS I-4-26 and 27
27. *See* Ārambhaṇādhikaraṇa in chapter 5 section 2
28. *See* Subala. Up.II-1
29. Tait. Up. III-1.
30. VS II-1-27.
31. VS II-1-28
32. *See* chapter 5 section IV
33. VS II-I-22
34. *See* AS verse 198. *See* also chapter 6 pp. *See* also FVV p.390.
35. VS 1-4-19. *See* also chapter 4 section VI.
36. VS 1-4-20 *pratijñā siddheḥ liṅgam āśmarathyaḥ*
    VS 1-4-21 *utkramiṣyata evaṁ bhāvāt iti auḍulomiḥ*
    VS 1-4-22 *avastriteḥ iti kāśakṛtsnaḥ*
37. VS II-3-42. *See* also chapter 7 section V
38. *See* verses 245 –249. *See* also chapter 7 section V
39. RB II-3-18 *ataḥ sarvadā cid-acid-vastu-śarīratayā tatprakāraṁ bramha*
40. *See* Śatadūṣaṇī vāda 33. *Tasyāḥ sarvamāna anāghratatvena khapuṣpamāṇatvāt*. *See* also RB. I-1-1 p. 114-115
41. VS II-1-15. See also chapter 5 section II.
42. *See* chapter 5, section III.
43. VS III-2-26 and III-2-27, III-2-28
44. *See* R.B. III-2-28
45. *See* TMK verse 496. *Dṛṣṭe apahnatyabhāvāt anumiti viṣaye lāghavasyānurodhāt*
    Śāstreṇaivāvaseye vihativirahite nāstikatva prahāṇāt;
    Nathopajñam pravṛttaṁ bahubhir upacitaṁ yāmuneya prabandhaiḥ
    Trātam samyag-yatīndraiḥ idam akhilatamaḥ karṣaṇam darśanaṁ naḥ;
46. *See* Vedārthasaṁgraha – p.100 *śiṣṭa-parigṛhīta-purātana veda vedānta vyākhyāna*. *See* also introduction pp. xx.

APPENDIX-I

THE NAMES OF ADHIKARAṆAS

with brief description of the subjects covered in them in the order presented in the *Adhikaraṇa-sārāvalī.*

Adhyāya 1- Samanvayādhyāya or the chapter devoted to establish the correlation of the various texts of the Upaniṣads with Brahman as the primary cause of the universe (jagatkāraṇa).

Pāda 1

1. Jijñāsādhikaraṇa (VS. I-1-1)

It justifies the need and importance of philosophic enquiry into the nature of Brahman by a spiritual aspirant after he has completed the stdy of *pūrva-mīmāṁsā,* which deals with the ritualistic portion of the Vedas and realized the impermanent value of the fruits achieved by the Vedic rituals and the eternal value of the Supreme Goal to be attained by the study of Vedānta.

2. Janmādyadhikaraṇa (VS I-1-2)

It discusses the soundness of the definition of Brahman offered by the Upaniṣads as the oprimary cause of the creation, sustenance and dissolution of the universe.

3. Śāstrayonitvādhikaraṇa (VS I-1-3)

It establishes that *śāstra* or the sacred texts is the only pramāṇa for knowing Brahman.

4. Samanvayādhikaraṇa (VS I-1-4)

It establishes that all the Upaniṣadic texts are purportful since they teach about Brahman as the Supreme Goal of attainment.

5. Īkṣatyadhikaraṇa (VS I-1-5 to VS. I-1-12)

It is devoted to prove that the term *sat* referred to in the Chāndogya Upanisad as the cause of the universe is not the *pradhāna* or the primordial cosmic matter admitted by the Sāṁkhya, but it is the Brahman, since the function of "resolving to create" the universe cannot be ascribed to the non-sentient cosmic matter.

6. Ānandamayādhikaraṇa (VS I-1-13 to VS I-1-20)

It discusses the issue whether the description of *Ātman* as *ānandamaya* in the Taittrīya Upaniṣad (II-5) is *Jīvātman* or *Paramātman* and affirms that it is Brahman, since it is essentially constituted of bliss par excellence.

7. Antarādhikaraṇa (VS I-1-21 to VS I-1-22)

It establishes that the *puruṣa* which resides in the orbit of the sun and also in the eye as described in the two passages in the Chāndogya Upaniṣad (I-1-6 and I-7-5)in terms of physical body with golden colors and eyes similar to the lotus flower is not the exalted *Jīvātman,* but the *Paramātman,* who is endowed with lustrous spiritual body not caused by *karma.*

8. Ākāśādhikaraṇa (VS 1-1-23)

It discusses that the concept of *ākāśa* referred to in the Chāndogya passage (I-9-1) does not denote the ethereal space but Brahman.

9. Prāṇādhikaraṇa (VS I-1-24)

It explains that the term *prāṇa* employed in the Chāndogya passage (I-11-5) is not the vital breath but Brahman.

10. Jyotiradhikaraṇa (VS I-1-25)

It explains that the terms Jyotis mentioned in the Chāndogya passage (III-13-7) does not refer to the physical light radiated by the sun and other luminaries but Brahman which is the Supreme Spiritual Light, three quarters of which cover the immortal higher domain.

11. Indra-prāṇādhikaraṇa (VS I-1-29 to I-1-32)

It establishes that the concept of *Indra-Prāṇa* mentioned in the passage of Kauṣītakī Upaniṣad as the object of meditation does not refer to the *Jīvātman* of Indra but Brahman as the *antarātmā* of Indra because the word *prāṇa* referred to here is correlated with the terms such as *ānanda, ajara* and *amṛta* stated in the later part of the passage.

Pāda 2

12. Sarvatra-prasiddhyadhikaraṇa (VS I-2-1 to I-2-8)

It discusses the implication of the statement of the Chāndogya passage "All this is Brahman" and the meditation enjoined on it as *tajjalān* etc. and brings out the important characteristic of Brahman as the Self of everything in the universe (*sarvātmā*).

13. Attrādhikaraṇa (VS I-2-9 to I-2-12)

It discusses the implication of the description of the ontological principle as the devourer *(attā)* of the entire universe in the Kaṭha Upaniṣad and brings out the characteristic of Brahman as *Saṁhartā* or the cause of the dissolution of the universe.

14. Antarādhikaraṇa (VS I-2-13 to I-2-18)

It discusses the implication of the Chāndogya passage in which *puruṣa* is stated to be abiding in the eye and affirms that this *akṣipuruṣa* is the very Brahman because it is described as *ātmā, amṛta* and *abhaya* and also as characterized by infinite joy.

15. Antaryāmy-adhikaraṇa (VS I-2-19 to I-2-21)

It discusses the significance of the *Antaryāmī Brāhmaṇa* which narrates how a higher principle abides in all entities in the universe and affirms that it is *Paramātman* (Brahman) who indwells in all beings including *jīvātmā* and controls them from within.

16. Adṛśyatvādi-guṇkādhikarana (VS I-2-22 to I-2-24)

It discusses the issue whether the metaphysical principal termed as *akṣara* which is described by the Muṇḍaka Upaniṣad as *adreśya, agrāhya* etc. refers to Brahman or *jīvātman* or *prakṛti* and establishes that *akṣara* qualified by negative attributes is Brahman since in the same passage it is stated as *sarvajña* and *sarvavit.*

17. Vaiśvānarādhikaraṇa (VS I-2-25 to VS I-2-33)

It discusses the issue whether *vaiśvānara ātmā* referred to in the Chāndogya Upaniṣad on which meditation is prescribed is Brahman or *Jīvātman* or some other entity and affirms that it is Brahman because of the mention of certain essential characteristics such as its cosmic form.

Pāda 3

18. Dyubhvādy-adhikaraṇa (VS I-3-1 to I-3-6)

It discusses the issue whether that which is described in the statement of the Muṇḍaka Upaniṣad as *āyatana* or the support of the heaven, earth, sky etc. which are woven in it, is *jīvātman* or *Paramātman* and establishes that it is Brahman, since the concerned passage *employs* the term *Ātman* which is regarded as *setu* or that which enables the person to attain immortality (*amṛta*).

19. Bhūmādhikaraṇa (VS I-3-7 to I-3-8)

It discusses the question whether the term *Bhūmā* mentioned in the Chāndogya Upaniṣad (VII-15-1) on which meditation is enjoined is *Jīvātman* or Brahman and establishes that it refers to Brahman since it is regarded as *satya* which is greater than *prāṇa* (*Jīvātman*) and also described as infinitely blissful (*niratīsaya-sukha-rūpa*).

20. Akṣarādhikaraṇa (VS I-3-9 to I-3-11)

It discusses the issue whether the metaphysical principle *akṣara* described in the Bṛhadāraṇyaka Upaniṣad in negative terms such as *asthūla, anaṇu* etc. is Brahman or other ontological entities such as *pradhāna* and *jīvātman* and concludes that it is Brahman since it is stated in the Upaniṣad that it is the supporter of the entire universe through its commanding power (*praśāsana*).

21. Ikaṣatikarmādhikaraṇa (VS I-3-12)

It discusses the issue whether the *Paramapuruṣa* referred to in the Praśna Upaniṣad as the object of meditation through the media of syllable '*Aum*' with all the three letters and who is also the object of realization (*Īkṣaṇa*), is Brahman or Hiraṇyagarbha and concludes that it is Brahman which is the object of enjoyment for the liberated soul.

22. Daharādhikaraṇa (VS I-3-13 to I-3.22)

It discusses the question whether the concept of *daharākāśa* or the subtle space within one's heart mentioned in the Chāndogya passage as the object of meditation along with certain attributes refers to Brahman or some other entity such as *bhūtākāśa* (ethereal space) or *jīvātman* and comes to the conclusion that it is Brahman since the *daharākāśa* is described as the supporter of the entire universe and that is it also free from all defilements (*apahata pāpmā*).

23. Pramitādhikaraṇa (VS I-3-23-24)

It discusses whether the *puruṣa* abiding in one's heart which is limited to the size of a thumb of a human being (*anguṣṭha-mātrapuruṣa*) as mentioned in the Kaṭha Upaniṣad (II-4-12) refers to Brahman or *Jīvātman* and affirms that it denotes Brahman since it is described as the Ruler of the past and future.

24. Devatādhikaraṇa (VS I-3-25 to I-3-29)

It points out after discussing the view of Jaimini, that even *devatās* are eligible for meditation since they too have the knowledge of Brahman and possess the body and the sense organs.

25. Madhvādhikaraṇa (VS I-3-30 to I-3-32)

It discusses the question whether the special deities such as *vasus* etc. referred to in the Chāndogya passage (III-1 to 11) dealing with *Madhuvidyā* are eligible for meditation and affirms that they too meditate on Brahman as their *Antaryāmin*.

26. Apaśūdrādhikaraṇa (VS I-3-33 to I-3-41)

It discusses the implication of the statement made in the passage of Chāndogya containing a dialogue between sage Raikva and Jānaśruti, a *kṣatriya* who lacks Brahman knowledge and who is addressed as *śūdra* and states in this connection that *śūdras* are not eligible for *Brahm-vidyā* since they are prohibited by *Śruti* from studying Vedas.

27. Arthāntaratvādhikaraṇa (VS I-3-42 to I-3-44)

It discusses the question whether *ākāśa* described in the Chāndogya Upaniṣad as *nāma-rūpakartā* or that which performs the function of giving names and form to the created objects is *muktātmā* or *Paramātmā* and affirms that it denotes Brahman since it is stated in the Upaniṣad that Brahman along with the *jīva* enters into the created entities and assigns names and form to them.

Pāda 4

28. Ānumānikādhikaraṇa (VS I-4-1 to I-4-7)

It discusses the claim of the Sāṁkhyas that *prakṛti* termed as *avyakta* in the Kaṭha Upaniṣad (I-3-11) is the cause of the universe and rejects it as untenable since the term *avyakta* contextually denotes the physical body.

29. Camasādhikaraṇa (VS I-4-8 to I-4-10)

It points out that the term 'Ajā' employed in Śvetāśvatara Upaniṣad which is construed in favour of Sāṁkhya theory of *prakṛti* as the cause of the universe does not support their claim since it is a general term without any specification, like *camasa*. a vessel used in the *yāga*.

30. Saṁkhyopasaṅgrahādhikaraṇa (VS I-4-11 t I-4-13)

It points out that the terms *pañca-pañca janāḥ* employed in the Bṛhadāraṇyaka Upaniṣad (VI-4-17) do not imply the twenty five categories of Sāṁkhya theory of *prakṛti* and its evolutes.

31. Kāraṇatvādhikaraṇa (VS I-4-14 and I-4-15)

It explains that the terms *avyakta* and *asat* used in the Brhadāraṇyaka and Taittirīya Upaniṣad respectively do not refer to the *prakṛti* of the Sāṁkhyas but Brahman as qualified with the unmanifest universe in the state of dissolution.

32. Jagadvācitāvādhikaraṇa (VS I-4-16 to I-4-18)

It discusses the implication of the terms *puruṣa* and its *karma* mentioned in the Kauṣītakī Upaniṣad (IV-18) and clarifies that *karma* denotes the *jagat* which is created by Brahman (*Kriyata iti karma*).

33. Vākyānvayādhikaraṇa (VS I-4-19 to I-4-22)

It discusses the question whether the term '*Ātman*' referred in the passage of Maitreyī Brāhmaṇa (Br. Up IV-4-6) discusses *jīvātman* or *Paramātman* (Brahman) and establishes that it is *Paramātman* who alone is to be meditated upon for attaining immortality.

34. Prakṛtyadhikaraṇa (VS I-4-23 to I-4-28)

It examines critically the theory of Seśvara Sāṁkhya (Yoga) that Īśvara is only the *nimitta kāraṇa* of the universe and establishes conclusively that Brahman is also the *upādāna kāraṇa* of the universe through the process of *pariṇāma* without affecting its *svarūpa* as *nirvikāra*.

35. Sarvavyākhyānādhikaraṇa (VS I-4-29)

It attempts to show that the Upaniṣadic statements which prima facie speak of the higher celestial deities such as Hiraṇyagarbha, Śiva, Rudra, Indra etc. as the cause of the universe are not opposed to the central theory of Vedānta viz. that Brahman as the Supreme Deity is the cause of the universe, if these texts are properly interpreted with due consideration to the context in which they are made and the principles of interpretation adopted in respect of the other passages.

Adhyāya II- Avirodhādhyāya or the chapter devoted to prove the soundness of the Vedānta doctrine of Brahman as the sole cause of the universe.

Pāda 1: Smṛti pāda dealing with the objections of Sāṁkhya and other Schools.

36. Smṛtyadhikaraṇa (VS II-1-1 and 2)

The *Kapila Smṛti* cannot be accepted as the authoritative source for determining the Vedānta doctrine of Brahman as the cause of the universe.

37. Yogapratyukty-adhikaraṇa (VS II-1-3)

The *Yoga Smṛti* is also unauthoritative for determining the purport of the Upaniṣadic texts dealing with the causation of the universe.

38. Vilakṣaṇatvādhikaraṇa (VS II-1-4 and 5)

In reply to the objection of the Sāṁkhyas that there cannot be any causal relationship between Brahman and the universe, since the two are of different nature, it points out that the causal substance and effect brought out of it need not be of the same nature.

39. Śiṣṭaparigrahādhikaraṇa (VS II-1-13)

The other schools of thought such as the Naiyāyikas, Jainas, Buddhists who subscribe to the theory of *paramāṇus* as the cause of the universe stand refuted since they are also opposed to the Upaniṣads and also suffer from logical inconsistency.

40. Bhoktṛāpatty-adhikaraṇa (VS II-1-14)

It attempts to prove that Brahman is not subject to the experience of pleasure and pain even though it is associated with the universe as its body.

41. Ārambhaṇādhikaraṇa (VS II-1-15 to II-1-20)

By way of refuting the theory of Vaiśeṣikas who maintain that cause and effect are absolutely different, it establishes the causal relationship between Brahman as cause and *jagat* as its effect on the ground that the two are non-distinct *(ananya)* in the sense that the effect is only a modified form of the causal sustance.

42. Itaravyapadeśādhikaraṇa (VS II-I-21 to II-1-23)

It refutes the objection of the Sāṁkhyas that Brahman being non-different from jīvas, the universe created by it is undersirable to it, since such a uviverse is full of suffering.

43. Upasaṁhārādhikaraṇa (VS II-1-24 and 25)

It attempts to show that Brahman is not in need of any accessory for creation of the universe.

44. Kṛtsnaprasakty-adhikaraṇa (VS II-1-26 to II-1-31)

It attempts to meet the objection that Brahman as the material cause of the universe would be subjected to total transformation into the universe, or alternatively if a part of Brahman undergoes modification, it would violate the Scriptural text speaking of Brahman as *niravayava* or devoid of parts on the basis of the explanation that Brahman possesses *vicitra śakti* or extraordinary power to create the universe without affecting its *svarūpa.*

45. Prayojanatvādhikarana (VS II-1-32 to II-1-34)

The objection that there is no useful purpose served by the creation of the universe which is filled with suffering is answered by explaining that the creation of the universe is a mere sport to the *Īśvara* (Brahman) and the creator is also not subject to cruelty or partiality since the individuals are created in a accordance with their *karma.*

Pada 2: Tarkapāda dealing with the logical untenability of the theories of other schools of thought regarding cosmic creation.

46. Racanānupapatty-adhikaraṇa (VS II-2-1 to II-2-9)

It is devoted to prove the untenability of the Sāṁkhya theory of *prakṛti* as the cause of the universe without the control of a sentient being.

47. Mahad-dhīrghādhikaraṇa (VS II-2-10 to 16)

It examines the theory of the Vaiśeṣikas who trace the origin of the universe to the *paramāṇus* and proves its untenability.

48. Samudāyādhikaraṇa (VS II-2-17 to II-2-26)

It is devoted to the refutation of the theories of Vaibhāṣikas and Sautrāntika Buddhists who also trace the origin of the universe to the *paramāṇus* and to prove their unsoundness.

49. Upalabdhy-adhikaraṇa (VS II-2-27 to 29)

It examines critically the views of the *Yogācāra* school of Buddhism, which does not accept the existence of external objects other than *vijñāna* or mental series, and proves their logical inconsistency.

50. Sarvathānupapatty-adhikaraṇa (VS II-2-30)

It critically examines the theory of *śūnyavāda* of the Mādhyamika Buddhists, according to whom *tattva* or what is considered to be a real entity is absolutely indeterminable, and rejects it on the ground that it is riddled with self-contradiction.

51. Asambhavādhikaraṇa (VS II-2-31 to II-2-34)

It is mainly devoted to prove the untenablility of the Jaina theory of *saptabhaṅgī* or seven fold formula and also the philosophical untenability of other doctrines advanced by the Jainas.

52. Pāśupatādhikaraṇa (VS II-3-35 to II-2-38)

It is devoted to the refutation of the school of Pāśupatas on the ground that their philosophical theories are unsound and their religious practices are also opposed to the Vedic teachings.

53. Utpatty-asambhavādhikaraṇa (VS II-2-39 to II-2-42)

It is mainly devoted to defend the validity of the system of *pāñcarātra* by setting aside a few criticisms against its teachings and in particular the origin of *Jīva*.

Pada 3: Viyat pāda dealing with ontological status of the cosmological entities and jīvātman.

54. Viyadadhikaraṇa (VS II-3-1 to II-3-9)

It discusses the question whether or not *viyat* or ether has an origin (*utpatti*) and affirms that it is an evolute of *prakṛti* and so also *vāyu* etc. since they are brought into existence by Brahman.

55. Tejodhikaraṇa (VS II-3-10 to II-3-13)

It discusses the process of evolution of each evolute in a particular order and clarifies that an evolute by itself does not cause the subsequent evolute but on the other hand, Brahman as inherent in an evolute that causes the next one.

56. Ātmādhikaraṇa (VS II-3-18)

It establishes that *jīvātman* is not subject to origin unlike *viyat* but it is eternal, as declared by the Upaniṣadic texts.

57. Jñānādhikaraṇa (VS II-3-19 to II-3-32)

It establishes that *jīvātman* is not merely of the nature of knowledge (*Jñāna-svarūpa*) but more importantly it is the knowing subject (*jñātṛ*). It is also *aṇu* or monadic in character and not *vibhu* or all-pervasive.

58. Kartṛadhikaraṇa (VS II-3-33 to II-3-39)

It establishes that *jīvātman* is the agent of action and refutes the theory that *kartṛtva* belonging to *buddhi* is superimposed on it.

59. Parāyāttādhikaraṇa (VS II-23-40 to 41)

It states that though the *kartṛtva* of *jīva* is caused by *Paramātman*, *jīva* as *kartā* has some freedom to act on its own in respect of the initial action in accordance with the influence of the past *karma*.

60. Aṁśādhikaraṇa (VS II-3-42 to II-3-52)

It discusses the relation of *jīvātman* to Brahman in terms of difference (*bheda*) and non-difference (*abheda*) and explains it as *aṁśa* of Brahman in the sense that it is an integral part of Brahman.

Pada 4: Prāṇapāda dealing with the nature of *Indriyas* and prāṇa

61. Prāṇotpatty-adhikaraṇa (VS II-4-1 to II-4-3)

It points out that *prāṇa* or vital breath has an origin similar to *viyat* and it is not eternal.

62. Saptagaty-ādhikaraṇa (VS II-4-4 and 5)

It rejects the view that *indriyas* are seven only and proves that it is eleven including the mind.

63. Prāṇāṇutvādhikaraṇa (VS II-4-6 and 7)

It points out that *indriyas* are *aṇu* or subtle organs since the Upaniṣad speaks of its movement along with *jīva* during its exit from the body.

64. Vāyukriyādhikaraṇa (VS II-4-8 to II-4-11)

It discusses the nature of the *mukhya prāṇa* or vital breath and points out that it is neither the mere elemental *vāyu* but it is a separate entity.

65. Śreṣṭāṇutvādhikaraṇa (VS II-4-12)

It points out that *mukhya-prāṇa* is also *aṇu or* monadic in nature since it is stated in the Upaniṣad that it also moves along with the *jīva* when it exits from the body after death.

66. Jyotirady-adhiṣṭhānādhikaraṇa (VS II-4-13 and 14)

It points out that the function of all *indriyas* and also *prāna* is regulated by *jīvātman* which is the controller of them (*adhiṣthātṛ*) and that this power of the *jīva* is bestowed by *Paramātman.*

67. Indriyādhikaraṇa (VS II-4-15 to 16)

It clarifies that *prāṇa* or vital breath is not an *indriya* or sense organ as in the case of ten sense organs and the mind since the Upaniṣad mentions clearly that it is distinct from the eleven sense organs.

68. Saṁjñāmūrtiklṛpty-adhikaraṇa (VS II-4-17 to 19)

It discusses the question whether the assignment of names and forms to the objects created by Brahma is done by Brahman or Hiraṇyagarbha and proves that this function is done by Brahman which causes the evolution of *prakṛti* upto five gross elements and then admixes them in certain proportion (*pañcīkaraṇa*) to constitute the variegated universe with names and forms.

Adhyaya III- Sādhanādhyāya or the chapter dealing with the means of attainment of Brahman

Pada 1

69. Tadantarapratipatty-adhikaraṇa (VS III-1-1 to III-1-7)

It discusses the question whether or not the *jīva* when it exits from the body after death, moves to the higher realm along with the subtle body (*bhūtasūkṣma*) and concludes on the basis of the details of *pañcāgni-vidyā* provided in the hāndogya Upaniṣad (V-3-3) that is moves into the realms of he moon with the subtle body to experience the fruits of good deeds.

70. Kṛtātyayādhikaraṇa (VS III-1-8 to III-1-11)

It is devoted to clarify that *jīvas* which have gone to the realms of the moon return to the earth with residual *karma* to be yet experienced in the next life.

71. Aniṣṭādikāryādhikaraṇa (VS III-1-1-12 to VS III-1-21)

It discusses the question whether even the souls of the individuals who have not performed meritorious deeds would go to the realm of the moon and answers that only those individuals who have performed meritorious deeds (*iṣṭādhikārī*) go to the *candraloka* to reap the benefits of the deeds.

72. Tatsvābhāvyāpatty-adhikaraṇa (VS III-1-22)

It clarifies a minor point that the soul, when it descends from the realm of the moon to the earth through the *ākāśa*, in the sense that it assumes similarity to *ākāśa*.

73. Nāticirādhikaraṇa (VS III-1-23)

This is also devoted to clarify a minor point relating to the duration of the stay of *jīva* in *ākāśa* and it states that it does not stay there too long.

74. Anyādhiṣṭitādhikaraṇa (VS III-1-24 to III-1-27)

It is devoted to explain the manner in which the *jīva* remains in the food grain before it enters into the human body in the form of *retas* (Semen).

Pāda 2: Ubhayaliṅga pāda dealing with the two-fold character of Brahman to create a craving for its attainment.

75. Sandhyādhikaraṇa (VS III-2-1 to III-2-6)

It discusses the question whether the objects experienced by the *jīva* during the state of dream *(sandhyā)* is created by *jīva* or *Paramātman* and explains that these are the wondrous creations of *Paramātman* to be experienced by the *jīvas*.

76. Tadabhāvadhikaraṇa (VS III-2-7 to III-2-8)

It discusses the question relating to the resting place for *jīva* during the state of *suṣupti* or the dreamless state and points out that all the three places mentioned in the Upaniṣads viz.–*hitā nāḍi, purītat nāḍi* and Brahman abiding in the heart–together serve as the resting place for *jīva* when it becomes united temporarily with Paramātman.

77. Karmānusmṛty-adhikaraṇa (VS III-2-9)

This is devoted to clarify that the same *jīva* which experienced the *suṣupti* comes back to its normal state.

78. Mugdhādhikaraṇa (VS III-2-10)

It describes the state of swoon which is sometime experienced by the *jīva* and it is described as *ardha-samapatti* or the state of half death in which *jīva* is neither alive nor dead.

79. Ubhayaliṅgādhikaraṇa (VS III-2-11 to III-2-25)

It is devoted to establish that Brahman though it abides in the *jīvas* and other entities as *Antaryāmin,* it is not affected by the defects found in the bodies of the *jīvas,* since by nature it is free from all defilements and is also endowed with numeraous auspicous attributes, as is evident from the Scriptural and *Smṛti* texts. It also discusses the implication of the Scriptural statement negating two forms of Brahman as *mūrta* and *amūrta* by the expression *'neti neti'* and states that Brahman is not devoid of attributes but on the contrary, it is endowed with attributes.

80. Ahikuṇḍalādhikaraṇa (VS III-2-26 to III-2-29)

It discusses the nature of the relation of the non-sentient universe to Brahman and explains that the universe caused by Brahman is related to it in the same way as an attribute to the substance or the body to the soul (*śarīra-śarīrī-bhāva*) similar to the relation of the *jīva* and Brahman as *aṁśa* and *aṁsī.*

81. Parādhikaraṇa (VS III-2-30 to III-2-36)

It discusses the question whethe there is any Reality higher than Brahman and affirms that Brahman is the highest Reality.

82. Phalādhikaraṇa (VS III-2-37 to III-2-40)

It discusses the question whether karma or deeds performed by an individual confers the desired fruits throught the unseen potency (*apūrva*) generated by it and comes to the conclustion that only *Paramātman* bestows all the desired fruits including *moksa.*

Pāda 3: Guṇopasaṁhāra pāda or the part dealing with the different vidyās or types of meditation on Brahman and the *guṇas* with which it is to be contemplated

83. Sarva-vedānta pratyayādhikaraṇa (VS III-3-1 to III-23-5)

It discusses the question whether the *vidyās* such as *dahara-vidyā* and *vaiśvānara-vidyā* taught in different Upaniṣads is the same or different and establishes that they are the same since there is no difference in the *codana* or the words enjoining it, the designation adopted for them, the nature of the goal to be attained and the description of the object of meditation.

84. Anyathātvādhikaraṇa (VS III-3-6 to III-3-9)

It clarifies that *udgītha vidyā* taught in the Chāndogya and Bṛhadāraṇyaka are different since the object and purpose of meditation on *udgītha* are different.

85. Sarva-abhedādhikaraṇa (VS III-3-10)

The *prāṇa-vidyā* enjoined for meditation in Chāndogya, Bṛhadāraṇyaka and Kauṣītakī Upaniṣad is the same *vidyā* since the *guṇas* with which it is to be meditated do not differ.

86. Ānandādyadhikaraṇa (VS III-3-11 to III-3-17)

With regard to the question relating to the *guṇas* with which Brahman is to be meditated upon, it is pointed out that the distinguishing *guṇas* of Brahman such as *ānanda, satya, jñāna, ananta* are to be necessarily contemplated along with Brahman in respect of all *vidyās,* since these are inseparable from Brahman and also useful to know its essential nature (*svarūpa-nirūpaka dharmas*)

87. Kāryākhyānādhikaraṇa (VS III-3-18)

It discusses the issue whether or not the performance of the *ācamana* or sipping of water three times prior to and after taking a meal is an unjuction laid down as part of the *prāṇavidyā* mentioned in the Chāndogya and Bṛhadāraṇyaka Upaniṣad and clarifies that it is not a *vidhi* but nevertheless the water taken as *ācamana* is to be contemplated as a garment (*vastra*) for *prāṇa.*

88. Samānādhikaraṇa (VS III-3-19)

It clarifies that the *Śāṇḍilya-vidyā* mentioned in the Agnirahasya and also in the Bṛhadāraṇyaka Upaniṣad though appears to be different *vidyās* in terms of the description of the *guṇas* with which Brahman is to be meditated upon are the same.

89. Sambandhādhikaraṇa (VS III-3-20 to III-3-22)

It clarifies that the *upāsanā* on Satya-brahma as abiding in the orbit of the sun and the same kind of meditation on Satyabrahma as abiding in the right eye are to be treated as two separate kinds of *upāsanā* and hence the *guṇas* mentioned in one Upaniṣad for contemplation are not to be include in the second meditation.

90. Saṁbhratyādhikaraṇa (VS III-3-23)

It clarifies that the special *guṇas* such as *jyeṣṭhatva, vīryatva* and *dyulokavyāptatva* with which Brahman is to be meditated upon as stated in the Taittirīya Śākhā and Chāndogya are not to be included in respect of all other *upāsanās.*

91. Puruṣavidyādhikaraṇa (VS. III-3-24)

It points out that the *puruṣa-vidyā* mentioned in the Taittrīya and also in the Chāndogya are different because there is difference in respect of certain details of the *vidyās.*

92. Vedyādy-adhikaraṇa (VS III-3-25)

The recitation of certain hymns in the form of prayer at the commencement of the *upāsanā* is not considered as a necessary *aṅga* or subsidiary part of the *upāsanā*.

93. Hānyadhikaraṇa (VS III-3-26)

It deals with the question whether the *Brahma-jñānī* at the time of his death should contemplate only on *hāna* or getting rid of his *duṣkrta* and *sukṛta* and also *upāyana* or its transfer to his friends and enemies, both of which are mentioned sparately in some of the Upaniṣads and clarifies that both are to be contemplated since *hāna* also includes *upāyana*.

94. Sāmparāyādhikaraṇa (VS III-3-27 to III-3-31)

It discusses the question whether the *Brahma-jñānī* gets rid of all his *sukṛta* and *duṣkṛta* at the time of his exit from the body prior to the movement through *arcirādi* path or some are to be got rid off after reaching the border of the higher abode (*paramapada*) and clarifies that both the *sukṛta* and *duṣkṛta* are thrown off at the time of exit since there is no scope to experience the fruits of the good deeds after the exit of the *jīva* from the body.

95. Aniyamādhikaraṇa (VS III-3-32)

It clarifies that the movement of the *Brahma-vit* through the *arcirādi-mārga* is not restricted to *upāsakas* of some specified *vidyās* but it is also applicable to all who observe *Brahmopāsana*.

96. Akṣaradhyadhikaraṇa (VS III-3-33 and 34)

It discusses the question whether the negative qualities such as *asthūla, anaṇu* etc. and also *adreśya agrāhya* etc. with which Brahman is to be meditated upon in respect of *upāsanā* on *akṣava* (Brahman), as taught in connection with the *akṣara-vidyā* by Bṛhadāraṇyaka and Muṇḍaka Upaniṣad respectively, are to be included in respect of other *vidyās* too and it is concluded that these negative qualities which are categorized as *heya-pratyanīkatva* are to be contemplated along with the four other essential attributes viz. *ānanda, satya, jñāna* and *ananta* for the reason that these too constitute an essential attribute of Brahman and are useful to know the nature of Brahman as free from defilements.

97. Antartvādhikaraṇa (VS III-3-35 to III--3-37)

It clarifies that the two ways of description of Brahman offered by Yājñavalkya to the questions raised by Uśastra and Kahola in the Bṛhadāraṇyaka Upaniṣad teaching *uśasta kahola vidyā* do not constitute two separate *vidyās* since both descriptions apply to Brahman which is the object of meditation.

98. Kamādyādhikaraṇa (VS III-3-38 to III-3-40)

It clarifies that the *dahara-vidyā* or meditation on Brahman abiding in one's heart which is mentioned in the Chāndogya and Bṛhadāraṇyaka with slightly varying description of the attributes with which it is to be contemplated do not constitute two separate *vidyās,* since the term *vaśitva* used in Bṛhadāraṇyaka is a specific form of *satyasaṁkalpatva* employed in Chāndogya.

99. Tannirdhāraṇa-aniyamādhikaraṇa (VS III-3-41)

It discusses an incidental issue relating to *udgītha upāsanā* and clarifies that it is not a necessary *aṅga* or subsidiary means to *vidyā.*

100. Pradānādhikaraṇa (VS III-3-42)

It discusses the manner in which *dahara-vidyā* or the meditation on Brahman as subtle space within the heart and clarifies that Brahman as qualified with the eight attributes as stated in the Chāndogya Upaniṣad is to be meditated upon and not *guṇas* alone separately.

101. Liṅgabhūyastvādhikaraṇa (VS III-3-43)

It establishes that the passage of the Taittrīya Nārāyaṇa in which it is stated that Nārāyaṇa is *parabrahma, paratattva, paraṁ jyotis* etc. is not intended to specify the nature of the object of meditation in respect of *dahara-vidyā* only mentioned in the preceding passage of the same Upaniṣad but on the contrary, it affirms that Nārāyaṇa as the Supreme Deity is the object of meditation in all the *vidyās* including *dahara-vidyā* because these statements contextually are of stronger validity *(prakaraṇāt balīyaḥ).*

102. Pūrvavikalpādhikaraṇa (VS III-3-44 to III--3-50)

This is an incidental topic which deals with the question whether certain religious rites to be observed mentally as mentioned in *Agnirahasya,* are part of the performance of the sacrifice done in the fire or are they part of *vidyā* observed mentally in the form of meditation and clarifies that these are of the nature of meditation.

103. Śarīrebhāvādhikaraṇa (VS III-3-51 and 52)

In connection with the subject of the *upāsanā* on *jīvātman* which is also part of the meditation on Brahman, it discusses the question whether *jīvātman* is to be meditated upon in its embodied state as *kartā, bhoktā* etc. or in its true form as qualified with its essential attributes such as *apahatapāpmā, satyasaṁkalpa* etc. and it concludes that *jīvātman* is to be meditated upon in its true form as different from its embodied form.

104. Aṅgāvabaddhādhikaraṇa (VS III-3-53 and 54).

It discusses a minor issue whether or not the *upāsanā* on *udgītha* which is enjoined in certain *Śākhās* of the Upanisads is applicable to all the other *Śākhas* and answers that it is applicable to all the *Śākhās.*

105. Bhūma-jyāystvādhikaraṇa (VS III-3-55)

In connection with the meditation on *Vaiśvānara Ātman*, the question is discussed whether the meditations on *dyuloka, āditya, vāyu, ākāśa* and *pṛthivī* which are parts of *Vaiśvānara Ātman* (Brahman) are also to be done separately and it is clarified that meditation on *Vaiśvānara Ātman* is to be observed in its cosmic form as one Reality comprising all parts.

106. Śabdādibhedādhikaraṇa (VS III-3-56)

It establishes that the several *vidyās* mentioned in the different Upaniṣads are different because of the difference in respect of the Scriptural statements in the form of injuctions (*codana*), the description in terms of *guṇas* with which Brahman is to be meditated, the designation offered (*ākhyā*) and other factors.

107. Vikalpādhikaraṇa (VS III-3-57 to III-3-58)

It points out that the different *vidyās* are alternative means to attain Brahman because the nature of the attainment is the same for all *vidyās*.

108. Yaṭhāśrayabhāvādhikaraṇa (VS III-3-59 to III-3-64)

It discusses a minor point relating to the *udgītha upāsanā* which is enjoined in some of the Upaniṣads and clarifies that it is not required to be observed necessarily in respect of all *vidyās*, as it is not enjoined as a subsidiary means to *upāsanā* on Brahman.

Pāda 4: Aṅgapāda or the part dealing with the *karma* as *aṅga* to *vidyā*.

109. Puruṣārthādhikaraṇa (VS III-4-1 to III-4-20)

It critically examines the theory of karma or the performance of the prescribed deeds as the direct means to the Supreme

Goal (*puruṣārtha*) and affirms that *vidyā* or (*upāsanā*) as aided by karma is the direct sādhana to *mokṣa.*

110. Stutimātrādhikaraṇa (VS III-4-21 to III-IV-22)

It deals with a minor matter relating to the glorificatory statements about *udgītha* and clarifies that these are to be taken as injuctions (*vidhi*) enjoining the *upāsanā* on *udgītha.*

111. Pāriplavādhikaraṇa (VS III-4-23 to III-IV-24)

It points out that the statements found in the Upaniṣadic passages dealing with the narration of *Brahma-vidyās* in glorifying terms are to be taken as part of the *vidhi* enjoining the *upāsanā.*

112. Agnīndhanādy-adhikaraṇa (VS III-4-25)

It examines the eligibility of the sanyāsins for observing the meditation on Brahman since they cannot perform the prescribed *karma* as *aṅga* to *upāsanā,* being ineligible to light the sacrificial fire (*agnīndhana*) and answers that they too are eligible for *upāsanā* since they observe such other *karmas* as prescribed for *sannyāsāśrama.*

113. Sarvāpekṣādhikaraṇa (VS III-4-26)

It discusses the case of the *gṛhasthas* and points out that they are required to perform all the prescribed *karmas* such as *yajña, dāna, tapas* etc. as aid to *upāsanā* since they are eligible to light the sacrificial fire.

114. Śamadamady-adhikaraṇa (VS III-4-27)

It points out that besides the performance of prescribed rituals the *gṛhasthas* are also required to cultivate *śama* or tranquility, *dama* or control of senses, *uparati* or inner satisfaction and *titikṣu* or patience, *samāhitatva* or equanimity as these are all auxiliaries to *vidyā.*

115. Sarvānnānumatyadhikaraṇa (VS III-4-28 to 31)

It clarifies that the general permission sanctioned by the Scripture for acceptance of all kinds of food by the *Brahmavit* is intended for special circumstance such as at the time of losing one's *prāṇa,* as is evident from the episode of Uśasti in Chāndogya Upaniṣad.

116. Vihitatvādhikaraṇa (VS III-4-32 to III-4-35)

It clarifies that the performance of *karma* such as *yajña, dāna* etc. is also to be performed by the *gṛhasthas* who are not seekers of *mokṣa,* since these are enjoined by scripture even for them.

117. Vidhurādhikaraṇa (VS III-4-36 to III-4-39)

It clarifies that even individuals who do not belong to the four *āśramas (anāśrami)* such as those who are widowers are also eligible for *Brahma-vidyā.*

118. Tadbhūtādhikaraṇa (VS III-4-40 to 43)

It points out that persons who have been thrown out of a particular *āśrama* for having committed sinful acts are forbidden from pursuing *Brahma-vidyā,* since the observance of *vidyā* by such persons is forbidden by the *śāstra.*

119. Swāmyādhikaraṇa (VS III-4-44 to III-4-45)

It deals with an incidental topic relating to the *udgīthopāsanā* and clarifies that this is to be accomplished by the priests appointed for the purpose by the person who intends to conduct it for the desired goal.

120. Sahakāry-adhikaraṇa (VS III-4-46 to III-4-48)

It clarifies that the term *mauna* which implies *manana* or reflection on the object of meditation is also enjoined along with *pāṇḍitya* or deep knowledge and *bālyatva* or child like innocence which constitute the accessories to *upāsanā.*

121. Āviṣkārādhikaraṇa (VS III-4-49)

It elucidates the term *bālyatva* mentioned in the Bṛhadāraṇyaka Upaniṣad by pointing out that it does not mean irresponsible behaviour like a child (*kāmacāra*) but it refers to the childlike innocence by not manifesting externally one's greatness as a *Brahma-jñāni.*

122. Aihikādhikaraṇa (VS III-4-50)

It deals with the question whether or not the *upāsanā* observed for the purpose of attaining benefits other than *mokṣa* such as heavenly bliss, wealth etc. and points out that the goal is attained soon after the completion of it, provided there are no obstacles in the form of *prārabdha karma.*

123. Muktiphalādhikaraṇa (VS II-4-51)

It points out that in the case of the *upāsanā* observed for attaining *mokṣa,* the goal is achieved soon after the completion of meditation, provided there are no obstacles in the form of strong *prārabdha karma* such as an offence to *Brahmavit.*

Adhyāya IV- Phalādhyāya or the chapter dealing with the Supreme Goal.

Pāda 1: Āvṛttipāda or the part dealing with the manner of upāsanā and its results

124. Āvṛttyādhikaraṇa (VS IV-1-1 to 2)

It points out that *vedana* which is the same as the *upāsanā* or *dhyāna* and which is the direct means to attain the Supreme goal is to be practised repeatedly and continuously until the goal is achieved and that it is to be accomplished with the aid of the *yogāṅgas.*

125. Ātmopāsānādhikaraṇa (VS IV-1-3)

It discusses the question whether the *upāsaka* should meditate on Brahman as different from him or as non-different from him and answers that he should meditate on it as its inner Self (*ātmetyeva*)

126. Pratīkādhikaraṇa (VS IV-1-4 to IV-1-5)

It clarifies that in the case of the *upāsanā* on other entities such as *manas, prāṇa* etc. the *upāsaka* should not regard them as his *Ātman* (Inner Self).

127. Ādityādimaty-adhikaraṇa (IV-1-6)

It considers an incidental topic relating to the contemplation on *udgītha* as the symbol of *Āditya* and states that *udgītha* is to be contemplated as *āditya* since the latter is a higher and superior entity (*utkarṣa*) than the former.

128. Āsīnādhikaraṇa (VS IV-1-7 to IV-1-11)

It specifies that the meditation is to be done in the sitting posture since it secures steadiness of the mind and body which is useful for concentraing on the object of meditation.

129. Āprayāṇādhikaraṇa (VS IV-1-12)

It points out that the meditation is to be pursued until the end of one's life, as stated in the Chāndogya Upaniṣad (VIII-15-1).

130. Tadadhigamādhikaraṇa (VS IV-1-13)

It establishes that *upāsanā* which has reached a state of perfection resulting in the clearer vision of Brahman, has the power to destroy all sins committed prior to its embarkation (*vināśa*) and that the sins committed unintentionally subsequent to the commencement of the *upāsanā* do not cling to him (*aśleṣa*).

131. Itarādhikaraṇa (VS IV-1-14)

It clarifies that *pāpa* or sins referred to in the Upaniṣad also includes *puṇya* or merit since *puṇya* also stands in the way of attainment of *mokṣa.*

132. Anārabdhakāryādhikaraṇa (VS IV-1-15)

It clarifies that the *sukṛta* and *duṣkṛta* which have not yet begun to give their results stand eradicated but not the *puṇya* and *pāpa karma* which have already begun to yield the results.

133. Agnihotrādy-adhikaraṇa (VS IV-1-16 to IV-1-18)

It discusses the question whether the prescribed rituals such as *agnihotra* are to be performed by the *Brahma-vit* for whom the results for such meritorious deeds do not bear any result and answers that these have to be observed since they are mandatory for him.

134. Itarakṣapaṇādhikaraṇa

It clarifies that the *prārabdha-karma,* that is , the *puṇya* and *pāpa karma* which has begun to bear its fruits, is to be experienced either until the end of the present life or even in a subsequent life until it is totally got rid of.

Pāda 2: *Utkrānti pāda* or the part dealing with the exit of the *jīva* from the body.

135. Vāgādhikaraṇa (VS IV-2-1 to IV-2-2)

While discussing the process of the exit of the *jīva* or the *upāsaka* at the time of death, it points out that the very organ of speech becomes merged in the *manas* in the sense that it becomes united with it.

136. Manodhikaraṇa (VS IV-2-3)

It clarifies that the mind combined with all the *indriyas* is not dissolved in the *prāṇa* or vital breath but it becomes united with it.

137. Adhyakṣādhikaraṇa (VS IV-2-4)

It points out that *prāṇa* associated with the sense organs becomes united with the *jīva,* which is the lord of all sense organs.

138. Bhūtādhikaraṇa (VS IV-2-5 to IV-2-6)

It clarifies that the term *tejas* with which *prāṇa* is united, according to the Upaniṣad, implies all the five subtle elements including fire.

139. Asṛty-upakramādhikaraṇa (VS IV-2-7 to IV-2-13)

It discusses the question whether the *utkrānti* is applicable to both persons who have realized Brahman and also those who have not undertaken the *upāsanā* to attain Brahman and affirms that *utkrānti* is common for the *upāsakas* and non-*upāsakas* upto the point of entering into *mūrdhanya-nāḍi* or the main artery leading from the heart to the cown of the head.

140. Parasampatty-adhikaraṇa (VS IV-2-14)

It explains how in the final stage of *utkrānti,* the *jīva* associated with the subtle sense organs, mind, *prāṇa* as well as the subtle elements becomes united with the Supreme Deity (*para-devatā*) and that this temporary union with the *para-devatā* abiding in one's own body as the *Antaryāmin* is intended for securing some relief for the afflicted *jīva.*

141. Avibhāgādhikaraṇa (VS IV-2-15)

It clarifies that the term *sampatti* or the union of *jīva* with *Paramātman* does not imply dissolution of it in the causal substance but on the contrary, it means that it becomes united with *Paramātman* in such a way that the two entities become indistinguishable (*avibhāga*).

142. Tadokodhikaraṇa (VS IV-2-16)

It describes how the *jīva* is enabled to exit through the *suṣumnā-nāḍi* radiating from the heart to the crown of the head which is illumined by *Paramātman* out of His grace in response to the devoted meditation on Him and also constant contemplation on the *arcirādi mārga* as part of an aid to *upāsanā*.

143. Raśmy-adhikaraṇa (VS IV-2-17)

It states that *jīva*, after its exit from the body proceeds to the realm of the sun through the course of its rays, which are present even in the night.

144. Niśādhikaraṇa (VS IV-2-18)

It affirms that the *Brahmavit* even if he dies in the night, attains Brahman.

145. Dakṣiṇāyanādhikaraṇa (VS IV-2-19)

The death of a *Brahmavit* in the half period when the sun moves southward (*dakṣiṇāyana*) does not affect his attainment of Brahman.

Pāda 3: Gatipāda or the part dealing with the movement of *jīva* through the divine pathway.

146. Arcirādy-adhikaraṇa (VS IV-3-1)

It examines the varying views found in the different Upaniṣads regarding the pathway leading to the *Brahmaloka* and concludes that there is only one pathway named *arcirādi mārga* commencing from *arcis* or light through which *jīva* traverses to the higher realm.

147. Vayāvādhikaraṇa (VS IV-3-2)

By way of clarifying the order in which the celestial deities are mentioned in the Upaniṣads, it points out that *devaloka* mentioned in one place is not different from *vāyu* or *vāyuloka* mentioned in another Upaniṣad.

148. Varuṇādhikarana (VS IV-3-3)

It clarifies that Varuṇa, the celestial deity ruling the rains (*parjanya*), is to be placed after lightning (*vidyut*) since the two are connected together.

149. Ātivāhikādhikaraṇa (VS IV-3-4 to IV-3-5)

It clarifies that the light (*arcis*) day, month, etc. do not refer to the physical entities nor are they places of enjoyment but they are the presiding deities over them and serve as guides (*ativahikas*) enroute the abode of *Paramātman.*

150. Kāryādhikaraṇa (VS IV-3-6 to IV-3-15)

It discusses two conflicting views relating to the types of *upāsakas* who are lead by the celestial deities to *Brahma-loka* held by Bādari and Jaimini, and establishes conclusively that neither those who meditate on *Caturmukha Brahmā* nor those who meditate exclusively on Brahman are lead to the *Brahma-loka* but as sated by Bādarāyaṇa, only those who meditate on Brahman and also on the individual self (*jīvātman*) conceived as inherently related to Brahman (*Brahmātmaka*) are led by the *ātivāhikas* through the *arcirādi-mārga.*

Pāda 4: Muktipāda or the part dealing with the nature of the mokṣa attained by jīva.

151. Saṁpadyāvirbhāvādhikaraṇa (VS IV-4-1 to IV-4-3)

It discusses the issue whether *jīva* which attains Brahman acquires any new form in the state of *mukti* or does it remain in its own form and affirms that *jīva* after reaching Brahman (*sampadaya*) manifests itself in its own natural form (*svena rūpa*) with all the eight attributes which were eclipsed during the state of bondage but now the same being fully manifested.

152. Avibhāgena-dṛṣṭatvādhikaraṇa (VS IV-4-4)

It discusses the question whether the *jīva* in the state of *mokṣa* enjoys the *guṇas* of Brahman as being separate from Brahman (*pṛthag-bhūtam*) or it experiences the same as being non-distinct (*avibhaktam*) and concludes that the *mukta-jīva* enjoys itself as non-distinct from Brahman since it now actually realizes that it is integrally related to Brahman (*avibhāgena dṛṣṭatvāt*).

153. Brahmādhikaraṇa (VS IV-4-5 to IV-4-7)

It examines the two views relating to the specific form in which *jīva* manifests itself after attaining Brahman viz (i) whether it manifests itself with all the eight attributes stated in the Chāndogya, as held by Jaimini or whether it manifests itself as consciousness only (*cin-mātra*), as held by Auḍulomi and affirms, as pointed out by Bādarāyaṇa, that *jīva* though it is by nature of pure consciousness, also possesses all the eight attributes in the state of *mukti*, since there is no contradiction between the two views.

154. Saṁkalpādhikaraṇa (VS IV-4-8 to IV-4-9)

It discusses the question whether the *mukta jīva* which is stated to perform any activities it desires in the state of *mukti*, fulfills all its desires out of its own free will or with some effort as in the case of ordinary individuals and answers that it fulfills its desires out of its own free will and no additional effort is needed for this purpose.

155. Abhāvādhikaraṇa (VS IV-4-10 to IV-4-16)

It examines the two conflicting views of Bādari and Jaimini regarding the possession of the body and the sense organs for performing activities by the *mukta jīvas* and points out, as stated by Bādarāyaṇa, that *mukta jīva* can assume a body, if it so desires and also can remain without a body, if it so wills.

156. Jagad-vyāpāravarjādhikaraṇa (VS IV-4-17 to IV-4-22)

It discusses an important question whether the *mukta jīva* which is stated in the Upaniṣad to enjoy equal status *(paramasāmya)* with Brahman in the state of *mukti* has the capacity to create the universe and answers that it does not have this capacity since the cosmic function of creation exclusively belongs to *Paramātman*. It also clarifies that equality with Brahman is only in respect of the enjoyment of bliss of Brahman and its glory (*bhogamātra-sāmya*). When once *jīva* attains *mukti*, there is no return of it to the mundane esistence (*anāvṛtti*).

APPENDIX-II

THE NAMES OF BRAHMA-VIDYĀS

referred to in the Upaniṣads and the Adhikaraṇa-sārāvalī
in the alphabetical order[1]

Names	Reference to Upaniṣads	Reference to Vedānta Sūtra	Reference to Adhikaraṇa-sārāvalī
1. Ākāśa-vidyā	Ch. Up I-9 and Viii-14	VS I-1-23 and VS I-3-42	AS 69 and 128
2. Akṣara-vidyā	Muṇḍ. Up I-1-5	VS I-2-22	AS 93
3. Akṣistha Satyabrahma-vidyā	Br. Up VII-5-1&2	VS III-3-20 and 21	AS 344
4. Ānandamaya-vidyā	Tait. Up II-5	VS I-1-13	AS 59 and 60
5. Anguṣṭha-pramita-vidyā	Kaṭha Up. II-4-12	VS I-3-23	AS 116
6. Antaryāmī-vidyā	Br. Up. V-7-1	VS I-2-19	AS 91
7. Antarāditya-vidyā	Ch. Up I-1-6	VS I-1-21	AS 62 & 63
8. Bālākī-vidyā	Kaus. Up IV-18 Br. Up. IV-1-16	VS I-4-16	AS 139
9. Bhumā-vidyā	Ch. Up V-15-1 to VII-16-1	VS 1-3-7	AS 104 and 105
10. Dahara-vidyā	Ch. Up VIII-1-1, Tait. Nārāyaṇa II-5	VS I-3-13 & VS III-3-38	AS 111 and 112
11. Gargy-akṣara-vidyā	Br. Up V-8-8	VS I-3-9	AS 108
12. Gāyatrī-vidyā	Ch. Up III-12 to 6	VS I-1-25 and I-1-26	AS 72
13. Jyotiṣaṁjyotir-vidyā	Br. VI-4-16 and 17	VS I-3-31 and I-4-13	AS 136
14. Īśāvāsya-vidyā	Isa Up.	VS III-4-1, VS III-4-9	AS 397
15. Pañcāgni-vidyā	Ch. Up V-10 Also Br. Up. VIII-2-15	VS III-1-1 and III-3-32	AS 274
16. Paramjyotir-vidyā	Ch. Up. III-13-7& 8	VS I-1-25	AS 71 and 72
17. Parampuruṣa-Vidyā (also named Trimātrapraṇava-vidyā)	Praśna Up. V-5	VS I-3-12	AS 109

18. Paryaṅka-vidyā	Kauṣ Up. I	VS IV-3-11	AS 514
19. Prāṇa-vidyā	Ch. Up. I-II-5	VS I-1-24	AS 70
20. Pratardana-vidyā	Kauṣ Up. III-2 & III-9	VS I-1-29	AS 74
21. Madhu-vidyā	Ch. Up III-1	VS I-3-30	AS 124
22. Maitreyī-vidyā	Br. Up VI-5-6	VS I-4-29	AS 141
23. Naciketa-vidyā (also named Attṛvidyā)	Kaṭha Up. I-2	VS I-2-9	AS 86 & 87
24. Nyāsa-vidyā	Tait. Nārāyaṇa 51	VS III-3-56 (implied according to Rāmānuja[2])	AS 385
25. Sad-vidyā	Ch. Up. VI-2-1	VS I-1-5	AS 55 and 56
26. Saṁvarga-vidyā	Ch. Up. IV-3-1 to 6	VS I-1-33	AS 125
27. Śāṇḍilya-vidyā	Ch Up. III-14-1 Br. Up. VII-6-1	VS I-2-1 and III-3-19	AS 85
28. Satyakāma-vidyā (also named Ṣoḍaśakalaśa-Brahma-vidyā)	Ch. Up IV-14-9	Not referred to in VS	Not referred to in AS
29. Vaiśvānara-vidyā	Ch. Up. VII-11 to 24	VS I-2-25 and III-3-55	AS 94 and 95 also 381-82
30. Vyāhṛti-vidyā (also named Ādityamaṇḍalastha-Brahma-vidyā)	Br. Up. VII-5-1	VS III-3-20	AS 344
31. Upakośala-vidyā	Ch. Up. IV-10-5 & IV-15-3	VS I-2-13	AS 88
32. Uśastakahola-vidyā	Br. Up V-4-1 and V-5-1	VS III-3-35	AS 361-362

1. There is no unanimity among the commentators regarding the names of the *Brahma-vidyās* though they generally agree that the total number of *vidyās* as means to *mokṣa* is thirty two. The names given in this list are in accordance with the *Adhikaraṇa-Sārāvalī* published by Ahobilamuṭṭ, Madras (1940).
2. See *Śrutaprakāśikā* on RB III-3-56. *Akṣaravidyādikā iti ādiśabdena nyāso vivakṣitaḥ. See* also AS verse 385.

GLOSSARY

Abheda : Non-difference.
Abheda-jñāna : Knowledge of the identity of *jīva* and Brahman.
Abheda-śruti : Scriptural texts speaking of the non-difference between *jīva* and Brahman.
Abhiniṣpatti : Manifestation.
Abhyāsa : Repetition.
Ācārya : Preceptor.
Acit : Non-sentient matter; primordial cosmic matter.
Ādhāra : That which serves as the basis; the Supporter.
Ādheya : That which is sustained; the supported.
Adhikaraṇa : Topical section comprising one or more *sūtras* dealing with a specific subject.
Adhiṣṭhāna : Substratum; objective basis for illusion (acc. SB).
Adhyāsa : Superimposition.
Adhyāya : A chapter in *Brahma-sūtras.*
Āditya : The Sun.
Adṛṣṭa : Unseen potency.
Adreśya : Imperceptible.
Adṛśyatvādhikaraṇa : Topic dealing with the subject of Brahman as imperceptible etc.
Agni : Fire.
Agnindhana : One who is eligible to light the sacrificial fire.
Ahamartha : The entity denoted by the notion of "I"; the *jīvātman* (acc. RB).
Ahikuṇḍala : The serpent and its coils.

Ajaḍa : Sentient.
Aja : Unborn, *Prakṛti* (acc. Sāṁkhya).
Ajñāna : Ignorance, absence of knowledge.
Ajara : Free from old age.
Ākāśa : Cosmic ether, space.
Ākhya : Designation; name.
Akṣara : Imperishable; Brahman; *jīvātman; prakṛti.*
Akṣarādhikaraṇa : The topic dealing with Brahman as *akṣara.*
Akṣi : Eye.
Akṣipuruṣa : The deity seen inside the eyes (by the yogi).
Amṛta : Immortal.
Ambara : Sky.
Aṁśa : A part; an integral part of a complex whole (acc. RB); close resemblance (acc. MB); appearing as part (acc. SB).
Aṁśādhikaraṇa : Topic dealing with *jīva* as an *aṁśa* or Brahman.
Amānava Puruṣa : The celestial deity who leads the liberated souls to *Brahmaloka.*
Anādi : That which has no origin.
Ananta : Infinite; that which is not conditioned by time, space and another entity.
Ānanda : bliss.
Ananya : Non-distinct; non-difference.
Ānandamaya : Blissful;
Ānandamayādhikaraṇa : The topic dealing with Brahman as *ānandamaya.*
Ānanda-tāratamya : gradation in respect of the enjoyment of bliss by liberated *Jivas* (acc. to MB)
Anāvṛtti : Non-return to bondage.
Anguṣṭhamātra : Size of the thumb.
Anivacanīya : Indeterminant; inexplicable.
Aṅga : Subsidiary.
Antaḥkaraṇa : Internal sense organ; mind.
Antara : Inside; within.
Antarādhikaraṇa : The topic dealing with the nature of the *puruṣa* seen within *āditya* and *akṣi.*

Antarātmā : Inwelling Self; *Paramātman* as immanent in all beings.
Antaryāmin : The inner controller; The immanent Supreme Being which controls everything from within; Brahman.
Antaryāmyadhikaraṇa : The topic dealing with Brahman as *Antaryāmin*.
Aṇu : Monadic.
Anumāna : Inference.
Ānumānika : That which is established by inference; *prakrti* admitted by the Sāṁkhyas.
Anupapatti : Logical untenability.
Anupraveśa : Entry of Brahman into all created objects along with *jīva*.
Apacceda-nyāya : The principle according to which what is later is to be accepted in preference to the earlier.
Apahata pāpma : Free from evil.
Apara : Lower.
Aparokṣajñāna : Direct knowledge of Brahman derived from meditation (acc. RB); Intuitive knowledge of identity of *jiva and* Brahman (acc. SB); direct vision of Brahman (acc. MB).
Apṛthakbhūta : Not existing as separate.
Ārambhana : Being connected with speech (acc. RB)
Ārambhaṇādhikaraṇa : The topic dealing with the subject of Brahman as material cause of the universe.
Arcis : Light.
Arcirādimārga : The pathway presided over by celestial deities through which *mukta jīva* traverses to the higher abode.
Aśabdam : Not supported by scripture but proved by *anumāna*.
Asakṛt : Repeated observance.
Aspaṣṭa : Ambiguous.
Āśrama : Stages of life.
Āśraya : Locus, basis, support.
Ativādi : One who speaks greatness of a principle.
Ātman : The individual self; also *Paramātman* (Brahman).
Attā : The devourer; one who is the cause of the dissolution of the universe.

Avasthā : the modified state of a substance.
Avasthiti : Abiding as one thing in the other.
Avibhāga : Non-distinct; Identity (acc. SB)
Avidyā : The cosmic principle which causes the appearance of Brahman as the universe (acc. SB); *Karma* in the form of *puṇya* and *pāpa* (acc. RB).
Avikāra : Not subject to any modification.
Aviduṣa : One who does not practice meditation on Brahman.
Āvirbhāva : Manifestation.
Āvṛttiḥ : Repeated practice.
Avyakta : Unmanifest primordial cosmic matter (*prakṛti*);
Avyākṛta : Unmanifest state of *prakṛti*; Brahman as associated with subtle *cit* and *acit*.
Āyatana : Abode; that which holds togther.
Avirodha : Absence of contradiction.
Avirodhādhyāya : The chapter II of *Brahmasūtras* proving the absence of contradiction in respect of Vedānta theories.
Baddha : Bound, The *jīva* in bondage.
Bhakti : Devotion; unceasing meditation on God.
Bhakti-yoga : unceasing meditation adopted as a direct *sādhana* for attaining *mokṣa*.
Bhāṣya : Commentary (on *Vedānta sūtras*).
Bheda : Difference.
Bheda-śruti : Scriptural texts teaching difference between the Brahman and *jīva*.
Bheda-vāda : The theory emphasizing the difference between the ontological entities.
Bhedābheda : Difference-cum non-difference.
Bhedābheda-vāda : The Theory upholding *bhedābheda*. between Brahman and *jīva* as well as *jagat*.
Boddhā : The knower.
Bhoga : Experience of bliss of Brahman.
Bhoktā : One who experiences the individual self.
Bhūmā : Infinitely great; bliss par excellence; Brahman.
Bhutākāśa : Physical ether.

Bhūtasūkṣma : Five subtle elements and *indriyas.*
Bhūtayoni : Source of the universe.
Bimba-darśana : Direct vision of the image of God.
Brahmā : The Vedic deity entrusted with the task of the creation of the universe.
Brahma (Brahman) : The Ultimate Reality in Vedānta.
Brahma-loka : The abode of Brahman.
Brahma-sākṣatkāra : Direct realization of Brahman.
Brahma-vidyā : The *Upāsanā* (meditation) on Brahman culminating in the direct vision of Brahman (acc. RB); the spiritual knowledge of Brahman.
Buddhi : Intellect; internal organ; mind.
Cakṣus : eyes.
Camasa : A special type of vessel used in *yāga* for drinking soma juice used in the *yāga.*
Candra : moon.
Chāyā : shadow.
Cintana : Repeated contemplation of the object of meditation; *dhyāna* (meditation).
Cit : Sentient being; the individual self.
Dahara, also *Daharākāśa* : Subtle space within the heart; Brahman.
Daharādhikaraṇa : The topic dealing with the meditation on *daharākāśa* as Brahman.
Dama : Controlling of sense organs.
Dāna : Charity.
Darśana : Vision or the realization of the self; specific type of meditation characterized with vividness (acc. RB); system of Philosophy.
Devatā : Celestial deity.
Dhāraṇa : Concentration on the object of meditation; sixth limb of *yogāṅgas.*
Dharma : Attribute : quality.
Dharmabhūta-jñāna : Knowledge as an essential attribute of the self. attributive knowledge.
Dharmī : Substrate; substantive aspect of a *viśiṣṭa* entity.
Dhruvānusmṛti : Steadfast meditation.

Dhyāna : Meditation.
Dīpa : Light of the lamp.
Doṣa : Defect.
Draṣṭā : The seer; *Paramāmtman;* also *jīvātman.*
Dravya : Sustance; that which serves as the substratum for modification.
Dṛṣṭānta : Illustration.
Duḥkha : Suffering; grief.
Duṣkṛta : Sin; sinful deeds; evil.
Dvaita : Dualism; the system of Vedānta expounded by Madhva.
Dyuḥ : Heaven.
Dyubhvādyadhikaraṇa : The topic dealing with Brahman as the *Āyatana* of heaven, earth etc.
Dvyaṇuka : Combination of two primary atoms; binary compound.
Eka : One.
Gati : Movement of *jīva* after its exit from the body to the higher realms.
Gauṇa : Secondary.
Gauṇārtha : Secondary meaning of a term.
Guhā : Cave; inner recess of the heart.
Guṇa : Quality; attribute.
Hetu : Reason.
Heya-guṇa : Defiling qualities or attributes.
Heya-pratyanīka : Opposed to everything that is defiling.
Hiraṇmaya : Golden.
Hiraṇyagarbha : Vedic deity entrusted with the function of creation.
Hita : Means or *sādhana* to achieve the Supreme Goal.
Hṛsva : Short.
Iṣṭādhikāri : Those who have performed meritorious deeds.
Indra : The name of the chief celestial deity.
Indriyas : The sense organs.
Īkṣaṇa : The act of seeing or resolving.
Īśvara : The Ruler of the universe.
Jaḍa : Inert matter.

Jagat : Universe.
Jagat-kāraṇa : Being the primary cause of the universe.
Jāgrat : Waking state of the self.
Janma : Origin; birth.
Jantu : A living being.
Jaṭharāgni : Digestiv fire.
Jijñāsā : Desire to know; enquiry into the nature of Brahman.
Jijñāsādhikaraṇa : The topic dealing with the enquiry into the nature of Brahman.
Jīva, also *Jīvātmā* : The Individual self.
Jīvanmukti : Liberation of an individual self from bondage while he is still embodied.
Jñāna : Knowledge.
Jñāta : The Knowing subject; the individual self as the knower.
Jñātṛtva : Knowership.
Jñeya : What is known; object.
Jyotis : Light, spiritual light.
Kalyāṇa-guṇa : Auspicious attributes (of Brahman).
Kāma : Sensual desires; what is desired or aspired for.
Kartā : Agent of action; the self as doer.
Kartṛtva : Process of action; activity.
Kāraṇa : Cause.
Karma : Action, ritualistic deeds; the result of past deeds.
Karma-kāṇḍa : Portion of the Vedas dealing with rituals.
Kārya : Effect; what is brought into existence.
Kṛti : Effort.
Kṛtsna-praśakti : Total transformation.
Kratu : Ritualistic deeds.
Laya : Dissolution of the universe.
Laukika : Empirical.
Līlā : Sport.
Liṅga : Identity mark; characteristic.
Mahat : The great; evolute of *prakṛti*.
Mahimā : Greatness; glory.
Manana : Logical reflecton.

Manas : Mind.
Mauna : Silence; repeated reflection on the object of meditation.
Māyā : Cosmic principle which gives rise to the world of illusion (acc. SB); the phenomenal character of the universe; the primordial cosmic matter; that which is an instrument of wonderful creation (acc. RB).
Māyāvāda : The doctrine of *Advaita* which advocates that everything other than Brahman is illusory.
Māyin : One who wields *māyā; Īśvara.*
Mīmāṁsā : Enquiry into the meaning of the Scriptural texts.
Mithyā : Illusory.
Mithyātva : Illusoriness.
Mokṣa : Liberation of the *jīva* from bondage; union with the Supreme Being and enjoyment of the bliss of Brahman.
Mṛt : Clay.
Mṛttikā : Made of clay.
Mṛtyu : Death.
Mukhyārtha : Primary meaning.
Mukta : One who is liberated from bondage; the liberated soul.
Mukti : The state of final liberation from bondage.
Mūlaprakṛti : The primordial cosmic matter.
Mumukṣu : An aspirant for *mokṣa.*
Nābhi : Hub of the wheel.
Nāḍi : Subtle artery.
Nairghanya : Cruelty.
Nāmadheya : Designation by name.
Nāma-rūpa : Name and form.
Nānā : Manifold; different.
Nānā-vyapadeśa : Texts teaching in the primary sense that *jiva* is different from Brahman (acc. RB).
Nididhyāsana : Steadfast meditation.
Nimitta-kāraṇa : The instrumental or efficient cause.
Nirañjana : Free from bondage.
Niravayava : Incapable of physical division; partless.
Nirdoṣa : Defectless; free from all defilements.

Nirguṇa : Devoid of attributes; undifferentiated.
Nirguṇa Śruti : Scriptural text describing Brahman as devoid of attributes.
Nirlepa : Unaffected by the experience of *sukha* and *duḥkha*.
Nirupādhika : Unconditioned.
Nirvikalpa : Indeterminate; devoid of all qualities (acc. SB).
Nirvikāra : Immutable.
Nirviśeṣa : Devoid of all characteristics; undifferentiated.
Niṣkala : Devoid of parts.
Niṣkramaṇa : Exit of the *jīva* from the body.
Niṣkriya : Devoid of activity; free from self-effort (acc. RB)
Nitya : Eternal.
Niyamana : Control.
Niyantā : One who controls all beings; God.
Pañca-bhūta : Five physical elements.
Pāda : Part; part of an *adhyāya* in the *Brahma-sūtras*.
Pāpa : Sin.
Pāñcarātra : Treatises dealing with the mode of worship and allied matters relating to Vaiṣṇavism.
Pañcīkaraña : The process of quintuplication of five elements.
Para : The higher element.
Para Brahma : The ultimate Reality; the higher Brahman (acc. SB); the Supreme Being (acc. RB).
Paramapada : The eternal abode of God.
Parama-puruṣārtha : The Supreme Goal.
Paramāṇus : The atoms which are conceived by the Vaiśeṣikas as partless, eternal, infinitesimal and supra-sensuous reals.
Pāramārthika : That which is absolutely real (acc. SB); real (acc. RB).
Param-jyotis : The transcendental light; Brahman.
Parama-puruṣa : The Supreme Being; Paramātman.
Paramātman : The Supreme Self; Brahman; God.
Paratantra : That which is dependent.
Parimāṇa : Dimension.
Pariṇāma : Evolution; Modification.
Parāyatta : What is endowed by God such as *kartṛtva*.

Phala : Fruit or result of an endeavour.
Pradhāna : The primordial cosmic matter (*prakṛti*), admitted by the *Saṁkhya.*
Prakāra : Mode of a substance; an attribute.
Prakārin : That which has modes or attributes; Brahman.
Prakāśa : Illumination.
Prakṛti : Primordial cosmic matter; also the material cause (acc. SB and RB)
Pralaya : Dissolution of the universe.
Prameya : The theory established by *pramāṇas.*
Prāṇa : Vital breath; *jīva;* Brahman.
Praśāsana : The power to command.
Prasiddha : What is well-established.
Prāpya : What is to be attained; Goal of attainment.
Pratibimba : Reflection; similar to (acc. MB)
Pratīka : The symbol of Brahman adopted for meditation.
Prayatna : Effort.
Pṛthak : Distinct; separate.
Pṛthivī : Earth.
Prāyaścitta : Expiatory rite.
Puccha : Tail; support.
Puṇḍarīka : Lotus.
Puṇya : Merit.
Puruṣārtha : The goal of human edeavour.
Puruṣottama : The Supreme Person; Brahman.
Puruṣa : Person; individual self; *Paramātman.*
Purvāgha : Sins committed prior to the commencement of the *upāsanā.*
Pūrvapakṣa : Prima facie view.
Pūrva-mīmāṁsā : The treatises which deal with the ritualistic portion of the Vedas.
Śabda : Sound; verbal testimony; revealed scripture.
Sādhana : Spiritual discipline; means adopted to attain Brahman.
Sādharmya : Equality; Similarity.
Sad-vidyā : Meditation on Brahman conceived as *sat,* as taught in the Chāndogya Upaniṣad.

Sādṛśya : Similarity.
Saguṇa : Endowed with attributes.
Saguṇa Śruti : Scriptural statement describing Brahman as qualified with attributes.
Sahakāri-kāraṇa : Accessory cause.
Sāmānadhikaraṇya : Syntactic equation of terms denoting the same entity but connoting different qualities.
Samanvaya : Concurrence with the main purport.
Samanvayādhikaraṇa : The topic dealing with the correlation of the Upanisadic texts with Brahman.
Saṁbandha : Relationship.
Saṁhartā : Brahman as the cause of the dissolution of the universe.
Samprasāda : *Jīvātman* (acc. RB); state of deep sleep (acc. SB).
Saṁyoga : Conjuction; external relationship.
Samvṛti : The principle conceived by the Buddhists to explain the phenomenal appearance of the manifold universe.
Saṁsāra : Bondage.
Samaṣṭi-sṛṣṭi : Creation of the aggregate universe.
Sāmya : Equality; equal status of the *mukta-jiva* with Brahman.
Sandhyā : The state of dream.
Saṁkalpa : Will.
Sanmātra : Constituted of knowledge only.
Śarīra : Body; that which is necessarily supported and controlled by the self and also subserves its purpose (acc. RB).
Śarīrī : The self of the *śarīra;* Brahman.
Śarīra-śarīrī-bhāva : The organic relationship between Brahman and the universe of *cit* and *acit* (acc. RB).
Sarvajña : Omniscient.
Sarvavit : Knower of everything.
Sarvātmā : Self of all.
Śāstra : Sacred texts.
Sattā : Existence.
Satya : Truth; Brahman as Reality (acc. SB); Unconditioned existence of Brahman (acc. RB).

Satyakāma : One whose needs or desires are self-fulfilled.
Satya-saṁkalpa : One whose will is not obstructed (acc. RB).
Saviśeṣa : That which is characterized; Brahman as characterized with attributes.
Sāyujya : The state of *mokṣa* in which the individual self enjoys equal status of Brahman.
Setu : Causeway.
Siddhānta : Final view; the established conclusive theory.
Siddhavastu : That which is already established.
Smṛti : Texts based on the revealed scripture such as *Itihāsas, Purāṇas* etc.
Sṛṣṭi : Creation.
Śravaṇa : Comprehending what is taught by a teacher.
Sthūla : Gross; manifested form.
Śuddhasattva : Spiritual substance characterized by unalloyed *sattva.*
Sukha : Happiness.
Sukṛta : Merit earned by the performance of good deeds.
Sūkṣma : Subtle; unmanifest form.
Śūnya : Void; indeterminable (acc. Buddhist)
Suṣupti : Dreamless state.
Suṣumnā-nāḍi : The subtle artery which radiates from the heart to the crown of the head through which the *jīva* exits from the body.
Sūtra : An aphorism; a concise aphoristic sentence expressed in a few words.
Sūtrakāra : The author of the Vedānta-sūtras.
Svaḥbhāva : The essential nature of an object; essential characteristic of an object (acc. RB).
Svābhāvika : Natural form; unconditioned.
Svapna : Dream.
Svarūpalakṣaṇa : Definition of an object in terms of its essential attributes.
Svatantra : One who is independent such as Brahman.
Svayam-prakāśa : Self-luminous; self-established (acc. SB.)
Syādvāda : The theory of the Jainas regarding the sevenfold description of an entity.

Tamas : The primordial cosmic matter (*prakṛti*); also one of the three qualities (*guṇa*) of *prakṛti*.
Tapas : Austerity; also Brahman.
Taṭastha-lakṣana : Definition of an object by means of identity.
Tatkratu-nyāya : The principle according to which in whatever form a person meditates, the goal attained should be the same.
Tattva : Metaphysical Reality; Ontological entity.
Tejas : Splendour; the element of fire.
Triguṇa : Three qualities of *prakṛti–sattva, rajas* and *tamas*.
Tyāga : Renouncement.
Ubhayaliṅga : Two-fold characteristic of Brahman as free from all defects and also endowed with *kalyaṇa-guṇas* (acc. RB)
Ubhayaliṅgādhikaraṇa : The topic dealing with Brahman as *ubhayaliṅga*.
Unmāna : Dimension.
Upādāna-kāraṇa : Material cause.
Upādhi : Adjunct; a limiting condition.
Upakrama : Commencement.
Upalabdhi : Comprehension.
Upalakṣaṇa : Qualification per accidens.
Upalakṣya : What is denoted by *upalakṣaṇa*.
Upapatti : Logical tenability.
Upakaraṇa : Accessories.
Upāsaka : One who practises meditation.
Upasaṁhāra : Conclusion; conclusive statement.
Upāsanā : Steadfast meditation; unceasing loving meditation on Brahman (acc. RB).
Upāya : Means to attain a goal.
Ūrdhvaretas : One who practises strict celibacy.
Ūrṇanābhi : Spider.
Utpatti : Production; origin.
Uttara-mīmāṁsā : The treatises which deal with the Upanisadic portion of the Vedas; Vedānta.
Vaidharmya : Dissimilarity; different from.

Vairāgya : Non-attachment.
Vaiśvānara : The Ruler of all souls; elemental fire; the digestive fire.
Vaiṣamya : Partiality.
Vākyārtha-jñāna : Knowledge derived from the study of the sacred texts.
Varṇāśrama-dharma : Religious duties prescribed according to castes and stages of life.
Veda : Revealed scripture.
Vicitra-śakti : Variegated power.
Vidyā : Upāsanā leading to the direct knowledge of Brahman (acc. RB); knowledge of the identity of *jīva* and Brahman (acc. SB).
Vākyānvaya : The correlation between the earlier and later statements.
Vijñāna : Knowledge.
Vijñātā : Knower.
Vilakṣaṇa : Of different nature.
Vikāra : Change; modification.
Vipaścit : Omniscient.
Virodha : Conflict; contradiction.
Viṣaya : Subject-matter of discussion.
Viṣaya-vākya : The Upaniṣadic statement which serves as the basis for the Vedānta-sūtra.
Viśeṣaṇa : Qualification; attribute.
Viśeṣya : The substrate for an attribute.
Viśiṣṭa : What is qualified.
Viśiṣṭa-abheda-vāda : The theory upholding oneness of Brahman as *viśiṣṭa* or organically related to *cit* and *acit* (acc. RB).
Viśiṣṭaikya : Oneness of substance as inseparably related to the attributes.
Viśvakartā : Creator of the universe.
Vivarta : Illusory manifestation.
Vivarta-vāda : The theory adopted by Śaṁkara to account for the illusory manifestion of Brahman as the manifold universe.

Vyapadeśa : Meaning in the primary sense.
Vyāvahārikā : Empirical.
Yajña : Offering of sacrifice in the consecrated fire.

BIBLIOGRAPHY

Basic Source books in Sanskrit

Adikaraṇa-sārāvalī of Vedānta Deśika with Adhikaraṇa-cintāmaṇi (commentary of Śrī Kumāra Varadāchārya) and *Padayojana* (commentary of Śrivaṇ Rāmānuja Yati, 42nd Jeer of Ahobila Mutt, Madras, 1940).

Adhikaraṇa-sārāvali of Vedānta Deśika with *Adhikaraṇa cintāmaṇi* (commentary of Sri Kumaara Vedāntacārya and *Sārātha-ratna-prabhā*) (commentary of Sri Uttamur Veeraraghavacharya), Ubhayavedanta granthmala, Madras, 1972.

Śārīraka Adhikaraṇa-ratna-mālā with *Prakāśā* of Mm. Kapisthalam Desikacharya, ed. Sri Srinivasa Raghavan, Pudukkotai 1938.

Śrībhāṣyam of Śrī Rāmānuja with *Śrutaprakāśikā* of Sudarśana Sūri (commentary on *Śribhāṣyam*), Ed. Uttamur Veeraraghavacharya, 2 volumes, Madras, 1967.

Other books in Sanskrit

Bramhasūtra-bhāṣya of Śaṁkara with *Bhāmati, Kalpataru* and other commentaries. Bombay, 1938.

Brahmasūtra-bhāṣyam of Madhva with *Tattva-prakāśikā* of Jayatirtha and other commentaries, Ed. K.T. Pandurangi 7 Vols. Bangalore 2002.

Daśopaniṣadbhāṣya of Śaṁkara. Ed. Govinda sastry, Delhi-1964.

Nyāyasiddhāñjana of Vedānta Deśika, Ed. Uttamur Veeraraghavacharya ed. Madras. 1976.

Nyāyāmṛta of Vyāsatīrtha with *Advaitasiddhi,* Ed. K.T. Pandurangi 3 Vols. Bangalore, 1994-96.

Paramārthabhūṣanam by. Uttamur Veeraraghavacharya, Madras.

Śatadūṣaṇī of Vedanta Deśika, Ed. Srivatsankaracharya, Madras 1973.

Śatabhūṣaṇī, by Mm. Anatakrishna sastriar, Calcutta.

Siddhitraya of Ālavandar, Ed. R. Ramanujachari, Annamalinagar, 1972.

Tātparya-Candrikā of Vyāsatīrtha, Ed. K.T. Pandurangi, 3 Vols. Bangalore, 1999-2001.

Tattva-muktā-kalāpa of Vedānta Deśika with Sarvārtha-siddhi (commentary by Vedānta Deśika), Ed. Uttamur veeraraghavacharya, Madras, 1973.

Upaniṣadbhāṣyam with *Tīkā* of Jayatīrtha and *Khaṇdārtha* of Sri. Raghavendratirtha, Ed. Poornaprajna Samsodhana Mandal, Bangalore 1997.

Upaniṣadbhāṣyam of Śrī Raṅgarāmānuja on Bṛhadāraṇyaka, Chāndogya, Īśa, Kena and other Upanisads. 3 Vols. Ed. Uttamur veeraraghavacharya, Madras.

Vedārtha-saṁgraha of Śrī Rāmānuja with *Tātparyadīpikā* of Sudarśanasūri, Ed. T.T. Devasthanam, Tirupati, 1954.

Viṣaya-vākya-dīpikā of Raṅgaramānujamuni, a commentary on the Upaniṣadic texts discussed in the Brahma-sūtras. Ed. Chakravarty Iyengar, Mysore, 1892.

Vedāntadīpa of Rāmānuja, Ed. P.B. Annangaraçharya. Conjeevaram, 1956.

Vedāntasāra of Rāmānuja, Ed. P.B. Annangaracharya, Conjeevaram, 1956.

Works in English

Radhakrishnan, S. *The Bramhasūtras,* London, 1960.

Radhakrishnan, S. *The Principal Upaniṣads,* London, 1953.

Raghavachar, S.S Śrībhāṣya on the *Philosophy* of the *Brahmasūtras,* Bangalore, 1986.

Raghavachar, S.S. *Śrī Rāmānuja on the Upaniṣads,* Madras, 1972.

Raghavachar, S.S. *Introduction to Vedārthasaṅgraha,* 2nd ed. Mangalore, 1973.

Rangacharya, M. *The Vedāntasūtras* with the *Śrībhāṣya* of Rāmānuja, English translation, 3 vols. 3rd edition, New Delhi, 1988-91.

Sharma, B.N.K. *The Brahmasutras and Their Principal Commentaries,* 3 Vols. New Delhi-1986.

Sharma, B.N.K. *Philosophy of Śrī Madhvācārya,* Bombay 1962.

Srinivasachari, P. N. *The Philosophy of Viśiṣṭādvaita.* Adyur, Madras, 1978.

Srinivasachari, S.M. *Advaita* and *Viśiṣṭādvaita,* A Study based on Vedānta Deśika's Śatadūṣaṇī. IIIrd Edn. Delhi, 1999.

Srinivasachari, S.M. *Fundamentals of Viśiṣṭādvaita*–A study based on Vedānta Deśika's *Tattvamuktākalāpa.* Delhi, IIIrd Edn. 2004.

Srinivasachari, S.M. *The Philosophy of the Vedānta-sūtra*–A study based on the Evaluation of the commentaries of Śaṁkara, Rāmānuja and Madhva. Delhi, 1998.

Srinivasachari, S.M. *The Philosophy of the Upaniṣads*– A study based on the Evaluation of the comments of Śaṁkara, Rāmānuja and Madhva. Delhi 2002.

Thibaut, G. *The Vedāntasūtras with Rāmānuja's Śrībhāṣya,* English translation, SBE series, Vol. 48. (reprint), Delhi-1962.

Thibaut, G. *Vedānta-sūtras* with the commentary of Śankarāchārya parts I and II. English translation with Introduction, SBE series, vols; 4, 38, (reprint) Delhi, 1962.

INDEX